The Business of Life and Death

Volume I: Values and Economies

Collected Philosophical Essays

by

Giorgio Baruchello, PhD

NORTHWEST
PASSAGE
Books

Gatineau, Quebec, Canada

The Business of Life and Death
Volume 1: Values and Economies

Collected Philosophical Essays

by Giorgio Baruchello, PhD

Copyright © 2018 by Giorgio Baruchello. All rights reserved.

ISBN: 978-0-9939527-6-0

Published by
Northwest Passage Books
Gatineau, Quebec, Canada

Cover photo: Arch doorway, formerly of a bank in downtown Ottawa, Canada, installed in the Mackenzie-King Estate, Gatineau Park, Quebec, Canada. Photo by Brendan Myers.

To Kieran Logi and Lorenzo Kiljan

Table of Contents

Preface v
Acknowledgments vi
Introduction viii
Original publication credits xviii

PART I – Introductions 1

    Chapter 1: The Cancer Stage of Capitalism 2
    Chapter 2: Value Wars 21
    Chapter 3: From Crisis to Cure 37

PART II – Applications 48

    Chapter 4: What Is to Be Conserved? An Appraisal of
    Political Conservatism 49
    Chapter 5: Good and Bad Tourism 80
    Chapter 6: Paul Krugman's Banking Metastases 101
    Chapter 7: Social Philosophy and Oncology 111
    Chapter 8: On the Mission of Public Universities 125

PART III – Implications 132

    Chapter 9: Adam Smith, Historical and Rhetorical 133
    Chapter 10: Cornelius Castoriadis and the Crux of Adam
    Smith's Liberty 154
    Chapter 11: The Price of Tranquillity: Cruelty and Death in
    Adam Smith's Liberalism 186
    Chapter 12: Adam Smith Can Never Be Wrong 223
    Chapter 13: Five Books of Economic History 246
    Chapter 14: A History of Economics 258
    Epilogue: Good and Bad Capitalism 269

Endnotes 285

Preface

My previous two volumes for Northwest Passage Books were, basically, philosophical explorations. Whether dealing with the traditional topic of death (*Mortals, Money, and Masters of Thought*) or the less commonplace topic of cruelty (*Philosophy of Cruelty*), the essays contained therein did investigate, organise and make some sense of the vast legacy of the Western philosophical canon—or at least they attempted as much. In the process, they did not aim at achieving more than merely suggest that a foundational conception of value might lie underneath it all. As this third collection of essays is concerned, however, that first and merely suggested conception of value finds finally full expression and open backing. In this book, as the reader is going to find out, I am no longer exploring, but engaging in philosophical advocacy. Life-value onto-axiology, namely the theory of value that I had merely hinted at in the two previous collections of essays of mine, is articulated and applied here to highly representative social dimensions, while some of its implications for intellectual and economic history are discussed.

As I look back at the years during which the essays collected and revised hereby were written, i.e. between 1999 and 2016, I realise how the diverse projects gathered and restyled for the present volume—review essays, book chapters, conference papers, scholarly articles, short notes—are all informed by my familiarity with, and tacit commitment to, life-value onto-axiology, even though this theory of value may not have always been the focus-point of each of them. Because of this realisation, I considered using the technical expression itself in the title of this book but, following conversations with Northwest Passage Books' chief consultant, I concluded that it would be unnecessarily abstruse and rhetorically ineffective. "Life-value onto-axiology" is theoretically correct, but it is not consistent with the spirit of this book. Insofar as the present volume is part of a project aiming at making philosophy less ivory-tower-based and biased, fostering reflection on what really matters in people's lives individually and collectively, then speaking of "the business of life and death" is equally correct and far more immediate. It is what our existence consists in, in a nutshell. The subtitle, "Values and Economies", captures further the contents of the present book and expresses the two main axes of scrutiny to be found in it by the reader, i.e. what really counts ("values") and what this recognition entails for concrete social organisation ("economies"), not just their abstract representation, which would be better labelled "economics". So numerous are the works of mine informed with the principles and concerns of life-value onto-axiology, that a careful selection was made in relation to the present volume and an additional one is going to be issued in the near future.

Acknowledgments

First and foremost, I must thank two persons, without whom this volume would not exist. The former is Dr. Brendan Myers, chief consultant at Northwest Passage Books, who has been most positive in his scholarly appreciation of my research, compelling in his editorial advice to consolidate my many past publications into few new books, persistent in his professional dedication to their dissemination, and generous in his expert assistance *vis-à-vis* the extensive redrafting needed to pursue such goals. The latter is Prof. John McMurtry, i.e. the true father of life-value onto-axiology, which does count today many adherents in the human, social and health sciences—Drs. Jeff Noonan, Jennifer Sumner and Bichara Sahely deserve a special mention in this context—but is also inextricably entwined with McMurtry's intellectual undertakings. Among them stands out his pivotal role *qua* Honorary Theme Editor and key-contributor for UNESCO's *Encyclopedia of Life Support Systems* (2002–2017), which is today's largest online repository of information on sustainable development. It is in this compendium of encyclopaedias that life-value onto-axiology finds its richest, widest and most nuanced presentation.

Secondly, I must thank the rector and the senior management of the University of Akureyri for allowing me to enjoy a sabbatical leave in the academic year 2016–2017, during which I could devote myself to a substantial number of research projects, including the volumes penned for Northwest Passage Books. In this connection, Dr. Enrico Albanesi and Prof. Carlo Penco of the Università degli Studi di Genova should be thanked too, for they provided me with access to key facilities at their university: office space, computer terminals, online catalogues, libraries, printers, etc.

Thirdly and finally, I should thank the editors and publishers of the works of mine that I have selected, amended and republished in this volume. Being granted such privileges is neither obvious nor inevitable, given the existing copyright restrictions under most legal jurisdictions. My own entries for the *Encyclopedia of Life Support Systems*, though certainly relevant for the present project, cannot be part of it, for instance. Therefore, I wish to thank most warmly Dr. Charles Tandy of Ria University Press, since he allowed me to include here nothing less than a forthcoming contribution of mine to the *Death and Anti-Death* book series, which he has been editing for several years. Analogous thanks go to all the publishers who have been as generous with respect to the more recent publications included in this volume.

As usual, if any imprecision or error happens to be found in the pages that follow, the responsibility lies solely with me. As also usual, despite my best efforts, I know from the onset that there will be some, for which I apologise right away. Repeated rounds of revision, peer review and editorial scrutiny cannot straighten completely the crooked timber of my prose. If there is any philosophical wisdom that I have acquired over many years of intellectual research and academic writing, it is that my own imperfection runs deeper than I can fathom, and it is sadly far more tenacious than I could ever fear it to be.

Introduction

A direct descendant of the Ontario Agricultural College, the University of Guelph can boast among the members of its vast academic family two great Canadian intellectuals, who have never been afraid of tackling public affairs and economic matters with unswerving courage, subtle acumen and dazzling style.

The first one is John Kenneth—"Ken"—Galbraith (1908–2006). During his very long career, he came to be admired internationally *qua* economist, social scientist, novelist, Oriental art historian, diplomat, political advisor, media personality, relentless champion of progressive causes, and unsurpassed master of witty prose. Being myself the son of a long-time bank manager, a projected employee of the same bank, and having been named after a member of the prominent Genoese family owning it—my baptismal godfather—, I grew up surrounded by banking issues and regular talks about these issues, by occasional heated debates on economic questions and, not least of all, by Galbraith's books, which were literally scattered around my paternal home. It is therefore also, if not primarily, because of his books that I developed a deep interest in economic matters and trusted the humanities to afford better insights into them than run-of-the-mill economics or business studies. As a teenager, I could already notice how a comparison of undergraduate textbooks revealed an alarming gap between economics' assumed anthropology and the variety of views on human nature available in the humanities at large. Any novel by Dostoyevsky, Balzac or Laxness was infinitely more instructive on this point than any textbook in economics or business studies, and much closer to the human reality that I could observe around myself. Similarly, the acknowledged forms of economic organisation and behaviour exhibited by human societies in the long history of our species appeared grossly oversimplified, if not plainly wrong, in the textbooks peddled to undergraduate students in economics and business studies. The very history of Genoa and the Genoese, the likely cradle and inventors of capitalism, could hardly be grasped by means of the categories of thought provided in those textbooks, which in my view marginalised or ignored pivotal factors of historical self-affirmation and economic expansion such as strict family bonds, military conquest and predominance, outright slavery, class-skewed taxation, relentless mono- and oligopolistic practices, intentionally asymmetric information, the cunning use and abuse of credit, and the bottomless depths of religious belief.

If anything, I knew as well that the young recruits in my godfather's bank, upon entrance into the austere institution that was going to employ them, were told quite bluntly to simply forget what they had studied. Real life, apparently, had little to do with what they had read in their textbooks—none of which was authored by Galbraith, incidentally. Whether wise or unwise, and probably rhetorically inflated, such an injunction was certainly not a good piece of advertising for the economic and business disciplines. Thus, though my professional path never led me into the banking world awaiting me since birth, I ended up pursuing undergraduate and graduate studies in philosophy and deal nonetheless with issues such as, *inter alia*, private property, money, preference satisfaction and consumer behaviour. As a middle-aged family man, I still read plenty of literature on economic subjects, I review books on them, I am a fellow of the American Association for Economic Research, and I still like returning to classics such as Adam Smith (1723−1790), Vilfredo Pareto (1848−1923), the brothers Karl (1886−1964) and Michael Polanyi (1891−1976), and Carlo Cipolla (1922−2000). Clearly, I could not escape my family's background and expectations, notwithstanding my unconventional choice of seeking a career in such a bohemian, if not monastic, field of study as philosophy—to the initial dismay of my father, I must add.

Few years ago, after yet another financial crash that most professional economists had not seen coming, a dear friend and research partner of mine—a British professor of economics—gave me great comfort by telling me that, when young people ask him what disciplines they should study in order to understand actual economic phenomena, he answers unfalteringly that history, philosophy and politics are far better options than a degree in economics. In his view, his own discipline has become too far removed from real human life, including actual economic activities. Though parading themselves as serious social scientists, he has come to believe that most of his colleagues favour self-entrenching *a priori* mathematical modelling upon rigid, limited and fantastic sets of admissible assumptions, over candid empirical observation, conceptually richer inter-disciplinary study, and plain, open-minded, honest reflection. Engaged in impressive displays of mathematical skill determining their discipline's internal pecking order, my friend and research partner claims that most economists have ended up forgetting about their defining realm of investigation, which they either misconstrue or neglect altogether. *Pace* much widespread prejudice, economics is by and large ceremonial; the humanities, on the contrary, can be instrumental, at least with regard to making sense and operating within actual economies.

The blindness of mainstream economists to the nature and workings of actual economies is a theme that Galbraith himself had hammered upon incessantly since at least the 1940s and up to his very last book, *The Economics of Innocent Fraud*, published in 2004. The great irony in my colleague's recent echo of his thought is that Galbraith was not the first famous economist in North America to accuse his peers of real-life irrelevance by self-inflicted methodological myopia. Galbraith was himself inspired by Thorstein Veblen (1857–1929) who, long before him, had uttered the same vibrant accusations, this time against William Stanley Jevons (1835–1882) and Alfred Marshall (1842–1924) rather than Milton Friedman (1912–2006) and Robert Emerson Lucas (b.1937). Similarly Veblen, to whom we owe the notions of "ceremonial" and "instrumental" institutions that I have just utilised, had also tried to reform the way in which economics was pursued within academia. Instead of the neoclassical emphasis on deduction, he believed there should be one on induction. Instead of the neoclassical choice of mathematical engineering and physics as paradigm, he thought that evolutionary biology should replace it. A new school of economics had eventually emerged, following Veblen's initial efforts, the so-called "institutionalist" or "institutional economics", which is still in existence today. However, Veblen did not succeed overall, and neither did Galbraith, who is regarded as a significant member of this school. The mainstream of economic research has continued along its conventional path and, having rejected Marxism and emasculated Keynesianism, it has never truly surrendered its neoclassical roots, which are most marked in introductory textbooks and in the accepted dogmas of business studies. Veblen's and Galbraith's school of thought is today nothing but a 'minor', 'marginal' and blasphemously 'heterodox' approach. Evidently, the blades of Marshall's scissors are made of very tough steel, capable of withstanding the attacks of several professional inheritors of Veblen's and Galbraith's scepticism, such as Joan Robinson (1903–1983), Gunnar Myrdal (1898–1987) and Steve Keen (b. 1953). Had institutionalist economics become the new normal, then my British friend and research partner would have not been so dismal about his own discipline just a few years ago.

The second illustrious Guelphite is John McMurtry (b. 1939), Professor Emeritus of Philosophy, fellow of the Royal Society of Canada and, as already acknowledged, Honorary Theme Editor for UNESCO's gargantuan *Encyclopedia of Life Support Systems*. McMurtry is also a former football player, educator, journalist, an academic star in Marxist studies during the 1970s[1]—which he later superseded *via* life-value onto-axiology—and a fiercely engaged public intellectual, who has become the *maître à penser* of Peter Joseph's internationally active *Zeitgeist* movement. Thanks to the several documentaries, roundtables, conferences and media projects launched by this progressive non-profit organisation, which is the brainchild of a former US stockbroker turned financial reformer, McMurtry's philosophy, or at least some tenets of it, have become familiar to millions of people around the planet. In particular, Peter Joseph's 2011 film entitled *Zeitgeist: Moving Forward* has been crucial in making McMurtry's philosophy well-known. In it, extensive interviews with McMurtry are comprised and his life-value onto-axiology endorsed as the correct path to understand the world's actual economies, By the end of 2016 it had been viewed on YouTube alone by more than 23 million people, not to mention the other websites and media supports available for its fruition, plus the many dubbed and texted versions circulating worldwide. This sort of mass visibility is very rarely attained by academics.[2]

Controversial, combative, committed and consistent, McMurtry has never shirked criticism, whether coming from him or directed at him—possibly a legacy of the tough spirit that one must develop when playing football at high levels. Above all, as far as I am concerned, McMurtry is the founder of life-value onto-axiology, namely the most comprehensive theory of value articulated by any philosopher in our century. Fascinated by it, I had the privilege and the hard charge of studying under McMurtry at the University of Guelph, the man being as tough *qua* doctoral supervisor as he is *qua* public intellectual—and as he must have been when he was a football player. Later in my life, this time as an academic, I have done much in terms of spreading the knowledge of life-value onto-axiology inside and outside philosophy departments, scrutinising its legal and economic implications, and expanding the fields for its fruitful application. Tellingly, the publications hereby revised and reissued were printed in six different countries (Canada, the US, Iceland, the UK, Israel and Greece) and as many different disciplinary areas (philosophy, economics, politics, law, health sciences and development studies).

As regards these diverse publications, the first part of the present volume introduces the reader to life-value onto-axiology by way of three review essays—duly revised, of course—covering respectively the first edition of McMurtry's *Cancer Stage of Capitalism* (1999; chapter 1), his 2002 book entitled *Value Wars: The Global Market Versus the Life Economy* (chapter 2), and the second edition of *The Cancer Stage of Capitalism: From Crisis to Cure* (2013; chapter 3). Though they are not the most articulate presentation of life-value onto-axiology, which I have already stated to be McMurtry's own contributions to UNESCO's *Encyclopedia of Life Support Systems*, these three books offer in all probability the most immediate and understandable, for they address, analyse and assess today's global economies in light of McMurtry's value theory, from the so-called "end of history" to the Great Recession, *via* the alleged "clash of civilisations" that, whether spontaneous or forced onto the nations by unwise militaristic policies, finds blatant and gruesome manifestation in contemporary Islamic extremism and resurgent fascism.

The second part of the present volume collects two earlier book chapters, one conference proceeding, a review essay and a short note, each of which displays the application of life-value onto-axiology to a specific area of inquiry: political conservatism (chapter 4), the tourist business (chapter 5), Europe's recent banking crises (chapter 6), oncology (chapter 7), and higher education (chapter 8). The nature, scope, aims and motives of life-value onto-axiology are thus disclosed by way of case studies in diverse fields of expertise, some of which are bound to resonate more (or less) forcefully with each reader.

The third part comprises nearly as diverse a spectrum of previous publications of mine, but tackles only two specific topics for which life-value onto-axiology has implications that I find fascinating. The former topic is the history of economic and political thought and, precisely, the intellectual legacy of Adam Smith, who has been playing a pivotal role, at least rhetorically (chapter 9), in buttressing the now dominant liberal ideology (in the European sense of "liberal"), its alternatives having been lost or marginalised (chapter 10) despite the many thorny issues marring Adam Smith's own thought (chapter 11) and economic liberalism at large (chapter 12). The latter topic is economic history, which has been 'colonised' more and more by the methods and assumptions of mainstream economics, to the point of losing sight of the idiographic complexity of its study subject (chapter 13), possibly because of its devotees' self-serving goals (chapter 14). To further stress the specificity of the two topics selected and dealt with in the third part, the book's chapter titles differ considerably from those of the original publications.

Finally, a 2009 article issued in *Economics, Management and Financial Markets* serves as an epilogue offering a synthetic appraisal of life-value onto-axiology *vis-à-vis* the overall aims of economic agency in principle, and the adverse environmental and social impacts of predominant economic activities in current practice.

Given the centrality of life-value onto-axiology and the recurrent references to its main proponents—its founder above all—there is inevitable overlap among the texts collected and revised here. Considerable redrafting went into assessing and reducing repetitions, yet without sacrificing excessively the internal coherence of each chapter. Besides, though essentially the same, the key-notions of life-value onto-axiology have been stated over the years in slightly different forms by McMurtry himself, which the present volume *ipso facto* records and acknowledges in their evolution and manifestations. The reader who is interested in tracking these forms can patiently read all the initial chapters and their specific take on such key-notions. The reader who is already familiar with life-value onto-axiology, or that is chiefly curious about some of its specific applications and implications, should skip the parts where accounts of life-value onto-axiology are reiterated. (In truth, the reader can do whatever she likes, once she's got this volume in her hands!)

What is more, in a collection of essays such as the present one, the old texts are meant to be polished up rather than written anew. Because of these competing exigencies, I erred on the side of caution in the initial five chapters and changed therein less rather than more. Deleted sections and substantive revisions become more and more pronounced in the ensuing chapters, which rely on what is presented to the reader in the preceding ones. The third part stands out in this sense, its texts involving a considerable amount of redrafting, though I did not fall victim of the temptation of writing altogether new material. As a result, the chapters in this volume are uneven in length and some are rather short in comparison with the original publications. The original structures, focuses and scopes have been preserved throughout, however.

Conceptually, little was in genuine need of thorough modification, insofar as the critical analyses offered by McMurtry since at least the mid-1980s were proven correct by subsequent events. And someone did take notice of this fact. Though never orthodox and always challenging, McMurtry's own involvement with UNESCO, his election to Canada's most prestigious scientific society, and the enormous international visibility gained after 2008 make one wonder whether John Maynard Keynes (1883–1946) was perhaps overly pessimistic when stating: "Worldly wisdom teaches that it is better for reputation to fail conventionally than to succeed unconventionally."[3]

On the one hand, the global financial collapse of 2008 and the ensuing Great Recession have led even mainstream pundits, institutions and scholars to take belated stock of the conspicuous problems that had long been denounced by McMurtry. The life-destructive inner logic of our economic order, which McMurtry's works painstakingly reveal, may not be as openly acknowledged by them yet. However, after such gargantuan traumatic events as the fall of Lehman Brothers or the Panama Papers scandal, even the popular press writes today about the ills of unbridled financial capitalism, ballooning gross inequality, troubling State capture by private interests, shameless and seamless corporate tax-dodging schemes, industry's murderous environmental irresponsibility, and the pitfalls of indiscriminate free trade. All these topics had been taboo for a long time. Only variously labelled and *ipso dicto* publicly disqualified "nostalgic", "socialist", "anachronistic", "radical", "discontent", "soft", "utopian", "pie-in-the-sky", "bleeding-heart", "crackpot" or "unscientific" academics would have dared proffer, before 2008, outspoken "jeremiads" or "rants" against the triumphant liberalism of the age embracing Reagonomics, the Washington Consensus, New Labour, the 2.0 economy, and the Great Moderation. Liberal rhetoricians have never been poor in verbal daggers with which to pierce, debase and discount their critics. Who, in her right mind, would challenge the system capable of defeating the so-called "evil empire"? Who would challenge the assumedly self-evident engine of prosperity, which cannot but be secured by the miraculous combination of private self-interested initiative with freedom from the "Leviathan" and its "protracted interference", i.e., from the rapacious State?[4]

Such was the self-congratulatory conventional wisdom of broadly neoliberal world leaders and academic sycophants for almost three decades, until public authorities had to step in and rescue the previously self-evident engine of global prosperity from its own faulty machinations, the greed that the same engine had been incessantly selecting for, and the awfully creative wizardry of its best and brightest innovators. Almost ten years have elapsed since the iconic collapse of Lehman Brothers, and the world's economies, their central banks, and large scores of under- or unemployed people are still struggling with the consequences of the crash. *Ad hoc* exculpations can be as numerous as the aforementioned liberal daggers, and many a rhetoric involving "crony capitalism", "bad apples", "national character", "transitions" and "one-in-a-lifetime crisis" have already been heard many times since the 2008 crash.[5] Nonetheless, possibly because of the length and breadth of the ensuing economic crisis, the seeds of critical doubt and intelligent reflection have had time to germinate. As a consequence, it is now publicly allowed and reasonable to talk adamantly of "the 1%", the scourge of tax havens, the perils of extreme wealth disparity, and the criminogenic frenzy of high finance.

This sort of talk was certainly not so permissible and mainstream in the 1980s and 1990s, when McMurtry was braving, with only few companions (including the old maverick Ken Galbraith himself), the conventional wisdom of the age. Given enough time and suffering, though, conventional wisdom can mutate, at least to a degree. Emblematically, after three decades of uncritical free-trade and liberal mantras, a self-declared "socialist" politician competed with considerable success in the latest primaries of the US Democratic Party, while an unashamed "old-labour" activist has become the head of the second largest political party in the UK. Ironically, in today's US, the current President is the real-estate tycoon and TV-celebrity Donald Trump (b. 1946), who won a fierce electoral campaign by promising, *inter alia*, American jobs for American citizens and protection from unrestrained free trade, whilst also criticising the 2003 US invasion of Iraq and his predecessors' overseas adventures. Whether Trump shall deliver on such electoral promises or not, we do not know yet. Nevertheless, protectionist populism and, in particular, outspoken isolationist postures had not been seen in

American politics for a century, i.e. since Woodrow Wilson (1856–1924) won re-election in 1916 with the slogan "He kept us out of war!". Times have clearly changed. When McMurtry published *Understanding War* (1989) and *Unequal Freedoms* (1998), or when he openly attacked George W. Bush's (b. 1946) militaristic foreign policy, the US Republicans, and most Democrats too, were squarely *not* on the same side as McMurtry.

On the other hand, over the same past few decades, we have been witnessing repeated high-level attempts at stemming in the most worrisome effects of climate change, which in the official parlance is no longer "avoidable"—as it was implied back in the 1990s—but only "adaptable to". As gloomy as this semantic shift may sound, some influential business interests are still willing to ignore it at our own collective peril. In point of fact, I am writing these lines on the day that the aforementioned US President Donald Trump announced his administration's decision to withdraw from the Paris Agreement on climate change. Technical exculpations aside, the withdrawal is a politically potent statement, as well as an unfriendly act toward most other nations and, above all, Mother Earth and Her children. US exceptionalism notwithstanding, the European leaders' scathing rejoinders to Donald Trump's decision, China's quick ascent to the world's leadership in renewable energy production, and the flourishing of countless projects for novel and environmentally sounder economies and economics—variously dubbed "green", "evolutionary" (a label that is as old as Veblen) and "doughnut"—are proof of McMurtry's being on the ball all along.

McMurtry's being correct with regard to the ecocidal character of contemporary economies is most clearly exemplified by the unaware and somewhat bizarre literal reinvention of his concept of "civil commons", which Burns H. Weston and David Bollier operated in the 2010s in a book entitled *Green Governance: Ecological Survival, Human Rights, and the Law of the Commons*.[6] So urgent and so poignant is this notion under the ongoing ecocidal circumstances, that these two researchers ended up reaching the same conceptual conclusion and verbal connotation as McMurtry had done many years before them.[7] Naturally, it remains to be seen whether the consistency between McMurtry's time-tested arguments and admonitions on the one side, and the eco-friendly trends on the other, is going to be substantial or not. McMurtry's identification of the private sector's inherent inability to lead to an ecologically sane order, unless forced into it by public authorities at several levels, is pivotal in this respect. There are certainly many positive signs in both technological and political developments today, but the damages of for-profit economic activities upon the planet's life support systems have neither been cancelled nor stopped yet, and even less have they been reverted in their grinding inertia. Living species continue to go extinct at spasm rates. Living spaces keep being polluted at all micro- and macro-levels. Livelihoods are still being callously sacrificed to investors' returns on equity and corporate quarterly reports. For every breath of fresh air that we successfully reclaim, at least twice as many are taken away.

The value-calculus offered by McMurtry's philosophy is as simple as it is damning: if the ecological and social systems allowing for life-ranges to exist and expand are damaged by the ongoing economic activities, then these economic activities cannot be deemed positive, even if they prove most profitable to the investor communities or to large sections of the population of some nations. This realisation was valid in the 1980s and it is still valid today. What is good is good; what is bad is bad. By grasping the fundamental conditions for value and disvalue, life-value onto-axiology does not lose relevance with the passing of time. As such, it is paradigmatic philosophy.

Original publication credits

Formally, considerable effort went into homogenising the frustratingly dissimilar academic referencing and citation styles of the original publications. As done already in my second volume for Northwest Passage Books, all bibliographic information is provided in the endnotes; there is no separate bibliography.[8] Original publication dates, translators' names and edition numbers are stated only when deemed relevant. Equally, as done throughout the book series, no analytical indices are included. Cited thinkers' dates of birth and death were kept, when available, while bracketed translations of foreign phrases were dropped. This economy of information allows the present book to be much more slender than it would otherwise be, considering also its target audience, which is not the same as the one of the original texts. Readers looking for a bulkier and more detailed critical apparatus can refer to the original texts, which are listed below.

PART I – Introductions

Chapter 1
A review essay of John McMurtry's The Cancer Stage of Capitalism, *Canadian Journal of Development Studies*, 22(1), 2001, 255–69.

Chapter 2
A review essay of John McMurtry's Value Wars: The Global Market Versus the Life Economy, *Appraisal*, 4(3), 2003, 147–52.

Chapter 3
A review essay of John McMurtry's The Cancer Stage of Capitalism: From Crisis to Cure (2nd ed.), *CCPA Monitor*, 20(6), 2013, 26–9 (Spanish translations by Andrés F. Célis are available in *Dilemata*, 15, 2014, 361–71, and *Espacio Crítico*, 19, 2013, 102–8; a Portuguese translation by Jorge Goncalves is available in *O activista*, September 2013, <http://www.oactivista.com>).

PART II – Applications

Chapter 4
What is to be Conserved? An Appraisal of Conservatism in Light of the Life Ground, in D. Özsel (ed.), *Reflections on Conservatism*, Newcastle upon Tyne: Cambridge Scholars Publishing, 2011, 289–314.

Chapter 5
Good vs. Bad Tourism. *Homo Viator's* Responsibility in Light of Life-value Onto-axiology, in E. Hujibens & M. Gren (eds.), *Tourism in the Anthropocene*, London: Routledge, 2015, 111–28.

Chapter 6
The Presupposed Oncological Model of Paul Krugman's Banking Metastases: An Introduction to John McMurtry's Philosophy, *Annuaire International des Droits de l'Homme*, VII, 2013, 353–71.

Chapter 7
Social Philosophy and Oncology (with Dr. Elísabet Hjörleifsdóttir), *Social Theory and Health*, 12(3), 2014, 313–38.

Chapter 8
Reflections on the Mission of Public Universities, *Appraisal Newsletter*, 6, October 2012, 1–2.

PART III – Implications

Chapter 9
The Caricature of Adam Smith: Ideal and Actual Capitalism in Noam Chomsky and John McMurtry, in H. Þráinsson & M. Whelpton (eds.), *Chomsky: Mál, sál og samfélag*, Reykjavík: Háskólaútgáfan, 2013, 325–50.

Chapter 10
Capitalism and Freedom: The Core of a Contradiction. An Essay on Cornelius Castoriadis and John McMurtry, *Nordicum-Mediterraneum: Icelandic E-journal of Nordic and Mediterranean Studies*, 3(2), 2008, <http://skemman.is/handle/1946/5921>.

Chapter 11
Violence and Tranquillity: Adam Smith on Death and Mortality, in C. Tandy (ed.), *Death and Anti-Death, Vol. 15*, Palo Alto: Ria University Press, forthcoming (2018).

Chapter 12
The Hopeful Liberal. Reflections on Free Markets, Science and Ethics, *Nordicum-Mediterraneum: Icelandic E-journal of Nordic and Mediterranean Studies*, 8(2), 2013, <http://skemman.is/handle/1946/15822>.

Chapter 13
"Economic Histories", a review essay of three books (F. Boldizzoni, The Poverty of Clio; S.J. Collier, Post-Soviet Social; and A. Kruck, Private Ratings, Public Regulations), *The European Legacy*, 18(5), 2013, 1–3; and "The Money Mystique", a review essay of two books (W.N. Goetzmann, Money Changes Everything. How Finance Made Civilization Possible; and Volker Berghahn, American Big Business in Britain and Germany), *The European Legacy*, 2017, <DOI: 10.1080/10848770.2017.1326663>.

Chapter 14
A review essay of Norbert Häring's and Niall Douglas' Economists and the Powerful, *Economics, Management and Financial Markets*, 8(1), 2013, 216–24.

Epilogue
Good and Bad Capitalism. Re-Thinking Value, Human Needs, and the Aims of Economic Activity, *Economics, Management and Financial Markets*, 4(3), 2009, 125–69.

PART I – Introductions

Chapter 1: The Cancer Stage of Capitalism

The Cancer Stage of Capitalism is an ambitious, committed and powerful work by John McMurtry, who aims at revealing and analysing both the inner logic and the structural consequences of contemporary market theory. As this theory is concerned, McMurtry's approach is not the most sympathetic. In his view, contemporary market theory is responsible for supporting a degenerate global market, whose development is the socio-economic equivalent of a carcinogenic pathology in medical science. McMurtry criticises its process of worldwide affirmation as destructive environmentally, socially and culturally, and he explains that its allegedly necessary conquest of the planet under multiple forms is the avoidable result of the institutionalisation of an economic and ethical paradigm that is characteristic of modern history, albeit unrecognised as such by economists and philosophers. As McMurtry writes: "In a different way from economics, philosophy also repels critical examinations of the dominant market system while at the same time assuming its order as a given. Its most influential figures not only tacitly assume the market system regulating world existence as a general fact, they never question. More deeply, they posit its first principle of self-maximization as the meaning of reason itself."[9]

Far from being a dogmatic condemnation, McMurtry's book presents logically well-constructed and empirically well-buttressed arguments to justify its negative evaluation of the market's planetary takeover. With an almost obsessive care for the factual foundation of his arguments, McMurtry depicts the dramatic implications of contemporary capitalism through concrete examples drawn from institutional and scientific sources on, *inter alia*, the environment, working conditions, epidemiological trends, un- and underemployment levels, and urban hygiene standards. In a constant search for illuminating interdisciplinary references, McMurtry combines scientific rigour with philosophical depth. The attention paid to the crucial inputs of medical science, biology, physics, economics, social and political science, reflects a rare operation of synthetic understanding of the problem at issue, bringing together an impressive number of researchers from diverse scientific fields that reflect the interdisciplinary nature of McMurtry's enquiry.[10]

The Life-Blind Money Sequences of Standard Market Theory and Practice

McMurtry claims that contemporary market theory entails a fundamental conflict between the requirements of the dominating economic forces, pursuing endless replication of money sequences, and those of planetary life. Life exists not only at the biological or ecological levels (e.g. biodiversity and environmental quality, which are necessary conditions for survival and growth of Earth's life-forms), but also at the anthropological, social and cultural levels (e.g. peaceful international relations, social order, reduction of criminality, and high literacy rates). To better understand what terms such as "money sequence", "life", and their mutual conflict mean, it is worth recalling here briefly McMurtry's 1998 book, *Unequal Freedoms: The Global Market as an Ethical System*.[11]

In the chapter entitled "The Economics of Life and Death", McMurtry explores the essential features of the traditional Marxist analysis of the capitalist economy, where money is invested in the production of commodities to raise more money at the end of an economic transaction (i.e. profits; or $\$ \rightarrow C \rightarrow \$^1$). Such is the *money-sequence economy*, firmly established worldwide by the 19th-century bourgeois Industrial Revolution *cum* colonial expansion. Then, the money-sequence economy replaced on a global scale the pre-capitalist conception of money as a mere means of exchanging commodities for other commodities ($C \rightarrow \$ \rightarrow C^1$). McMurtry furthers Marx's model into three post-Marxist sequences of the capitalist circuit:

[1] Commodities are analysed in terms of relevance for life, i.e. money→commodities as means of life→more money ($\$ \rightarrow MoL \rightarrow \$^1$). The considerations following this conceptual

operation are rather dramatic: many of the commodities produced in the existing global market do not improve or even sustain life-forms, but harm them (e.g. junk food and cigarettes).

[2] More alarmingly, some highly profitable commodities in the money-sequence economy are explicitly designed to destroy life (e.g. weapons and toxic pesticides). McMurtry symbolises the money-sequence as money→commodities as means of destruction→more money ($\$ \rightarrow DC \rightarrow \$^1$).[12]

[3] Another variation of the money-sequence economy is not mediated by any commodity that is not money itself. In other words, it is decoupled from any sort of productive activity. In contemporary parlance, this is the so-called "virtual" or "paper economy" (e.g. equity investments, currency speculation), as opposed to the "real economy" (i.e. [1] and [2]). Its algebraic expression is $\$ \rightarrow \$^1 \rightarrow \$^2$ (i.e. money→more money→more money, *ad infinitum*).[13]

Once characterised as [1]–[3], McMurtry's preoccupations become quite evident. None of the life-distinctions that these sequences embody is or can be recognised by the money-sequence economy and by standard economic thinking. Commodities, even when lethal, are revealingly called "goods" nonetheless in both theory and practice. As such, the entire capitalist economy can be said to be detached in principle from any life-based defining criterion. The very idea that, somehow, the nefarious impact of for-profit activities may be conventionally called "externalities", i.e. external to what is properly economic by definition, hence deemed a matter for regulators and public authorities acting upon the economy from its outside rather than from its inside, reveals the intrinsic life-blindness of standard market theory, not just that of its material manifestations.

McMurtry concentrates most of his analyses on [3], since this third instance has become the leading force in today's market economy, as indicated in various ways by the enormous international fluxes of financial capital, including investments in the stock market, private lending to public institutions, currency speculation, concentration of financial capital in investment funds of different types, and continued access to strategic credit by large corporations spearheading the globalisation and standardisation of production, sales and consumption patterns. In other words, [1] and [2] have turned, to a significant extent, into appendices of [3]. The financial market has become the actual arbiter of the real economy. Significantly, the main arena of contemporary capitalist competition —competition for profits—takes place on the stock market, not the direct production and sale of commodities, and financial services are often the largest part of manufacturing businesses themselves.[14]

What propels McMurtry's life-grounded perspective into ethical alarm at the widespread success of the so-called "paper economy" is that the life-protecting powers of the public institutions—the sole institutions that directly promote the common good as such—are being weakened or even annihilated by [2], but even more so by [3]. This is happening not only because of the patent life-destructive practices of states involved in conflicts enriching arms industries and dealers, which are far from absent on the world's scene, but also because of the progressive subjugation of the public sector to the private sector, which is in great part the result of the former borrowing capital from the latter in order to be operative. The private sector's paramount interest becomes then to increase the public sector's debt and maximise financial returns from it in the form of compound interest. This is the iron logic of the phenomenon at issue, whose consequence is a structural weakening of the public sector and its subsequent incapability of performing its constitutionally mandated life-protecting tasks, insofar as its revenues are siphoned instead to the creditors, who often escape taxation and hardly reinvest their profits into the local economies.

Life *qua* fundamental criterion does not enter at all into the computations of the private sector investing in the public sphere, because [3] selects for financial returns on investment as its ultimate, constitutive and defining task, irrespective of the social problems that often arise in its wake. Fund managers are definitely more likely to lose their job for being unable to enrich adequately the fund's already-rich shareholders, not for impoverishing the population of a debtor country or municipality, increasing manic-depressive pathologies, or leading to a spike in suicides. Also, whereas public institutions operate mainly at a local or national level, [3] is supernational. Consequently, because of this gap between the market and the institutions that could protect the general welfare, the money-sequence economy has become in effect a transnational sovereign overriding the life-protecting control of national and regional goods.

The relationship between globalisation and systemic damages to life-hosts is, however, not discerned as a problem from the market's point of view, and this is not revised, both because the economic trends are often considered as necessary as physical laws—a claim that is as old as David Ricardo (1772–1823)—and because the market has also a role in determining the social consciousness of these economic phenomena themselves (i.e. through the corporate-owned media whose market regulation is too in accordance with the money-sequence goal of maximising returns to shareholders). With the insidious pervasiveness typical of a cancerous disease agent, the money-sequence economy is not recognised as the cause of the life-damages it actually selects for in order to reduce costs and increase revenues. The immune defences of the social host, i.e. its public authorities, do not function to halt the cancerous development, but rather serve the advance of its life-decoupled sequences as a requirement of "returning to growth", "competing in the global market.", being "efficient", etc. It is in this sense that McMurtry's reference to a *cancer stage* of capitalism must be understood. He does not use "cancer" as a metaphor, but rather as an explanatory model for understanding the modalities whereby the virtual economy has been taking over the real economy, and whereby the rule of the former over the latter is also damaging the life-structures of the planet through its cost-reducing and revenue-increasing regime, which at the same time hampers and reduces those life-protecting public institutions as "unaffordable costs", "distorting competition", "interfering in the free market", etc.

McMurtry argues that economic and social paradigms have been historically taken as the obvious and necessary framework of both the commonsensical and philosophical—or more generally scientific—view of reality. Because they are so obvious, they not only stop being questioned, but they also stop being seen as human constructions implying values, preferences and interests. The first chapter of the book provides a detailed historical elucidation of this process of critical oblivion. McMurtry describes a number of instances of intellectual acceptance of economic and social structures as necessary givens, or "closed value programmes".[15] McMurtry's examples portray an imprinted resistance to any deep questioning of the established social regimes and two cases from the history of thought are highlighted: Socrates' (470−399 BC) and David Hume's (1711−1776).

Both of them, according to McMurtry, are major philosophical iconoclasts who, despite their corrosive thinking, never dared doubt the necessity or value of the basic social and economic structures of their own societies—slavery in the case of Socrates, and private property in the case of Hume. Only with Jean-Jacques Rousseau (1712−1778) and Karl Marx (1818−1883), argues McMurtry, did philosophy become capable of criticising *radically*—that is, to the root—the existing economic and social paradigm. These two radical cases notwithstanding, McMurtry concludes that the philosophical-scientific enterprise has mostly been, and still remains, timorous about rising doubts of Rousseauvian or Marxian magnitude. A general escape from this intellectual and personal challenge is testified by contemporary academic research, whereby a form of "methodological censorship" is regularly enacted by scholars and scientists between, among, upon, and within themselves.

McMurtry's notion of censorship is not to be understood in the mode of a tribunal of inquisitors selecting and punishing trespassers —which, nevertheless, may sometimes be the case—but rather a methodological exclusion of any intellectual space where trespassing is possible. Academia's self-confinement within the "closed value program" of contemporary market theory, McMurtry argues, is achieved in several ways: by ignoring those problems that could reveal the axiological contradictions of the ruling paradigm (e.g. about the notion of freedom, as explained in what follows); by making any such deep-structured critique unreachable through the promotion of narrow-sighted hyper-specialist scholarly approaches;

by taking the paradigm for granted as a necessary historical, physical or divine structure beyond human choice. With this last move, the economic and social paradigm becomes a structure founded on necessity, whose criticism as a "value programme" would be as unreasonable as questioning the moral rightfulness of Einstein's relativity. As a result, any Rousseauvian or Marxian intellectual challenge becomes implausible and all the easier to invalidate whenever arising among allegedly "odd", "disgruntled", "unprofessional" and otherwise rhetorically disqualified critical minds.

Regaining Sight and Resolving Problems

The second and third chapter offer a detailed account of how the free market's value programme has developed and taken over the regulation of planetary life over the last three centuries. This historical account is intended to move beyond trans-historical *generalia* and individuate the causal nexus between the existing economic system and the harms suffered by individuals, populations, cultures and environments, in specific hosts and periods.

The first step of McMurtry's scrutiny strikingly demonstrates an apparently outrageous statement: "the free market has been turned into its effective opposite".[16] McMurtry claims that contemporary globalisation has betrayed utterly the classical model of the free market—what Adam Smith described as the self-regulating economic system where a multitude of responsible individuals are free to exchange priced goods and services in order to maximise their own individual profit and unintentionally promote the common good. McMurtry carefully lists and outlines the basic conditions that Smith presupposed for this system to work properly: the absence of any individual's major influence over price or supply in production and distribution; the normal non-emigration of capitals to foreign countries; the primacy of the real economy over the paper economy; the productive reinvestment of capitals to put labour to work; the public enforcement of taxation proportional to the citizen's wealth; and the sharp distinction between private trade and sovereign jurisdictions, i.e. between merchants and governments.

After a poignant analysis of Smith's texts and of the structural data of the contemporary global markets, McMurtry convincingly concludes that the latter meet none of these conditions, either in theory or in practice. Instead of a free market with many free competing agents, a plutocracy of big corporations exists in realty, which increasingly prevent the competition of producers and sellers, save when this may be advantageous to them (e.g. increased competition among workers for lower wages). McMurtry argues step by step that almost none of the supposed freedoms of the free market is actually left: not that of the consumer, for several World Trade Organisation's (WTO) agreements deny it; not that of the seller, for enduring unemployment represents a logical paradox (the sellers of their labour, namely the largest group of sellers on the market, are not free to sell); not that of the producer, for a wage-earner producing goods is subject to the employer's directives, while a corporate manager is bound to obey to the "fiduciary duty to stockholders" to maximise profits; not that from government interference, for private companies ask for and regularly obtain tax deferments and many other convenient loopholes, publicly funded subsidies, *ad hoc* legislation, and governmental investments in infrastructures, research, shares and any other good or service that these companies may wish to be the beneficiary of the public purse.[17]

The second step in McMurtry's scrutiny is the elucidation of the pathological logic operating beneath the global market. Even if most of Adam Smith's necessary conditions for the free market have been subverted, one is still present, namely, the market agent's maximisation of profit. However, since multinational corporations are the true effective agents left in the global market, where cut-throat price wars are carefully avoided by such giants, this remaining condition takes the form of abatement of costs for private corporations. Under this perspective, some of the most alarming elements of the global market come to light. In fact, once disengaged from all other conditions of classical market theory, corporate agents enter a process of unlimited self-reproduction, aimed at increasing profits at any cost to life outside their proprietary columns.

Anything that may represent an obstacle to their money-sequence growth becomes an obstacle to trade that must be eradicated, even if it may be good under several other respects (e.g. environmental regulation, work-safety standards). Corporate plutocracy can even reject democracy whenever its absence may be more profitable. In their eyes, public authority can turn into an annoying interference in the market, whilst all public-sector functions become legitimate if and only if they contribute to so-called "market competition", no matter how uncompetitive and skewed this is in reality.

These dramatic horizons are not the expression of McMurtry's political concerns but rather, as he accurately demonstrates, a long record of recurrent historical cases. For instance, with regard to the erosion of existing states' margin of control over the money-sequenced growth of corporations, McMurtry observes how major private financial groups have managed to free themselves from public constraints by means of complex tax avoidance schemes, opaque ownership structures and, above all, privatised money supply all over the world. With precise references and data, McMurtry shows the systematic strategies through which corporate oligopolies have progressively subjugated public institutions, creating, by way of leveraged credit, the money upon which these institutions depend at the cost of accumulating compound interest. Enriched in this way, private financial interests, which already own the bulk of private corporate stocks, have occupied public structures too, squeezing out of them vertiginous profits, eliminating regulatory impediments to their own expansion, and compelling the State itself to work against its own constitutional goals.

The money-sequence "virtual economy" has conquered more and more power over a plethora of private enterprises, public spaces and resources, following a pattern of development that McMurtry eventually diagnoses as a carcinogenic pathology on the social level of life-organisation:

> [A]n uncontrolled and unregulated reproduction and multiplication of an agent in a host body; that is not

committed to any life function of its life-host; that aggressively and opportunistically appropriates nutriments and resources from its social and natural hosts in uninhibited growth and reproduction; that is not effectively recognized or responded to by the immune system of its hosts; that possesses the ability to transfer or to metastasize its growth and uncontrolled reproduction to sites across the host body; that progressively infiltrates and invades contiguous and distant sites of its life-hosts until it obstructs, damages and/or destroys successive organs of their life-systems; and that without effective immune-system recognition and response eventually destroys the host bodies it has invaded.[18]

Carefully applied to each degenerative phase of civil and environmental life-organisation, McMurtry's medical model explains the connection between the pervasive affirmation of the global market and the impotence of most governments in coping with the harms produced by market deregulation and uninhibited universalisation in the name of liberty and free choice: mass unemployment, environmental collapse, social insecurity, and increasing gaps between rich and poor persons and nations. McMurtry explains and documents the ways in which states have become co-operating agents of the disorder affecting them, incapable of patrolling, recognising and responding to the threat of the carcinogenic patterns divesting them of assets and control.

The third step of McMurtry's historical account is the determination of a cure for the disease. Ultimately, once the disease is revealed, the previously invisible contradiction between global market demands and life requirements becomes open to a solution, at least in principle. McMurtry's formulation of a cure moves through two distinct moments: first, the identification of the theoretical criteria for a paradigm shift; second, the determination of operative criteria that can guide the paradigm shift.

The first moment—providing theoretical criteria for a paradigm shift–requires the introduction of life within the life-blind Newtonian model of market theory. This is possible, argues McMurtry, if and only if one recognises that the dominating economic paradigm is also and fundamentally an ethical paradigm, i.e. a value programme. Paradigms can be changed if and only if they are a matter of choice, not of necessity. McMurtry's concern about choice and necessity explains why he opens his book with an illustration of how value programmes arise, develop, take over, and become invisible. The paradigm shift McMurtry advocates implies the passage from a money-sequence economy to a life-sequence economy. The latter type of economy can be expressed as follows: life→money as means of life→more life (or $L{\to}MoL{\to}L^1$). The life-sequence economy substitutes the priority of the money-sequence economy—i.e. more money at the end of each transaction ($\$^1, \$^2...\$^n$)—with a new one, namely more life at the end of each transaction (L^1). "More life" means, in this revised understanding of economic activities, money that is successful in terms of meeting genuine life needs, where a need is defined as that whose regular deprivation "results in an absolute reduction of its owner's life-range capabilities".[19] Under the alternative paradigm that McMurtry proposes, economic transactions would become truly profitable in a completely new way: "profits" would not to be judged by corporate incomes above all else, but by fulfilment of life-hosts' requirements.[20]

According to the logic of the "life-sequence economy", life is increased, or at least maintained at the same level, at the end of its transactions. Increases or decreases in terms of life, argues McMurtry, are measurable by the degrees or ranges of biological movement, felt being and thought that they enable or disable. Conceptual and material instruments required for these measurements are furnished by, *inter alia*, medical science, biology and several other disciplines (e.g. measurements of functionality for organs, surveys on literacy levels, comparative records on infant mortality or life-expectancy rates).[21] In order to show how the contemporary global market economy is not profitable in terms of life-sequences, the initial part of the fifth chapter identifies systemic deteriorations or destructions of social and environmental life-hosts following from its advance. The evidence McMurtry provides is not intended to display simply the conflict between private interests and life-needs; rather, it is deployed to argue that the existing problems can be solved. This evidence reveals the existence of an infrastructural, reactive life-ground, whose exigencies cannot be damaged by "the cancer stage of capitalism" without some form of life-protective response.

The second moment—the determination of the operative criteria for the shift—argues from the nature of the life-ground toward recognisable guidelines for reorganising the present economy. Unlike Marx, who bases his resolving principles of social revolution as productive force development and the political movement of the working class towards the creation of society anew, McMurtry works from the basis of life-value as such, especially the evolved "civil commons" and "social immune system" already in place requiring the recognition and response of societies across class divisions.[22] What is this life-ground, though? How can it help us modify the existing economy into a life-serving one?

McMurtry bases his answer on the *explanans* of his most original philosophical notion—the "civil commons".[23] The *commons* are any "nature-given land or resource not regulated by human agency to serve life", whereas the *civil* commons imply a co-operative social construct whereby, *inter alia*, "such natural or human-made goods of life... are regulated".[24] In other words, the concept of "civil commons" refers to the array of human life-aimed resources regulated by the community benefitting from them, ensuring their preservation over time, and granting to all community members continued access to them. In McMurtry's own words: "[T]he civil commons is human agency in personal, collective or institutional form which protects and enables the access of all members of a community to basic life goods."[25]

McMurtry cites many examples, including the pre-agribusiness village commons in England and the Turkwei's acacia forests in modern Kenya, worldwide funeral customs (intended as practices to avoid epidemics caused by rotting corpses) and children's primary education (the ABCs needed to be able to interact with the other members of the community). Other examples reach beyond the more evidently regulated "commons" of a community: the Internet (as an area of expression based on free software and voluntary cooperation), indigenous music, sidewalks and footpaths, and, most profoundly, vernacular language.[26] In McMurtry's opinion, the difficulty in recognising all these cases as expressions of the civil commons arises from the fact that we presuppose them, hence forgetting them as preconditions of the community's own existence. In his words: "We do not see the civil commons underneath us [on which] our lives stand."[27]

Under this perspective, the civil commons are not an idealistic principle of good will, or a declaration of universalistic intent, but something already present in the world's life-protecting institutions. This is true, for example, of phenomena as different as the welfare state, the Nuremberg Charter, the Ozone Protocol, public gardens and city plans. Hence, McMurtry concludes, if we want to respond to the pathogenic privatisation of the global market, we must turn our gaze towards the civil commons, which operate in their primary moment as a social immune system.

In the final part of his book, McMurtry defines a series of operative criteria to be implemented over the already-existing life-protecting human structures. First, he articulates principles to select among public offices, for "whatever is required for the civil commons to serve life is a legitimate function for public financing and support".[28] These offices would have then to respect their constitutionally mandated ends, i.e. those life-enabling ends that qualify as civil commons. Instead of working in favour of the reproduction of money-sequences, as the life-uncommitted cells of an organism affected by cancer do, they would respond in accordance with the life-host requirements against the cancer's life-reducing effects. Second, McMurtry describes the sort of constitutional and legal framework to be applied in order to respond. The Universal Declaration of Human Rights, the International Covenant on Civil and Political Rights (ICCPR) and the International Covenant on Economic, Social and Cultural Rights (ICESCR) are highlighted as the already-existing constitutional and legal framework expressing precisely the defining principle of the civil commons in codified form. Nothing new or revolutionary is needed: all key-resources are already in place. The crucial point becomes recognising their unifying life-protective telos and enforcing it effectively as "the rule of law".[29]

In contrast, the existing regimes of international trade regularly override the enforcement of the legal principles stated in these charters and covenants as a trend of dreadful "metastases".[30] International trade, as McMurtry demonstrates by its exclusions, permits any sort of crime against humanity because no recognition by prior law against these crimes is included in the thousands of articles that supposedly regulate it. Applying already-instituted international charters on the same level as, say, international copyright conventions, would achieve important advances, though. More deeply, argues McMurtry, control over the source of the carcinogenic pathology, i.e. the proliferating money-sequence economy, is the fundamental ground of resolution to society's war against itself.

In practice, then, McMurtry has specific policy proposals to offer, for example the introduction of an international system of minimal taxation on financial transactions, along the lines of the so-called "Tobin tax". This is seemingly a minor and merely technical adjustment in the financial game as this is played today, which involves however more wealth in a day than the United States' (US) Gross Domestic Product (GDP) amounts to in a year. With the revenue from these taxes alone, the states could limit already the disastrous outcomes of currency speculation, boom/boost cycles, and the strangling pressure of private money-lenders.[31]

Concluding Remarks

After acknowledging the many poignant arguments offered by McMurtry in his *Cancer Stage of Capitalism*, a few critical points need to be raised. Any excellent scholarly work, in fact, cannot but produce new questions. Specifically:

(a) Which market theory is McMurtry criticising?
(b) How plausible is his alternative economic model?
(c) What is his understanding of the notion of life?

As regards (a), McMurtry's analysis of the free market relates essentially to a precise historical phenomenon capable of life-destruction at unprecedented speed and range—today's global market, as this has been unfolding since at least the 18th century. In particular, his book criticises the devastating consequences of contemporary globalisation and identifies the main sources of its success: transnational corporations, collusive public institutions and hypocritical libertarian ideologues. In other words, his work cannot be said to present arguments against market theory and the free market in general, i.e. in abstract terms, but rather against a particular socio-historical instantiation of it, i.e. market theory and the free market as they have actually evolved until now. Connectedly, McMurtry's impressive elaboration of biological, sociological, economic and political data can surely prove the flaws of the existing market and the many contradictions of its defenders, but it cannot reject market theory and the free market as such, i.e. on a more theoretical level. McMurtry's book does track the evolution of market theory of the last three centuries and envisages connections between its 18th-century origins and its recent carcinogenic eruption and metastases.[32] However, its critical focus is clearly centred on the latter, namely the global corporate system, which has appropriated the traditional free market for its self-description, though it opposes it in every principle.[33]

In consequence, an economic model intended to be an alternative to today's global market need not necessarily be McMurtry's life-sequence economy, which he claims to be the way out from the cancer of 21st-century capitalism. For instance, a money-sequence alternative could be congruously developed from McMurtry's notion of the unseen mutation of Adam Smith: a healthy capitalism. An alternative model based on the achievement of an actual free market can be imagined, where all the structures and requirements envisaged by Smith are in the right place and operate on a global scale, instead of being perverted or eliminated by the uncontrolled greed of monopolists that he opposed and by the improper intervention of local states, which Smith criticised as well. Then, and only then, might actual wealth be produced *via* capitalist means and become likely to be fairly distributed between capital and labour. Furthermore, if such a real free market with perfect competition were ever attained, then the realm of economics would also be kept apart from that of politics, both in theory and in practice. Acting consistently with its own telos, market theory would regard only matters of trade and not of collective decision-making, or, whenever it did otherwise, it would be evident that it is not doing economic analysis, but something else, e.g. politics or advocacy. This way, the market would be left as free as possible, while the problems external to, or unresolved by, trade alone would be tackled in their proper political terms.

As regards (b), it can be argued that the alternative model sketched in (a) is doubtfully achievable, but the same can be said of McMurtry's. Whereas his criticism of the global market is factually supported, detailed, up-to-date, clear and down-to-earth, his alternative economic model—the life-sequence economy—seems far less easy to grasp and less obvious to adopt. Even if one could easily agree with McMurtry on the existence of realities such as vital needs, life-enhancing goods and life-defending institutions, the unveiling of a universally shared life-ground being regulated as the civil commons and encompassing things as diverse as public parks, Robin Hood of Sherwood Forest and language, would remain a much bigger step to take.

In other words, not only would there be the problem of reaching a unanimous agreement on what constitutes a vital need, a life-enhancing good or a life-defending institution, plus the problem of organising such things in a functional hierarchy, but there would also be the problem of understanding all these various realities in terms of life-sequences, life-ground responses and the civil commons. Whether he is aware of it or not, McMurtry gives his readers and the world's political agents a very demanding task: to get rid of a significant part of their current conceptual framework, of their culture, of their *Bildung*, in favour of another one—a 'McMurtryian' one. He asks for a paradigm shift that is not merely a piece of hermeneutics or a mental experiment, like being 'trapped' within a novel or playing a character, but one that changes the overall interpretation of economic and political affairs. McMurtry does much more than simply detect the imperfections of contemporary capitalism and suggest *ad hoc* remedies, which indeed exist in such forms as trade unionism, international legislation and public welfare structures. He actually tries to revolutionise the generally adopted economic *Weltanschauung* by intellectual means. He tries to let us see and understand in full the civil commons underneath us that our lives stand on.[34]

Now, nothing and no one should be prevented from doing so; but if one aims at challenging and changing the present reality, as McMurtry surely does, is a complex theory-laden reinterpretation of economic and political interrelations the most suitable tool? Even without denying the value of McMurtry's attempt, and even accepting the aptness of his life-centred paradigm, the practical results are highly unlikely to become visible in the short run, if ever. A conceptual change of this magnitude seems much more related to the sphere of culture and its long time-spans of growth and transformation than to the sphere of politics and its short time-spans, to which McMurtry devotes his attention.

As regards (c), by assuming life as a given, primary and uncontroversial value, McMurtry's criteria for understanding, measuring, comparing life-gains and life-losses are far from self-evident. In fact, at least two orders of criticism can be applied to them:

(i) They do not exclude conflicts or difficult evaluations; and
(ii) They rely on other disciplines that can be epistemologically unreliable.

Concerning (i), McMurtry claims that life must be protected and, when possible, enhanced. Consequently, biological motility, felt being and thought have to be protected and, when possible, enhanced. Clearly, the first term is a condition for the possibility of the other two. However, nothing ensures that, when two or three terms of this triplet are at stake at the same time, no reciprocal competition can arise. For instance, should a sophisticated gourmet quit an abundant consumption of red meat, from which she derives great pleasure (felt being), because of its negative consequences for her health (biological motility)? How can any diminution in felt being on the gourmet's side be compared with that of her own biological motility? In which measure should one term of the triplet be favoured with respect to another? Should the gourmet renounce red meat completely or just partially? And what about the slaughter of animals and consequent reduction of biological motility and felt being that her enjoyable activity implies? How will we calculate the increase or decrease of life-ranges?

Another example: was the great Romantic poet Samuel Taylor Coleridge (1772–1834) increasing his life-ranges when using opium to expand the capacity of his mental faculties (felt being and thought), in spite of the negative effects that the drug had on his physical health (biological motility)? Of course, it could be said that, had he avoided such practices, he would have probably lived five or even ten years longer. Would that have been a gain in terms of life-ranges? Would humankind be better off, always in terms of life-ranges, with an older but presumably less inspired, imaginative, creative Samuel Taylor Coleridge?

My question on Coleridge and humankind leads to a more dramatic one: when is it right to judge a gain or a loss in terms of life-ranges? Should this be done before an action is performed, while it is being performed, or after it has been completed (or at all these moments)? If it is evaluated after an action is completed, how long after? Immediately, one year, one generation, or one century? Was not war (implying life-reduction) the main instrument for the expansion of the Roman civilisation (implying life-increase)? Similarly, could the contemporary market require not a dramatic amount of life-reduction now, in order to achieve a better future, richer in life? Who can evaluate and suggest the best decisions to take? McMurtry's book, though offering conceptual pathways whereby to deal with these issues, does not articulate a precise set of categories whereby to meet such critical questions.

Concerning (ii), McMurtry refers to the medical and biological sciences, as well as social and political sciences, *qua* useful disciplines to help us evaluate how to gauge, protect and enhance life. Quite evidently, McMurtry needs an inter-subjective instrument to be able to draw a line between life-destruction and life-promotion, and these sciences represent such an instrument. However, doubts can be cast on the disciplines that play such a crucial role in McMurtry's work. First, throughout the history of humankind, almost every science has known periods of political and economic control selecting what researches should do and determining which results should be obtained. McMurtry accuses contemporary scientists of colluding with the market value-system, while at the same time he must rely on their findings for empirical substantiation of his own claims. Can we trust the existing scientific community to be up to the task? Or, less sceptically, how far can we rely on the existing disciplines? Can they solve the examples of conflict given above? McMurtry's *Cancer Stage of Capitalism*, which certainly provides food for thought aplenty, does not provide a clear answer to these critical questions either.

Chapter 2: Value Wars

[O]ver 60 per cent of international trade is between offices of the same firms or interlocked partners[35]... [A]n estimated 75-90 per cent of cancer afflictions are now environmentally induced[36]... [D]ominant private banks and financial institutions have wrested away over 95 per cent of existing currency and credit creation... and have increased both public and private indebtedness to higher levels than in 1929[37]... [their] currency-reserve requirements... [being] 0-4 per cent[38]... [T]here has been over a tenfold multiplication of automobiles since 1950, and a well over 100-fold increase of leisure motorcrafts, with these multiplying units typically increasing in horsepower, mileage driven, non-renewable energy consumption, fume effluents[39]... $2.6 trillion of unaccountable documented damages a year are imposed on [US] citizens by their own corporations, whose fortune 500 do not create but reduce net American jobs. American workers' hours are the longest hours in the industrialised world[40]... Taxpayers' subsidies to these corporations are at least $135 billion per year and growing in the weapon business[41]... Average wages have fallen by 12 per cent since 1980, while the average working week is 60 hours a year longer[42]... Every 12 months 245,000 people are killed by air pollution, corporate hospital malpractice and toxic exposures in corporate workplaces... as 90 per cent of the economic growth was appropriated by 1 per cent of the population[43]... 2 million poor people and parents are in corporate state cages, while infant mortality rates are higher than Cuba and longevity is near the worst of all OECD countries[44]... This "free flow of capital" in 1997 Asia transferred $100 billion to currency speculators from their domestic banks, doubled unemployment in leading Korea and bankrupted 90 per cent of its construction companies, destroyed the economy of Indonesia so that vectors of its 220 million people are now plundering the world's most species-rich rainforests in desperation, and occasioned the buy-up of the assets of the Asian tiger 'market miracles' at bankruptcy rates[45]... Murdoch's News Corporation made £1,400,000,000 from the production and sale of newspapers in Britain between 1987 and 1999, and paid no corporation taxes[46]... Far from blocking such tax evasion, New Labour granted further tax giveaways to other rich capitalists, slashing taxes on capital gains from 40 per cent to 10 per cent[47]... 165,000 corporate public relations professionals now outnumber the total number of journalists who work for all newspapers, radio, and television stations, with 9000 PR firms the source of an estimated 50-80 per cent of the news presented.[48]

Above all else, McMurtry's *Value Wars* is an impressive scholarly collection of data on the phenomenon of globalisation, which is thereby displayed in its complex array of economic, social, political, and biological implications. Looking at today's mainstream Western media, such data seem to be rarely, if ever, as widely publicised and discussed in any depth as David Beckham's latest injury or as Microsoft's new operative system. Yet, these data speak of social and economic tensions concerning billions of human and non-human lives that are being affected, sometimes, in the most ruinous ways. These social and economic tensions are the reality about which morally responsible intellectuals are expected to care; at least insofar as they maintain their commitment to the understanding of the fundamental grounds of value along which human agency unfolds. Indeed, just because of the amount and of the urgency of the information provided, McMurtry's book is a most remarkable text.

Secondly, McMurtry's *Value Wars* is an impressive scholarly collection of data that are analysed philosophically. Cutting across different fields of inquiry and human activity, McMurtry's study argues that the corporate take-over of the world's resources increasingly fails to satisfy the original, etymologically grounded defining criterion of "capital": living wealth producing more living wealth. McMurtry proceeds to expose and resolve this foundational confusion by distinguishing different forms of capital, their regulating sequences of determination, and their systemic effects on life. The result of this analysis is the detection of an ongoing conflict between the requirements of today's leading economic forces and the requirements of life itself. In addition to this result, McMurtry formulates a number of practical guidelines for policy-making to be implemented by the existing world's governments upon the basis of the international legal framework already available to them.

The Conflict of Money and Life

The starting point of McMurtry's distinction is the individuation of the regulating sequence of determination of the capitalist economy, which Marx first outlined and which neoclassical economists have retained to the present day. McMurtry refers to it as the *money-capital sequence*, insofar as monetary wealth is invested (input) in commodity production and/or stocks, in order to command more monetary wealth (output). The formal expression of this sequence, which McMurtry had developed in his previous two volumes on globalisation (*Unequal Freedom* and *The Cancer Stage of Capitalism*) and that we encountered in the previous chapter, is the following: $\$ \rightarrow C \rightarrow \$^1$. "$\$$" refers to the initial money input, "C" to the commodities or stocks in which the money input is invested (e.g. the automobile industry, agribusiness, market-margin speculation), and "$\$^1$" to the money output, which must be higher than the input, either by reduction of the input (e.g. cost abatement by downsizing or avoidance of labour standards and taxes) or by increase of the output (e.g. revenues increase by reinvestment in short-term currency speculation or avoidance of capital gain taxes). The obligation to determine an output that is higher in monetary value than the original input derives from the so-called "fiduciary duty" existing between the corporate subject and its stockholders, whose assets are expected to increase in value *ad infinitum*, beyond simple profitability, unless the corporate subject ceases to exist.[49]

To the money-capital sequence McMurtry adds the *life-capital sequence*. Regularly, throughout the system of economic transactions, ranges of biological movement (or action), felt being and thought are also invested in the production of means of life, sometimes furthering broader and deeper ranges of biological movement, felt being and thought. Recycling industries, public management of community water aquifers and universal education are examples of what McMurtry conceives of as life capital producing means of life producing more life capital in return. The formal expression of the life-capital sequence, which was also introduced in the previous chapter, is the following: $L \rightarrow MofL \rightarrow L^1$. "*L*" refers to the initial input of life-capital invested in the means of sustenance and promotion ("*MofL*") of wider ranges of life-capital to be obtained as an output ("L^1").

With regard to the calculation of this capital, McMurtry expands on the recent, alternative econometrics that have been developed by the UN as well as by other high-level institutions in order to deal with the dimensions of human capital and natural capital (e.g. the UN's Human Development Index and the Statistics Canada System of Environmental and Resource Accounts). Specifically, McMurtry outlines a comprehensive *Well-Being Index*, which is based on a basic minimum parametric of eight life means: "air quality... access to clean water... sufficient nourishing food... security of habitable housing... opportunity to perform meaningful service or work of value to others... available learning opportunity to the level of qualification... healthcare when ill... [and] temporally and physically available healthy environmental space for leisure, social interaction, and recreation".[50]

Far from being the daily standards upon which governments, institutional policy-makers and mainstream economists base their decisions or measure value, the ontological and axiological dimensions that these alternative econometrics deal with have not been and cannot be computed by the Newtonian-physics-modelled econometrics of either classical or neoclassical market theory, which, as McMurtry highlights, deal instead with "uniform, invariant sequences" of "externally observable and quantifiable" objects.[51] Life is blinkered out *a priori* by such standard system of economic calculus, for it does not display the necessary features of the particular objects that can be handled by such a calculus, namely inanimate objects following unvarying patterns of behaviour.[52] If, from a logical point of view, the disconnection of the money capital from the life capital does not imply necessarily any conflict between them, the same disconnection does not imply mutual flourishing either. The variable of life is simply alien to the money-capital sequences.

In practice, the conflict between the two capitals is rife, as McMurtry's cross-disciplinary researches reveal amply, almost obsessively, *pace* any facile presumption of boundless prosperity secured by a providential logic of unintended consequences.[53] Moreover, McMurtry observes how, in the last twenty years, money-capital growth and accumulation has been taken more and more often as the only structure of understanding and directing any assumedly rational and scientific process of policy-making. Neoclassical economics has become much more than a possible interpretation of certain economic phenomena: it has become the paradigm of human rationality itself.[54] Through a grotesque repeated combination of *non-sequitur* statements, rhetorical rejections of alternative views, mass-media propaganda, culpable denials of historical evidence, and the eschatological (and non-falsifiable) assumption of a deistic invisible hand that will solve all problems, the world's most powerful "group-think" has locked many minds within a set of equations reading: "Global Corporate System = Free Market = Freedom = Democracy = Prosperity = Development".[55] I would be prone to concede that such a set of equations becomes hardly tenable before any serious intellectual scrutiny, but it can prove very effective if "no alternative" is allowed to exist *ab initio*, for any alternative is bound to be, by the very definition of the paradigm, "irrational" and "unscientific".[56]

McMurtry's study helps us to see how the underlying, unanalysed, *de facto* metaphysical stance of the world's leading institutions—with the International Monetary Fund (IMF) and the WTO singled out *in primis*—has become a contractarian doctrine depicting a universe of self-maximising, informed, responsible, and free individuals who trade material goods in the competitive market. All this being done and believed in despite the contrary facts collected in *Value Wars*, which depicts an actual economic reality made of:

- Inter-dependent, self- and all-minimising individuals (e.g. ecocidal global warming, depletion of fresh-water sources, industrial-activity-related cancers, life-capital losses in general);[57]
- Who are deprived of the information required to make rational choices (e.g. WTO-dictated labelling prohibitions)[58] and who, for a large part, are not trading at all (i.e. the unemployed masses that cannot trade their labour for wages, or the millions who must accept precarious jobs since pauperism, social exclusion or starvation are the alternatives);[59]
- While it is corporate subjects, not individuals, that perform most of the world's trade (e.g. the largest 300 corporations control 98 per cent of all foreign direct investment, and 60 per cent of all land cultivated for export);[60]
- With such a trade being mainly virtual in nature (e.g. financial speculations counting for at least three quarters of all commercial transactions from the beginning of the 20th century, and regularly squeezing resources from the debt-ridden largest part of society in favour of the world's 1% creditor élite controlling the levers of financial and, often, political power);[61]
- Such corporate subjects being neither responsible (corporations enjoy limited liability, as no other citizen does, both at the domestic and, in particular, at the transnational level),[62] nor free (the managers of corporate subjects, though certainly capable of egregious larceny, are bound to their stockholders by fiduciary duty),[63] nor involved in any competitive market;
- Because what we have in existence is an oligopoly of corporate companies[64] dictating the rules of the game unilaterally to bribed and/or financially dependent

governments,⁶⁵ which enforce such rules upon their citizens and these citizens' business activities, i.e. by operating continuous market interferences favouring the creditor élite.⁶⁶

Most governments have followed the neoclassical paradigm blindly or, more appropriately for McMurtry's analysis, life-blindly. Whether doing so willingly or because under financial and/or military threat, they all have reshaped the very fabric of their communities. Typically, this reshaping has had dramatic effects on the lives of the populations involved. The quest for maximised money-capital outputs does not stop before anything, in fact, and can and does impair intellectual growth, health and democracy, if any such non-computable entity operates as "barriers to trade" or as life-enabling but profit-reducing "protectionism". As McMurtry reports, for instance, "Sub-Saharan African and East Asian countries like Indonesia and Pakistan now pay up to five times more for debt-servicing foreign banks or military-industrial providers than they do for public education and healthcare".⁶⁷

Value Wars provides an incredible amount of additional evidence, as McMurtry investigates the social and economic misfortunes of Argentina, Bolivia, Brazil, Canada, Colombia, Ecuador, Guatemala, India, Iraq, Japan, Korea, Mexico, Nicaragua, Russia and its former Soviet sister republics and satellites, Thailand, the former Yugoslavia, and the US. Life-capital significant figures in environmental losses, job insecurity, lack of healthcare and education, pathological depression and suicide rates have regularly increased in these countries as a consequence of the compliance with the life-blind logic of money-capital sequences—all these being losses that, as McMurtry's volume points out, standard GDP figures cannot individuate by their very nature.⁶⁸

Most tellingly, as we keep hearing in mainstream information media, the language itself used by the governments involved in this global pattern of allegedly rational re-shaping of entire countries speaks of "restructuring" and "reengineering" societies through "necessary sacrifices", in order to "compete in the new global market", as if even the blindest subservience to the neoclassical paradigm could not completely hide the life-destructive implications of its application. Only the European Union (EU), in McMurtry's view, has not succumbed entirely to the neoclassical "Stalinisation" of the world's economy, and is thus regarded as a model of more life-respectful socio-economic development, albeit under threat.[69]

The conceptual limitations of the neoclassical model are most evident when we de-construct the four basic money sequences of money capital along McMurtry's lines of life-capital analysis, which he first developed in *The Cancer Stage of Capitalism*—as also seen in the previous chapter:

(1) $\$ \rightarrow C+ \rightarrow \$^1$ ($C+$: to the degree that C is a life-enabling commodity to people and/or to the environment by its production and/or consequences, e.g. organic foods production, self-powered vehicles)

(2) $\$ \rightarrow C- \rightarrow \$^1$ ($C-$: to the degree that C is a life-disabling commodity causing life-reduction to people and/or the environment by its production and/or consequences, e.g. junk food, fuel-driven recreational vehicles)

(3) $\$ \rightarrow DC \rightarrow \$^1$ (DC: a commodity C so constituted as to reduce or to destroy life-organisation by its nature, e.g., armaments and cigarettes)

(4) $\$ \rightarrow \$^1 \rightarrow \$^n$ (Money is transformed into more money with no life-enabling good or service produced in between, e.g. transnational currency speculation)

Money sequence (1) is benign, and to be selected for by internalising the steering mechanisms provided by McMurtry's life-capital econometrics within economic practice (e.g. green taxation, enforced legislation). Money-capital sequences (2) and (3) are the material processes of the "Corporate Commodity Cycles", whose cumulative depredations of human and environmental life-organisation are not factored into the market-value calculus at any stage of their repertoires of eco-dismantling, extraction, processing, transportation, packaging, advertising, consumption, and non-recovered disposal.[70] (4) is the extreme case of an utterly life-detached economy, as it does not even deal with material goods, but only with virtual ones, by means of which, however, it can command over all other operations of the Corporate Commodity Cycles and therefore intensify the life-disablement that such Cycles are responsible for. Financial speculation, private money-creation by inflated assets, and unregulated credit generation are the unseen pumps of the debt-ridden, merger-obsessed "corporate juggernaut" dictating the path of globalisation, which crushes uncooperative e societies and ecosystems standing in its way.[71] The unifying economic principle of all steps of this process is one alone, namely externalisation of the costs of for-profit commodity cycles onto those who do not profit from them.[72]

The Reconciliation of Money and Life

To counter-balance the harmful pattern of unrestrained self-replication of money sequences, especially of the type (4), McMurtry proposes a *life turn*. The defence of human and environmental life organisation can be achieved by systematic accountability procedures of: (A) corporate internalisation, rather than externalisation, of costs; and (B) regulatory reduction or prevention of life harms by the Corporate Commodity Cycles through instituted obligations to comply with life-protective regulations as binding articles of international trade and access to other societies' markets.[73]

Trade sanctions are continuously enforced on a global scale. Modern computer technologies allow for instantaneous cross-checking of all major transactions. Hence, as McMurtry suggests, the same ought to be done with regard to the assessment of new types of sanctions to be introduced, these being directed to the fulfilment of life-protecting and life-promoting ends. Further, McMurtry's life turn implies restoring national and international legal sovereignty over corporate fictitious persons, 'who', for instance, are recognised human rights in their defence (e.g. the right to hold private property in particular), but against 'whom' no legally valid accusation of violation of human rights can be formulated, insofar as only State agents in the exercise of official duties can be charged with human rights violations. Similarly, legal responsibility must be reinstituted by removing or thoroughly revising limited liability privileges, which allow investors to ignore whether they finance private companies involved in murderous or ecocidal activities.[74]

It may be wondered whether the transformation of existing capitalism into a life economy is affordable. McMurtry's life turn clearly responds by four lines of argument, which my remarks have implied throughout:

1. It is the current systematic destruction of life capital by the unaccountable externalities of corporate money capital that is disastrously unaffordable, for they make present life worse and future life less likely;
2. Life-protective standards can be enforced through trade agreements as cost-effectively as the protection of private patents and other corporate rights are ordinarily by way of incentives and penalties of trade access, tariff or fines;
3. The current competitive advantage of externalising vast costs onto those who cannot afford them, and the cost-penalisation of responsible corporations, are simultaneously removed by a level-playing field of market competition regulated by strictly enforced life standards;
4. The macro recessionary/depressive trend of world economies requires a major demand stimulus of life-capital protection and formation to ensure the health and security of global citizens in place of the spectacularly wasteful and destructive public investments in, and subsidies for, military commodities and industrial agriculture.[75]

A succinct exposition of the possible legal procedures to be followed is provided by McMurtry in his concluding chapter, entitled "Life-Economy Manifesto". With respect to the factual urgency of McMurtry's life turn, I suggest the reader to consider that, while I was drafting the original review essay upon which the present chapter is based:

- The oil tanker *Prestige*, which was involved in the most profitable of trades, i.e. oil, was sinking off the Spanish coast, pouring tons of highly viscous polluting liquid into the sea;
- US President George W. Bush was speaking at a North Atlantic Treaty Organisation (NATO) meeting in Prague about the necessity of a new attack on oil-rich Iraq, whose population had already been suffering from massive aerial bombings in 1991, eleven-year-long economic sanctions causing a UN's Children Fund (UNICEF)-estimated 5,000 child-deaths per month, and twenty-three years of dictatorial rule by a murderous tyrant armed by the Western weapons industries and supported for most of his career by the US government;
- Several Indonesian citizens had been arrested under the charge of having organised a homicidal attack in Bali, i.e. possibly abiding to the sadly growing logic of terrorist response to the life-blind corporate neo-colonial policies exemplified by the Iraqi case;
- North-Western Italy had been devastated by yet another flood, the frequency of which had been increasing steadily as a result of global warming;
- Members of the Southern-Italian organisation *No-Global Rete* were imprisoned and charged with so-called "ideological crimes" [*reati d'opinione*], instituted in the penal code in the fascist era, such as planning to disrupt the economic order and interfering with State activities: these activists had issued electronic and printed messages criticising the policies promoted by the G-8 powers.

The issues with which McMurtry's book deals are probably the most serious, for they are issues about life and death. Too often, even in the scholarly world, insightful voices remain unheard because of political prejudice or personal convenience. In this sense, since 1989, many liberals have been uncritically prone to side with the libertarian rejection of the Marxian body of knowledge, rather than with the Marxist critical re-examination of the same. Yet, as McMurtry's furthering of Marx's money-capital sequence illustrates, much can still be learnt and developed from his writings. Moreover, McMurtry clearly operates beyond Marx, who presupposed wage labour throughout his analysis of economic reality. The life-ground to which McMurtry appeals is prior to both libertarian and Marxist frames of understanding, touching a fundamental level of reality whose analysis is precluded by their assumptions. Hopefully, this depth of investigation may lead scholars to derive useful insights from McMurtry's text, independently of political preconceptions. In particular, I am interested in highlighting how liberals can benefit from texts like McMurtry's *Value Wars* in order to verify how today's globalisation is jeopardising centuries-old structures of social co-existence.

First of all, the free market is at risk. In spite of the dominating rhetoric of "liberalisation" and "deregulation", we are undergoing a process of more and more thorough regulation of international trade in all of its forms. This process is dictated by corporate lawyers to governments, who are made subservient to the whims of the planet's corporate oligopoly by means of financial blackmailing. Debt-strangled countries like Chad or Nigeria can be seen as the most telling examples of how successful corporate financial means of command over entire societies can be. In a 10th October 2001 interview to *The Observer*, the former Chief Economist of the World Bank Joseph Stiglitz (b. 1943) summarised the merciless logic of this financial *itinerarium ad diabolum* in four steps, which McMurtry himself mentions in conclusion of his book (I follow here the latter's wording):[76]

1. "[B]riberisation-privatisation" (i.e. corporate-profiting "market reforms" implemented by corrupt or ideologically aligned officials),
2. "[C]apital-market liberalisation" (i.e. foreign capitals are allowed in the country so as to drain the national reserves and take control over the nation by debt creation),
3. "[M]arket-based pricing" (i.e. raising prices on basic life goods in

order to create political instability and further weaken domestic authorities),
4. "[P]overty reduction by Free Trade" (i.e. mandatory imports of corporate goods, including life-destructive ones, and cheap sale of domestic produce on the international markets).

More powerful and proudly independent countries can also be compelled to follow the demands of the corporate oligopoly. In Germany, where revenue from corporate taxes had fallen by over 50 per cent since 1980 and private profits risen by 90 per cent, transnational corporations such as Deutsche Bank and Daimler-Benz ensured that the taxes would not rise again by threatening Finance Minister Oskar Lafontaine (b. 1943)—soon forced out of his cabinet —with a possible loss of 14,000 German jobs to lower tax zones available under new transnational trade agreements.[77]

The rhetoric-inflated global free market is a less and less a free market in which many self-maximising, informed, responsible, and free individuals are competing in the trade of material goods, such that if any of them fails, she is easily replaced and the system continues unaltered. As McMurtry argues, in line with the observations provided already in his *Cancer Stage of Capitalism*, hardly any of Adam Smith's essential freedoms for genuine capitalist trade have been left on the scene:

1. Not that of the consumer, for several agreements deny it (e.g. WTO's prohibition of labels disclosing what their lawyers call "discriminatory information" on the labour and environmental standards under which commodities were produced; non-transparent discussions and/or decisions on international trade regulations later forced through parliamentary processes and not subjected to popular vote);
2. Not that of the seller, for most sellers are not free to sell (e.g. the paradox of mass unemployment: sellers of their labour are, in fact, unfree to sell);
3. Not that of the producer, whether she is the humblest worker or the proudest top manager (e.g. the wage-earner producing goods is

subject to the employer's directives, whilst managers are bound to maximise profits by fiduciary duty towards the stockholders);
4. Not that from government interference, for private corporations themselves ask for it regularly (e.g. tax deferments, publicly-funded subsidies, government investment in infrastructures, creation of market opportunities by military action, private-public partnerships, etc.).

Nor are left on the scene three fundamental conditions for genuine free trade—at least according to Adam Smith's conception of it:

1. That it creates work (e.g. unemployment figures have increased in most re-engineered countries in the past twenty years and full employment is no longer sought as a national priority, whilst the so-called "natural rate of unemployment" is accepted inasmuch as it prevents inflation, which would eat into the assets of the financial élites);
2. That it creates tangible goods (as seen, the short-term speculative paper economy has by far overgrown the real economy and/or long-term financial investments);
3. That it increases the wealth of the nations (cf. any list of countries affected by sudden "meltdowns", which were unknown under the Bretton Woods system, and any one of countries chronically indebted to foreign capital, to which they must then defer when it comes to economic, fiscal and other sovereign policies).

Secondly, several fundamental liberal freedoms are at risk, if not even the entire framework of rights entrenched within liberal, democratic constitutions. The political goals praised by Benjamin Constant (1767–1830), John Stuart Mill (1806–1873) and Isaiah Berlin (1909–1997), which had been strenuously defended by Western governments against the fascist and Soviet menaces, have been progressively abandoned after the cessation of the latter menace. Indeed, on the basis of the evidence collected in McMurtry's book, it could be argued that after the fall of the Berlin Wall, Western societies, rather than exporting liberal ideals, have been importing conspicuous degrees of Soviet-like labour and environmental malpractices, and the very possibility that certain persons—the Leader, the Party, or the Corporation, its top managers and those of the investment funds controlling much of the shares—may exist, at least *de facto*, above the law.

Also, it could be argued that, in the same years, the enjoyment of personal freedom has become more and more difficult, as it is more and more difficult for vast sectors of the population to possess enough material, temporal and intellectual resources to afford any significant self-expression, stand up alone against the employers' will, avoid lifelong marketing bamboozlement and make use of democratic institutions that are routinely bought and sold by the economic potentates. McMurtry's text helps us to see how the collapse of life-protecting public infrastructures of social wellbeing (e.g. by privatisation and/or strategic defunding of public transports, healthcare, policing, education and water resources), the ruin of entire eco-systems, the secretive top-down *faits accomplis* masterminded by non-elected central bankers or corporate-lobbied governments, and the imposition of corporate commodities on financially devastated countries are the macro-level mirror of the liberticidal realities of which more and more citizens have experience as micro-level tragedies, which involve endemic poverty, ever-growing depressive pathologies, non-unionised insecure occupations, and Pavlovian homogenisation of individual behaviour by corporate media.

Concluding Remarks

The global media are most representative of the illiberal tendencies contained in today's corporate industry, insofar as their sophisticated behaviourist techniques of marketing propaganda target all, children and teenagers included, in order to create life-long conditioned comportments (i.e. the so-called "branding", which is the same verb describing what is regularly done to cattle and that used to be done to slaves). If little open discussion of these issues is visible in the mainstream public arena, despite efforts in this sense dating back at least to Galbraith's 1967 *New Industrial State*, it is because the very same corporate media contribute in a more and more decisive way to the generation and distribution of the relevant information.[78] This is a risk about which 20th-century liberal icon Karl Popper (1902–1994) had warned his contemporaries just a few years before his death.[79]

In the academic sphere, we may still enjoy enough intellectual nurturing and freedom of speech to be able to publish critical texts such as McMurtry's or the present one, although we do not have any realistic chance of reaching regularly as wide an audience as the one reached daily by Apple or Visa with their scientifically crafted advertising campaigns. Whether we will be able to enjoy this freedom for long is not at all clear, as civil liberties are being eroded by anti-terrorist regulations such as the 2001 American Patriot Act, the 2001 Canadian Bills C-35 and C-36, or the 2002 Italian re-exhumation of ideological crimes from Mussolini's penal code.

Chapter 3: From Crisis to Cure

The first edition of John McMurtry's *Cancer Stage of Capitalism* needed no amendment; nonetheless, the second edition massively updates and advances its diagnosis. The great global turns of 9-11, the 2008 Wall Street crash, Latin America's socialism for the 21st century, and the ongoing implosion of social-democratic Europe are all here analysed in depth. The new anchor concept of "life capital—life wealth that produces more life wealth without loss"— spells out the life-ground so long missing from economic theory. The book's Preface ("What is Capital?") and long opening chapter ("Decoding the Cancer System and its Resolution") are completely new, while the new subtitle "Cure" is spelled out in light of the last 12 years of corporate assault on the life-ground and the rising global resistance to it.[80]

Despite McMurtry's 1978 *Structure of Marx's World-View* being a classic in Anglophone Marxist studies, the second edition of *The Cancer Stage of Capitalism* is neither a Marxist nor a neo-Marxian work. Quite the opposite, the Marxian assumptions of David Harvey (b. 1935)—not to mention Karl Marx himself—and the Critical Theory approach of Jürgen Habermas (b. 1929) are exposed to devastating re-grounding analyses. On the right, the inherently "life-blind" categories of neoclassical theory and neoliberalism are exploded, while Friedrich A. Hayek (1899–1992) and Milton Friedman are surgically deconstructed.[81] Even the work by Naomi Klein (b. 1970), which followed the first edition of McMurtry's book, is found to miss the underlying carcinogenic normality of so-called "disaster capitalism". Critique, however, is not the goal of the book. It is finding a life-coherent way out of the greatest collapse of both the biosphere and human civilisation that the world has ever known.

McMurtry decodes "the Great Sickness" as driven by private "transnational money sequences" multiplying in ever new and bizarre types through life hosts at every level.[82] For him, the system disorder emerged back in 1973 with the US defeat in the Vietnam

War, which led to the abandonment of the gold standard in America and the gradual demolition of the post-war Bretton Woods architecture, whereby free capital trade had been thwarted and financial speculation kept in check. At the same time, the Chilean experiment of forcibly non-unionised labour relations and top-down privatisations was conducted under General Augusto Pinochet (1915−2006) and related worldwide as a success story, which launched the absolutist rule of free-market dogma that Italy's long-time conservative MP and Finance Minister Giulio Tremonti (b. 1947) has recently dubbed "white" or "financial fascism".[83] Then, from the 1980s of Thatcherism and Reaganomics, down to the years of unipolar 21st-century world rule, the "Great Sickness" is carefully unpacked—almost step by step—following the waves of life-depletion unleashed by deregulated finance capitalism. Against its expansion, which has already claimed entire ecosystems, imperilled planetary as well as social life support systems (LSS), and *a fortiori* taken countless lives, McMurtry poses the universal and interrelated "human and natural life-requirements", whose necessities to reproduce are cumulatively deprived and despoiled.[84] This conflict is the ultimate theme of his study.

The Cancer

In summary, the "cancer system" diagnosed in the new opening chapter is the deregulated and exponentially growing global money-sequences to limitlessly more.[85] Re-grounding in "life sequences of value" and the "civil commons" is the inner logic of recovery.[86] McMurtry's "Diagnostic Summary of the Degenerate Trends" spells out in detail the elements of the "causal mechanism" at work behind the sickness, yet one paragraph of this study suffices to summarise the all-front corporate money-system attack on both biosphere and civilisation:

> The air, soil and water cumulatively degrade; the climates and oceans destabilize; species become extinct at a spasm rate across continents; pollution cycles and volumes

increase to endanger life-systems at all levels in cascade effects; a rising half of the world is destitute as inequality multiplies; the global food system produces more and more disabling and contaminated junk food without nutritional value; non-contagious diseases multiply to the world's biggest killer with only symptom cures; the vocational future of the next generation collapses across the world while their bank debts rise; the global financial system has ceased to function for productive investment in life-goods; collective-interest agencies of governments and unions are stripped while for-profit state subsidies multiply; police state laws and methods advance while belligerent wars for corporate resources increase; the media are corporate ad vehicles and the academy is increasingly reduced to corporate functions; public sectors and services are non-stop defunded and privatized as tax evasion and transnational corporate funding and service by governments rise at the same time at every level.[87]

This diagnosis may seem hyperbolic. But any search for one exception to these trends reveals how exact and precise they are. Overall, one basic lesson emerges. The "common interest" of nations and "competitive economic growth" are not one and the same, as regularly assumed.[88] On the contrary, they are in full-scale war of corporate money-sequence occupation with no bound against life, and life-value resistance at all levels.

Against the avoidant ideologies of relativism and subjectivism, McMurtry articulates "a universal and objective ground of value"; from it he "recovers step by step the missing life-ground of values and the ultimate meaning of how we are to live."[89] As shown in McMurtry's glossary for the philosophy theme of UN's Educational, Scientific and Cultural Organisation's (UNESCO) *Encyclopedia of Life Support Systems* (EOLSS), the life-ground is simply defined: "Concretely, all that is required to take the next breath; axiologically, all the life support systems required for human life to reproduce or develop."[90] Without enough bread, clean water, breathable air, open spaces in which to move and have regular sleep, progressive learning and meaningful socialisation, no value we cherish can live on. All values, whether ethical, political, legal, economic, epistemic, spiritual or aesthetic, rely upon this vital platform. Even those who deny such a value ground presuppose it by the very act of breathing.

The ultimate problem is stated in one axiomatic sentence: "Money-sequence growth throughputs that produce no life-necessity and run down non-renewable resources multiply waste and incapacitate life and life-support systems."[91] The disorder has many pathways of attack and despoliation: ever more wasteful production and consumption in leading consumer societies; growing non-contagious pathologies from intentionally marketed, life-damaging addictive commodities; and decline in environmental and social standards across the planet. The diagnosis investigates many sites of the carcinogenic system at work in plural modes, including Chile, China, Iraq, Canada, Japan, New Zealand, the former Yugoslavia, sub-Saharan Africa, Rwanda, Libya, Guatemala, Mexico, Peru, and —most systematically—the once prosperous US and EU. A comprehensive index provides easy access to crucial concepts, definitions, trends, and many examples. Throughout, McMurtry distinguishes between good and bad government in principle. Legitimacy of government depends on its fulfilling constitutionally mandated "preventative" and "enabling" life-functions ("the social state"), while bad or illegitimate government fails in, or even strips away, these life-serving functions in order to let the private money sequences of the rich grow further ("the corporate state").[92] But what serves life and what does not?

Failure to answer this question has long allowed élites and governments to ignore people's life needs. McMurtry's criterion of need resolves this longstanding conundrum. A need is, and only is, "that without which life-capacities are always reduced" (and, eventually, destroyed).[93] Armed with this understanding, he shows that globalising capitalism, since at least the 1980s, has become blind to any life needs in both theory and practice. As a result, the most severe ecological and social problems follow from it—from water aquifers and rivers lost to industrial pollution and agribusiness's overexploitation, to corporate market rights poisoning foods and making life-saving medications and knowledge unaffordable to those who need them, not to mention more and more powerful weapon commodities intentionally constructed and sold to maim and kill life. All these and other malignant growths of the great sickness show that the widespread faith in the "happy coincidence" between profit-making and the common interest by a providential "invisible hand" is at best pseudo-science.[94] But why should all this count as a cancerous system?

The first crucial step in McMurtry's diagnosis is the defining goal of the world's ruling economic agents. Whether cast as "value added", "profits", "return on equity", "quarterly earnings reports", or "shareholder value", the sole "ruling value code" is in fact "to maximize by any vehicle, method, or channel open to its entry the ratio of its owners' money-demand increases to money-demand inputs."[95] In the words expressing this underlying value principle, Chicago economist Milton Friedman is direct and absolute: "The one and only responsibility of business is to make as much money for stockholders as possible."[96] As McMurtry deconstructs the problem: "Grounded in an engineering model of perfectly divisible inputs and outputs, life itself is in principle ruled out... What money wants is all that exists."[97] Specifically, thousands of corporate-treaty rules override all else, often backed by US- or NATO-controlled armed forces, in order to collect debt, threaten, isolate, or invade societies resisting corporate money-sequence multiplication through them.

The second main step of diagnosis lies in recognising that any exponentially multiplying and uncontrolled demand serving no life-function is cancerous by definition. This is why private transnational money sequences with no committed life-function overrunning more and more domains of nature, society and the human organism are cancerous by definition. In the clinical terms of this study: "The atmosphere, freshwaters and oceans, topsoils, trees, animal habitats, and species and mineral resources degenerate in life-carrying capacities and biodiversity" while "the rising majority becomes ever more insecure, stressed, dispossessed, and malnourished beneath GDP and market measures."[98]

The third main step of diagnosis observes that in all cancers the immune defences of the host fail to recognise the invasive growth. Instead, they increasingly yield all their resources to the out-of-control self-replication of the parasitic demand. Thus, societies' long-established life-protective institutions are defunded, redirected and unresponsive to the cumulative assault upon life-hosts and support systems. They mutate instead into servants of private money-sequence growth. Governments, the media, universities, and even UN agencies do not recognise the system disorder, but collaborate with it. This is why, as McMurtry argues, we have seen a long succession of disastrous policies bleeding societies into depression since the Reagan-Thatcher turn:

> Ruin of government programs, workers' jobs and small business with the cranking up of interest rates to over 20% prime in the 1980s… repeal of Depression-installed regulations like Glass-Steagall… the race to the bottom of wages, benefits, and social legislation by global competition with no life-standards… cannibalist interest rates and debt charges… "market reforms," trade-treaty edicts prohibiting legislation reducing "profit opportunities," wars on resource rich regions with social control… supranational treaties in vast all-or-nothing tranches of "investor" rights… according all rights only to transnational corporations… [and] binding regulations… [overriding] all human and natural life-requirements through generational time… private bank displacement of sovereign control over currency and credit.[99]

As for the central discipline charged with understanding the macro system, the focus upon money-value in lieu of life-value runs so deep that "economic thought is in principle incapable of recognising what has gone wrong."[100] How can societies ever recover, then?

The Cure

The answer is by life-capital re-grounding at every level. The money-greed pathology is as old as civilisation, but never before had it been sovereign over nations. In this systemic sense, it is new. Its nonstop attacks on historic working-class rights, government regulation, progressive taxation, public welfare investment, and biosphere requirements are built in. To respond to its advance, McMurtry re-grounds human thought in what he calls "the evolution of the civil commons" which, he contends, defines civilisation itself, i.e., all the real gains of our species across generational time.[101] This is a major argument of the book and it goes all the way back to the nature of language itself.

A vast array of natural and human life-giving organisations that we can conceive of as worthy of protection, but ordinarily take for granted, are shown to express an underlying "civil commons principle": whether tangible or ideal, they are "all social constructs which enable universal access to life goods".[102] It is not a bygone or utopian idea, but includes, *inter alia*, the clean air that we still breathe, life-protective laws, universal health plans, the world wide web, common sewers, sidewalks and forest paths, games and fields of play, the open and cooperative development of science, public streetscapes, effective pollution controls, city squares and sidewalks, old-age pensions, universal education, universal hygiene practices, fair democratic elections, unemployment insurance, maximum work hours and minimum wages, public parks, clean water, community fish-habitats, and public broadcasting. Far from being merely an ideal, McMurtry demonstrates that "civil commons formation in provision of life-goods" has long been in existence and proved superior to "any for-profit system", including "corporate partnerships", which are laid bare as public-wealth looting schemes.[103]

Behind the global corporate occupation, on the cognitive level lie profound fallacies of reason still unrecognised at the highest level of intellectual inquiry. Primary is the absurd assumption that "private money" alone counts as "demand" in "the economy", thus erasing "all needs and demands of organic, social and life-systems themselves."[104] This connects to the ludicrous assumption that all corporate commodities are called "goods", however damaging to people's health and the environment they may be. Perhaps, under this respect, most controversial is McMurtry's identification of conceptual confusion between the "over-demand" of the global corporate market and the "over-population" of Earth.[105]

What is addressed most centrally, however, are the reigning assumptions that the "global market" is in fact "a free market" and works for the "common good"—ultimate value premises that he demonstrates to be systematically false.[106] More challengingly still, what counts as "productivity" and "greater efficiency", even to the political left, increasingly runs down "life capital" at every level.[107] Here, the second edition's central concept of life capital leads to a "Copernican revolution of economics", which is spelled out both in principle and in policy terms: "The three R's of true economy— Reduce, Re-use and Re-cycle—[constitute] the inner logic of preserving and advancing life capital in natural, social and technological terms."[108]

What of contemporary China, though, which is apparently winning the great global competition for so-called "growth"? According to McMurtry, this apparent victory leads to:

> [E]ver more industrially devastated environments and peoples whose large-scale ruin—produces mass cheap commodities serving no life-need. Ever more monumentally life-blind cycles have dwarfed Western industrialization and inequality in scale. The Three Gorges defining China's wondrous natural beauty have been destroyed, its largest freshwater lake turned into mud and dust; Tibet is looted and overrun, one can hardly breathe or see through the megopolis air, corruption is far more rampant, and hundreds of millions of poor are more life-means deprived than before the U-turn.[109]

Under standard economic thinking and practice, life and life-capital costs are factored out in fatal large scale. The system derangement of the era rules the Chinese Communist Party itself: that transnational market money-demand is the ultimate value, and ever cheaper commodities are the supreme goal of human society on Earth. But what is the point of this devastating critique? It sounds a lost cause. Where anywhere do humanity's life-capital advances come before private transnational money-capital growth?

McMurtry identifies underlying civil commons and life-capital trends expressed in four pivotal changes of policy that have long worked and that do so again when effectively implemented:

1. "[H]igher taxes for the corporate rich", in order to pay for the social and environmental life-support systems and vast public wealth subsidising them at every level, whilst also draining resources for unproductive speculation;[110]
2. "[A]ggressive national recovery of control over public owned resources", in order to secure revenues for life-enabling public bodies and protect them from the vagaries of private profit-seeking activities;[111]
3. "[P]ublic banking and investment", in order to fund life-enabling services;[112] and
4. "[P]olicy-led elimination of structural depredation of the poor and the environment", upon whose fate depends the sustainability of any economic order on Earth.[113]

Lucid criteria inform the definitions of "human", "natural", "knowledge", and "social" capital underpinning these policies,[114] while "life capital" and its "universal parameters of diagnosis" specify "determinants of social health and disease" to guide action.[115] "Recovery from the Great Sickness" is therefore possible, though by no means easy, as McMurtry concludes.[116]

Certainly, social response is demanded by rising pain and worldwide oppression, as expressed in massive uprisings in countries as diversely central as Greece, Spain, Egypt, France, and the US. All effective policy shifts nurture life capital, not State power. But who or what else can lead recovery if not State power?

Who or what, if not combined state power, can make Ray Anderson's (1934−2011) celebrated case of 100% sustainable industrial production the norm for all businesses on Earth?[117]

According to McMurtry, honest public authorities' life-enabling intervention in the economy is the only real option. The policy logic required has already been tested repeatedly across continents, if not understood in principle. Shift in taxation for public spending on common life bases has been proven to work by Scandinavian countries over many decades, and public reclamation of public resources has worked wonders in modern Norway and Ecuador. More broadly, the "public option" serves "the known needs of… people and their life-conditions" by public investment in life capital at every level that this account reports in synoptically connected pattern.[118]

As far as the third policy shift is concerned, McMurtry insists on the crucial role that credit plays and the urgency of restoring public control of it after the disastrous effects of internationally deregulated banking. He compares the long string of post-Bretton-Woods meltdowns with the time when "nations loaned to themselves and spent themselves productively into prosperity across the world during and after the 1939-45 war."[119] Also, he highlights the positive experiences of "Abraham Lincoln's" greenbacks, "German Landesbanks" and North Dakota's "public-banking and debt system", the "1935 Bank of Canada Act… [providing for] the central bank lending to government as its sole shareholder", as well as all leading economies using "variations of public investment" sustained by reclaimed public credit.[120]

The ultimate moral policy shift identified is the final one, though: "the progressive elimination of structural depredation of the poor and the environment".[121] Its relation to the previous three is straightforward: financially, it is enabled by the other policy shifts. Here the post-1945 reconstruction of Europe by public investment in human capital, as well as Latin America's many socio-economic success stories since 1999, show the way in overcoming absolute poverty while recovering the real economy at the same time. Lest the Earth's environment collapses beyond recovery, the analysis points to the "no-pollution schedule of the Ozone Protocol" and the long-neglected "binding [I]nternational Covenant on Economic, Social and Cultural Rights" as proven steps in life-capital protection and advance by binding inter-state policy and laws.[122] Only international norms as binding conditions of trade can enforce what is already known to be essential.

A Concluding Remark

The economy must work for humankind, not humankind for private money-demand.[123] McMurtry observes how, in 2010, conservative French President Nicolas Sarkozy (b. 1955) called for basic life-enabling reforms in free-market capitalism at the World Economic Forum in Davos, and immediately became the target of the corporate media, just as Bill Clinton (b. 1946) had become himself when he called for "levelling up, not down" globalisation, back in 1998. Any reform of the sick system is resisted and is bound to be resisted by those who benefit from the sickness, at least in the short term. But far worse for life on Earth is not recognising and not responding to the lethal disorder affecting it.

PART II – Applications

Chapter 4: What Is to Be Conserved? An Appraisal of Political Conservatism

Conservatism is by no means univocal. Since the dawn of humankind, psychological conservatism has characterised the attitude of many people, whose opposition to change flags out their nearly instinctive reaction to anything that may threaten long-lived habits of thought and action. More articulate and internally diverse has been political conservatism, whereby philosophers and political thinkers have reasoned upon which given institutions ought to be maintained or restored against the rising tide of reform and revolution. Legal conservatism has expressed the cautious approach of all those jurists and, mostly, men of law, who believe that any new piece of legislation must be vetted cautiously and within an established constitutional framework, and/or that judicial activity must be restrained by precedent, strict standards of interpretation, and/or time-honoured professional praxes. Fiscal conservatism has rejected State intervention in the economy by various means, including taxation, which should be either minimal or non-existent. Religious conservatism has emphasised the important roles and values of given religious and theological traditions, which must be maintained, lest humankind be doomed to suffer in this world and/or in the next. Moral conservatism too has stressed the important roles and values of given codes of behaviour, which must be preserved and cherished, independently of otherworldly considerations. Social conservatism, in a parallel fashion, has highlighted the important roles and values of given praxes and habits, which alone are deemed capable of explaining the enduring success of certain human associations *vis-à-vis* the dangers and difficulties that fate has been throwing at them.

Rhetoric

On their part, scholars in rhetoric have observed that conservatism fares well when it comes to producing persuasive arguments. The "locus" of "order" based upon comparisons of "earlier" and "later", such that the former is described as preferable to the latter, abounds in all spheres of human communication.[124] This "locus" or "commonplace" appears to be particularly successful within those professional contexts where individual and/or group identity and/or recognition rely upon the specificities of the "technical language" that has been acquired by its professional members, who may have engaged as well in sacred "oaths" or "rituals" that further strengthen "inertia" or adherence to "precedent".[125] Deviation from established norms becomes therefore an exercise in "futility", if not even a token of utter "perversity" that may place in "jeopardy" the cherished institutions of a given community.[126]

It is true that the opposite line of argument has been employed repeatedly too. Modernity seems to have favoured change and chance to conservation, up to the point that even the most banal marketing campaign of yet another consumer goodie is presented today to potential buyers as 'revolutionary' and *ipso facto* most desirable. Similarly, a recurrent and exemplary complaint has been voiced of late by several economists, and even more Wall Street firms, after the 2008 collapse of international finance. According to them, governmental re-regulation of the financial sector is despicable, for it may stifle innovation. Change and chance are thereby revealed to be so powerful a rhetorical commonplace that they can challenge the seemingly obvious and unassailable inference that the global, dramatic, and ongoing economic crisis, which was caused by the deregulated financial sector in the first place, should be compelling enough a reason for its re-regulation. Gifted with such a persuasive ability, change and chance have been so appealing and successful in the modern age that many self-professed political "conservatives" have become nothing but proponents of yesterday's reformist ideologies, such as representative democracy and economic liberalism. Thus, the paradoxical situation has been engendered, whereby self-professed political conservatives eagerly attempt to preserve human institutions that have demonstrated time after time to be forces for major transformation.[127]

A parallel twist can be observed in the field of contemporary conservationism, that is to say, the broad philosophical and political family of environmentalists. Despite their frequent association with today's reformist parties and even revolutionary left-wing ideologies, the original spirit of conservationism is far from being either reformist or revolutionary. In nearly all of its known forms, conservationism has opposed science-technology and/or industrial society, insofar as either or both of them have threatened ecosystems, life forms, and/or living species. The 19th-century roots of Western conservationism—at least according to Donald Gibson's erudite account of its history—lie with reactionary "aristocrats" and "gentlemen" that were disquieted by several of the destructive effects of the industrial revolution.[128] Self-professed conservative environmentalists did become a minority during the 20th century, but they were not altogether absent, such as *Lord of the Rings* author and Oxonian linguist John Ronald Reuel Tolkien (1892–1973) and German-born ethicist and historian of religion Hans Jonas (1903–1993).

In the present chapter, the contribution by the latter 20th-century thinker is discussed as an eminent token of conservative conservationism. Subsequently, the notion of "life ground" is presented, with reference to life-value onto-axiology, which is then applied in order to show how good and bad conservatism can be identified in principle. Finally, Hans Jonas' contribution is assessed.

Hans Jonas

Hans Jonas took very seriously the issue of environmental degradation, which he regarded as the result of humankind's overblown "ingenuity".[129] In this he followed the steps of his mentor Martin Heidegger (1889–1976), whom Jewish and Israeli war-veteran Jonas admired as a thinker and loathed as a committed German national socialist. Both of them believed science and technology to form an indissoluble binomial, at the theoretical level as well as at the practical one. They thought that science-technology had been successful at providing unprecedented means to shape and reshape natural and human reality; but also that it had been dangerously weak, if not utterly unequipped, *vis-à-vis* determining the ends for the proper employment of such wondrous means. Throughout his career, Jonas ceaselessly warned his readers and students against this binomial's tendency to:

- Isolate itself from other realms of human insight, such as religion, the arts and philosophy; and
- Self-engross as a life-threatening end-in-itself.

According to Jonas, well-established and often idolised science-technology had been engaging in a prolonged self-referential process of "permanent self-surpassing toward an infinite goal."[130] In this pursuit, it had been "neither patient nor slow", for it had "compresse[d]… the many infinitesimal steps of natural evolution into a few colossal ones and forgo[ne] by that procedure the vital advantages of nature's 'playing safe'."[131] Jonas did not fear the binomial's failure, but its boundless triumph: "the danger of disaster attending the Baconian ideal of power over nature through scientific technology arises not so much from any shortcomings of its performance as from the magnitude of its success".[132]

In primis, Jonas' concerns are the expression of an ethical conservatism that is reminiscent of René Descartes' (1596–1650) provisional morality. Any leap forward—no matter how glorious it is said to be—or any substantial change—no matter how momentous—are looked upon wearily by prudential reason because, if any such transformation proves to be misdirected, then to correct its harmful effects becomes arduous, if not impossible. Much wiser is to imitate nature's "playing safe", thus taking small steps and so long enough a time as to be able to ponder upon and examine carefully what happens and/or may happen. There need be no needless hurry: "progress is an optional goal, not an unconditional commitment, and… its tempo… has nothing sacred about it."[133]

Being an outspoken advocate for reasonable and reasoned prudence, Jonas opposed the commonly heard notion whereby collective wellbeing and the advancement of human knowledge could justify *per se* painful or morally ambiguous sacrifices. In his view, human dignity and the sanctity of life have been placed in danger far too often and culpably light-heartedly, whenever swift instrumentalist calls for progress resound loud and wide, e.g.:

- Cases of "selective abrogation of personal inviolability and the ritualized exposure to gratuitous risk of health" due to scientific experimentation upon vulnerable human beings;[134]
- The development of techniques for organ transplantation, particularly heart transplants, and the related expeditious novel criteria for death introduced in the latter half of the 20th century;[135] and
- The dramatic character of genetic engineering, which, unlike common engineering, acts irreversibly upon living creatures in the very process of experimenting.[136]

Preventing disaster may require extreme remedies, but improving the human condition does not and, according to Jonas, it ought not to. This holds true even if accepting such a principled restraint implies perishing of old age or disease, like our ancestors did before us: "grievous as it is to those who have to deplore that their particular disease may be not yet conquered."[137] The stringent deontological principles of proper conduct handed down by our forefathers should not become the victims of a much-trumpeted and hurried quest for brighter, better futures: "Society would… be threatened by the erosion of… moral values… caused by too ruthless a pursuit of scientific progress".[138] Besides, aging and dying have always been part of the human horizon, and they too contribute to making life valuable *qua* "incentive to number our days and make them count."[139] Though appreciable, future-driven technical-scientific possibility and its social desirability carry less normative weight than moral duties grounded in what has been recognised as good across generational time, and particularly the continuation of nature and humankind: "Unless the present state is intolerable, the melioristic goal is in a sense gratuitous… Our descendants have a right to be left an unplundered planet; they do not have a right to new miracle cures."[140]

Jonas' plea for prudence notwithstanding, both scientific knowledge and new technological devices expanded enormously in his lifetime and he had no wish to deny the evidence placed before his eyes. Hence, his reflections and his teaching endeavoured to lead his readers and his students to acknowledge that "responsibility with a never known burden and range ha[d] moved into the center of political morality."[141]

In the modern age, according to Jonas' analyses, we have become disenchanted yet super-powerful creatures, whose hands can mould as easily as destroy the environment surrounding and sustaining us. We must grow into responsible masters, then, for we are no longer slaves. Neither God nor the Creation can be the outright sources of moral and political wisdom capable of directing modern, disenchanted humankind's behaviour. Humankind alone can and ought to be such a source, for its own survival is at stake.[142] As Jonas wrote: "the very same movement which put us in possession of the powers that have now to be regulated by norms—the movement of modern knowledge called science—has by a necessary complementarity eroded the foundations from which norms could be derived."[143] The frailty-born divine presence in nature or "sacrosanctity" that had told our ancestors what to do is no longer available to us.[144] Secular, rational, and alone, modern humankind has to reckon with the duties arising from its novel position of mastery over nature and, *a fortiori*, over itself. This is no easy task, for "[w]e have sinned" much already by damaging "at full blast" our planet, which is the true "inheritance" of our descendants.[145] Nevertheless, since "mankind has no right to *suicide*", we must engage in "the pursuit of virtue", that is to say, the cultivation of "moderation and circumspection", thus hoping to rescue ourselves and our own planet from us.[146]

In secundis, Jonas was never entirely positive about the epistemic successes of modern science-technology. Its disastrous implications for planetary survival mirrored a deeper failure. Reflecting upon the mathematically abstract and the dispirited mechanistic approach that had been informing science-technology since its inception, Jonas noticed and highlighted how basic biological phenomena like individuation *via* metabolism, the felt side of being, or human freedom itself, had regularly escaped the grasp of the modern scientist. In his view, a novel "philosophical biology" was needed, which could recognise "life" for what it is, unlike mainstream "biologists and behaviourists", who had been training themselves to toying with sheer "abstractions" and "mathematical values".[147]

Since Galileo's (1564−1642) day, science-technology had either neglected the corporeal realm in its living dimensions or attempted to reduce these dimensions to more manageable inorganic aspects *via* "physical description".[148] Rather than tackling the living *qua* living, biology—though one could say the same of much contemporary medicine and economics—had been trying to follow the lead of physics and chemistry, which describe and predict their objects of study as mathematically formalised regular uniformities, that is to say, inanimate abstractions. Then, as Jonas concluded, we may even acquire "a minutely detailed inventory of the composition of the eye, the optical nerve, the cerebral centre for vision, and of the modifications taking place therein when visual stimulations occur, yet" this is not even to begin to "know what 'to see' may mean."[149]

In tertiis, Jonas claimed—unexpectedly for a 20th-century religious conservative thinker—that a Marxist economic system would make a better candidate than a capitalist one *vis-à-vis* sustainable development.[150] It was his pondered view that beneficial self-denial, identification with one's own community, and a sophisticated philosophical anthropology that addresses the human being *qua* sensuous living creature can be retrieved in Marx's writings far more easily than in any liberal economist's. Moreover, a dictatorial Marxist government could reach the desired goals much more swiftly than a liberal one, which must allow ample room for parliamentary deliberations, profitable business strategies, and paradoxical advertising-saturated consumer sovereignty.[151] As Jonas stated, the latter type of government involves an astounding amount of "waste attendant upon the mechanics of competition, and… the nonsense of a market production aimed at consumer titillation."[152] On the contrary, the former type of government expresses "the promise of a greater rationality" given its "centralized bureaucracy".[153]

Nevertheless, Jonas did observe the actual practice of Marxism in the 20th century and detected therein an invariable flourishing of Baconian utopias that paid no heed to moderation, circumspection, or prudence. Quite the opposite, in the name of some glorious future, self-proclaimed Marxist nations promoted a form of development akin to the one pursued by liberal countries, and such that "the most colossal mass extinctions can appear as a necessary, alas painful, but beneficent surgical operation."[154] Jonas' conservative and conservationist assessment leads then to the curious conclusion that Marxism may indeed be a better candidate than liberal capitalism as concerns preventing the ecological devastation of the planet; but also that the People's Republic of China and Soviet Union have had conspicuously less to do with Marxism than their constitutions declare. Theory and practice, in an additional disavowal of Marx's thought, had been kept separate in the tangible history of these countries.[155]

20th-century Marxist countries were not alone in betraying their founding principles. As far as liberal countries are concerned, Jonas believed them to have failed in many and tragic ways too. The fascist dictatorships of Europe, born after the collapse of the liberal economic order, were the clearest examples of this betrayal. Jonas himself had been affected by them, for he was a German-born Jew who sought refuge abroad while Nazism triumphed in his homeland, fought in a volunteer Jewish brigade of the British Army engaged in the Italian campaign of 1943–1945, and witnessed the post-colonial quagmire of the Middle East as a volunteer soldier in the Israeli army. As he admitted in a 1993 speech about racism held at Percoto (Italy): during "the darkest night of Europe… [only] some solitary lights" were visible.[156] The liberal's Enlightenment and the capitalist's industrial revolution, that is to say, the two pillars of the "developed and much-celebrated Euro-American white civilization" had failed in eradicating or controlling the ancient, deep-rooted racist propensities of the human soul.[157]

Fascism was not the only tragedy that Jonas had in mind when he spoke about the failure of liberal, capitalist countries *vis-à-vis* racism. As though the "hell" of the Holocaust in the ravaged Europe of the inter-war period had not been terrifying enough, liberalism had equally been unable to prevent the "scabrous heritage of slavery in contemporary America", that is to say, the prosperous and militarily sheltered country in which Jonas spent most of his adult life.[158] To avoid the continuation or repetition of similar tragedies, Jonas thought that we ought to employ "all forces of moral education and a vigil political attention", which should never underestimate the power of the "beast hidden within our imperfect human condition."[159]

In this respect, Jonas stated that a somewhat puzzling aid in the fight against racism could emerge from "the planet's ecological meltdown" characterising "the second half of the twentieth century".[160] Race, in the face of this terrible new "challenge" should become "anachronistic, irrelevant, almost farcical", whilst "a shared guilt" should "bind us" and reveal "a shared responsibility" such that "either we react and act together as 'one', or we will perish and, with us, the Earth as we know it."[161] Sparing no strong language, Jonas concluded his 1993 speech as follows:

> In the old days religion told us that we were all sinners because of the original sin. Today it is our planet's ecology that accuses all of us of being sinners because of the overexploitation of human ingenuity. Back in the old days, religion terrified us with the Last Judgment at the end of times. Today our tortured planet predicts the coming of that day without any divine intervention. The final revelation... is the silent scream emerging from things themselves, those things that we must endeavour to resolve to rein in our powers over the world, or we shall die on this desolate earth which used to be the creation.[162]

Consistently with the secularised character of modernity, the ancient images of fear, doom and damnation would seem to have found for Jonas new, modern faces. It is difficult to disagree with him. Throughout the 20th century, our planet's environment was spoiled by the scientifically and technologically assisted processes of financing, extraction, production, transportation, marketing, consumption and disposal of the goods traded worldwide.

The spoliation denounced by Jonas has persisted in the 2000s. With the exception of occasional lower carbon emissions in the EU and the reduction in the thinning of the planet's ozone layer—protected since 1989 by a unique piece of top-down international legislation—none of the other basic dimensions of the Earth's biosphere has been spared by the enduring combined processes mentioned above. Not the planet's forests; not its marine flora and fauna; not its hydrologic cycles; not its sources of fresh water; not its top-soil mantle; not its biodiversity; not its air quality. These are the essential ecological dimensions upon which humankind relies for the satisfaction of its most basic and universal vital needs, such as breathing, eating and drinking. They are the "things themselves" that, according to Jonas, "scream" because of the "overexploitation of human ingenuity."[163]

Life-blind Economics

Confronted with the twin crises of our day, the UN's Secretary-General Ban Ki-moon (b. 1944) denounced on the 22nd May 2009: "The economic and financial turmoil sweeping the globe is a true wake-up call, sounding an alarm about the need to improve upon old patterns of growth and make a transition to a new era of greener, cleaner development."[164] Evidently, twenty years after the collapse of the ecologically dubious experiments of Soviet Union and its satellite countries, "things themselves" keep screaming at us.

Moreover, if we look at the world today, Jonas' "waste attendant upon the mechanics of competition" and "the nonsense of a market production aimed at consumer titillation" have actually increased over the same decades.[165] They now affect even Earth's most populous country, which is nominally one of the few Marxist regimes still standing: the People's Republic of China. As amply shown in words and practice, contemporary Chinese enterprises and the Chinese government have accepted profit as a valid motive for human agency, as well as capitalist competition on the international markets as a crucial goal for the nation's economic policies. What is more, by being a willing recipient of highly polluting industries and a provider of cheap labour on unhealthy and hazardous workplaces, contemporary China offers concrete examples of the life-destructiveness of for-profit economic activity.[166]

We need not gaze upon China to observe this sort of life-destructiveness, though. Wherever "competition" and "market production" are in place, the causal nexus between the pursuit of profit and life-destruction is given away each and every time the business community and/or its political representation opposes and/or circumvents environmental and/or health-and-safety regulation, and/or effective enforcement thereof. "Costs", "rigidity" and "competitiveness" are the usual slogans that demonstrate the inability to consider, or the eventual unwillingness to take aboard, any substantive life-based considerations that may endanger profitability, such as the long-term environmental sustainability of the industrial or financial processes involved, the wellbeing of future generations, or the mental health of the societies affected by the same industrial and/or financial processes. Sales rule, not vital parameters—*ergo* Ban Ki-moon's hope for "transition to a new era of greener, cleaner development."

Most revealing of the etiological nexus between the pursuit of profit and life-destruction is the way in which the governments of liberal countries such as the US and the UK spent the years following the international financial collapse of 2008 bailing out private banks that were co-responsible for the ongoing global economic downturn. By this policy alone, these governments made sure that otherwise failed banks would retain or recover profitability, while at the same time thinning or withdrawing public resources from life-protective and life-enabling institutions (e.g. healthcare facilities, public education, wildlife protection, international aid) in order to fund the bailouts themselves, protect the money-measured value of existing assets, servicing debt, and display an attractive profile to treasury bond holders, amongst whom are the bailed-out banks themselves.[167]

Environmentally and vitally sound restrictions upon business activities do exist, and sometimes they are thoroughly applied too. Nevertheless, the crux is that no intrinsic life-based restriction is deducible from the profit-driven machinery of the global economy *per se*. As both the jargon of standard neoclassical economics and concrete economic activity reveal incessantly and ordinarily, human beings, plants, animals, water aquifers and ecosystems are mere "externalities" to the economic processes; and external do they remain unless they are translated into:

(A) "[C]osts" (e.g. novel tax burdens, fines by monitoring authorities); or
(B) "[B]usiness opportunities", whether these be found in
  (B1) Life-enabling forms (e.g. increased labour productivity by safe and secure workers, ecotourism, organic farming, innovative recycling methods), or
  (B2) Life-disabling forms (e.g. child labour, pesticide-protected monocultures, factory-farmed chickens, plastic-bottled water and greenhouse-effect-increasing mining operations in glacier-free Greenland).

Treating life and the living either as external or as instrumental, it comes as no surprise that a very large number of economic "commodities" are extremely "incommodious" to life and the living, such as junk food, cigarettes, carcinogenic construction materials and speculative financial products.

Emblematically, former White House economic advisor and World Bank Chief Economist Lawrence—"Larry"—H. Summers (b. 1954) asserted on this point: "the economic logic behind dumping a load of toxic waste in the lowest wage country is impeccable, and we should face up to that."[168] An orthodox heir to the received views of classical and neoclassical liberalism, he too fails to acknowledge life's intrinsic worth, going instead by the lifeless "mechanics of competition" denounced by Jonas. Under this perspective, life's value is, *au fond*, instrumental.

History bears ample witness to this fact. From Charles

Dickens' (1812–1870) England to today's China, environmental and workplace-related life-saving restrictions have been imposed upon the market economy from the outside. For example, it was the combined action of Christians, socialists, chartists and compassionate or enlightened capitalists like Robert Owen (1771–1858) that made it possible for the 19th-century British factory system, so vividly described by Fyodor M. Dostoyevsky (1821–1881) in his 1863 travel diaries as a man-eating "Baal", to become the life-provider of the West celebrated by Austrian economists Ludwig von Mises (1881–1973) and Friedrich A. Hayek.[169] Back then, right-thinking liberals like Herbert Spencer (1820–1903) and his many followers criticised loudly as unwarranted State interference in market equilibria nearly all the primeval forms of welfare provision that had been surfacing across the industrialised nations, especially in the final decades of the century:[170]

> [T]o administer charity, to teach children their lessons, to adjust prices of food, to inspect coal-mines., to regulate railways, to superintend house-building, to arrange cab-fares, to look into people's stink-traps, to vaccinate their children, to send out emigrants, to prescribe hours of labor, to examine lodging-houses, to test the knowledge of mercantile captains, to provide public libraries, to read and authorize dramas, to inspect passenger-ships, to see that small dwellings are supplied with water, to regulate endless things from a banker's issues down to the boat-fares on the Serpentine.[171]

Echoing Spencer's biocidal conception of market freedom, Harvard economist Larry Summers argues that the developing nations are countries in which the inhabitants are paid "the lowest wages" and die younger than "people" in richer nations, who instead "survive to get prostrate cancer", despite the developing nations' natural environments being "UNDER-polluted… compared to Los Angeles or Mexico City".[172] Consequently, the same developing nations are also the countries in which "health impairing pollution" can be "done… [at] the lowest cost", for such already poorer and shorter-lived populations have less to lose, i.e. they have lower "foregone earnings from increased morbidity and mortality".[173]

Summers' memo does not address the fact that such an impeccable logic, if followed, would also be self-reinforcing, hence condemning shorter-lived populations to remain shorter-lived. Equally, the likely damages to the natural environments caused by the sort of trade advocated by Summers are not considered either, despite their obvious economic implications: mired in growing polluted environments and worsened health, developing nations would never become developed, whilst developed nations would accrue an even bigger advantage over the developing ones. Reconsidering the validity of economic categories of thought producing such an "impeccable logic" in light of their paradoxical implications is not something that Summers is willing to do.

What Summers does in his memo, instead, is to follow such categories of thought to the utmost and therefore reduce the scope of conceivable socio-economic relations to short-term, horizontal, two-party exchanges, that is, to commutations. A species of particular justice, commutative justice is all the justice that Summers can conceive of. There is no awareness of the different allocations of resources, or of the rights and duties that would be required in order to level the playing field on which wealthy and poor nations enter into contractual exchanges. There is, in short, no awareness of the fair redistributions demanded by the logically corresponding latter kind of particular justice, i.e. distributive justice, as recognised long ago by Aristotle (384–322 BC) or the natural law tradition (e.g. by means of international cooperation, productive credit provisions, fair trade, etc.).

Nor is there any notion of general or social justice, whereby any community, in order to function properly, is owed first of all continued good environmental conditions, enforced good laws and adequate fiscal resources in view of both the present and the future common good. Such genuine goods can be obtained *via* well-meaning cooperation with other communities, not *via* the exploitative and plausibly lethal exchanges advocated by Larry Summers.[174] Summers is actually so blind to general or social justice, as to write "'[d]irty' industries" between quotation marks, i.e. as though polluting and health-damaging dirt were not as real an issue as the profits that the polluters can make.[175] Similarly, he describes "a clean environment" and "pretty air" for "aesthetic and health reasons" as matters of "demand", i.e. as tradable goods to be bought and sold by contractual parties, rather than as mandatory preconditions for a well-functioning society aiming at the common good.[176] Life, whether individual, collective, local and global, is itself reduced to a matter of profitable trade, which is *ipso facto* regarded as more valuable.

The history of Lawrence Summers's infamous memorandum is also intriguing *per se*. After the memo was leaked to the public in February 1992, Brazil's Secretary of the Environment José Lutzenburger (1926–2002) sent the following comments to Larry Summers, who was back then at the helm of the economists' team at the World Bank: "Your reasoning is perfectly logical but totally insane... Your thoughts [provide] a concrete example of the unbelievable alienation, reductionist thinking, social ruthlessness and the arrogant ignorance of many conventional 'economists' concerning the nature of the world we live in... If the World Bank keeps you as vice president it will lose all credibility."[177] Lutzenburger lost his job shortly after writing his letter. Larry Summers, instead, was appointed in 1999 the U.S. Treasury Secretary, and later became President of his *alma mater*, where he still teaches *qua* Professor and Director of the Mossavar-Rahmani Center for Business and Government. No better example of what constitutes mainstream, self-rewarding, well-paid, life-blind, right-thinking orthodoxy could be concocted.

Nonetheless, facing prolonged media inquiries and some political backlash, Summers has been trying to disavow it.[178] In the late 1990s, a former young member of Summers' staff at the World Bank and soon-to-be colleague of his at Harvard—the economist Lant Pritchett—claimed to be the actual author of the memo, which he had merely shown and given to Summers to sign, its tone being sarcastic, its aim being to spur internal debate, and its leaked version having been used malevolently to discredit Summers and the World Bank.[179] Whatever the case, which reminds one of the popular TV series *House of Cards*, the memo crystallises poignantly the callous character of laissez-faire liberalism and, whether sarcastic or not, it has been taken seriously by many scholars, including economists affiliated with the libertarian Cato Institute.[180]

The Earth's Life Support Systems

Today's environmentalism in its many manifestations, including Jonas' own contribution, is attempting to counter and/or integrate precisely this short-term-oriented, self-maximising perspective of theoretical and practical economic agents and let them grasp fully, not to say resolve, the aetiology of the ongoing ecological collapse. Without external assistance, these agents are quite simply blind to the biological and ecological requirements of life, despite presupposing them throughout their operations.

In a forward-looking attempt to assess and revise "old patterns of growth" and promote the "greener, cleaner development" advocated by UN's Secretary-General Ban, UNESCO had already established in 2002 the world's largest source of information on sustainable development currently available to scholars and governments worldwide. This source, as seen in the first part of this book, is EOLSS, which defines its study object as follows:

> A life support system is any natural or human-engineered (constructed or made) system that furthers the life of the biosphere in a sustainable fashion. The fundamental attribute of life support systems is that together they provide all of the sustainable needs required for continuance of life. These needs go far beyond biological requirements. Thus life support systems encompass natural environmental systems as well as ancillary social systems required to foster societal harmony, safety, nutrition, medical care, economic standards, and the

development of new technology. The one common thread in all of these systems is that they operate in partnership with the conservation of global natural resources.[181]

The definition of LSS supplied and endorsed by UNESCO acknowledges two main typologies. On the one hand, there are natural LSS, such as the hydrological cycles of the planet and the oceans' plankton-based ecosystems. On the other hand, there are LSS created and maintained by collective human agency, such as the nations' educational institutions and the UN treaty bodies assessing and fostering the enforcement of ratified human rights covenants. Together, these two typologies of LSS embrace and draw attention to those ecological and social dimensions upon which human life depends for its very being and/or wellbeing.

Qua EOLSS' Honorary Theme Editor, John McMurtry refers to all LSS on Earth as "civil commons". This notion, which has become part of the technical armoury of Anglophone social scientists, comprises all "social constructs which enable universal access to life goods".[182] According to McMurtry—and consistently with Jonas' assessment of humankind's mastery over nature and over itself—both natural LSS and those created and maintained by collective agency are civil commons. Insofar as all LSS are acknowledged and conceptualised as LSS, and insofar as all LSS require human protection, promotion or recovery, then all LSS are socially constructed in order to secure and/or foster human life.

There are, in other words, no LSS that can be left outside the scope of our life-serving social forms of consciousness, agency and regulation, unless any such LSS have not yet been recognised as LSS. In this perspective, we can appreciate why McMurtry lists a most diverse and far-reaching variety of civil commons:

> [C]ommon sewers, international outrage over Vietnam or Ogoniland, sidewalks and footpaths, the Chinese concept of jen, the Jubilee of Leviticus… water fountains, Robin Hood of Sherwood Forest… old age pensions, universal education, Sweden's common forests… the second

commandment of Yeshua… the rule of law, child and women shelters, parks, public broadcasting, clean water… the UN Declaration of Human Rights… village and city squares, the Brazilian rainforests, inoculation programmes, indigenous story-telling, the Ozone Protocol, the Tao, the peace movement, death rituals, animal rights agencies, community fish-habitats, food and drug legislation, garbage collection, the ancient village commons before enclosures.[183]

As tokens of socially conceived LSS, all of the civil commons listed above contain a single defining function. All of them are concerned with securing life means to all the members of a community whose members' wellbeing depends on them. Also, taken together, all of these tokens of civil commons indicate how deep and how broad in both time and space can be the "life ground", which is defined below.

The Life Ground

According to McMurtry, the life ground is "concretely, all that is required to take the next breath; axiologically, all the life support systems required for human life to reproduce or develop."[184] UNESCO's LSS are understood by him as denoting those civil commons that humankind has established conceptually and/or materially in different times and places in order to secure universally the means necessary for human life to continue and, possibly, blossom.

Given that all value depends ontologically upon such LSS/civil commons, McMurtry attributes the highest importance to them: "Life support systems – any natural or human-made system without which human beings cannot live or live well – may or may not have value in themselves, but have *ultimate* value so far as they are that without which human or other life cannot exist or flourish."[185]

As regards the understanding of life, McMurtry discusses three main ontological modalities in which life regularly unfolds within and across living individuals, that is to say:

(1) "[A]ction" (also called "biological movement" or "motility");
(2) "[E]xperience" (also called "feeling" or "felt being"); and
(3) "[T]hought.[186]

No ontological dualism or radical disunity is involved: "Although we can distinguish the cognitive and feeling capacities of any person, this does not mean dividing them into separate worlds as has occurred in the traditional divisions between mind and body, reason and the emotions. Life-value onto-axiology begins from *their unity as the nature of the human organism.*"[187] Henceforth, actual civil commons protect and promote life as action (e.g. legal standards for nourishing food, public provision of potable water), felt being (e.g. freedom from fear *via* job security, counselling services for the youth), and/or thought (e.g. increased access to academic institutions, independent media).

Civil commons are to accomplish their life-grounded task whilst having genuine vital needs as the baseline criterion. As McMurtry explains: "'n' is a need if and only if, and to the extent that, deprivation of n always leads to a reduction of organic capacity."[188] It is only that without which life capacity is harmed that may count as a real need. We can survive and perhaps even flourish without cars and computer gadgets, but we can hardly take another step without nourishment, protection from natural elements, regular sleep, or temporally sustained participation in inter-subjective networks such as families and human communities.[189]

In connection with the notions of "civil commons", "life ground" and "need", McMurtry's "Basic Well-Being Index" (WBI) aims at identifying the complete and universal set of goods serving vital needs. These are the needs that must be met in order for human life to be possible and its genuine fulfilment attainable; the corresponding life goods being:

1. Air quality
2. Access to clean water

3. Sufficient nourishing food
4. Security of habitable housing
5. Opportunity to perform meaningful service or work of value to others
6. Available learning opportunity to the level of qualification
7. Healthcare when ill
8. Temporally and physically available healthy environmental space for leisure, social interaction and recreation.[190]

McMurtry's WBI exists in a variety of slightly different versions and constitutes his most visible contribution to the establishment of socio-metrics for human wellbeing, along the lines of the life-capabilities approach championed since the 1980s by Amartya Sen (b. 1933) and Martha Nussbaum (b. 1947).[191]

However, the WBI does not wish to be solely a standard of evaluation that integrates those of mainstream economics. The WBI serves also the end of pinpointing fundamental dimensions of human existence—namely the life ground—that are threatened by mainstream economic activity and the comprehension of which is obfuscated by mainstream economics. As McMurtry observes: "Claimed 'economic goods' which disable or do not enable life abilities are not means of life; they are economic 'bads'".[192] Machine guns, conversion of bio-diverse forests into monocultures, and global-insecurity-creating securitisation packages are not good. They may maximise, in the short term, the revenues of select economic agents, which is why they are regarded as valid and positively valuable in both current economic theory and practice. Nevertheless, like slave labour in previous centuries, speculation on prime agricultural sources of nourishing carbohydrates and toxic industrial chemicals such as oxirane, glyphosate and ethylenedibromide are bad, because they unquestionably reduce existing as well as possible wider ranges of action, felt being and thought. Albeit these items of trade may satisfy someone's preferences, they fail to satisfy another's fundamental and, from a life-grounded standpoint, axiologically prior need.

Aware of the recurring and avoidable destruction of life in current market economies, McMurtry concludes that the ongoing threat to living creatures and ecosystems is so deep, pervasive and unchallenged, that the oncologic paradigm is the best way to explain it.

First of all, McMurtry describes the logic of economic activity as the relentless generation of money returns to money investors. This is, in essence, the founding principle of so-called "free-market" activity. Reducible to this principle are, in his view, all those common expressions of economic commendation, which are often presented as value-neutral scientific descriptors, such as "wealth", "efficiency", "competitiveness", "productivity", "growth" and "development". Guided by this founding principle, profit-pursuits replicate themselves across Earth's societies and ecosystems through sequences of investments and returns mimicking the pathological self-replication of cancerous cells.

Secondly, like cancerous cells, the relentless profit-driven sequences of the global economy show no self-limitation for the sake of the host body's organic wellbeing. Indeed, these sequences are expected to proceed without limit, for all economic agents are assumed to be self-maximising indefinitely: their craving for more knows no satiety. Thus, not even the planet's environmental meltdown, to which they contribute decisively, serves as a stopping point. As conducive to "growth" as they may be for the standard conception of economic activity, regular profit-pursuits lack any alternative or deeper guiding principle grounded in life, that is to say, in those biological, ecological and social conditions that are needed for human life to continue and, if possible, flourish. The host body, i.e. Earth's ecosystems and societies, is therefore bound to suffer and it might even die because of them, for they are blind to the host's needs: "The system is by its inner logic a horizonlessly expanding money-demand machine engineering all that lives to extract more money value from it, to reduce the costs of continuing its existence, or to extinguish it as of no money worth."[193]

The unrestrained self-replication of profit-sequences is profoundly anti-economic too. In the long run, the unstopped sprawling of profit-pursuits disrupts the natural and the social fabric underpinning any stable economic activity fostering human and humane development. This is no novel or radical realisation. Long ago, in the wake of the calculating mentality of the revolutionary liberal man of commerce, Edmund Burke (1729–1797) had already feared for the survival of those religious and moral values that had made Europe great: "Even commerce, and trade, and manufacture, the gods of our economical politicians, are… themselves but effects, which as first causes, we choose to worship. They certainly grew under the same shade in which learning flourished. They too may decay with their natural protecting principles."[194] Today, faced with the environmental spoliation of the planet, John McMurtry fears for the survival of that invaluable source of all values, which makes everything human possible, economic activity included: the life ground.

The oncologic paradigm may appear hyperbolic, at least *prima facie*, not unlike Jonas' own depiction of an approaching man-made apocalypse. Yet, as substantiated by the ongoing ecological and economic crises recognised by none less than Ban Ki-moon himself, the effects of the theoretically endless, non-satiable self-replication of profit-pursuits have been detrimental to life at many different levels of analysis:

- Since the dawn of the industrial revolution in the Atlantic nations, the Earth's LSS have been put under unprecedented pressure, whether by contamination or overexploitation of underground aquifers, pollution-caused cancers, or desertification and loss of arable soil;
- Despite or even because of new scientific discoveries and technological applications, this pressure has mounted further during the latter half of the 20th century, to the point of being acknowledged as a threat to human survival by scientific and diplomatic bodies at the highest levels of international representation;
- Fuelled by finance-driven globalisation, this pressure has extended in recent decades to several of those life-protecting and life-enhancing social civil commons that had been

developed by previous generations as instruments to steer the course, and select the effects of, otherwise life-unprincipled profit-pursuits. As a result, life-destructive social phenomena have become commonplace worldwide, such as:
- Sudden meltdowns of countries that deregulated capital and currency trade;
- The disappearance of allegedly expensive public housing programmes;
- Selloffs of and/or cuts to publicly provided culture, education, sanitation, environmental protection, health-and-safety monitoring and healthcare;
- Privatised hence less inclusive and legally less regulated security provision, both domestic and international;
- Privatised hence less secure old-age pension schemes; and
- Reduced and less secure occupational options and/or longer working hours in countries affected by stress-related yet profitable increases in mental ill-health.

Representatively, as the last example in the list is concerned, one of Argentina's leading experts in medical science has recently remarked:

> According to neoliberal dogma, the market is the perfect allocator of resources and the ideal arbiter of priorities and policies. Beginning in the unfortunate decade of the 80's, the market, in both general society and in health, weakened labor, increased unemployment, dismantled universal social coverage, lowered salaries, reduced public health expenditures, privatized services, mandated user fees, and decreased supervision of private health care providers and of the pharmaceutical industry. All these initiatives deteriorated the collective physical health. As to mental health, the replacement of more or less predictable individual lives with the uncertainties and unpredictability

of unchecked market forces quite clearly deteriorated it.[195]

The profitable reconstruction of mental illness and ill-health further exemplifies Jonas' own recognition of the fact that the scientific-technological apparatus that has been responsible for the sustained demographic boom of modern nations, both capitalist and Marxist, can be utterly blind to life and to the causes of its depletion.

In combination with this recognition, McMurtry's oncologic paradigm elucidates why the same can be said of other complex social apparatus that are institutionally committed to the common good. For instance, over the past few decades, democratic governments, research centres and central banks have regularly failed to acknowledge the ongoing assault on life-protective and life-enhancing civil commons. Almost without exception, these civil bodies have cooperated with the assailant, namely with the endless replication of profit-pursuits, as amply exemplified by:

- Conceptualising public investments in education or healthcare as costs;
- Conceptualising and dismantling life-protecting regulation as 'red tape';
- Addressing business ethics as yet another instrument towards higher profits;
- Dismantling the currency trade regulations implemented after the experience of the Great Depression and its mass-murderous political offshoots, i.e. fascism and World War II (WWII);
- Interpreting "rights" in trade treaties solely as a subset of civil rights concerning property and contracts;
- Conflating life-grounded terms such as "wellbeing" and "prosperity" with life-decoupled economic "growth" and "efficiency"; and
- Fostering the privatisation of public banks and other public assets guaranteeing a steady flow of revenues to the public purse that sustains the nations' civil commons.

According to McMurtry, this sort of recurrent institutional behaviour shows how many of societies' long-established life-aimed agencies have given further proof of the cancer-like character of standard economic reality. Specifically, they have acted analogously to the immune defences of a living organism that did not detect the presence of self-replicating cancerous cells as pathological and therefore facilitated their ominous self-replication. These institutions' ties to the life ground, from which they all emerged and upon which they rely for their continued existence, have been either forgotten or tragically misunderstood.

Good Political Conservatism

The emphasis placed upon the role of public institutions and public resources might suggest that McMurtry's onto-axiology is incompatible with so-called "free market" economies, whose cancer stage he denounces so forcefully. This incompatibility subsists as current implementations of such economies are concerned, but it is not a logical necessity. From a life-grounded perspective, which economic system is in place is not of crucial importance. What matters, instead, is that life-capabilities are protected and promoted. The obligations derived from the recognition of the paramount character of vital human needs concern the results, not the means. From a life-grounded perspective, any economic system is successful if and only if: "[It] secure[s] provision of means of life otherwise in short supply (i.e. the production and distribution of goods and the protection of ecosystem services which are otherwise scarce or made scarce through time)."[196]

If properly selected and aptly regulated "free markets" were able to deliver these means of life universally and across generations, then such "free markets" would be successful. Yet, as far as the prevailing version of "free markets" has been assessed, this delivery has not taken place to an adequate degree, which explains Ban Ki-moon's emblematic call for "transition" as recently as in 2009. Proposing more of the same alleged "development", dubbed variously as a "return to growth" or renewed "efficiency" and "competitiveness", means proposing further life-blindness and likely life-destruction, which increased logging of pluvial forests and austerity programmes exemplify respectively in both so-called "developing" countries and "developed" ones.

Indeed, long before Ban and the current global economic crisis, Jonas had already concluded that the very survival of humankind as we know it had been put into question by the now predominant liberal model of economic activity. Alternatives are therefore *needed* in the genuine sense of the word, for life is at stake in its biological and ecological preconditions. The planet's LSS are in peril; and if "free markets" are incapable of distinguishing between good and bad, then someone else will have to do it for them.

Given the current conditions of world affairs and the history of the world's modern nations, public bodies appear to be the most plausible institutions invested with the power or, at least, the legitimacy required to perform this service. After all, they have already provided it on previous occasions, such as the already-mentioned international agreement on the ozone layer. Elected governments, publicly funded monitoring bodies and courts of law can and ought to, *inter alia*, function *qua* civil commons. This vital function of theirs is particularly urgent if Jonas' fears for the continued existence of our species are realistic. Clearly, EOLSS' expert founders and contributors testify to these fears.

Under the current socio-economic conditions, it is difficult to get such potentially life-serving institutions to operate as genuine civil commons. We live in a world dominated by the TINA-like demands of for-profit 'free' market agency in practice—a first contradiction—and yet devoted in theory to democratic and postmodern 'pluralist' difference—a second contradiction.[197] With the exception of so-called "subjective" and "individual" market choices, any alternative determination of good and evil is looked upon with suspicion, especially if it claims to be "objective", which McMurtry does in fact claim, since he cannot imagine how there could be any pluralism, any democracy, any economy, any value, indeed anything human at all, without the life ground.

Obstacles notwithstanding, McMurtry's axiology has been made available by UNESCO to individuate a sharp, principled way to discern what is good from what is bad, while having sustainable development in mind as the northern star for collective decision-making. As it is stated in the central paragraph of his 2009–2010 EOLSS Theme Essay, "*X is value if and only if and to the extent that x consists in or enables a more coherently inclusive range of thought/experience/action*", while "*X is disvalue if and only if and to the extent that x reduces/disables a range of thought/experience/action.*"

In short, that which allows for life to persist and flourish is good. That which does not is bad. Such is the core of McMurtry's onto-axiology. A thorough discussion of the two axioms above would exceed the limits of the present work. Hopefully, it suffices here to stress how McMurtry's life ground entails that a good economic system:

(1) Must secure the provision of vital goods for as many citizens (ideally all of them) and for as long a time as possible (sustainability being no short-term goal); and

(2) It must generate the conditions for a fuller enjoyment of life along the same spatio-temporal coordinates.

Whereas (1) indicates that which is most important in order to live, (2) points towards the conditions for living well. Unless a cruel fate or human callousness dictates otherwise, the ideal horizon of the human person is cast well beyond the mere level of vital needs. We do engage regularly and recurrently in both actions and interactions that, it is hoped, will enrich us physically (action), spiritually (felt being) and intellectually (thought), thus making our life worth living.

Human communities have established a great variety of civil commons that aim not solely at securing access to basic goods such as food, care and shelter, but also to those goods that make us more human, if not better humans, such as education, sports and the arts.[198] Additionally, it is hoped too that the enrichment enjoyed by each agent may extend to her communities, which have constructed and/or allowed for the performance of such actions and interactions.

The "free market" itself has been justified in this way, insofar as a providential "invisible hand" is said to combine market agents' individual pursuits into collective wellbeing—the persisting failure of which is what Jonas and McMurtry highlight in their works. The life ground discloses in principle which praxes and policies may be genuinely enabling and which, instead, disabling.

Conservatism, in each of its many declinations, is therefore good if it serves life, i.e. if it *conserves* those LSS that enable universal access to life goods and foster action, felt being and thought. It is bad if it reduces access to these goods or destroys them and/or the conditions for their production and reproduction through time. In more concrete terms, good conservatism endeavours to *conserve* genuine civil commons, such as:

- The planet's ecosystems;
- The public centres of universal schooling and education at their different levels of complexity and achievement;
- The local theatres and community libraries that have disseminated culture for generations;
- The hospitals and healthcare facilities that have provided care to the infirm in urban and rural areas;
- The laws and regulations that have steered economic activities towards the construction of healthier, longer-living, more cohesive and peaceful nations;
- The policing and law-enforcing institutions that have granted security to citizens, guests and visitors of modern states; and
- The moral virtues and religious piety that inspire life-enabling attitudes and behaviours such as mutual respect, justice, compassion, solidarity and humaneness.

From a life-grounded perspective, good conservatism conserves the international community's longstanding official commitment to the rights enshrined and ratified in life-enabling centrepieces of worldwide legislation such as the ICCPR and the ICESCR. Bad conservatism does the opposite of all this.

If an individual can lose sight of what is good or cause harm in the pursuit of a misconstrued good, so can conservatism fail in conserving the conditions for the preservation and extension of the given ranges of thought/experience/action. This is what has happened to today's most popular form of self-proclaimed conservative political ideology, i.e. neoliberalism. Jonas' work substantiated the notion whereby the application of this ideology during the 20th century proved ecologically unsustainable, analogously to its political counterpart, namely Soviet Marxism. McMurtry's work further helps to comprehend the reasons for this failure: insofar as neoliberalism accepts wholeheartedly and unwaveringly the main tenets of standard ("neoclassical") economics, then it is conceptually unequipped to tackle human needs and life-grounded considerations. Furthermore, as exemplified by Robert Nozick (1938−2002), one of the most representative theoreticians of this ideology, neoliberalism has been capable of arguing positively that actual life is of secondary importance, especially *vis-à-vis* the abstract right to own life goods privately:[199] "[A] right to life is not a right to whatever one needs to live; other people may have rights over these other things. At most, a right to life would be a right to have or strive for whatever one needs to live, provided that having it does not violate anyone else's rights.[200]

No equally biocidal theory and practice is retrievable in Jonas' streak of conservatism, or certainly not as patently. Responsible prudence was, for Jonas, the fundamental move in the right direction, not the primacy of property rights or of any particular economic system. A religious man, Jonas revered nature as God's creation, not man's parcelling and ownership of it, which can find adequate justification in much conservative thought, but as a means to a higher end (e.g. Thomism), not only as an end in itself or as a supreme social value (e.g. Objectivism).[201]

Quite the reverse, Jonas concerned himself with the risks associated with continuing in the fast-paced "melioration" of humanity by science-technology, which he concluded to be conducive to what he termed a "suicide". All other political considerations were subsidiary to this prime concern: preventing humankind's suicide. By choosing so forceful a formulation, Jonas' appeal for the establishment of a political morality centred upon responsibility selected life as the ultimate ground of value available to human comprehension.

Grounding humankind's hopes for salvation in life was no random case or unreflective circumstance on Jonas' part. On the contrary, Jonas did believe that it is from the phenomenon of life that morality and, *a fortiori*, responsibility emerge. According to him, there exists a "timeless archetype of all responsibility, the parental for the child", which can be retrieved in all historical and human settings, despite apparent exceptions to and variations of parental care.[202] This timeless archetype is the one paradigm for moral action that ought to apply to all spheres and roles of human existence requiring responsibility, such as "the artist [*vis-à-vis*] his work" and "*the statesman [vis-à-vis] the state*".[203] Jonas claims the "timeless archetype of all responsibility" embodied in parental care to be nothing less than "an ontic paradigm in which the plain factual 'is' evidently coincides with an 'ought'—which does not, therefore, admit for itself the concept of a 'mere is' at all."[204] As he argues: "We can point at the most familiar sight: the newborn, whose mere breathing uncontradictably addresses an ought to the world around, namely to take care of him."[205]

Even if we may explain away this ontic—i.e. lived or experienced—paradigm by means of some inhumane exercise in abstract sceptical reason—hence bringing it to the onto-logical level—the new-born's breath of life is bound to reverberate in our flesh, in our heart, in the deepest and most diverse depths of our being. The new-born's breath is a powerful, natural statement of absolute value; it is an embodied categorical call for responsibility. As Jonas wrote: "Here the plain being of a *de facto* existent immanently and evidently contains an ought for others, and would so even if nature would not succour this ought with powerful instincts or assume its job alone."[206]

Concluding Remarks

In his appeal to the "timeless archetype" of parental care, as well as in his opposition to humankind's overingenious ongoing suicide, Jonas' philosophy resonates forcefully with life-value onto-axiology, despite the personal, chronological, and theoretical differences between Jonas and McMurtry. In this archetype, our ties to the life ground are not severed, but revealed and set as the benchmark for informed, reasoned deliberation. Science-technology is itself assessed in connection with life-grounded concerns and Jonas' reformulation of Kant's Categorical Imperative is most explicit on this point: "Act so that the effects of your action are compatible with the permanence of genuine life… Act so that the effects of your action are not destructive of the future possibility of such life." Or also, "[i]n your present choice, include the future wholeness of Man among the objects of your will."[207]

Jonas' philosophy is crystal-clear on life's axiological primacy, as also are his condemnation of the planet's plundering by irresponsible human beings and his qualified acceptance of illness, aging, suffering and death as conducive to a fuller appreciation of life. On the one hand, plundering the Earth that we have inherited endangers life as action and, with it, the preconditions for all felt being and thought. On the other hand, the awareness and the experience of our mortality are seen by Jonas as instrumental toward acquiring a richer feeling of aliveness and a deeper understanding of life's intrinsic value. All three ontological modalities of life individuated by McMurtry are present and foundational in Jonas' call for responsibility and prudence, which wishes to secure "the future wholeness of Man." In the end, whether Jonas' reinterpreted Kantian Categorical Imperative can be easily instantiated in each specific case or not, the basic parameters for evaluation are such that life's needs and value are clearly posited as primary and paramount. By application of life-value onto-axiology, Jonas' conservatism is likely to be good.

Chapter 5: Good and Bad Tourism

A founding father of French existentialism, Gabriel Marcel (1889–1973) rediscovered the Augustinian notion of *homo viator*, whereby the human condition is understood as akin to a traveller whose true being is defined by the journeys that she chooses to pursue and, above all, by the relationships that she establishes along her journeys.[208] Unless a person is condemned by early death or severely disabling conditions, choosing no journey at all and engaging in no relationship whatsoever are not an option, for we are naturally bound to inhabit a specific place in time and space as well as a human community of sorts, as sedentary or even as suicidal as we may eventually decide to be. Whether we like it or not, we are cast in this world and will have made many choices, trodden many paths, endorsed many values and met many people, our own family relatives or guardians *in primis*, before we can even begin reflecting upon the possibility of taking a step into the nihilistic abyss of self-seclusion or self-destruction.[209]

Yet, it is not the "absolute despair" driving some individuals to isolation or suicide that Marcel concentrates upon, unlike other famous French existentialists such as Jean-Paul Sartre (1905–1980) and Albert Camus (1913–1960).[210] Rather, it is the "unconquerable hope" that, mysteriously, animates most human lives.[211] Neither the nauseating awareness of inevitable mortality and seemingly absurd Sisyphean toil, nor the painful testimony of physical, mental and moral degeneration can disarm most people's ability to retrieve some value in their experiences, or the "substance of *life*", as Marcel dubs it.[212] Fired by a hope-fuelled "enthusiasm or ardour for *life*", we are generally capable of finding a modicum of fulfilment in our existence, as troublesome and as finite as we understand it to be.[213]

According to Marcel, by informing our mental abilities with hopeful ardour for life, we set in motion a "creative process" whereby we establish our 'I' through time (i.e. our individuality) and move beyond our immediate circumstances by conceiving of our own future constructively, recognising value both around and within us, while at the same time opening ourselves to other persons like us, "our neighbours".[214] In this manner, we may be able to overcome the "temptation to despair" induced by the consciousness of our unavoidable transience, constitutional frailty and possible solitude.[215] Echoing Saint Augustine of Hippo (354–430), Marcel depicts a human reality in which sin is always afoot; but so too is the path to salvation. The latter requires acknowledging inter-personal relationships and how we are going to go about them, not least about the one that we may discover and accept to have with a divine person, as Marcel himself did in his adult life (Marcel converted to Catholicism in the late 1920s, distinguishing himself once more from French existentialists like Sartre and Camus, who were professed atheists).[216]

Homo Viator

Given the inherent inescapability of our journeys on this Earth, the notion of *homo viator* is nothing but another philosophical definition of the human being, alongside Friedrich Schiller's (1759–1805) *homo ludens* and Henri Bergson's (1859–1941) *homo faber*. Whichever journeys we may be on, whichever relationships we may engage in, for as long as we live and act, we are travelling. Furthermore, we are not alone on our journeys, even if we may not like every or any fellow traveller, or choose not to believe that some of them do actually exist, such as present society, future generations, the Earth's local and global ecosystems, or these ecosystems' unified totality as a living entity.

Consistently with Augustine's original emphasis, Marcel's notion of *homo viator* focuses eventually upon the immortal soul's journey from its earthly dwelling to *post-mortem* otherworldliness, and the significance of our earthly moral standing for this journey. Under this perspective, crucial is the relationship that we may or may not decide to establish with the supreme *fons vitae*, i.e. God. In daily experience, many journeys are undertaken in an apparently much more prosaic way, such as those of contemporary tourists. What we commonly associate with these journeys, are evasion, relaxation, breaks from work routines, last-minute deals and a modicum of legal rights when things do not work as they should. The crushing power of mortality, frailty and solitude are not part of tourist brochures. God is hardly ever mentioned in connection with EasyJet or Ryanair, unless the traveller experiences much turbulence during a flight. The commonplace experience of tourism sounds not only anti-climatic *vis-à-vis* Marcel's *homo viator*; it seems totally unrelated.

This un-relatedness is obvious only *prima facie*. No matter how profound or exceptional the key-questions of existentialism may sound, ordinary tourism is also affected by how we give shape to our own identity, how we think about our future, what type of values we opt for and what kind of inter-personal relationships we cherish. As banal as people's summer holidays may seem at first, these too are journeys that impinge upon matters of life and death; they too define our identity and the authenticity of our existence. For one, albeit catered as an alternative among many in conventional tourist marketing, pilgrimages in Christian, Muslim and Buddhist cultures are a patent example of journeys that aim at more than sheer entertainment. Supposedly, the fate of one's own soul may depend on it. For another, choosing to travel in order to hunt down or eat animals listed among an ecosystem's endangered species, or to seek sexual gratification with adults or minors in poverty-stricken communities, says a lot about the person that we are, that we become, and how we associate ourselves with other persons.

As to less faith-inspired and morally extreme examples, the way in which we decide to travel (e.g. by more or less polluting means of transportation), the way in which we look—at, upon or after—the persons that we meet (e.g. waiters or travel guides) and the way in which we select our souvenirs and memorabilia (e.g. by purchasing archaeological artefacts of dubious origin) can tell us something about the ilk of persons that we are, become and associate with. The same can be said of whether one travels to discover oneself, be oneself or amuse oneself into oblivion of her circumstances. The very fact that we may or may not think about some of the moral implications of our not-so-extraordinary journeys reveals much about ourselves. Tourism, like any other dimension of human agency, is no stranger to ethical and axiological assessment. As the pivotal World Tourism Organization's (UNWTO) 1999 *Global Code of Ethics for Tourism* (GCET) asserts, if ethically conducted, "tourism" is capable of "contributing to economic development, international understanding, peace, prosperity and universal respect for, and observance of, human rights and fundamental freedoms".[217] By implication, if tourism is not ethically conducted, some of the above goods may be diminished. Fundamentally, depending on who gives shape to it and how, tourism can be good; or it can be bad.

Who is to say what is good and bad, though? On what grounds can this kind of judgment be passed? How can assertions like those contained in GCET, which was adopted in 2001 by the UN, be assessed and, if challenged, defended? Questions of this variety have kept philosophers busy for centuries and a number of answers have been provided over the long history of the discipline—far too much for a sheer book chapter like the present one. Rather, in what follows, while keeping the ground-breaking GCET in the background, I endorse, outline and apply life-value onto-axiology, which is in all probability the most articulate theory of value developed in the 21st century. By doing so, I offer firstly a detailed yet succinct presentation of a significant development in contemporary philosophical thought. Secondly, I offer a set of criteria whereby the reader can think about, and discriminate between, good and bad tourism, grounding GCET and any analogous normative approach to tourism in as deep a source of value as philosophical thought can retrieve. I conclude this chapter by reflecting upon our being *homines viatores* in light of the implications of life-value onto-axiology for human agency, tourism included.

Life-value Onto-axiology

John McMurtry's entire endeavour is based upon the reasoned belief that, *pace* fashionable relativism and subjectivism, it is possible to identify a universal and objective ground of value. There may exist a 'marketplace of ideas' about what is good and what is not, but some preferences are actually better than others. Marcel's existential hopefulness is not lost on McMurtry, according to whom we can "recover step by step the missing *life-ground* of values and the ultimate meaning of how we are to live."[218]

As we saw in the first part of the present book, the definition of the life-ground is not overly complicated: "Concretely, all that is required to take the next breath; axiologically, all the life support systems required for human life to reproduce or develop." It is so basic a point that it is often taken for granted in scholarly studies. Without enough bread, clean water, breathable air, open spaces in which to move, regular sleep, acceptable education and meaningful socialisation, no value whatsoever that we cherish will ever be expressed in reality. No value whatsoever, whether ethical, political, legal, economic, epistemic, spiritual or aesthetic, can be given independently of this vital platform. Life is the fundamental precondition for any and every other value that there can be (hence the prefix "onto-" i.e. "concerning being") and, *a fortiori*, it is itself valuable and inescapable whenever reflecting upon evaluations (hence "axiology" i.e. "value theory"). There can be no life as such, not to mention any good life, outside the life-ground: "Life support systems—any natural or human-made system without which human beings cannot live or live well—may or may not have value in themselves, but have ultimate value so far as they are that without which human or other life cannot exist or flourish."[219]

If Earth *qua* totality of its biodiversity-sustaining ecosystems is akin to a living individual, which James Lovelock (b. 1919) famously dubbed "Gaia", then the planet's LSS are akin to the functioning metabolic, psychological and socio-cultural apparatuses allowing a living individual to lead a life as such and, possibly, a good life.[220] To all effects, they are vital functions allowing concrete individuals to be alive as animals and active *qua* human beings.

To deny the life-ground's import constitutes a token of performative contradiction, for she who denies it has been meeting her vital needs for the very long time entailed in developing the faculties required to deny its import. Even pessimists, the suicidal and gnostics affirm it, albeit *via negativa*, for they take their departure from a better life that is no more, that is dreamt or conceived of, or that is to be gained *post mortem*.[221] Logically, it is possible to distinguish between life's intrinsic value and the life-ground's instrumental value. Ontologically, it is not: "All that is of worth consists in and enables life value to the extent of its experienced fields of thought, felt being and action (intrinsic value), and what underlies and enables these fields of life themselves, life support systems."[222]

As also revealed in the preceding quote, McMurtry maintains that life manifests itself in three modes of being: "action" (also "biological movement" or "motility"), "felt being" (also "experience" or "feeling") and "thought".[223] In the religious sphere, these modes of being are exemplified in the believer's gratitude for one's being alive, the comforting or even exhilarating presence of the divine within one's heart, and the illuminating or thought-provoking subtleties of theological argumentation. In the secular sphere, health professionals come across these ontological modes under the guises of physical, psychological and mental well-/ill-being. Tourists encounter them too, for instance as healthy, pleasant, meaningful ethnic food in its original historic setting. All that is intuitively saluted as genius, justice, happiness or health is—if truly good—a constructive and comprehensive expression of life-value, in one or more of these modes of being: action (e.g. fitness), felt being (e.g. wonder at nature's intricate complexity) and thought (e.g. proportionality in judiciary adjudication).

No sharp ontological tri- or dualism is implied by McMurtry's tripartite distinction: "Although we can distinguish the cognitive and feeling capacities of any person, this does not mean dividing them into separate worlds as has occurred in the traditional divisions between mind and body, reason and the emotions. Life-value onto-axiology begins from their unity as the nature of the human organism."[224] Thus, as already seen in this book, the fundamental axioms in McMurtry's "life-value onto-axiology" read as follows:

- "X is value if and only if, and to the extent that, x consists in or enables a more coherently inclusive range of thought/

feeling/action than without it"
- "X is disvalue if and only if, and to the extent that, x reduces/disables any range of thought/experience/action."[225]

These axioms apply to all types of human agency. For instance, as contemporary environmentalism is concerned, McMurtry distinguishes between "zero growth" and "zero bad growth", claiming the former to be negative and the latter to be positive, since "growth of production that serves universal human life-needs is necessary and good the more there is deprivation."[226]

To all intents and purposes, life-value onto-axiology achieves a traditional goal of philosophical inquiry, since it allows for the determination in principle of good and evil, cutting across received dualisms, e.g. nature vs. culture, geoengineering vs. sustainable retreat, *res extensa* vs. *res cogitans*, utilitarianism vs. deontology, free choice vs. paternalism, free trade vs. protectionism, individualism vs. collectivism, liberalism vs. conservatism, cooperation vs. competition, theism vs. atheism, description vs. prescription, present vs. future, economic value vs. environmental value, etc.

In theory, the definitive axiological criterion is sharp: life-enablement is good; *vice versa,* life-disablement is bad. In practice, there are going to be simpler and more complex evaluations to be made. Thorny cases and dilemmas are part of the fabric of the human world. Not even the most perceptive philosophy can save us from having to face them. Nevertheless, if life-value onto-axiology is correct, then the better option is bound to be always the result of comparisons of coherent life-value, since no good can be given outside the life-ground, the composition and scope of which McMurtry clarifies by means of two key-concepts: "need" and "civil commons".

As the former key-concept is concerned, McMurtry observes that not anything that we may claim to "need" is, after closer scrutiny, a need: "'n' is a need if and only if, and to the extent that, deprivation of n always leads to a reduction of organic capacity."[227] Only that "without which life-capacities are always reduced" counts as need.[228] We can live, and even prosper, without travel cheques or credit default swaps, but we cannot live, not to mention prosper, without "sufficient nutriment, clean water, sewage facilities, learning of society's symbol systems, home and love, and expert care when ill".[229] To strengthen the point, life-value onto-axiologist Jeff Noonan neatly separates "needs" from economic "preferences" (aka "wants"):[230]

- "[D]eprivation of needs always leads to harm whereas deprivation of wants is only harmful in light of revisable self-interpretation".[231]
- "[N]eeds are satiable whereas wants are not".[232]

No much-desired expensive consumer goodies will ever be vital like water and bread, even if their lack may be hurtful and the conditioned desire for their acquisition so intense as to lead to hysterical, murderous behaviour, or even suicide. Critical revision of one's own beliefs can change such desires, but not the needs for adequate hydration and nourishment.

McMurtry's WBI, which we have already encountered, identifies humanity's fundamental "means of life" or "vital need[s]… for none can be deprived without reduction of vital life capability."[233] In its formulation for UNESCO's EOLSS, McMurtry lists seven vital goods that refer to as many vital needs:[234]

1. The atmospheric goods of breathable air, open space and light;
2. The bodily goods of clean water, nourishing goods and waste disposal;
3. The home and habitat goods of shelter from the elements;
4. The environmental good of natural and constructed elements all contributing to the whole;
5. The good of care through time by love, safety and health infrastructures;
6. The good of human culture in music, language, art, play and sport; and
7. The good of human vocation and social justice – that which

enables and obliges all people to contribute to the provision of these life goods consistent with each's enjoyment of them.

If these goods are not provided, then vital needs are not met; and if these needs are not met, then human capabilities disintegrate, to the eventual point of individual and/or social annihilation. If these needs are met, instead, then human capabilities do not merely endure: they can "flourish" into the good life, individual as well as social.[235]

As the latter key-concept is concerned, McMurtry defines "civil commons" as "[a] unifying concept to designate social constructs which enable universal access to life goods."[236] In the second edition of *The Cancer Stage of Capitalism*, McMurtry lists once more an enormous array of concepts, arrangements and artefacts aimed at fulfilling life-enabling ends under diverse socio-historical contexts (I italicise here those that seem particularly relevant with regard to tourism):[237]

> The nature of language, *the air we breathe*, the common fire, *food recipes*, universal health plans, *the world wide web*, common sewers, international campaigns against US war crimes, *sidewalks and forest paths, sports and sports fields*, the open science movement, the Chinese concept of jen, the Jubilee of Leviticus, *public streetscapes*, effective pollution controls, *birdwatching, city squares and sidewalks*, Buddha's principle of interdependent origination, old-age pensions, the rule of life-protective law, universal education, universal hygiene practices, *footpaths and bicycle trails*, fair elections, unemployment insurance, *the global atmosphere, maximum work hours and minimum wages, public parks*, clean water, the Tao, community fish-habitats, public broadcasting, the ancient village commons before enclosures, the unnamed goal of the Occupy Movement.

Albeit usually devoid of an explicit overarching theory of value as their intellectual foundation, societies have been valuing, protecting, respecting and fulfilling life-requirements and LSS for millennia. Possibly built upon the cooperative inclinations that have helped the survival of many animal species, including ours, these many concepts, arrangements and artefacts have established "commons" that are characterised by the predicate "civil". This predicate reveals the socially constructed and socially aimed dimensions of the institutions nurturing "real capital" i.e. "life-capital – the natural and human-made wealth that produces more through time without loss".[238] McMurtry is not talking, say, of pastures available to all without supervision and sanctions for misuse, but of pastures that the community consciously or pre-consciously (i.e. akin to linguistic syntax) recognises in its symbolic systems and manages in order to yield life-supporting fruits through time for all its members, thus reducing a prime cause of internecine competition.

McMurtry's "civil commons" should not be confused with Garret Hardin's (1915–2003) unregulated natural "commons", whose tragic doom justifies their appropriation for private ends.[239] McMurtry's works are consistently critical of such an appropriation, since it has regularly taken place for class or élite benefit (e.g. 19th-century Highlands clearances), and/or converted the existing civil commons into means of non-universal (e.g. costly for-profit academic indexes) and/or life-disabling ends (e.g. employing higher human knowledge for the production of speculative "financial weapons of mass destruction").[240]

As to what constitutes "real" or "life capital", McMurtry treats it consistently as the evolving onto-axiological base for measurable life-loss and life-gain through generational time. It is the totality of the biological species, their LSS, human cultures and technologies as they produce, reproduce and enable more life capacities. The Anthropocene implies *per se* no destructive agency on humankind's part. However, it has witnessed an exponential increase in the significance of human agency for this life-capital accumulation, which the human economy directs by its own corresponding order—and disorder—of production, reproduction and growth.[241] How to steer human agency on Earth, and therefore the economy itself, constitutes the ultimate context for the exercise of freedom, as anxiety-laden and burdensome as such a responsibility may be.

Assessing Tourism

Given the fundamental axioms of life-value onto-axiology, tourism can be deemed good or bad depending on whether it enables life-means provision and enjoyment or not. Also, given the composition and scope of the life-ground, we can better grasp GCET's intended positive function for "responsible tourism".[242] GCET is a token of civil commons, insofar as it is a social construct attempting to steer human activities nationally and internationally so that life-enabling goods—in this instance those related to tourism—may be provided universally. As article 7(1) of GCET reads: "The prospect of direct and personal access to the discovery and enjoyment of the planet's resources constitutes a right equally open to *all* the world's inhabitants."[243]

Life-value onto-axiology can also help the discerning mind not to take even GCET's declared aims of "economic development, international understanding, peace, prosperity and universal respect for, and observance of, human rights and fundamental freedoms" at face value, but to discriminate in principle between good and bad forms of each. This principled discrimination may sound counter-intuitive, yet it is most relevant in connection with "economic development", to which I confine the present discussion, for not all activities that fall under this notion are genuinely life-enabling. Consider, for instance, the effects that GDP-engrossing tourism can have *vis-à-vis* the "environmental crisis" denounced by the international scientific community at its highest levels.[244] Depletion of fresh-water sources and pollution of the atmosphere by fossil fuel consumption are not the exclusive province of more commonly vilified industries, such as agribusiness and mining. They can apply to the tourist industry too (e.g. high water consumption in tropical resorts and increased aerial traffic).

These negative contributions to the environmental crisis of the Anthropocene are not the result of any inherent malevolence or callousness in the business sector, even though such cases do exist (e.g. hydro-intensive golf courses built in desert regions). Rather, they are the result of the inherent incapacity of private enterprise at large to act in accordance with ultimate, endogenous, life-grounded criteria. Somewhat convolutedly, the preamble of the GCET itself admits this inherent incapacity by stating that "the world tourism industry as a whole has much to gain by operating in an environment that favours the market economy, private enterprise and free trade" for the sake of "the creation of wealth", which is not life-grounded *per se*.[245]

On the contrary, in order to bring forth life-enablement, such a wealth-driven "tourism industry" must bow to "a number of principles and a certain number of rules".[246] Without exogenous constraints, "responsible and sustainable tourism" would be "*incompatible* with the growing liberalization of the conditions governing trade in services and under whose aegis the enterprises of this sector operate".[247] Left to their own devices, business agents in the tourist sector would concern themselves chiefly if not solely with making money, not with protecting and enabling life at large; the former is their paramount *telos*, the latter is not. It is only by means of criteria external to prevailing economic logic "that it is possible to reconcile in this sector economy and ecology, environment and development".[248]

The conflict between standard business logic and what is actually needed for life-enablement lies at the heart of life-value onto-axiology in its application to world affairs, tourism included. Spanning across, and delving into, an immense amount of scientific literature, McMurtry's research since the 1980s constitutes an empirically solid demonstration of how "common interest" and "money-demand growth" are not one and the same thing, as so often claimed under the superstitious assumption of an all-optimising invisible hand.[249] Quite the opposite, in spite of the theodicy hidden within mainstream economics' assumed *equilibria* and much-repeated notions of "positive spill-overs" and "trickle-down" boons, common interest and money-demand growth have been increasingly at war with each other, as poignantly summarised in the long quote from the second edition of McMurtry's *Cancer Stage of Capitalism* offered in chapter three of this book—under the poignant subheading "The Cancer". As it was stated, McMurtry's picture of contemporary reality may sound hyperbolic to some, yet a search for even one exception to these empirical generalisations reveals how exact and precise they are.[250] So bleak are the bio-environmental and socio-economic trends of the past decades, that McMurtry diagnoses the Anthropocene's malaise to be a *cancer*.

We saw in the same previous chapter that the first, crucial step in McMurtry's oncological diagnosis is the determination and assessment of the defining *modus operandi* of the world's leading economic agents, i.e. national and transnational corporate businesses, of which tourism ones are but a small fraction. However cast in accounting formulae, and taking account of the actual behaviour of private bureaucracies, the one and essential characteristic or "ruling value code" that best describes what paramount goal these agents pursue is: "to maximize by any vehicle, method, or channel open to its entry the ratio of its owners' money-demand increases to money-demand inputs."[251] As the aforementioned Chicago economist Milton Friedman stated: "The one and only responsibility of business is to make as much money for stockholders as possible."[252] Yet, this "responsibility of business" is very far from GCET's declared pursuit of "responsible tourism", i.e. a "tourism development" that "safeguard[s] the natural environment with a view to achieving sound, continuous and sustainable economic growth geared to satisfying equitably the *needs* and aspirations of present and future generations."[253]

In Friedman's iconic formulation, no vital needs are mentioned, whether present or future, only making money. Consistently with this understanding, common economic practice refers to carcinogenic pesticides, junk food, cigarettes, armaments, pollution quotas and many pathogenic types of labour as economic "goods", for they generate profits to businessmen and investors, even if bad for life. As McMurtry concludes: "The ruling paradigm is in principle life-blind."[254] Such an economic logic pursues relentless self-expansion and yet can draw "no distinction between what serves organic, social and ecological life-hosts and what poisons, dismantles and loots them."[255] In oncology, that is precisely what cancerous cells perform: *a theoretically endless process of self-replication within a host body, whose health or eventual survival is not and cannot be perceived by the self-replicating cells as an effective control response.*

The second step in the diagnosis consists in the recognition that the effects of this theoretically endless self-replication are also analogous in practice. As any oncological record can show, *the uncontrolled sprawling of cancerous cells leads eventually to loss of organic capacity*, down to the very point of killing the cancer's living host. As McMurtry writes: "As global capitalist exploitation of the environment has advanced and advances across global life-conditions and elements, all of these global life-conditions and elements… degenerate in direct proportion in their life-carrying capacities and biodiversity."[256] Life-blindness may not signify hostility to life in theory, but it does so in practice.

The third step in the diagnosis relates to the fact that, in cancerous pathologies, *the immune defences of a living organism fail to identify the cancerous cells as harbingers of death and keep facilitating their self-replication*. Analogously, as explained already in chapter 3, societies' civil-commons institutions have been largely unresponsive to the ongoing assault upon local and/or global life-conditions. Instead of providing and enforcing life-grounded distinctions in the business sphere, these institutions have cooperated with the process of life-blind and life-destructive sprawling by facilitating, *inter alia*:

> [R]uin of government programmes, workers' jobs and small business with the cranking up of interest rates to over 20 per cent prime in the 1980s…[,] the repeal of Depression-installed regulations like Glass-Steagall… the race to the bottom of wages, benefits and social legislation by global competition with no life-standards… cannibalist interest rates and debt charges… 'market reforms', trade-treaty edicts prohibiting legislation reducing 'profit opportunities', and wars on resource rich regions with

social control... supranational treaties in vast all-or-nothing tranches of 'investor' rights... according all rights only to transnational corporations... [and] binding regulations... [overriding] *all human and natural life-requirements through generational time*... private bank displacement of sovereign control over currency and credit.[257]

Some genuine civil-commons responses have been attempted, undoubtedly, as exemplified by GCET in the tourism sector. They have been very timid, though. The measure of their timidity is easy to gauge: have they stopped or reverted the life-losses that McMurtry's oeuvre compiles *vis-à-vis* the Earth's atmospheric degradation, arable-topsoil desertification, water-aquifer impoverishment, biodiversity reduction, rising income inequality, food contamination, production and consumption of addictive pathogenic commodities, non-contagious disease multiplication, growing private-debt levels, public-sector investment cuts, or proliferating tax evasion schemes? No, they have not. Apart from occasional local progresses, which indicate how alternative courses of action are possible, the answer is still globally negative.[258]

Redressing Tourism

Thus far, as McMurtry's publications adamantly record and explain, the depletion of LSS in the Anthropocene has been so severe that the international scientific community has repeatedly denounced the threat posed by human agency to the present wellbeing and the long-term survival of our species. Over the past four decades, we have been told over and over again that if the governments of the world do not act in a concerted, life-enabling way, major suffering will unfold inevitably and many of humankind's achievements will be lost, if not humankind itself. And with humanity being lost, who will ever have consciousness of what we have done, and failed to do?

The threat of species-wide suffering, extinction and oblivion can have a terrifying, paralysing effect. They are certainly dreadful thoughts to entertain, unless we are engulfed by a nihilistic death wish. Indeed, the threat at issue mirrors in collective form the terrifying, paralysing awareness of mortality, frailty and solitude that Marcel observed in the sphere of individual existence. Yet, reasoning by analogy, the temptation to despair can be overcome by means of hope.

If anything, Marcel's *homo viator* reminds us of the mysterious resilience that we display before that which makes us fear and tremble. There is hope. Perhaps it is a fool's hope, but it is hope nonetheless. McMurtry, despite the dismal facts and trends that he painstakingly collects and conveys in his oeuvre, states that "recovery from the Great Sickness" is possible, though by no means undemanding.[259] His research does not aim solely at regaining sight of the common root of both the environmental and the economic crises, but also at finding ways to let the human economy be life-enabling rather than life-disabling.

Collective choice might opt eventually for the former path; or it may not. Freedom's burden, which existentialists like Marcel explored thoroughly, contemplates the possibility of misused freedom, to the point of self-destruction. As tourism is concerned, GCET itself can either remain a mere list of good intentions or become a well-established set of guidelines inspiring binding regulations. When life-enabling, the frequently censured "red tape" for businesses is actually a lifeline for humankind.

As already seen in the third chapter, the first step towards "the cure" is the conceptual re-grounding of "human", "natural", "knowledge" and "social" capital, as well as "globalisation" and "development", which are understood in terms of "real capital", i.e. "life capital".[260] After reconsidering these key-concepts along life-grounded lines of interpretation, three "universal parameters of diagnosis" of the "general determinants of social health and disease" can be identified that should guide any ensuing social actions and, *a fortiori*, modern tourism too:

[I] "Continuity of life-necessities and means to members of society",

[II] "Functioning contribution of citizens to society's life-requirements", and

[III] "Sustaining the life-carrying capacities of the environmental life-host".[261]

Whatever viable community we may choose to conceive of, its members must have their vital needs met, which can be done by letting all able members participate in life-sustaining economic activities, which in turn must not be harmful to the natural and human-made preconditions for need-satisfaction, i.e. natural and human LSS or civil commons.

It should be emphasised that nature's LSS, insofar as they are thought of and/or managed for life-enablement, are *ipso facto* civil commons. As soon as any natural or human activity is conceived of as having an import upon life and is managed so as to let this import be comprehensively and coherently positive, then that activity becomes a token of civil commons.

The great challenge of the Anthropocene is for humanity to acknowledge to itself that nature's LSS themselves, such as the Earth's water and nitrogen cycles, are now well within the province of human understanding and steering, however varying the latter may be in degree, and can turn all too easily into life-disabling systems when poorly managed. The deep and extensive intermingling of natural and human factors in the Anthropocene can then be deemed good or bad depending on its life-valued implications. No realm where human agency is involved can be excluded. Tourism itself, by fulfilling parameters [I]–[III], could become a true token of civil commons.

As also shown in the third chapter, the second step towards a cure is a set of four shifts in prevailing economic policy that would turn money-making into a means of life-enablement, instead of continuing to treat life-hosts as a means of money-making:

[1] "[H]igher taxes and disincentives for the very rich",[262]
[2] "[A]ggressive national recovery of control over public owned

resources",²⁶³

[3] "[P]ublic banking and investment",²⁶⁴ and

[4] "[P]olicy-led elimination of structural depredation of the poor and the environment".²⁶⁵

All four shifts are articulated for the sake of nurturing "real capital", not for the sake of predatory "State power" or even "equality" as such.²⁶⁶ Still, in today's world, only State power *qua* civil commons is likely to achieve such ambitious shifts. Who or what else, if not State power, could actually streamline the tourist industry along the parameters [I]–[III] by means of consistently enforced GCET's "principles" and "rules"?²⁶⁷

If anything, the Great Recession has shown the world what life-destructiveness deregulated markets are capable of. Besides, none of the advised policies is unknown to modern humankind. They are not trite utopias, but policies that have been tested practically and successfully in the recent past on several occasions, showing how "the right of states, charged with vigilance for the common good" can be employed to a vastly life-enabling effect.²⁶⁸

In the case of tourism, the principles and regulations invoked by GCET fit squarely within the fourth policy shift discussed by McMurtry, given above all the explicit connection made therein between "responsible tourism" and existing human-rights legal "instruments", especially the ICESCR.²⁶⁹ Furthermore, without watchful monitoring and concrete enforcement of life-grounded principles and regulations, there would be little chance for any truly responsible tourism, the economic "competitiveness" of which would be easily undermined by business practices cutting corners *vis-à-vis* environmental standards or "the fundamental rights of salaried and self-employed workers in the tourism industry".²⁷⁰ The first and third policy shifts are relevant with regard to the costs associated with monitoring and enforcement by societies' civil-commons agencies, since more substantial and more readily available public funds could support these agencies, the ambitious aims of which the UNWTO's code extends to "saving rare and precious resources", "avoiding... waste production" and "preserving and upgrading monuments, shrines and museums as well as archaeological and historic sites".[271]

Concluding Remarks

McMurtry's focus, unlike Marcel's, is set upon collective dimensions of agency. However, life-value onto-axiology applies equally to the individual dimension, particularly with respect to existential choices and moral behaviour. The fundamental axioms of life-value onto-axiology tell us what is good and what is bad. Therefore, they offer ultimate criteria for each person's existential and moral evaluations. Accordingly, we can make sense of McMurtry's bold claim that through life-value onto-axiology we can "recover step by step the missing life-ground of values and the ultimate meaning of how we are to live". It is also on a personal level that life-enablement constitutes the good and life-disablement its opposite. The good life is a life in which life-capacity is nurtured as extensively as possible, as exemplified emblematically by the life-nurturing healing and caring acts of religious prophets and saints.

Given the social and natural milieus in which individuals live and act, the individual's good life means for her to operate as a life-capacity multiplier: "The more human beings subsume the requirements of their fellows' and their environment's life-capital capacities into their organizational regulation, the better they are."[272] In the pursuit of the good life, we cannot limit ourselves to fostering our own life-capacity in isolation. We must equally nurture other persons', living creatures' and ecosystems' life-capacity *qua* extensions of our own, as instantiated daily in the subjectively and inter-subjectively rewarding experiences of parenthood, education, nursing, care, genuine friendship, empowering leadership and service, constructive cooperation, inspiring artistic performance, compassion to people and animals, humane animal husbandry and environmentally sound behaviour. Responsible tourism *qua* individual agency falls under this line of understanding.

Although McMurtry acknowledges extensively the commonalities between the recognition of life's supreme value to be found in many spiritual traditions and the one articulated in his own philosophy, neither the bulk of his work nor life-value onto-axiology are focused primarily on the meaningful relationship that individuals may establish with a personal God. In this, Marcel's discussion of *homo viator* emphasises quintessentially religious themes that are not central within McMurtry's philosophy. Nevertheless, the recognition of life's supreme value is sufficient to clarify how the awe and existential import *vis-à-vis* life's majesty characterising many spiritual traditions persist within life-value onto-axiology, which extrapolates "the ultimate meaning of how we are to live" from the life-ground.

On this point, the alarmed words of 20th-century environmentalist, bio-ethicist and historian of religion Hans Jonas, whom the reader encountered in the previous chapter, are most illustrative, and they go to show how the ruling economic paradigm is not only blind to life-needs, it is also deaf to the peculiar scream that the "tortured" Earth emits. Worshipping Mammon rather than Gaia, many human beings seem oblivious to the sacred primacy of life. This peculiar scream is therefore a call to renewed personal responsibility *vis-à-vis* creation itself. It is a secular path to salvation or, if failing, damnation.

Responding constructively to the threat to life caused by the "Great Sickness" is therefore not merely a social task, but one that involves, and gives ultimate meaning to, individual agency as well, just like the pursuit of redemption has done traditionally for countless believers. First of all, no social task would ever be accomplished without widespread individual agency. Secondly, and more distinctively, to be conscious of, and positively responsive to, the ecological crisis of the Anthropocene is part of what the individual's good life requires, since the properly directed expression of an individual's life-capacity cannot but enable to some extent the surrounding individuals, living beings and life-conditions. In order for a specific individual's life to be truly good, her contribution to life in general must be truly good, now and in the future.

As odd as such a notion may have sounded at the beginning of this chapter, it should be clear by now that the same ethical and existential considerations apply to individual choices within the realm of tourism, whether entrepreneurial, recreational or occupational. Tourism is no vacation from personal responsibility. Morality does not vanish into thin air when we consider each individual as an investor, a manager, a producer, or a consumer. Nonetheless, we have no guarantee that the individual should opt always, primarily or even frequently for the good life. Freedom's burden entails having the concrete prospect of opting for its opposite too. Ignorance, greed, stupidity, ennui and capriciousness are but a few of the failures conspiring to draw the worst out of humankind. Uncompromisingly, the sprawling cancer diagnosed by McMurtry shows how systematically humankind has been capable of taking a path that is not good. Yet, humankind's long-evolved civil commons, GCET included, remind us also of our potential for taking a positive one. Following Marcel, we can hope that this latter path may be the decisive one for most of us in the face of the Anthropocene's greatest challenge: our own survival as a species.

Chapter 6: Paul Krugman's Banking Metastases

Given the severity and the duration of the international economic crisis ushered by extensive financial trade of "toxic assets" in the 2000s, phrases such as "banking cancer" or "financial metastasis" are being uttered more and more commonly in the popular press.[273] At the same time, medical descriptors and oncological metaphors can be encountered in scholarly literature too. For example, shortly before his death, British historian Eric J. Hobsbawm (1917–2012) stated that today's "laissez-faire capitalism" has reached a stage that should be deemed "pathological", for it runs divergent from—if not counter to—fundamental "human needs".[274] Chicago University's Law-and-Ethics Distinguished Professor Martha Nussbaum compares to "a cancer" the transformation of American and British higher education into sheer training for employment in, or service to, private businesses.[275] Nobel-laureate economist Paul Krugman (b. 1953) brings together the popular press and scholarly literature in his blog for *The New York Times* and proffers comments such as the following ones:[276]

> Experts say the cycle of anxiety, forced selling and surging borrowing costs is reminiscent of the months before the collapse of Lehman Brothers in 2008, when worries about subprime mortgages in the United States *metastasized* into a global market crisis.

> [W]e've now seen three island nations around Europe become huge international banking hubs relative to their GDPs, then get into crisis because their domestic economies don't have the resources to bail out those metastasized banking systems if something goes wrong. This strongly suggests, to me at least, that we have a fundamental problem with the whole architecture (to use the preferred fancy word) of international finance.

Similes, metaphors and rhetorical figures in general play a very important role in the way we talk and think. Indeed, it would be impossible to talk and think without them.

Rhetoric

Rhetoric gives us tropes or figures through which we interpret the world; it gives us shapes, structures—"gestalten", in psychology's jargon—delineating the contours of identifiable items in an otherwise undifferentiated mass of perceptual stimuli.[277] Insofar as words representing concepts representing discrete sections of potential or actual perceptual reality constitute the bulk of language, it has been argued that rhetoric is inescapable in thinking and communication.[278] Moreover, rhetorical figures and metaphors in particular have always played an important role in both scholarship and scientific research;[279] e.g., by addressing politically organised societies as "the body politick",[280] or by referring to the solar system in order to explain how electrons orbit around the nucleus.[281]

Some metaphors hit the nail on the head and stick around for a long time, as with the body politic, which has been with us since at least the days of Aesop's (620–564 BC) *Fables*.[282] Others blossom into explanatory models of reality, as with Bohr's pioneering study in atomic physics.[283] A few become so ingrained in disciplinary fields that those who use them tend to forget their metaphorical origin, e.g. "force", "field" and "vector" in physics; "cell", "corpuscle" and "nucleus" in biology; "market", "growth" and "capital" in economics. Some even migrate from one field of specialised knowledge to another, e.g. engineering-born "mechanism", "overheating" and "flow", which have found ample use in rhetoric-prone economics.[284]

There is therefore nothing new or utterly surprising as regards Paul Krugman's use of metaphors in connection with markets and banking crises. What is interesting, however, is:

- That the repeated use of such tropes logically presupposes the possibility of applying oncological notions to socio-economic

affairs; and
- That there exists already one attempt to do precisely this sort of operation extensively, i.e. to apply the medical understanding of a cancerous pathology *qua* explanatory model to recent socio-economic phenomena, including debt crises.

In Anglophone philosophy, John McMurtry is known for analysing the aetiology tying together for-profit economic activity and life-depletion, both natural and social, as cancerous.[285]

In what follows, I reiterate in a stricter economic light his oncological analysis, which has already been offered in the previous chapters of the present book, and offer lists of tokens of both life-destructive and life-serving phenomena, so as to display how life-value onto-axiology does offer a valuable unifying frame of understanding meeting Krugman's own concerns *vis-à-vis* the banking sector. Hopefully, in not too distant a future, McMurtry's key-notions (e.g. "civil commons") and theory of value will be as commonplace amongst scholars worldwide, including economists, as John Rawls' (1921–2002) "veil of ignorance" and theory of justice have been over the past four decades.

Oncology

The first, crucial step in the oncological analysis of current world affairs is the determination and assessment of the defining *modus operandi* of the world's leading economic agents, i.e. a rather small cluster of large national and transnational private firms and corporations.[286] As already discussed repeatedly in the previous chapters, the defining aim of these agents is the following: to regularly bestow increasing money returns upon money investors and/or managers.[287] From an economic and even legal point of view, there is nothing strange or mistaken, at least *prima facie*, with this regulating code. As long as nothing illicit takes place, this code is taken to be reflecting the only rational course of action, which should theoretically proceed ad infinitum, since *homo economicus*' desires are deemed multiple, varying and non-satiable by textbook definition.[288]

According to standard economic theory, each sentient economic agent is a self-maximising pleasure-machine (non-sentient ones self-maximise too, but for the fiduciary sake of their shareholders' pleasure). Pleasure is obtained by fulfilling one's desires, i.e. textbook "preference satisfaction" (or the older ordinalist Paretian ophelimity).[289] The fulfilment of these desires translates into corresponding economic transactions under a money-based price system that, as a corollary of non-satiability, must continuously expand to secure regularly increasing returns, thus producing economic growth. But is such a growth always desirable? And, if so, are all types of growth equally desirable, or are some better than others? And what sort of criteria could distinguish among them?

From a biological point of view, one major problem is immediately visible in the economic logic at issue, insofar as there are *no* life-related coordinates, which discriminate between:

- Vital and deadly desires, desire fulfilments and/or corresponding economic transactions;
- Healthy and unhealthy ones; or
- Sustainable and unsustainable expansions of the money-gauged price system.

On the contrary, it is only through the intervention of rationalities and agents external to the purely economic sphere that discriminations of this kind can take place, e.g.: national legislators concerned with the public good; enforced *ergo* justiciable human rights provisions; scientifically solid and thoroughly applied health-and-safety standards; well-funded and well-staffed environmental agencies and State tribunals.

Taken in their abstract form *qua* legal *personae*, economic agents possess no life-related coordinates for biologically sound discrimination, as exemplified daily in concrete form by: profitable yet life-destructive trade in tobacco, junk food and pathogenic pesticides; expensive patents on life-saving medical treatments;

fossil-oil drilling in Arctic regions that have become ice-free because of global warming; and financial speculation on the price of vital staples such as wheat and maize. Not to mention legally more opaque cases, e.g.: disposal of developed countries' hazardous waste into developing countries;[290] "vulture funds" profiting from the sovereign debts of the Earth's poorest countries;[291] accounting experts devising tax-elusion schemes benefitting wealthy clients yet depriving home communities of resources that could fund, *inter alia*, State and municipal police forces, public prosecution offices, public hospitals, research centres, schools and universities.[292]

Under standard criteria of economic rationality, allegedly rational agents aim solely at self-maximising, i.e. getting more and more desire fulfilment or "preference satisfaction", whether mentally and/or physically healthy or not,[293] often in response to cravings that are craftily induced into consumers by means of conditioning techniques devised by marketing and advertising professionals.[294] Such supposedly rational agents engage consistently and continuously in money-based transactions that, in theory, must self-replicate endlessly, in order to secure regularly increasing returns onto investment and/or management.

This theoretically endless self-replication process is expected to go on indefinitely, whatever may eventually happen to public health, people's lives, and the planetary and social fundamental structures upon which their health and lives depend.[295] Biological categories of life and death, as well as health and sickness, are absent *in principle* within standard economic rationality. At the same time, "growth" continues and *must* continue *qua* paramount and legally accepted system-defining aim of the economy. In oncology, that is precisely what cancerous cells perform, namely a theoretically endless process of self-replication within a host body, whose health or eventual survival is not and cannot be perceived by the self-replicating cells as an effective control response.

The second step in the oncological analysis of current world affairs consists in the acknowledgment that the effects of this theoretically endless self-replication are analogous in practice too. As any oncological record can illustrate, the uncontrolled sprawling of cancerous cells leads eventually to loss of organic capacity, down to the very point of killing the host, whose demise implies also the demise of the cancerous cells within it. Similarly, the sequences of investment and returns in the global economy have been producing life-losses on a massive scale by, *inter alia*:

- Industrial pollution of the Earth's atmosphere;
- Agribusiness' contamination of underground aquifers;
- Cuts to healthcare provision *ergo* to living persons' health for the sake of securing wealthy creditors' pecuniary returns;
- Identically motivated cuts to environmental, public hygiene and workplace safety agencies;
- Less-inclusive privatised policing and old-age pension schemes;
- Industrial relocation and/or expansion in countries with lesser health, safety and environmental standards.

If anything, McMurtry's oeuvre is an impressive collection of empirical data on the losses suffered by natural as well as human-made LSS because of life-disconnected economic activity. Not one of these systems has been spared, for they include: the air we breathe; the water we drink; the topsoil needed for agriculture; the Ozone layer protecting us from lethal solar irradiation; the bio-diverse forests and oceanic algae generating oxygen through photosynthesis; the socially managed institutions that respect, protect and fulfil the civil, political, social, economic and cultural rights enshrined in the human rights legislation at its highest level (i.e. the ICCPR and ICESCR).[296]

McMurtry's oeuvre discloses also how the size of the cancerous mass has been increasing exponentially over the past three decades, thanks to the global financialisation of the world's economies. Having demolished intra- and international barriers to financial trade inherited from the Great-Depression and Bretton-Woods eras, the nations' currencies, sovereign debt emissions, credit creation, old-age pension savings, as well as public services (e.g. defence) and strategic natural assets (e.g. oil and gas reserves, living marine resources) have all been targeted for transformation into for-profit tradable items, both:

(1) Directly, *qua* bought-and-sold commodities; and, above all,
(2) Indirectly, *qua* collaterals of leveraged financial products, which constitute the lion's share of late-modern world trade.[297]

This has been done under global finance's pressing search for short-term pecuniary gain, i.e. leaving aside or underplaying the medium- and/or long-term social and biological sustainability of the processes of extraction, transformation, transportation, consumption and disposal operated in the continuous pursuit of "return on equity", "profits", etc.[298] The inherent economic logic at work has been money-driven, *not* life-driven. The economy has been conceived of, *in primis* and above all else, as generating money-based returns, rather than serving specific vital needs or life-enabling aims across generations. As leading Finnish jurist Aulis Aarnio (b. 1937) puts it: "Environmental values and economic values often clash, as in the protection of the forests and waterways. Almost without exception, the values that have prevailed have been economic."[299] (Not to mention that by harming their own ontological preconditions, such "economic values" prove themselves to be in essence anti-economic.)

Mostly, there has been no evil intention at play. Although sectors of the existing market economy do benefit from the direct dilapidation of LSS (e.g. pharmaceutical companies profiting from diseases caused by industrial pollution), this dilapidation is rarely the aim of the agents at play (e.g. arms manufacturers and arms traders profiting from societies' fall into civil war). Rather, textbook economics and actual businesses eschew *a priori* such fundamental onto-axiological structures and damage thereof. This avoidance is accomplished by either presupposing these structures uncritically *qua* free gifts of history;[300] or treating them as *externalities*, i.e. domains lying outside the contractual one in which the economic agents are formally confined in both standard theory and much legal practice.

Occasionally, these externalities re-enter the economic purview by turning into costs (e.g. "green" taxation) or profit opportunities (e.g. the aforementioned costly treatments for diseases caused by industrial pollutants). In any case, pressed by ever-mounting calls for increasing returns on invested capital, private companies have hardly ever requested and/or welcomed life-protective regulation and tax-based financing thereof. Quite the opposite, they have normally claimed them to be tokens of "fiscal unfriendliness", unwarranted "rigidities" in, or harmful "interferences" with, business activity—in a nutshell, evils to be avoided, unless they are exploited instrumentally to squeeze out competitors.[301]

The third step in the oncological analysis of current world affairs relates to the fact that, in cancerous pathologies, the immune defences of a living organism fail to identify the cancerous cells as harbingers of death and keep facilitating their self-replication. In an analogous fashion, societies' long-established life-protective institutions (e.g. democratic governments committed to the common good, universities as independent research centres, central banks *qua* socially responsible monitoring bodies) have been largely blind and unresponsive to the ongoing assault upon local and/or global life-conditions. Repeatedly, they have not recognised it for what it is: an assault on precisely such life-conditions. On the contrary, these institutions have pro-actively cooperated with the diffusion of the cancerous pathology by, *inter alia*:

- Treating public investments in healthcare and education as reducible costs;
- Dismantling currency trade barriers and other national and international life-protecting regulations under free-trade agreements;
- Creating *fiat* money and ironically dubbed "credit lifelines" for highly indebted private banks but not for States themselves or other public institutions constitutionally mandated to provide essential social services;
- Reforming fiscal systems in such ways that fewer life-serving resources are contributed by societies' wealthiest members

and potentially life-serving resources can be more easily syphoned into foreign tax shelters;
- Equating economic growth and/or private businesses' *desiderata* with human happiness and/or public prosperity; and
- Fostering the privatisation of public assets that guaranteed a steady flow of revenues to life-serving public bodies.

Institutions that should serve as the white cells and antibodies of the body politic—screening for, and selecting out, pathogenic intruders—have facilitated its weakening, whether *via* direct assault onto, or indirect destabilisation of, the LSS upon which the body politic relies.

Seeking for a cure to the ongoing pathology, McMurtry's WBI represents his most ostensible contribution to the development of standards for the measurement of human wellbeing, so that progress and regress may be interpreted in ways that mainstream economic criteria neglect or fail to ascertain, both in theory and in practice. The importance of determining novel standards and indicators is considerable, and widely acknowledged by many academics and politicians (e.g. the 2008–2009 Stiglitz-Sen-Fitoussi Commission created by the French government), but above all it is important to reconceptualise economic phenomena so as to re-orient them in line with life-based criteria. Awareness of looming environmental disaster is as old as the Club of Rome's pioneering 1972 report entitled *Limits to Growth*.[302] Since then, much progress has been achieved in "green" economics.[303] However, all this "green" production in theory has not dented neoclassical orthodoxy and, above all, standard textbooks, upon which is formed the knowledge of economics of most businesspeople, politicians, as well as economic and political advisors, i.e. crucial decision-makers, who still cling onto "growth" *qua* supreme end in practice.

A Concluding Remark

It has already been highlighted how the type of "growth"

conceptualised and pursued in today's global market has had systemic negative implications upon life at many levels, to the point of making the usage of cancer-based tropes frequent and the explanation of said implications by means of a cancer-based paradigm possible. Yet, in the wake of the latest major economic crisis, the same global market has been proven equally unable to attain "growth" on its own life-blind terms, i.e. in terms of pecuniary aggrandisement for money investors and/or managers.[304] Its rationality, which economics textbooks presuppose, is to be seriously questioned; and that is what McMurtry's work does, consistently with the poignant characterisation of the Socratic role that philosophers are expected to play in genuinely democratic societies. As the Greek polymath and long-time OECD economist Cornelius Castoriadis (1922–1997) phrases this Socratic role: "[it is] the possibility and the ability to call established institutions and significations into question."[305]

Chapter 7: Social Philosophy and Oncology

Since first outlining it in an article for *Social Justice*'s 1995 special issue on public health,[306] John McMurtry has been elaborating a "diagnosis" of the global economy's ongoing systemic depletion of natural and social resources "as carcinogenic".[307] This diagnosis was fully articulated four years later in the first edition of *The Cancer Stage of Capitalism*. Widely read and reviewed, sometimes years after it first appeared for Pluto Press,[308] the cancer diagnosis has been often misrepresented and misunderstood. Thus, McMurtry clarifies it in the second, revised, 2013 edition of his book: "the cancer stage of capitalism is *not* a metaphor", it is "an explanatory model".[309]

Unlike a mere image of likeness, the explanatory model applies thoroughly and with systematic correspondence the carefully discussed defining features of a serious carcinogenic disorder to economic phenomena. Additionally, McMurtry observes with numerous examples how this diagnosis is implicit in, or underlies, much recent discourse on the global economic crisis following the 2008 collapse of Wall Street, though the discourse itself is not yet capable of penetrating the systemic meaning of the disorder and indeed incoherently avoids it with revealing yet superficial terms like "financial contagion".[310]

In this chapter, I presuppose the previous introductions to life-value onto-axiology, whilst I reiterate McMurtry's oncological explanatory model of socio-economic affairs, in order to integrate it further, emphasise its medical aspects, and offer some reflections on the implications that standard oncological analysis reveals *vis-à-vis* current economic phenomena interpreted as a cancerous pathology.

Cancers

McMurtry's book argues repeatedly and at length that the most widespread forms of disease today, non-contagious pathologies and "cancer" in particular, are due primarily to intentionally marketed, life-harming, addictive, priced "consumables" such as cars, cigarettes and junk food, i.e. as "a capitalist disease epidemic".[311] Capitalism, in his view, lies also behind the carcinogenic decline in life-protective environmental and social standards across the planet over the post-Bretton-Woods decades.[312] The book cites countless authoritative sources in support of these theses, such as leading health scientists' assessments of the socio-economic determinants of ill-health in today's societies, and cancerous pathologies in particular,[313] as well as a few famous politicians' and one Wall Street mogul's dramatic assessment of the current economy's inability to produce genuine wellbeing—left and right of the political spectrum.[314]

There seems to be little or no doubt that the global economic system, which for convenience is called "capitalism", operates increasingly, though certainly not exclusively, against both natural and human-made LSS. Cancerous pathologies are the symptom of such a life-destructive systemic agency, which brings death aplenty in many other forms too. High-level gatherings and documents such as the 1992 UN Rio Declaration on Environment and Development bear public and official witness to one of them. Water aquifers lost to industrial pollution and agribusiness' overexploitation, and corporate patents making life-saving medications unaffordable to many countries' health-care services, are further tangible proof of the same phenomenon, not to mention highly profitable "weapons", i.e. commodities "intentionally constructed to maim and kill life", to which McMurtry had devoted the 1989 book *Understanding War*.[315]

All these examples show also that the faith in the "happy coincidence" between profit-making and "social or ecological goods" thanks to the providential "invisible hand" informing the market mechanism is naïve at best, insincere at worst, and empirically false anyway.[316] As regards the life-enabling goods (e.g. bread) and services (e.g. employment) supplied by the same system to certain living beings, there has been normally no alternative source; hence commending "capitalism" for such goods and services would be like praising the institution of slavery for having the slaves fed.

Perhaps, as unlikely as this would sound to trafficked slaves or exterminated indigenous populations, the ideal capitalism of "the local butcher, brewer, and baker" depicted by Adam Smith in his 1776 *Wealth of Nations* might have occasionally achieved such a happy coincidence somewhere at some hypothetical point in the past.[317] Since the 19th century, however, the real capitalism of Dickens' powerful industrialists, Veblen's large trusts and Galbraith's transnational corporations has been showing long successions of entrepreneurs, shareholders, landowners, top managers, as well as their political, academic and media apparatchiks, who "have over centuries militantly opposed maximum work hours, reduction of child labour, minimum wages, workplace safety, labour unions, public health care, unemployment insurance, old age pensions and social security support systems".[318]

It is actually difficult to think of a single civil commons institution of modern societies—be it public postal services or regulatory frameworks for the banking industry—that corporate interests have not tried "to eliminate… or price… for profit".[319] Valuing everything in terms of money and money alone, whatever may serve other values (e.g. health, hygiene, survival, dignity, fairness, beauty, religious probity) is an obstacle to business unless it can become a profit opportunity. Cancers are no exception: as long as it is more profitable, selling cures is systematically favoured over preventing them.

Under this respect, McMurtry is factually correct when recording the significant, pathogenic reduction of funds and personnel of "environmental agencies" in the US and Canada over recent decades. It is equally true that the "1998 Kyoto pact" to counter the destabilisation of the Earth's climate was turned into a "new market regime for private corporations to buy and sell rights to pollute the planet's atmosphere", instead of stopping the carcinogenic pollution as such.[320] In all these cases, the price for these systemic choices is paid in worse health and in lost lives.

Analogies

We read already in the previous chapters how the life-disablement caused by the systemic agency of capitalism can count as analogous to a cancer. It is worth recalling here the heart of this diagnosis by McMurtry and stress further in medical terms the pathological character of the dominant, global economic system.

First of all, a theoretically endless series of self-maximising economic transactions is sought in contemporary economic practice in the name of "growth", without any inherent life-based parameters, precisely like the sprawling self-replication of cancerous cells within a living host. As McMurtry writes: "Grounded in an engineering model of perfectly divisible inputs and outputs, life is in principle ruled out... What money wants is all that exists."[321]

Secondly, the effects of this theoretically endless self-replication are analogous to a cancer in practice too. As any oncological record can illustrate, the uncontrolled sprawling of cancerous cells leads eventually to loss of organic capacity, down to the very point of killing the host, whose demise implies also the demise of the cancerous cells operating the lethal "invasion".[322] No rational mind can deny that "life-capital reproduction through time" is being endangered on a massive scale by the continuing spoliation of our planet's "forests, waters, and animals as well as climate cycles"; yet "money-capital" keeps "[m]ultiplying" invariably in aetiologically damning processes of, say, for-profit mechanised logging, pesticide-intensive agriculture, and extensive fossil-oil consumption.[323] What is more, such processes are still deemed "rational" in economic terms, as though what we have come to call "the economy" could be separated and opposed to its ontological preconditions.[324] Regularly, this bizarre and life-depleting "rationality" prevails, as with Principles 2 and 16 of the aforementioned 1992 UN Rio Declaration on Environment and Development. On the one hand, the Declaration openly recognises the "environmental crisis".[325] On the other, it allows itself to press for environmental protection and restoration "without distorting international trade and investment".[326] *Ipso dicto*, "international trade and investment" are revealed to have priority over the Earth's environment, i.e. the key-determinant for good- and ill-health, also given that "States", hence private agents therein, "have the sovereign right to exploit their own resources".[327] As McMurtry laconically states: "'Capital' has come to refer to what deprives the world of life-goods without production of them."[328] Specifically, "[w]hatever the systemic destruction of human life and universally accessible life means of a society, and however they are provided by peaceful and self-governing life ordering, the ultimately driving transnational money-sequences dismantle them to multiply themselves."[329]

Capitalism does not only operate against LSS, but it does so *systemically*: capitalism is "pathological in principle because it *always selects for money-value over life* value".[330] Textbook economics and actual businesses eschew *a priori* such fundamental onto-axiological structures and damage thereof. This avoidance is accomplished by either presupposing these structures uncritically *qua* free gifts of history, or by treating them methodologically as "externalities", i.e. domains lying outside the contractual one in which the economic agents are formally confined in both standard theory and legal practice.[331] The very textbook concept of externality "reveals its pathogenic programme in principle by acknowledging that the invasion, occupation and destruction of *its life-hosts is 'external' to its growth*."[332]

Occasionally, these externalities re-enter the economic purview by turning into costs, such as "green" regulation and/or taxation of life-depleting activities. Given the predominant life-disconnected economic "rationality", business entities tend to resist and/or circumvent such regulation and taxation: "Life-serving standards are a liability in the global corporate system".[333] Revealingly, in standard textbooks for marketing and advertising, long-established SWOT analysis places life-protective laws and regulations under the "T" of "threats" to private businesses, not the "S" of "strengths", insofar as contributing to social and environmental wellbeing is not these businesses' binding aim, while selling for a profit is.[334] On other occasions, these externalities re-enter as profit opportunities, such as the future likely scarcity of life-giving water, which is going to become "the single most important physical commodity based asset class".[335] Either way, resistance to life-serving intervention and forecast profits from life-depletion indicate how "economic thought is *in principle incapable of recognizing what has gone wrong.*"[336]

This incapability is emblematically exemplified by the World Bank's apparent schizophrenia in its recurrent acknowledgements of the dramatic environmental and social issues discussed in McMurtry's book and the regular funding of projects furthering precisely such issues.[337] The life-blind value-logic conditioning the Bank's and market operations at large is such that the "global market paradigm… is confined to the simple, fungible inputs, throughputs and outputs of market money-sequences. That is why such a mind-set says 'society does not exist' or 'environmentalists obstruct business'".[338] Societies' life needs and fundamental environmental concerns do not and cannot compute *per se* in any meaningful way: "the first question is not is this measure desirable, but what will be the impact on the country's competitive position in the world's economy".[339] Only money-sequences compute, irrespective of loss in life or livelihood, as exemplified by "American CEO Albert Dunlap", who fired "11,000 workers to multiply the stock price" and celebrated publicly that he had "created six-and-a-half billion dollars."[340]

Yet societies, their basic civil commons formations (e.g. families and local communities *qua* fundamental centres for human acculturation, socialisation, individualisation and care) and the environment upon which they all rely, are presupposed throughout the operations of the global market. Specifically, under deregulated and/or business-friendly fiscal regimes, the global market free-rides upon "all the unpriced goods from natural and social life-support systems", lest it ceases to exist.[341] Moreover, "most profits are by property in land and knowledge [the global market] does not create".[342] From a biological and medical point of view, the money-sequencing "transnational regime" is *parasitic*, for it assumes "the right to enter and access other societies' markets across boundaries cost-free, with no obligation to pay any of the direct or indirect costs of building, maintaining or developing any of the conditions of these markets' existence... [while it] simultaneously seek[s] subsidies and incentives... [and] assume[s] effective immunity from and non-liability for the harms [it] do[es] to organic social and environmental life".[343]

Thirdly, in all cancerous pathologies, *the immune defences of a living organism fail to identify the cancerous cells as harbingers of death and keep facilitating their self-replication*. In an analogous fashion, societies' long-established life-protective institutions have been largely blind and unresponsive to the ongoing assault upon local and/or global life-conditions. Repeatedly, democratic governments, central banks, legislating parliaments, UN agencies and universities *qua* centres of "critical thought as social-immune system" have not recognised the sprawling of money-sequences across domains for what it is, that is to say, an assault on precisely such life-conditions.[344] On the contrary, these institutions have eagerly cooperated with the diffusion of the cancerous pathology, seeking "growth" above all else, and never wondering whether it is good or bad growth that is being sought after.

Fallacies

Given the symbolic systems in which human beings gain consciousness of themselves and of their own environment, McMurtry tracks a number of socio-cultural phenomena that reveal how it has been possible for the cancer to go undetected. Chapter 2 of the second edition of *The Cancer Stage of Capitalism* is devoted entirely to the ways in which the identification and critique of societies' deepest value-structures have been discouraged, though never altogether halted, in human history. As a result, the reader encounters in McMurtry's book a poignant record of widespread yet *fallacious lines of reasoning*, such as:

- "[P]rivate money" alone counting as "demand" in "the Economy", thus discarding *ab initio* "all needs and demands of organic, social and life-systems";[345]
- "[T]he confinement of social and economic agency to atomic

aggregates" despite societies' and environments' being the ontological preconditions for any meaningful individuality whatsoever;[346]
- [T]he misleading confusion between "over-demand" with "overpopulation";[347]
- "[D]ictator Hugo Chavez" *qua* "*ad hominem* diversion" from Venezuela's and Latin America' strides ahead in life-enhancement during the 2000s, after "the foreign money-sequences with no life-function were no longer permitted to hijack its social life organization to grow and multiply their parasitic compound interest debt services destroying the economy and social life organization";[348]
- "[V]ast greed" or "moral bankruptcy" *qua* causes of the latest major economic crisis, yet failing to explain "the surrounding system selecting for them";[349]
- Human beings being treated as means to "money-valued growth of the economy" rather than human-rights-endowed ends in themselves.[350]

In addition to fallacious lines of reasoning, McMurtry's book records and dismantles a good number of equally widespread:

- *Dogmatic slogans* (e.g. there is "no alternative";[351] "market magic" and "revolution[s]";[352] "this is what people want";[353] "big government" is bad;[354] a long list of US Republicans' attacks against life-serving "entitlements";[355] "efficiency";[356] the fossil-oil conglomerates "produc[ing] what we must have";[357] it is "human nature"[358]) and
- *Untested assumptions* (e.g. "the global market system as a technical given";[359] "the common good" *qua* "what the market decides";[360] "the global market value-system as normal";[361] "Hayek's canonical definition of 'the free market'" corresponding to the actual "corporate global market"[362]), as well as
- *Unfalsifiable* hence unscientific *hypotheses* (e.g. the global market's all-optimising "invisible hand"[363]) and

- Outright *lies* (e.g. "new efficiencies", "savings", "development", "well-being", "sustainability" meaning their opposite;[364] deregulated private banks' debt crisis turned into "Europe's debt crisis";[365] "life-system pillage, despoliation and destruction" heralding "productivity" and "greater efficiency";[366] "the pervasive equation of the global corporate system to 'the Free World'";[367] "the putative ' global market… promotes democracy'";[368] "nations of Europe 'being saved'" while "the private banks get all the public money";[369] the global market logic being "necessary" or equating "liberty" and "the social good";[370] a "renewed flow of credit" justifying the 2008 massive bailouts of over-indebted private banks[371]).

Blinded by fallacious lines of reasoning, dogmatic slogans, untested assumptions, unscientific hypotheses and outright lies, human repositories of collective knowledge and social agency expected to operate as the white cells of the body politic—screening for, and selecting out, pathogenic intruders—have facilitated its weakening. Unable to detect and to respond to the ongoing assault, they march on in many countries of the world, as blindly as before, towards self-demise: "Like Einstein's definition of insanity of 'doing the same thing over and over again and expecting a different result' – governments keep *abdicating public responsibility and privatizing public life-capital bases*."[372]

Therapies

We have already seen that McMurtry believes "recovery from the Great Sickness" to be possible, though by no means easy. As a first step towards a cure, McMurtry offers re-grounded concepts of "human", "natural", "knowledge" and "social" capital, as well as "globalisation" and "development", which come to be understood in terms of "real capital", so as to grasp what a sensible life-enabling economy is like.[373] Analogously, he identifies three "universal parameters of diagnosis" of the "general determinants of social health and disease" that should guide any ensuing social action: "Continuity of life-necessities and means to members of society... Functioning contribution of citizens to society's life-requirements... [and] Sustaining the life-carrying capacities of the environmental life-host".[374] Whatever community we may wish to think of, its members must have their vital needs met, which can be done by letting all able members participate in life-sustaining economic activities, which in turn must not be harmful to the natural and human-made preconditions for need-satisfaction, i.e. natural LSS and social civil commons. As McMurtry writes, truly rational "use of natural and human capital" must be "consistent with sustaining and developing them as life-capital".[375] In essence, lie-value onto-axiology bases the understanding of economic phenomena in their deeper life-functions: "life-demand is the driver, life-goods are the means of welfare, and the economy is the rational organization of factors to achieve equilibrium between life-needs and goods."[376]

Under current socio-historical circumstances, the criteria for a truly life-enabling economy translate into four major policy shifts, which have already been presented to the reader: "higher taxes and disincentives for the very rich"; "aggressive national recovery of control over public owned resources"; "public banking and investment"; and "policy-led elimination of structural depredation of the poor and the environment". None of the advised policies is unknown to modern humankind, since they have been tested practically and successfully in the recent past on many occasions (e.g. Scandinavia since the mid-20th century, Latin America as of the late 1990s, the US greenbacks, Germany's regional banks, the Marshall Plan, Brazil's "Bolsa Familia" programme in the 2000s, Canada's "Mincome" in the 1970s).

Under the same current socio-historical circumstances, the prime common causal mechanism of cancers and other non-communicative diseases is the money-sequence multiplication system in which all victims are embedded as moving parts. In today's medical practice, standard cancer treatment hardly helps in keeping cancerous pathologies from arising, since it does not tackle this prime common source of pathogenic toxins and stressors entering the organism and causing the cancers. Rather, the treatment of the resulting cancers focuses upon a number of subsequent factors, such as the type of cancer, whether it is localised or widespread, as well as the overall health status of the patient. The aim with most treatments is to either directly remove and/or kill the cancer cells, or to lead to their eventual death by impeding their abnormal and unbalanced division.[377]

There exist four fundamental kinds of cancer treatment under the prevailing methodology, which does not include systemic prevention:

(I) Surgery,
(II) Chemotherapy,
(III) Radiation therapy, and
(IV) Biologic or targeted therapy.

(I) Surgery can be used to diagnose, prevent and treat cancer. It consists in removing tissue, whether entirely or primarily cancerous, from the body. (II) Chemotherapy makes use of combinations of specific drugs for getting rid of cancerous cells from the patient's body. The drugs are aimed at rapidly multiplying cancer cells and affect also other cells that multiply fast, such as cells in our stomach and in the roots of our hair. (III) Radiation therapy kills cancerous cells by directing strong energy at them. Radiation does not distinguish between normal tissues and malignant ones; hence the irradiated energy may kill sick cells as well as healthy ones. Exact preparation is therefore required for the treatment to hit the tumour and leave out as much healthy tissue as possible. (IV) Targeted therapy has the ability to treat cancer by targeting delivery through angiogenesis (the physiological process through which new blood vessels form from pre-existing vessels). This method consists of drugs that go after specific characteristics of tumours and prevent the cancerous cells' self-replication, e.g. by blocking the chemical signals needed for cancerous cells to develop and keep growing or the blood stream sustaining them.[378]

Often, these four different types of treatment are used in

combination, either simultaneously or sequentially. All of these treatments, whether eventually successful or not, have side-effects, thus creating discomfort, pain or illness in the patient whose life is at stake.[379] In particular, surgery, chemotherapy and radiation therapy are aggressive interventions into the trajectory of cancerous pathologies, aimed at stopping the development of the disease. They are aggressive in the sense that they disturb the life of the patient, they cause unpleasant side-effects and, above all, they kill directly malignant cells. McMurtry´s policy shifts would also disturb many lives. Many people find radical changes overwhelming and they resist them, even if they are sorely needed and the need is recognised by many other persons, including experts and professionals. Faced with such a conspicuous change in the established socio-economic trends, as deadly as these may be, many people would feel like patients diagnosed with cancer: bewildered, shocked, vulnerable, resentful and losing hope, despite the chances for a suitable cure.[380] Thus, it is reasonable to assume that these policy shifts require careful preparation and explanation before becoming a reality.

Nonetheless, just as in curing cancer the treatment methods may be used together for full effect, so would McMurtry´s shifts be likely to have to be put into practice either all at once or over a relatively short time for them to have full effect, i.e. to prevent effective resistance from the financial élite. In fact, as such an élite is concerned, unless they are capable or willing to reconsider in a life-grounded manner their position within both society and nature, then the four policy shifts would kill *de facto* their opportunities to make a killing. If implemented, the four policy shifts recommended by McMurtry would change the lives of the wealthy beyond recognition, meaning that they would not be able to hoard valuable priced properties at will. Their lives would be much more similar to the lives of the planet's common people, i.e. driven primarily by satiable needs rather than insatiable wants.

It should be noted that, having thwarted the influence of the financial élite, McMurtry's four policy shifts would open a window of opportunity for the prevention of its resurgence. In other words, public control of banking and investment, variously combined with the other three policy shifts, could serve as civil commons preventing financial overgrowth, speculation and crises, along the lines of the Bretton Woods system, for instance. By doing so, McMurtry's recommendations would prove analogous to primary care, i.e. the prevention of cancer.

McMurtry recommends four policy shifts and there are four fundamental types of cancer treatment. However, there is no one-to-one correspondence between the two sets. Rather, "aggressive national recovery of control over public owned resources", "public banking and investment" *qua* recovery of credit creation and management from the private sector, and "policy-led elimination of structural depredation of the poor and the environment" correspond to all three aggressive interventions identified above, i.e. surgery, chemotherapy and radiation therapy. By removing entire chunks of business activity from the for-profit domain and restoring it to that of the common good, these policy shifts would simply cause entire sectors of economic agency to disappear, just like the three aggressive cancer treatments cause organic tissue to perish. They would be examples of what Keynes himself advised as the necessary "euthanasia of the rentier" to be pursued towards the creation of a sustainable form of capitalism.[381] On their part, "higher taxes and disincentives for the very rich" appear to work more like targeted therapy, e.g. by blocking revenue streams to the very affluent who lead the ongoing economic cancer by waves of financial investments.

A Concluding Remark

Life-value onto-axiology offers a contribution to the understanding, as well as to the development of standards for the measurement, of human wellbeing, so that progress and regress may be interpreted in ways that mainstream economic criteria neglect or fail to ascertain, both in theory and in practice. The conceptual framework provided by this theory of value is oncological, and life-enablement is the paramount concern guiding it. Still, by systemic application of the oncological framework to today's global market, life-value onto-axiology shows us what means can be employed in order to resolve the most pressing socio-economic woes of our time. Whether life-value onto-axiology will be paid heed to, however, we do not know. It is to be hoped that it will be. Responding to a cancer diagnosis by avoiding what alone can work is, in fact, fatal.

Chapter 8: On the Mission of Public Universities

Recurrent debates and discussions among staff and administrators at Iceland's higher-level educational institutions led me to ponder upon a perplexing yet common equivocation. This equivocation is nothing but the increasingly widespread assumption that public universities (hereafter "universities"), insofar as they participate in and co-operate with today's so-called "global economy", could, should, or even ought to be conceived of as market agents, i.e. as businesses, enterprises, industries, etc. Under this assumption, universities would provide profitable goods and services required by relevant market segments; at the same time, students would be customers of universities, which in turn would compete with other service providers in attracting investments and somehow lead to wealth creation, i.e. pecuniary returns to money investors. Such a characterisation of universities is, in my view, historically deficient and institutionally ludicrous.

Academia, Then and Now

Universities do have a budget and train citizen in various useful occupations, but describing them as running a business or being businesses is a cheap metaphor at best, whatever its misleading popularity may have been in recent decades. Universities are part of those civil commons that societies have evolved through centuries of historical progress. Indeed, the first university was established about a thousand years ago in the country where I was born, Italy, long before the emergence of any global economy whatsoever, or of capitalism itself in whatever early form we may wish to concede. Profitability was hardly a paramount concern in 11th-century Bologna, whatever entrepreneurial commerce could take place there at the time. Truth, and especially discerning the true sources and meaning of Roman law, were the defining aim of the institution.[382]

As tokens of civil commons, the paramount goal of academic

institutions has been to increase ranges of life capacity and, specifically, attain knowledge and understanding at the highest level of articulation, i.e. *qua* academic disciplines.[383] Initially, access was limited to the male members of a tiny élite. Later on, access was widened to the female members of the élite. Eventually, in several countries, access was extended to large sectors of the population upon selection by intellectual merit rather than birthright or pecuniary means. Along this path, the Polar Star of universities has been truth, not wealth or profit, especially in today's dominant short-run formulation of it.

Unfortunately, this short-run, finance-born and seemingly business-friendly formulation of wealth has been influencing more and more thoroughly the operations of public universities worldwide. With rare exceptions, the transformation of academic faculties, departments and research centres into tools for the eventual generation of money returns to private money investors and/or managers has been revealed throughout by a set of higher-education policies observable in nearly all countries over the last ten- to twenty-five years. This set of policies has regularly involved:

- Increased so-called private-public "partnerships" in research (e.g. private company A grants token funds to publicly run university B to have students researching an A-enriching issue; in short, A receives a public subsidy *via* B)
- Increased private-public "partnerships" in teaching (e.g. privately funded chairs);
- Outright privatisation of educational institutions;
- Market-oriented selection of research programmes and curricula (e.g. reduction or elimination of liberal arts and humanities in lieu of market-specific training lines);
- Selective privatisation of management, teaching and research positions (e.g. contracting out and part-time staffing);
- Promotion of the managerial mentality at all levels (e.g. bonuses for top administrators and lower staff salaries/higher student fees; private-fund attraction as promotion criterion);
- The use of campuses as business opportunities (e.g. junk food

dispensers, marketing surveys, pervasive billboards, renamed classrooms).

Often, these policies have been regarded as the expression of a relatively novel understanding of the long-established academic vocation of universities, namely the much-trumpeted "knowledge economy". I write "relatively" because a similar fad had occurred in the 1960s, primarily but not exclusively in connection with Peter Drucker's (1909–2005) writings about the allegedly novel "knowledge worker" characterising post-industrial economies. Fads, however, come and go with swift regularity, also in management and business studies.

The Knowledge Economy

According to the latest surge, the pursuit of knowledge goes hand-in-hand with the eventual generation of money returns to private money investors and/or managers. Unfortunately, this understanding, is severely flawed:

(1) Whereas the academic vocation is to engage in the pursuit of *universal* truths (hence the term "university", indicating utmost generality), knowledge is relevant to the economy if and only if it leads to the obtainment of profits for particular individuals or interest groups:
>(1a) Not only is the beneficial scope of intellectual life restricted to themes and issues related to the economic interests of specific individuals or groups, but
>(1b) also does its defining aim change: truth is no longer the fundamental criterion of knowledge in the knowledge economy, because sales are now that. Bluntly, what doesn't sell doesn't matter, even if it is true; *au contraire*, what sells does matter, even if it is false (e.g. the blossoming industry of fake news, WHO pandemic media scares, WTO-level resistance to product-labelling that could indicate embarrassing labour or environmental details, Florida's

recent ban on using the phrase "climate change" in the State's official documents).

(2) Whereas the academic vocation is to promote the free and open dissemination of knowledge, the economy-defining profit-motive calls for the restriction of information flows by, *inter alia*, private patents and copyright controls (e.g. "too-expensive" indexes that university libraries cannot afford).

(3) Whereas the academic vocation is to develop staff and students as intrinsically valuable *human* beings that are autonomous in thought and action (hence the term "humanities" indicating the set of disciplines furthering this development), the economy-defining profit-motive promotes the instrumental use of staff and students (e.g. as cheap researchers, consumers, credit-seekers, future labour).

(4) Whereas the academic vocation is to develop staff and students as *free* critical minds in nations constitutionally committed to individual *liberty* (hence the term "liberal arts" indicating the set of disciplines furthering individual liberty by, *inter alia*, cultivating the personal skills required for democratic polities to function and for people to be more self-aware *ergo* less enslaved to inherited social habit and animal proclivity), the knowledge economy implies the market-based selection of staff's research (e.g. choosing topics that are likely to be funded by private sponsors) and students' education (e.g. employability, i.e. being sought after by private interests), as well as the conditioning of their unconscious desires (e.g. scientifically crafted, slave-reminiscent branding of young minds, which are to react automatically to predesigned stimuli and lead to behavioural patterns advantageous to private companies).

As regards Peter Drucker, I believe that he would have disavowed the facile equation circulating around Icelandic universities today. His understanding of "knowledge economy" and capitalist economies was adamant about the essential differences between the defining values of the business reality under capitalism and those of human flourishing at large, which includes the pursuit of knowledge. In the 1969 book entitled *The Age of Discontinuity: Guidelines to Our Changing Society*, whence the expression "knowledge economy" originates, Drucker states: "The economic history of the last hundred years in the advanced and developed countries could be called 'from agriculture to knowledge'… knowledge is now the main cost, the main investment, and the main product of the advanced economy and the livelihood of the largest group of the population"; its ultimate goal is not "its intrinsic beauty [or]… wisdom" but to ensure "the ability of an economy to grow and compete", as exemplified by the unhealthy lifestyle of "the knowledge worker [who] is working more and more… [whilst t]he manual worker, the typical worker of yesterday, may have more leisure… go home at five in the evening".[384]

According to Drucker, there are good things happening in the modern knowledge economy, such as "farm surpluses… the division of the fruits of higher productivity… [social] mobility… access to education… the [large] employed educated middle class", but the novel "knowledge worker" is nonetheless only "the upgraded and well-paid successor to the skilled worker of yesterday" and, exactly like her predecessor, she is bound to experience "disenchantment", i.e. Drucker's rhetorically cautious rendition of Marx's alienation, unless capitalists and their executives "learn to manage the knowledge worker both for productivity and for satisfaction".[385] The nature of the productive "machine" has not changed, whatever transformation capitalism may have been experiencing, hence the "status, function, and position… of the knowledge worker" is bound to be "*the* social question of the developed countries for the twentieth and probably for the twenty-first century", analogously to the industrial worker's ones being the social question of the 19th century in Europe and North America.[386]

As regards the reader who may have lost touch with the long-established academic vocation of universities, it should be highlighted that university research and education ought to aim at better understanding as such, i.e. devoid of any ulterior motive—profit included—that does not enable further understanding, which is what the profit-motive hampers most visibly as of points (1)–(2) above. Also, if genuinely followed, the academic vocation fosters the acquisition of independent, literate and constructive thinking, according to subsets of human understanding known as academic disciplines (e.g. physics, philosophy, anthropology). Their fundamental criterion of knowledge is the consistent evaluation of evidence according to evolved praxes of interpretation, identification, classification, analysis and testing. Truth, not profitable sales, guides them.

Truth and profit may sometimes go hand-in-hand. By providing knowledge and understanding at the highest level of articulation, universities have certainly educated generations of entrepreneurs, executives, white-collar workers and productive citizens of all sorts and stripes. Universities have been unquestionable centres of innovative thinking, creative experimentation, thorough revision and ground-breaking vision translating at times into profitable business life. At a deeper level, universities have cultivated methods, skills and values facilitating moral socialisation, humane civilisation and intelligent communication, i.e. essential yet regularly neglected preconditions for any economic activity whatsoever. In brief, universities have been instrumental to market efficiency in many ways. Nevertheless, this market-oriented function of universities has been just one of many, often indirect, and possibly adventitious. In the 20th century, for instance, cutting-edge research in physics was led in academies of countries that did not have a capitalist economic order.

A Concluding Remark

To conclude, I wish to focus upon one function that makes universities unique and may remind the reader of the reason why universities ought to be protected from too direct a market involvement, as well as from the market's defining aim: profit. Universities, as long as they have been allowed to do their job with adequate funding and independence, have served as a monitoring body over the excesses, threats and falsities endangering the countries in which they were established, if not humankind at large. In this capacity, universities have produced research and issued warnings capable of preventing terrible catastrophes, e.g. the thinning Ozone layer in the 1980s. Other times, their evidence and warnings were ignored at great cost for all, e.g. Joseph Stiglitz's and John McMurtry's sophisticated critiques of deregulated financial wizardry in the 1990s and 2000s. Still, even when unheard or marginalised, academic disciplines have generated ideas, novel forms of reasoning and alternative approaches that were used later in order to cope with the disastrous effects of human and natural catastrophes. As long as funds and independence are guaranteed, universities can keep serving societies as life-saving monitoring bodies. Reduced to a mouthpiece of market forces, they cannot do it.

PART III – Implications

Chapter 9: Adam Smith, Historical and Rhetorical

Today's academic and popular literature is replete with references to Adam Smith, and in particular to his 1776 *magnum opus* known as *The Wealth of Nations* (hereafter WN), which is a recurrent source of private inspiration and public appeal, but above all a time-honoured means of political legitimisation and the theoretical justificatory ground for so-called "free market institutions".[387] For example, the long-time Chairman of the US Federal Reserve, Alan Greenspan (b. 1926), states:

> In one of the more notable coincidences of history, our *Declaration of Independence* was signed the same year in which Adam Smith published his *Wealth of Nations*. Smith's prescription of letting markets prevail with minimal governmental interference became the guiding philosophy of American leadership for much of our history. With a masterful insight into the workings of the free-market institutions that were then emerging, Smith postulated an 'invisible hand' in which competitive behavior drove an economy's resources toward their fullest and most efficient use. Economic growth and prosperity, he argued, would emerge if governments stood aside and allowed markets to work.[388]

This genre of public addresses, penned in this case by a high-profile man of the US financial establishment, is representative of the self-appointed free-market advocates' broad rhetorical reliance on Adam Smith. Greenspan played a crucial role in establishing the international financial architecture of late capitalism, especially as Chairman of the US Federal Reserve between 1987 and 2006. He therefore represents a prime example of how Smith's received views, as discussed in this chapter, can be decisive in the world of policy, power and politics, more than any sophisticated scholarly study by some higher-brow academic economist.

Like many self-declared champions of "free-market institutions", Greenspan too asserts a substantial continuity between the kind of ideal economic system presented in Adam Smith's work and the Wall-Street-centred global economic system established worldwide after the collapse of the Soviet Union.[389] Three years after delivering the speech quoted above, though, Greenspan was faced with another collapse, namely the global systemic crisis caused by the "toxic assets" designed and traded by the main protagonists of the businesses that he was meant to supervise, namely the "increasingly complex financial instruments" that Greenspan believed to be the source of "a far more flexible, efficient, and hence resilient financial system".[390] As Greenspan eventually realised, he had been tragically wrong. Only repeated massive interventions by the very visible hand of the State and the resulting investor confidence were able to save the so-called "masters of the universe" from bankruptcy and avoid an annihilation of the banking sector akin to the one the US had witnessed after the crash of 1929.[391] In a glaring twist of public stances, the same firms that had been lobbying political parties and legislators for decades, allegedly in order to deregulate business life and allow the free market to see to itself, started calling incessantly and loudly for the State's direct help and invoked a thorough change of business mores.[392] At a hearing held by the US Congressional Committee of Government Oversight and Reform, Greenspan confessed: "Those of us who have looked to the self-interest of lending institutions to protect shareholders' equity (myself especially) are in a state of shocked disbelief."[393]

Greenspan's shocked disbelief notwithstanding, his admission begs a deeper question. Is it actually the case that the 1980s–2000s global economy, in which he himself had so much clout, possessed any substantial continuity with the sort of market economy to be found in WN?[394] Given that an exhaustive survey of WN would exceed the scope of this chapter, I let a well-established contemporary Smith scholar, Maria Pia Paganelli (b. 1973), address this question from the right of the political spectrum.[395] Then, I move to the work of Noam Chomsky (b. 1928) and John McMurtry, gatekeepers of the political left in the US and in Canada. Not only do they anticipate and substantiate the main thesis of this chapter, i.e. that the real Adam Smith has hardly anything to share with today's "free-market" sycophants *à la* Alan Greenspan, but they offer also critical considerations *vis-à-vis* Smith's ideal as such. Unlike Paganelli, they argue that, even when recovered from historically mistaken or intellectually dishonest use, Smith's own original take on free-market institutions may not be a desirable ideal after all. A few remarks of my own conclude the chapter, stressing further the importance of Chomsky's and McMurtry's views for a nuanced understanding of both Adam Smith's 18th-century thought and toady's market institutions, ideal as well as actual.

Looking from the Right

Texas-based Smith scholar Maria Pia Paganelli is very sceptical about the substantial continuity postulated by Greenspan, whose quoted passage reveals eight commonly held beliefs of many contemporary self-professed "free-market" adherents:[396]

a. There is an implicit relationship between free markets and US democracy (a "notable coincidence");
b. All markets should enjoy "minimal government interference";
c. As it has been done for the most part in American history;
d. The unhindered "invisible hand" secures necessarily optimal results;
e. "[C]ompetitive behaviour" as such is praiseworthy;
f. "[S]elf-interest" as such is praiseworthy;
g. Including that "of organisations, specifically banks";
h. "[E]conomic growth and prosperity" are the ultimate goods resulting from b-g.

Although the world's and humankind's natures may still contain the same fundamental drives that they possessed in the 18th century, if not before, societies, politics and economic institutions can produce strikingly different results over time, including "convulsions, apoplexy, or death... of [the] body politic".[397] Looking at today's fine mess caused by the world's heavily financialised economies, Paganelli has no qualms in calling the current system the "caricature of Smith".[398] She does not explain whether this caricature is the result of wilfully dishonest misinterpretation, ideological bias, poor understanding of Smith's complex and sometimes ambiguous work, or a case of mistaken identity—such as taking Smith for Greenspan's intellectual mentor Ayn Rand (1905–1982), for instance.[399] Rather, through careful exegeses of the second chapter in the second book of WN and additional passages in both WN and the *Theory of Moral Sentiments*, Paganelli's studies show invariably that Smith was:[400]

- No uncompromising advocate of unregulated banking, which is not a market like any other (*contra* (b) and (g));[401]
- No uncritical admirer of unscrupulous self-aggrandisers, who attain social approbation by glittering wealth in lieu of modest virtue (*contra* (e) and (f), which Smith qualified in nuanced ways);[402]
- No blind believer in the "necessary... development of an order of natural liberty", which faces instead "accidents of history... [and] natural yet destructive passions" (*contra* (d));[403]
- No dogmatically confident believer in the ability of large business concerns:
    - To operate in compliance with the principle of market competition (*contra* (c));[404]
    - To seek no *ad hoc* legislation by adequately bullied or lobbied lawmakers, who therefore no longer serve the good of the commonwealth (*contra* (a) and (c));[405] and
    - To generate widespread prosperity as an inevitable result (*contra* h).[406]

According to Paganelli's analysis, Smith would not defend a global economic system dominated by a few, well-connected corporate juggernauts, and a few conniving individuals inside them, that have engaged routinely in national and international lobbying for favourable legislation (e.g. WTO's label exposure prohibitions and derivative-friendly regulations emanating from the Bank of International Settlements (BIS)), as well as "Ponzi schemes, insider trading, creative accounting, or questionable practices."[407] Just as the great master of the Scottish Enlightenment condemned the internationally trading British joint-stock companies of his day that reduced or annihilated genuine market competition,[408] which requires a large plurality of morally decent and legally liable individual entrepreneurs to subsist, so would he condemn today's analogues that do the same on an unprecedented scale, and particularly in Greenspan's US.[409]

I refer to Paganelli's work because it is a very recent example of high-level Smith scholarship that builds upon ongoing investigations in its area of inquiry and is:

- Published in leading academic journals (receiving in 2009 the prize for the Best Article of the Year, awarded by the European Society for the History of Economic Thought);
- Sympathetic to Smith's endeavour and, above all, to his economic liberalism;
- Armed with the notion of Smith's "caricature"; and
- Well-documented with regard to the history of 18th-century economics, thus placing Smith squarely within the trends and debates of his day.[410]

Paganelli is not alone in having noticed the conspicuous gap that exists between Smith's depiction of a proper market economy and the economic reality to which we have become accustomed. Implicitly, the qualitative distance separating us from Smith's time and ideal is revealed by all those economists and historians who have recorded honestly and labelled aptly the different phases or manifestations of Western economies, such as: "personal" or "entrepreneurial"; "managerial", "industrial" or "corporate";[411] "shareholder-value" or "fiduciary";[412] "mercantilist" and "neo-mercantilist";[413] "real" and "virtual".[414] Invariably, with these accounts, Smith's vision recedes into the background, also in connection with the history of Greenspan's US.[415]

Analogous considerations apply to those researchers who have shown how the same economies have moved unstoppably towards increased concentration of wealth, widespread conditions of monopsony, *de iure* monopoly, or *de facto* cartel, and therefore entrenched political influence whereby privileged status and guaranteed earnings can be secured irrespective of business performance, or rent can be extracted from other productive activities (i.e. unearned income).[416]

Even if the specialists may be aware of how remote Smith's ideal is *vis-à-vis* today's economic reality, mainstream political discourse and the guiding principles of influential policy-makers like Greenspan himself have been devoid of such an awareness. The economic order unleashed in Smith's name may be a caricature of his thought, as Paganelli writes, but the persistence of references to Smith in its makers' worldview and the legitimacy that his name alone bestows upon their actions are no silly joke at all. Self-appointed "free-market" advocates like Greenspan do believe, or have claimed to believe, that we live and should live under a "free-market" system that is bound to generate prosperity by keeping the government aside, precisely as Adam Smith instructs, such a system orbiting around the de-regulated and liberalised self-interest of highly competitive individuals operating within, as well as on behalf of, shareholder-value-driven corporate concerns, of which Adam Smith was weary. All this holding true, at least, as long as it is advantageous to the corporate giants and the financial élites determining the select areas and the limited ways in which governments are expected to play a role in the economy. In 2008, as we have seen, governments were hurriedly called back into play on the largest scale, *pace* three decades of unrelenting "free-market" political rhetoric and associated 'reform' policies, in order to prevent the collapse of the world's financial system and, with it, of much of the global economy.

Looking from the Left

Points analogous to Paganelli's had already been made long before her by two thinkers that are not associated with Smith studies or cited therein, possibly because of their open left-wing political stances, i.e. Noam Chomsky and John McMurtry.

According to Chomsky, Smith believed the human propensity to "truck[,] barter [and exchange]" to be the driving force of that "free market" which, under the right circumstances, would benefit all.[417] Such a free market would best serve "the beautiful system of natural liberty" praised by Smith, i.e. the commercial society made of a plurality of morally decent, legally liable, industrious entrepreneurs.[418] Chomsky observes that Smith believed this system to be threatened already in the 18th century by rapacious businessmen, who were prone to establish private monopolies as well as inefficient joint-stock companies, that is, corporations.[419] These companies would in turn corrupt governments and public officials at large, in order to pursue their self-aggrandisement under the banner of the common good, yet inevitably at its expense.[420] Additionally, Chomsky believes Smith to have regarded colonialism as objectionable and the specialised, efficiency-driven division of labour of industrial manufacturing to lead to inhumane working conditions, hence requiring State regulation.[421]

Chomsky's picture of Smith's views is mostly correct, but for a few details worth pointing out. It is erroneous to claim that Smith objected powerfully to colonialism, the cruelty of which he acknowledged, but which Smith also praised for imposing civilised trade and manners upon backwards nations, and for generating more florid animal and human populations.[422] Similarly, the idea that all would benefit equally from the wealth created by private enterprises is, at best, an overstatement. For one, Smith never denied that in a system based upon "free trade" the entrepreneurs would reap most of the benefits in good times, while the "race of labourers" would take most of the losses in bad ones.[423] What this latter race of humans could expect instead, was to be better off in their poverty and insecurity than the very king of a savage nation could ever dream of being.[424] Also, the issue of the division of labour is an ambiguous one, for Smith depicts it as both the key-factor "of the natural progress of opulence"[425] and a condition under which the labourer becomes:

> [N]ot only incapable of relishing or bearing a part in any rational conversation, but of conceiving any generous, noble, or tender sentiment, and consequently of forming any just judgment concerning many even of the ordinary duties of private life… [and] equally incapable of defending his country in war… But in every improved and civilized society this is the state into which the labouring poor, that is, the great body of the people, must necessarily fall, unless government takes some pains to prevent it.[426]

As far as Paganelli's "caricature of Smith" is concerned, Chomsky argues that, *pace* Greenspan's assumptions (a) and (c), the US have never established a genuine "free market", starting with the protectionism that characterised their 18th- and 19th-century history, and stepping further away from it over the last hundred years or so, which witnessed the affirmation of large oligopolies. US finance and many other areas of business life (e.g. agriculture, aero-spatial industry, media and entertainment) have long been in the hands of a well-established corporate network, whose self-interest directly opposes market competition (*contra* (e–g))[427] and leads their owners to control *de facto* the nominally democratic State by funding select political parties, lobbying elected representatives, and supporting/ attacking politicians through their media outlets and financial resources (*contra* (a–c)).[428]

Indeed, *via* the State's diplomatic and military apparatus, such *Fortune-500* oligopolies have frequently tried to impose their rule upon the whole world for their own benefit, fully capable and aware of condemning many others into a state of misery.[429] *Pace* Greenspan's (d) and (h), wealth and opulence have been enjoyed by the few, and the few alone—whether it is the planet's North *vis-à-vis* the planet's South, or the rich *vis-à-vis* the poor inside each nation, the US included. Chomsky recalls slaves, exterminated indigenous populations, and economically strangled and/or militarily invaded and/or bombed countries *qua* glaring denials of any open participation in whatever kind of mutually advantageous free trade there may be, or in any necessary path to overall economic wellbeing.[430] At the same time, mainstream economists are accused by Chomsky of having consistently avoided any serious computation of these enormous State-led "market distortions", which have been informing centuries of economic activity and corporate expansion.[431]

In this context, the enduring political language glorifying the "free market" performs the rhetorical function of legitimising the *status quo*, so that eloquent references to Smith's propensity to "truck, barter and exchange" may keep enriching the rich and prevent the State from intervening in ways that do not enrich the rich (e.g. tax-funded social programmes).[432] The function of such references is, in Marxian terms, ideological, for it persuades the general public to believe in something that is harmful to their real economic interests and that does not withstand serious intellectual scrutiny.[433] It is a token of hypocrisy, a contradiction between what is said to be going on and what actually goes on. Exemplarily, Chomsky recalls two self-appointed "free-market" champions of the 1980s, i.e. former president Ronald Reagan (1911–2004) and Secretary of Treasury James Baker (b. 1930), who made thorough, ample and repeated use of "import restrictions… import relief… non-tariff barriers to trade… and… government subsidies."[434]

Finally, Chomsky believes contemporary global economies to contradict Smith's historical presupposition of considerable labour mobility and relative confinement of capitals to the country of origin in the most egregious manner: billions upon billions of US dollars can be transferred almost instantaneously from one country to another, whereas migrant workers encounter higher and higher barriers, whether physical or bureaucratic, sometimes erected by self-proclaimed "free-market" adherents in both US government parties.[435]

According to McMurtry, as seen already in the first chapter, there have occurred seven "unseen mutations" of Smith, which are worth recalling here. Specifically, McMurtry shows how the current global "corporate system" fails regularly and patently to secure the following seven qualifying conditions, without which Smith's "free market proper" ceases to be:

1. "[N]o private monopoly or oligopoly of production or distribution" is in place.[436]
2. "[D]omestic capital would not migrate to foreign nations".
3. The "productive labour" of "manufacturers" creates "some particular subject or vendible commodity which lasts for some time at least after the labour is past" i.e. tangible, durable goods, which are no longer the norm today.[437]
4. Unearned income (e.g. "stock, bond and currency speculation", rent from land) is thwarted by taxation, given that Smith believes that "the sole use of money is to circulate consumable goods, provisions, material and finished work", i.e. not as a commodity but as a "medium of exchange".[438]
5. "[C]apital must be reinvested in productive jobs, or else it is 'perverted from its proper destination'".[439]
6. "[T]axation must fall on citizens 'in proportion to their respective abilities', and on those to whom 'the benefit is confined'".[440]
7. Business interests and business-like mind-sets stay away from law-making and government. As Smith asserts: "No two characters seem more inconsistent than those of trader and sovereign — the mean rapacity, the monopolizing spirit of merchants and manufacturers neither are, nor ought to be, the rulers of mankind".[441]

Some mutations are more endogenous than others. Specifically, as the second point in the list is concerned, there is adequate textual evidence that Smith would have not opposed the emigration of capital for the sake of higher profits.[442] Rather, given also that Chomsky makes the same observation as McMurtry, it is reasonable to assume that Smith considered the tendency for capital to remain in the country of origin more as a structural result of the technologies conceivable in his day and of the small-scale entrepreneurship that he praised, than an explicit feature of his ideal.

As regards the third point, Smith does not deny that there may be countless forms of "work... [that] perishes in the very instant of its production" and that he therefore deems "unproductive of any value", but he would not do away with them all, for they may be desirable as well as necessary, since they include, *inter alia*, "the sovereign... the officers of both justice and war... the whole army and navy... lawyers, physicians, men of letters."[443] Moreover, the notions of "productive" and "unproductive" labour are far from unambiguous in his work, although it is certain that Smith emphasised throughout his WN very concrete and productive dimensions of economic life as tokens of national wealth, such as well-cultivated land, animal stocks, child mortality and demographic trends.[444]

As concerns the other mutations, we have already encountered McMurtry's poignant reference to Joseph Stiglitz's four-stage process of government-enhanced penetration of corporate oligopolies into foreign markets. This too is worth recalling here:

(I) "Privatization" or "Briberization" (whereby governments are lobbied, bullied or outright bribed into privatising strategic assets of the State, especially public banks);

(II) "Capital Market Liberalization" (or the "Hot Money Cycle", whereby capital markets are opened to foreign investors and a bubble ensues);

(III) "Market-Based Pricing" (i.e. the bubble bursts and an economic crisis follows, leading to higher interest rates, fewer public expenditures, and higher costs of living, which in turn lead to income inequality, political instability, higher crime rates and reduced internal demand); and

(IV) "Poverty reduction strategy" by "Free Trade" (i.e. international financial institutions are brought in to provide so-called "aid packages" consisting in further privatisations and the complete opening of domestic markets to foreign investors, who thus may (re)colonise the country piecemeal).

As a former World Bank chief economist and Nobel-prize laureate, Stiglitz's adamant depiction of economic reality caused quite a stir in the early 2000s and it revealed, long before today's Wikileaks and Libor or Euribor scandals, how many corporate lobbies had been hijacking political processes both nationally and globally (*contra* (a) and (c)), in order to shelter themselves behind opaque ownership structures and limited liability legislation, reach and control new foreign markets, and foster their self-interest at the expense of competition (*contra* (e–g)) and development (*contra* (h)).

Critical Remarks

Taken together, Paganelli, Chomsky and McMurtry provide ample evidence that Smith's recipe has not been applied, despite frequent high-level statements to the contrary. A consumer society planned and regulated at the behest of finance-intensive corporate interests is not a commercial society emerging from free inter-personal transactions in tangible goods. Yet, Chomsky and McMurtry do not stop here.

It is not enough for them to show that the modern global economy is no adequate instantiation of Smith's ideal; nor that, because of such an inadequacy, Smith's ideal cannot be used to legitimise today's global economy. Unlike Paganelli, Chomsky and McMurtry also challenge Smith's own stance as a legitimate and desirable ideal, hence challenging further Greenspan's own enthusiasm for "free-market institutions". Even if the caricature of Adam Smith is dispelled, there can be reasons not to follow Adam Smith's advice: the actual picture may be still grotesque.

To begin with, Chomsky observes a mistaken yet dominant official philosophical anthropology whereby human beings are seen primarily as self-seeking consumption-oriented social atoms, or walking tokens of *homo economicus*.[445] This anthropology assumes that we are motivated exclusively or primarily by material rewards. Its origins are said to lie with Adam Smith and his belief that we are defined anthropologically by our propensity to "truck, barter and exchange". However, according to Chomsky, we all share as well:

- A natural ability to make moral choices: morality is natural, i.e. intrinsic to being human.[446]
- A tendency to justify our choices in terms of the common good in order to preserve a positive self-image before ourselves and others.[447]
- An often implicit philosophical anthropology ("human nature") upon which we base our choices, their justification and the positive character of our self-image.[448]
- A belief in "human rights" (e.g. appreciation of liberty, opposition to slavery) as testified among others by the thought of "Rousseau, and Humboldt" and by the widespread recognition of "a need and a right to freedom… free creative thought and its expression."[449]

In many ways, Chomsky's depiction of "human nature" is reminiscent of Smith's *Theory of Moral Sentiments*.[450] Chomsky does not seem to pay much notice to this similarity, however. After all, the mutual coherence of Smith's two main works, or rather their mutual contradiction, is a hotly debated issue. It is known among specialists as "the Smith problem", i.e. the uneasy relationship between the benevolent and moral human being of Smith's *Theory of Sentiment* and the significantly selfish and amoral one of Smith's WN, which Chomsky deems dangerously skewed and callous. Needless to say, "free-market" reformists and reform have taken aboard the latter rather than the former.

Also, Chomsky observes that the three most competitive sectors in the US economy (agriculture, high-tech and pharmaceutical industries) are heavily State-subsidised and, crucially, that no country has ever developed by free-market trade alone, i.e. without a system of protectionist tariffs, State credit, national economic plans, State aid to strategic sectors, etc.[451]

Finally, Chomsky claims that economies based upon "free-market institutions" deny most people liberty, for they entail inevitably:[452]

- Capitalist relations of production, whereby most people live

only by enriching the rich;
- Wage relations, whereby human beings must choose between renting their talents and time under imposed and often hazardous conditions in order to get the money needed to purchase market goods, or suffer deprivation as only alternative, sometimes to the point of starvation and death;
- Possessive individualism, whereby human beings are raised into thinking of themselves primarily or significantly as self-seeking consumption-oriented social atoms rather than caring, compassionate, solidarity-prone, friendly, creative members of a community;
- Totalitarian, top-down chains of command within commercial, industrial and financial enterprises, which show no organisational feature of democratic self-government;
- An apparatus for indoctrination that cultivates all of the above, for it aims at profiting from the preceding four conditions both directly (e.g. the entertainment industry) and indirectly (e.g. by removing resources from anti-capitalist media outlets and research centres; or by selecting only conformist people for the most lucrative, influential and revered positions in journalist punditry, university teaching and economic advice to governments).

Chomsky believes "libertarian socialism" (aka "anarcho-syndicalism"), as partially exemplified during the 1930s in Catalonia and in 20th-century Israeli Kibbutzim communities, to be a much better option, for two main reasons:

(A) It serves liberty by fostering material and immaterial resources (e.g. temporal, cultural, anthropological and ethical) for all to live, meaningfully and constructively, in the community to which they belong (e.g. by rotation of basic tasks; attribution of additional tasks upon personal interest; cultivation of self-respect as prime source of motivation, as well as friendship, sympathy, responsibility and solidarity).

(B) It serves society by promoting democracy, i.e. rule by the people over the people for the people, *via* grassroots councils, within as well as outside the political realm (e.g. in neighbourhood- or town-wide assemblies, factories, industrial branches, crafts, etc.).[453]

Chomsky provides only a sketchy picture of this kind of libertarian-socialist society. Certainly, achieving such a novel form of society would require profound cultural changes, comparable to those that took place in the age of the Enlightenment, when the possibility of equality between aristocrats and commoners became a plausible human aim—and took over two centuries of bitter political struggles to unfold. Chomsky is, in this respect, a visionary, not unlike those Western intellectuals who, though dubbed "utopians" or "radicals" by their opponents, foresaw and advocated the worldwide abolition of slavery, the pursuit of universal literacy, the drafting of democratic constitutions, the abolition of internal barriers to commerce, and the possibility of preventing poor workers and their families from being wiped out by famines and disease in times of crisis.[454]

As to the main instrument to attain the necessary changes, Chomsky claims the free use of an informed human reason to be the only genuine path to emancipation; hence condemning the primacy of violent insurrection or revolution paraded by other forms of anarchism and socialism, Marxism *in primis*.[455] Education aimed at nurturing solidarity over selfishness and responsible media are pivotal, in Chomsky's view, which on this matter is reminiscent of the brand of "socialism" championed by German Veblenite and celebrated physicist Albert Einstein (1879–1955), who wrote: "I am convinced there is only one way to eliminate these grave evils [of capitalism], namely through the establishment of a socialist economy, accompanied by an educational system which would be oriented toward social goals."[456]

McMurtry agrees with Chomsky on condemning the philosophical anthropology that underpins much of contemporary economics, whereby human beings are "properly and finally ordered as individual owners and exchangers seeking to maximise fulfilment of… individual desires."[457] McMurtry argues that it is an overly simplistic and empirically mistaken form of social Darwinism that reduces human agency to sheer "competition to survive" and ignores the bio-environmental and cooperative social preconditions for individuality itself, such as family life and childhood's linguistic, moral and psychological relational upbringing.[458]

Like Chomsky, so does McMurtry describe the world's economy as a network of idle owners' interlocked oligopolies controlling supply and demand *via* "operant conditioning" of the populations, benefitting from State subsidies and "money creation by private bank leveraging", and engaging mostly in rent-seeking virtual transactions.[459] Again like Chomsky, McMurtry is aware of the totalitarian character of such interests, which entail military and diplomatic punishments, discipline by government-sponsored boycotts, speculative financial attacks, and top-down impositions by transnational investment treaties.[460]

Both McMurtry and Chomsky point to common objective derangements of allegedly democratic societies subjected to the hegemonic control of corporate interests over universities, research centres and mainstream media, such that truly alternative views are hardly ever mentioned or taught, and no counterevidence is admitted that may contradict the system's assumed goodness, despite growingly visible social and environmental degradation.[461] To substantiate these claims, McMurtry observes that even the opponents of the corporate system often assume uncritically that we are dealing with "free trade" (instead of oligopolies), "globalisation" (instead of transnational corporatisation) and "development" (instead of the stripping of long-evolved life-systems, such as unsustainable large-scale agribusiness in lieu of sustainable small-scale organic farming).[462]

Unlike Chomsky, though, McMurtry does not seem to directly relate the dominant philosophical anthropology to Adam Smith. His declared critical target is the libertarian or neoliberal school (e.g. Hayek, Friedman and Nozick) that mistakenly, carelessly and/or cynically conflates Smith's ideal with the current corporate global system.[463]

Also, McMurtry does not go as far as Chomsky in advocating an altogether alternative economic system. Rather, he starts by reflecting upon what exactly a good economic system should do. He concludes, as seen repeatedly in the first three chapters of the present book, that a good economic system provides coherent universal access to life goods and services across generational time. Any and every economic system can be good, if it can secure the current and the future conditions for the sustenance of meaningful and possibly flourishing human lives. Next, McMurtry reflects upon the omnipresent and relentless environmental and social costs of the "Corporate Commodity Cycles", which reduce access to life goods and services both in the present (e.g. privatised medical services causing postponement of care) and in the future (e.g. depletion of the Earth's fertile top-soil mantle by intensive agribusiness cultivation). Given the patent extent of such costs and attendant life reductions, McMurtry infers that the current system is ostensibly bad. If anything, it is the first time in human history that our species could be the pivotal cause of its own extinction.

In connection with the risk of self-extermination, McMurtry discusses the deification of profit-maximisation in what he dubs "market theology", which appeals to Smith's notion of the "invisible hand" in order to claim that self-interest-driven markets are self-correcting and therefore bound to bring about all that is desirable, democracy included.[464] McMurtry regards this notion as a profound methodological flaw in Smith's WN, and even more so in today's orthodox economics, because of its scientific unfalsifiability. Smith's normative assumption, whereby free markets are bound to generate prosperity, admits of no counterevidence, since the future is unknown. We simply do not know and we cannot know, but we are told over and over again to avoid any "interference" with the market. Meanwhile, we can all die as well.[465]

According to McMurtry, having more-or-less free markets is not the only operating instrument that societies have created in their history to secure prolonged universal access to means of life. Many are the tools, both material and immaterial, that can secure vital goods and services for all the members of a community. They are the countless tangible and intangible "civil commons" evolved by societies through time, serving the paramount end of granting all members of a self-regulating community the concrete enjoyment of goods and services, upon which needs are met and better lives are made possible.

McMurtry's approach, far from being utopian or ideal, is thus rooted in the experience of innumerable world communities, many of which never developed fully a commercial society worthy of Smith's WN, and yet provided themselves with civil commons.[466] As for free markets, or even the corporate global system, McMurtry is empirically and pragmatically inclined: the proof is, so to speak, in the eating of the pudding. If and when certain economic arrangements secure continued universal access to means of life (e.g. by providing the tax base for the State's welfare provision), they are desirable and valuable. When they work against it (e.g. by avoiding or evading taxation), they are undesirable and loathsome. McMurtry's recipe is not "less interference" and "more free markets" whatever the circumstances, as it is heard so often in the public arena. On the contrary, it calls for:

- Consistent and thorough life-enhancing regulation of market transactions in means of life only;
- Preservation of non-market-based civil commons that guarantee universal access to life goods and services (e.g. public provision of waste disposal, universal healthcare plans, well-funded and well-staffed regulatory and monitoring bodies); and
- Abolition of economic sectors that prove life-destructive, whether they are in public hands, private hands, or act as independent from actual democratic governance (e.g. the chemical weapons industry, private investment banks).

McMurtry's stance is not directed against Smith. As focussed as it is upon today's and tomorrow's sustainability of economic activities, it simply steps beyond Smith. And in all likelihood, given the challenges facing our generation, Smith ought to be left behind. Although he did praise commercial society for raising the standards of living of all involved in it, Smith, like many other 18th-century thinkers, was quite simply oblivious to the environmental implications of commercial society, not to mention of the industrial, consumer and debt-ridden societies that were to evolve thereof. The technologies and the consumption rates conceivable at Smith's time were not yet as capable of large-scale depletion of LSS as we have come to realise and face today, early-modern disasters notwithstanding (e.g. Dodos and Steller's Sea Cows being hunted into extinction, the 1770s Great Bengal Famine, the two Copenhagen Fires). Smith saw no problem whatsoever with the "clearing of a country over-grown with [forests]".[467] Analogously, the main forms of destruction that he contemplates in WN are those of exterminated "savages" in European colonies and of ravenous children of the "inferior ranks of people" in times of recession.[468] Both are, in his view, acceptable, if better commercial circumstances ensue. Today, I believe, most people would find them morally repulsive and practically avoidable.

Concluding Remarks

Chomsky's and McMurtry's concerns *vis-à-vis* Smith's excessive confidence in a free-market system's ability to generate genuine human wellbeing are worth pondering upon, especially as we face today the "threat to the environment" resulting from so-called "economic development".[469] As Chomsky claims, this threat "can't be ignored much longer, because if facing it is delayed too much longer there isn't going to be a lot more to human history."[470] Adam Smith has hardly anything to offer in this connection. Indeed, the "maximization of short-term gain" characterising WN's philosophical anthropology is at the heart of the "capitalist conditions" that are "going to destroy the environment".[471] Therefore, other perspectives must be adopted to counter the biggest danger to human survival of our time and that is where McMurtry's work can offer an articulate solution that is consistent with Chomsky's overall approach: life-value onto-axiology.

Under this respect, even if environmental degradation is not something that Smith predicted and wrote about, and even if he could be callously accommodating of countless deaths amongst native populations and the poorest of the poor, one single, isolated and surprisingly 'McMurtryian' pearl of wisdom can be excavated and adapted from Smith's WN. Curiously enough, it arises when discussing the rationale for regulating the banking sector:

> To restrain private people, it may be said, from receiving in payment the promissory notes of a banker, for any sum whether great or small, when they themselves are willing to receive them, or to restrain a banker from issuing such notes, when all his neighbours are willing to accept of them, is a manifest violation of that natural liberty which it is the proper business of law not to infringe, but to support. Such regulations may, no doubt, be considered as in some respects a violation of natural liberty. But those exertions of the natural liberty of a few individuals, which might endanger the security of the whole society, are, and ought to be, restrained by the laws of all governments, of the most free as well as of the most despotical. The obligation of building party walls, in order to prevent the communication of fire, is a violation of natural liberty exactly of the same kind with the regulations of the banking trade which are here proposed.[472]

Protecting life—from fires, in this specific case—is more important than asserting freedom at all costs, including freedom to trade as one may wish. It may not be Smith's preferred point of emphasis in WN. Nonetheless, and in contradiction with other claims and hopes of his, Smith happens to recognise the paramount value of human life over free trade and private property, at least this time.[473]

Despite their different political inclination, Paganelli, Chomsky and McMurtry concur upon the notion that the global economic system that has been in place under its banner over recent centuries is a caricature of Smith's commercial society. After longer than two hundred years, his ideal appears archaic. The alleged "free market" of Greenspan and many other self-appointed champions does not rest upon the same premises as Smith's own one and actually contradicts Smith's conception in many significant and persistent ways. State-subsidised, tax-dodging, limitedly liable self-maximisation by corporate giants setting prices and dealing mostly in virtual goods and services is clearly not what is required to establish an actual free market of many, morally decent, legally responsible, small entrepreneurs, who manufacture and trade mostly durable goods and reinvest their profits into job-creating local industries.

Greenspan and the other self-proclaimed champions of "free trade" may use Smith's name because of its rhetorical implications, but in doing so they resemble the Chinese Communist Party displaying portraits of Karl Marx in their headquarters, or Emperor Constantine's (306–337) publicly professed adherence to the precepts of Christianity while engaging in the murder of his relatives. If someone wishes to justify today's global economy as it has actually unfolded over time, she had better refer not to Adam Smith. Doing that would be a travesty; or, as Paganelli writes, a "caricature".

Chapter 10: Cornelius Castoriadis and the Crux of Adam Smith's Liberty

Capitalism and Freedom is not only the title of a 1962 book by Milton Friedman playing a pivotal role in the worldwide assertion of the neoliberal paradigm, but also the slogan that leading statesmen, politicians and opinion-makers have been heralding in recent years, in order to justify, amongst other things, the slashing of welfare states and the invasion of foreign countries.[474] Often, within this rhetorical discourse, "capitalism" has been rephrased as "free trade" or "free market",[475] and coupled regularly with "democracy", this essentially contested concept denoting the political system that is believed to better entrench and promote "freedom", "liberty" or "autonomy". Thus, capitalism and democracy have been described as the two sides of one and the same project for human emancipation, colouring the ideology and the political agenda of governments left and right of the political divide, and showing how deeply neoliberal beliefs have become part of the dominant public mind-set. Bill Clinton, for example, asserts:

> Fair trade among free markets does more than simply enrich America; it enriches all partners to each transaction. It raises consumer demand for our products worldwide; encourages investment & growth; lifts people out of poverty & ignorance; increases understanding; and helps dispel long-held hatreds. That's why we have worked so hard to help build free-market institutions in Eastern Europe, Russia, and the former Soviet republics. That's why we have supported commercial liberalization in China-the world's fastest-growing market. Just as democracy helps make the world safe for commerce, commerce helps make the world safe for democracy. It's a two-way street.[476]

Whether the capitalist experiment promoted in the 1990s by Bill Clinton and Boris Yeltsin (1931–2007) in the former Soviet Union has been successful or not is an issue that cannot be addressed in this chapter. Rather, Cornelius Castoriadis' work is to be addressed, for it reminds us of the fact that capitalism and democracy have had a different historico-geographical origin and a different orientation of value or defining aim. As concerns these two points, the following pages present and discuss some of Castoriadis' teachings, sometimes directly, other times in connection with other thinkers, especially Adam Smith. This way, in addition to deepen our understanding of the latter's views and legacy, this chapter pays homage to one of the most original Greek thinkers of the 20th century, whom Anglophone philosophers are still largely unaware of.

Neoliberalism

Terms such as "capitalism" and "neoliberalism" are often left undefined. In order to reduce the scope of possible ambiguity and the likelihood of misunderstanding, I provide a clearer connotation of what I mean with "neoliberalism" by means of a critical summary outlining what I believe to be its main tenets. Nearly all of these tenets are shared by liberal or classical economics as well; the last two, however, are typical only of its 20th-century renaissance *qua* neoliberalism:

- All value is ultimately understood as, or reducible to, money-capital; hence the neoclassical equation between prices paid for commodities and satisfaction of preferences, whatever they may be (Pareto's ophelimity, a standard presupposition of the neoclassical paradigm, does not distinguish qualitatively between the want of golden toilet seats and the need for potable water).
- The individual maximisation of money-capital returns from invested money-capital is regarded as natural (i.e. an anthropological *datum* already endorsed by Adam Smith), rational (i.e. not to follow this principle is insane), and it can even be normatively binding (e.g. corporate managers have a fiduciary duty to shareholders to the maximisation of the

latter's returns).
- No limit to the maximisation of such returns is set, as revealed by the neoclassical principle of non-satiety (a reformulation of Jean-Baptiste Say's (1767–1832) so-called "law" in classical economics, i.e. supply necessarily and invariably creates its own demand).
- This maximisation is believed to be accomplished most effectively through a system of free sale and purchase of commodities (i.e. the "free trade" commended already by Adam Smith).
- The free market is believed to guarantee the fairest distribution of commodities, i.e. their optimal allocation, approaching an ideal balance between supply and demand, thanks to its alleged ability to self-adjust and regulate (Adam Smith's invisible-hand mechanism is thus assumed to make it possible for the pursuit of individual self-interest to become the chief originator of collective wellbeing i.e. the wealth of nations).
- It is inferred from the previous point that public authority should interfere as little as possible with the free market's operations, whether by means of taxation, subsidy, or public ownership of assets that could be privately owned instead.
- An exception is made for those interferences that are deemed to serve the free market, thus ultimately leading to its paramount goal, i.e. the individual maximisation of money-capital returns (Adam Smith, for example, regarded progressive taxation of income and the public provision of both domestic and international security as necessary to the wealth of the nations).
- Since all value is ultimately understood as, or reducible to, money-capital, then the free market is regarded as the source of all that is valuable hence good and desirable.
- Market competition makes sure that the fittest alone survive, to whom wealth is thereby justly accrued, in line with a process of selection as natural as the one that Darwin observed in nature (the Darwinian characterisation of socio-

economic affairs became far less pronounced among 20th-century liberals after the repeated mass murders perpetrated by fascist dictatorships in the name of Darwinian anthropology and racial worldviews).
- Whenever undeniably negative effects are produced by the free market (e.g. carcinogenic pollution, life-threatening obesity, sexual exploitation of paupers and minors), then these effects are either discarded as externalities (i.e. the causal connection between the free market and its effects is nominally denied) or accepted as unavoidable costs that the alleged market's self-adjusting and regulating ability is bound eventually to resolve (hence frequent expressions such as "transition", "in the long run", etc.).
- Since the free market is regarded as the source of all that is valuable hence good and desirable, those who criticise or threaten it are condemned as either irrational (e.g. incompetent, unscientific, ignorant) or evil (e.g. terrorists, communists, anarchists).

Democracy

Castoriadis recalls that the earliest forms of democracy were toyed with by several Greek city-States and partially Hellenised communities in pre-Christian antiquity.[477] Further experiments saw the light in Continental Europe "at the end of the Middle Ages, in the interstices of the feudal world, [when] communities that wanted to be self-governed collectivities were reconstituted—new cities or bourgeois communes, in which a protobourgeoisie (long before any idea or real existence of capitalism!) created the first seeds [*germes*] of modern democratic and emancipatory movements."[478] These experiments in democratic rule were meant to guarantee the citizen's liberty from tyrannical rule, hence reducing the space for alienation, since they were aimed at establishing societies in which was granted to individuals and groups "the possibility of and the capacity for calling the established institutions and significations into question."[479] This was no small feat, for such openness to critical self-scrutiny and reconfiguration has represented, according to Castoriadis, "a tiny exception in the history of humanity."[480]

Castoriadis' notion of "significations" is particularly important in this context, for it shows how the sought-after liberty goes beyond the sphere of legal-constitutional affairs, reaching that of existential-spiritual affairs, as the citizenry are recognised the freedom to revise cherished traditions, beliefs and values in their pursuit of a meaningful existence. In this perspective, it recalls the Marxist notion of alienation, which addresses at least four types of loss suffered by the wage labourer because of the profit-driven prevailing interests of the employer:

1. Of the product (i.e. the final artefact does not belong to those who made it and often those who made it cannot even afford to buy it);
2. Of the production (i.e. slower, individual, unique, creative craftsmanship and mastery are replaced by faster, cost-effective, mechanised, routinised activities);
3. Of individuality (i.e. workers perform activities that a host of other persons can also perform nearly identically, whether younger, older, female or male, and irrespective of time-honoured and time-demanding craftsmanship; workers become easily replaceable and extremely vulnerable to competition on the labour market, hence their individual bargaining power is reduced and their cost to the employer, as a result, is also reduced);
4. Of humanity (i.e. workers perform activities such that hardly anything distinctively human is required of the worker; sometimes machines can replace the worker altogether; other times the only way to work is by adjusting unnaturally one's human skills, whether physical or intellectual, to the machine; new work-related pathologies emerge; the intensity, duration and/or conditions on the workplace are so tiring and/or stressful that the worker's free time is left to the satisfaction of the worker's animal needs, rather than to the cultivation of more distinctively human faculties).

Capitalism and its forms of alienation were only partially anticipated in late-medieval southern Europe, where Genoa,

Florence and Venice served as chief financial and bureaucratic engines for innovative international commerce and export-based agriculture and mining,[481] whilst also experiencing social and political tensions between classes foreshadowing later ones.[482] However, according to Castoriadis, mature capitalism flourished only in modern northern Europe, particularly in Britain, and was such that: "All human activities and all their effects", hence politics as well, "c[a]me to be considered more or less as economic activities and products, or, at the very least, as characterized and *valued* essentially through their economic dimension. No need to add that this *valuing* is done solely in monetary terms."[483]

As a direct consequence of this value-orientation or defining aim, capitalism selects for/against that which is monetarily valuable/disvaluable and, *a fortiori*, that which is/is not computable in monetary terms. Castoriadis does recognise that many capitalist "societies include a strong democratic component. But the latter has not been engendered by human nature or granted by capitalism or necessarily entailed by capitalism's development. It is there as residual result, as sedimentation of struggles and of a history that have gone on for several centuries."[484] Were we even to concede that, in its expansion in modern times, the capitalist axiological revolution was accompanied throughout by an affirmation of democratic forms of government, this hypothetical *datum* would not diminish or contradict the fact that the attribution and active pursuit of monetary value is not the same thing as, nor is logically implied by, "the possibility of and the capacity for calling the established institutions and significations into question."[485] Capitalism and democracy, read through Castoriadis' lenses, are two different entities.[486] Not only the "rights and liberties" celebrated in liberal democratic constitutions, "did not arise with capitalism, nor were they granted by the latter."[487] Also, their defining orientation of value has been too divergent to be necessitated by capitalism. For Castoriadis: "Capitalism as such has nothing to do with democracy": whereas the latter aims at autonomy, the former aims at money-making—a point to be unpacked further in the following paragraphs.[488]

Liberalism

The geographically-located historicity of capitalism is not a new theme or realisation. Castoriadis cites Claude-Henry de Rouvroy, Comte de Saint-Simon (1760–1825) and his personal secretary Auguste Comte (1798–1857) as enthusiastic supporters of the industrial revolution in France and its colonies, genuinely aware of the novelty of the economic system that they commended to their fellow Frenchmen.[489]

In Scotland, Adam Smith observed and studied the particular and unique "events", as he calls them in WN, making it possible for the new economic system to develop in Britain and some of the British colonies, especially the soon-to-be-independent American ones. Indeed, in his "Digression concerning the Variations in the Value of Silver during the Course of the Four last Centuries", Smith divides the history of modern Europe into three periods, explaining how "the market of Europe has become gradually more and more extensive" and why "since the discovery of America", itself but a historical event devoid of patent inevitability or intrinsic necessity, "the greater part of Europe has been much improved."[490]

As concerns the different nature of capitalism and democracy, Adam Smith never suggests that free trade would translate necessarily into democratic regimes; in which, to be true to his thought, he did not place his trust wholeheartedly. Adam Smith was a liberal, not a republican. In the 18th- and 19th-century, these terms had sharply differing meanings.[491] Under crucial political perspectives, Gilbert du Motier, Marquis de Lafayette (1757–1834) was not Jean-Paul Marat (1743–1793), John Stuart Mill was not Robert Owen, and Camillo P. F. G. Benso, Conte di Cavour (1810–1861) was neither Giuseppe Mazzini (1805–1872) nor Giuseppe Garibaldi (1807–1882). What liberals and republicans believed to be democracy and its proper realisation to consist in varied a lot, with the liberals concerning themselves primarily with the rights of small circles of educated and propertied citizens, and the republicans attempting to broaden the circle to those who owned little or nothing at all and often lacked basic schooling. As the liberal Cavour stated:

"'Democracy' is a very elastic notion that can be equally applied to very different systems, and that corresponds to thoroughly distinct ideas when pronounced by Gioberti or Mazzini, Louis Blanc or some American belonging to the school of Washington or Jefferson".[492]

The great divide between liberals and republicans colouring and characterising the debates and struggles of modern Europe is largely, perhaps conveniently, overlooked in today's ordinary treatment of the history of democracy, as though universal suffrage, unhindered equality before the law, universal schooling and access to healthcare were obvious steps in the history of liberalism. These and many other steps, however, were hardly obvious to the radical men and women that, from the days of the American Revolution to the granting of the right to vote in federal elections to all Swiss women in the 1970s, fought hard and long to be allowed to take each of them. If one wishes to understand what today's much-trumpeted "liberalisations" may signify, then one should look at and into the history of liberalism with a candid eye, especially as regards its iconic proponents and the privileged attention that they paid to the interests of the new wealthy elites who, especially in the day of the industrial revolution, challenged the old wealthy elites controlling Europe's aristocratic regimes.

For his part, according to the Scottish liberal Smith, "democracy" means to enlarge slightly the franchise for political participation amongst the "race of proprietors", who would therefore see the order of "those who live by rent" joined by the order of "those who live by profit" in the control of civil and political institutions.[493] At the same time, the "race of labourers", namely the vast majority of the population in commercial societies, would be left in a state of subjection, marked by such a forbidding toil for survival that the time and resources for genuine self-improvement would be nil.[494] This state of subjection being also life-threatening in times of economic deterioration: "in civilized society it is only among the inferior ranks of people that the scantiness of subsistence can set limits to the further multiplication of the human species; and it can do so in no other way than by destroying a great part of the children which their fruitful marriages produce."[495] Whenever the "real wealth of society becomes stationary" and eventually "declines… there is no order that suffers so cruelly from its decline… than that of labourers."[496]

Life-destructive as it may be, Smith sees no alternative to this state of affairs, upon which relied the whole economic system unfolding in Britain in his lifetime and, *a fortiori*, British society at large. After all, according to Smith, there is hope that the pursuit of private profit could prevent the real wealth of society from declining too frequently, if left unhindered and guided by Providence's invisible hand—Smith being a Scottish Presbyterian as well. On the contrary, there is no hope whatsoever for the "race of labourers" to aspire to actual political participation:

> But though the interest of the labourer is strictly connected with that of the society, he is incapable either of comprehending that interest, or of understanding its connection with his own. His condition leaves him no time to receive the necessary information, and his education and habits are commonly such as to render him unfit to judge even though he was fully informed. In the public deliberations, therefore, his voice is little heard and less regarded, except upon some particular occasions, when his clamour is animated, set on, and supported by his employers, not for his, but their own particular purposes.[497]

Much more bluntly than most of today's self-declared followers of his doctrine, Adam Smith admits that "[c]ivil government, so far as it is instituted for the security of property, is in reality instituted for the defence of the rich against the poor, or of those who have some property against those who have none at all."[498] And from the fact that Adam Smith never criticises either the private pursuit or the public defence of property *via* civil government, one can easily infer that he was not planning or promoting any major change in these matters, which instead republicans, Jacobins, Quakers and other 'radicals' pursued instead. After all, as the reader can read in the next chapter, Smith believed that God's Providence can take care of humankind's lot without need of radical change or revolution.

Marxism

The case of Adam Smith is extremely significant, insofar as he is a major representative of classical liberalism and remains a major point of reference for today's neoliberals. The much more moderate liberal stances of, say, Leonard T. Hobhouse (1864–1929), who defended universal suffrage and the right of workers to unionise in the face of powerful employers, are hardly ever recalled in contemporary debates, even if they are chronologically much closer to us than Smith's and have found direct expression in many a national constitution.[499]

Adam Smith's case is at least as significant as Karl Marx, whose work finds however a direct and patent echo in Castoriadis' own activities as a Trotskyite partisan, a social scientist, a philosopher, and a psychoanalyst. Critical at times, accommodating at others, Castoriadis retrieves in Marx "the robust awareness of the historicity of this phenomenon", i.e. the affirmation of capitalism, whose constitutive contingency was dishonestly and "quickly covered over by the apologists for the new regime, who were recruited especially among the economists."[500]

According to Castoriadis, as soon as the feudal world started to wane, a "denial of capitalism's historicity" appeared on the scene, which "has prevailed among the economists from David Ricardo until the present day. Political economy as well as its object have been glorified as an investigation into 'the pure logic of choice' or as a study of 'the allocation of limited means for the achievement of unlimited objectives'", which has abstracted the historical, socio-cultural and geographical reality of the actual economies observable in the world around us and turned them into impalpable fictions translatable into apparent laws expressed in mathematical terms.[501]

Marx had witnessed almost the same phenomena as Smith, though on a much larger scale, since in Marx's day the bourgeoning capitalist machinery described in WN was affirming itself worldwide, no longer solely in Great Britain and its colonial empire, and it had reached levels of articulation and productivity that Smith could not even begin to fathom. Marx too regarded the discovery of the Americas as a unique, crucial event, which had made it possible for the process of "primitive accumulation" to be ignited—this process being geographically and historically specific and, as Castoriadis writes, "conditioned by factors that have nothing 'economic' about them and that owe nothing to 'the market': specifically, extortion, fraud, and violence, both private and state-led."[502] Aware of these factors, Marx desired ardently to achieve a new social order whereby to guarantee the citizen's freedom to the fullest extent, quantitative as well as qualitative—a goal that Castoriadis, unlike Smith, shared with Marx throughout his life.

Not only did Marx aspire to establish a society in which all citizens were free from despotic control, whether due to *de iure* legal-political oligarchic rule or by *de facto* oligarchic control of the available means of life; but also a society in which each citizen would be free to explore and cultivate her inclinations, interests and abilities. In other words, Marx's liberation from alienation comprises a horizontal component (or breadth), whereby freedom is to be distributed to all citizens equally (e.g. by liberating labourers from wage slavery, i.e. depending on the rich for their survival), as well as a vertical one (or depth), whereby each citizen must be free to intensify her enjoyment of life (e.g. by being given free time and recreational opportunities, which the rich have often deemed superfluous and unproductive, hence contesting for decades any legislation aimed at limiting child labour and daily working hours). In this perspective, as later noted by Oscar Wilde (1854–1900), the realisation of socialism would have been the precondition for the actual realisation of liberalism, as each and every individual would have had then and then only a real chance to lead a meaningful existence, not just those few who, under a regime of private ownership, could afford it.[503]

For Castoriadis and Marx, "the possibility of and the capacity for calling the established institutions and significations into question" means the departure from an economic and social reality condemning the majority of the world's population to *de facto* political subjection and frequent precariousness of livelihood. According to Marx's analyses, it was exactly what the workers' discontent revealed: the masses—the *demos*—were not served well by capitalism, contrarily to what Smith might have ever indicated. Thus, as known, Marx tackled the element that Smith claimed to be residing at the core of the economic and social arrangement allowing for the vast majority of the world's population to depend on wages for their survival: private property. Marx's criticism of private property did not mean to do away with all forms of private property, but rather to control and limit it so as to serve human life without distinction of class:

> Capital is a collective product, and only by the united action of many members, nay, in the last resort, only by the united action of all members of society, can it be set in motion… We by no means intend to abolish [the] personal appropriation of the products of labor, an appropriation that is made for the maintenance and reproduction of human life, and that leaves no surplus wherewith to command the labor of others. All that we want to do away with is the miserable character of this appropriation, under which the laborer lives merely to increase capital, and is allowed to live only in so far as the interest of the ruling class requires it.[504]

Darwinism

Whether Marx's attempt was successful or not, it is too complex an issue to be discussed here. The concrete manifestations of Marxism have been at least as varied as those of liberalism. Similarly, I am not interested in discussing the differences between Marx's top-down, State-centred communism and Castoriadis' bottom-up, self-managing system of social ownership. Rather, I limit myself to mention how Castoriadis, moving his analysis from another angle, criticised back in the 1980s and 1990s the dominant neoliberal mantra saying—much more vocally than ever after the fall of the Berlin Wall—that the "capitalist society… proved its excellence—its superiority—through Darwinian selection."[505]

According to Castoriadis, any serious historical study would show the pointlessness of using such a simplistic notion in order to make sense of the development of capitalism, and he mentions several authoritative intellectual figures substantiating his remark: "Max Weber… Werner Sombart… Richard Tawney… Karl Polanyi."[506] This issue is nonetheless most relevant to him because the Darwinist justification of capitalism, if widely adopted in dominant political discourses, would attain a terrifying threefold rhetorical goal:

1. It would attribute some sort of historical necessity to the advent of capitalism, thus emptying whatever value human autonomy may have in these matters.
2. It would state this historical necessity in apparently rational, scientific terms, thus casting the shade of irrationality and 'unscientificity' to any alternative economic system.
3. It would imply an overall positive evaluation of the same phenomenon, thus accusing any alternative economic system to be contrary, whether intentionally or not, to the wellbeing, if not the very survival, of the human species.

For Castoriadis, *pace* the neoliberals' hopes and claims, "applying the Darwinian schema to social forms in history" constitutes an "absurdity… and the repetition of the classic fallacy (the survival of the fittest is the survival of the fittest to survive; the domination of capitalism shows simply that it is the strongest, ultimately in the crudest and most brutal sense of this term, not that it would be the best or the most 'rational')."[507] Moreover:

> What one observes in the sixteenth, seventeenth, and eighteenth centuries is not a competition among an indefinite number of regimes, out of which capitalism would have emerged the victor, but the enigmatic synergy of a host of factors that have all conspired toward the same result. That, later on, a society founded upon a highly

evolved technology might have been able to show its superiority by exterminating Amerindian nations and tribes, as well as Tasmanian or Australian aborigines, and by enslaving many others, presents no great mystery.[508]

If we were to take seriously the application of Darwinian selection to human societies, then the next Genghis Khan (1162–1227), Joseph Stalin (1878–1953) or Osama bin Laden (1957–2011) that were resolute, lucky and merciless enough to reshape the face of the planet according to his own murderous whim would prove *ipso facto* the superiority of his nightmarish New Order. *Pace* the fervent proponents of liberal institutions, personal freedom and daring entrepreneurship, any proficient tyrant's alternative should then be hailed as the crowning achievement of human evolution on Earth.

It can be argued that there exists a Darwinian ethos in sectors of the business world, especially high-level finance, which self-fulfils the idea that the business community is nothing but a wild 'jungle' of so-called "throat-cutting", "back-stabbing" "money-grabbers" engaged in endless "competition", hence unavoidably "cruel", impermeable to "pie-in-the-sky", "bleeding-heart", "utopian" humaneness, and requiring "opportunism", "cynicism", "toughness" and "having-balls" *qua* "necessary evils" or "realism". Any restraint on, or improvement of, this sorry scheme of things is seen as hopeless *a priori*. (In yet another example of human self-alienation, the cynical cause the world to be a hell, and then they argue that they are cynical because the world is hell.) This 'dog-eat-dog' pursuit of wealth, as displayed most patently by high finance, is *nihil novum sub sole*. Castoriadis observes that empire-building as well as "hoarding [have been] practiced in many historical societies, and attempts by latifundist landowners to exploit the land on a grand scale with servile labor are also known (in particular, during a period close to us, in imperial Rome)."[509] What is specific to the capitalist type of accumulation is "the continual transformation of the production process with a view toward increasing output, combined with a reduction of costs."[510] There can be never enough, no matter how much wealth has already been attained.

Rationality

Capitalism aims relentlessly at maximising profit by increasing revenues and reducing costs—what is taken nowadays to be the standard for rationality itself. According to Castoriadis, "that is the decisive feature. This characterization contains the basics of what Weber would later call 'rationalization,' and about which he will say, correctly, that under capitalism it tends to seize hold of all spheres of social life, doing so in particular as an extension of the empire of calculability."[511] In this process, "Capitalism [becomes] a regime that cuts off virtually every relationship between the institution and an extrasocial instance of authority. The sole instance of authority it invokes is Reason, to which it gives a quite peculiar content."[512]

Anything or anyone that contradicts this peculiar form of 'enlightened' imperialism, which sheds oblivion's darkness on any alternative form of reason, is blamed as "irrational", "sentimental", "utopian", "out of date", "standing in the way of progress" or, if insistent, as "threats to law and order": there is no lack of rationalisations for the capitalist standard of rationality. In this fashion, capitalism embodies "one of the most deep-seated traits of the singular psyche—the aspiration to omnipotence."[513] Under this perspective, 20th-century "totalitarianism is only the most extreme point of… the demented capitalist project of an unlimited expansion of pseudorational pseudomastery… which, moreover, is inverted into its own contradiction, since in it even the restrained, instrumental rationality of classical capitalism becomes irrationality and absurdity, as Stalinism and Nazism have shown."[514]

Castoriadis writes "psudorational" and "pseudomastery" because capitalist rationality pursues uncritically endless growth as an end in itself (never wondering why or to what end) and cannot control constructively the noxious results of its operations (e.g. the environmental crisis) as well as of its own operations (i.e. the recurrent systemic crises requiring the State to rescue capitalism from itself). Concerning omnipotence, instead, Ludwig Feuerbach (1804–1872) had already suggested in the 19th century that religion arose from humankind's dream of omnipotence. Specifically, as this dream got continuously frustrated by reality's resistance to human will, humankind began a process of self-alienation, at first individuating spiritual entities in nature to be 'bought' with sacrifices and rites, and then reaching the ascription of absolute omnipotence to an utterly superior God, thus leaving humankind powerless. Humankind, in other words, alienated herself of her own world-changing powers by projecting them all onto a divinity that humanity herself had generated.[515]

John McMurtry, in the 21st century, suggests that classical (or liberal) and neoclassical (or neoliberal) economics have led many governments and human communities along analogous lines of self-alienation. Specifically, given the governments' alleged inability to sustain or even bring about the much-desired common good or "social optimum", classical economists started positing "a doctrine of unintended consequences" whereby "the perfect orchestration of countless changing factors" is guaranteed "by the apotheosized Market Hand" and such that "the causal sequence is predestined without human reason involved".[516] In keeping with this line of argument, human involvement has been blamed routinely as undue interference, and later even condemned as the "road to serfdom", i.e. the title of a well-known volume by neoclassical 'giant' F.A. Hayek. Recovering and intensifying Adam Smith's overall emphasis, markets have come to be said to be better left to themselves, whereas governments should correspondingly shrink in size—the State itself coming to be seen as nothing but an aggregation of individual consumers rather than cooperating citizens—eventually leaving entire human communities with hardly a shred of planned economic policy aiming at the much-desired common good, or even with the concepts to formulate it. Instead, the common good should come about automatically, handed down by a perfectly self-organising combination of market forces, which are assumed to deliver it at some later point, at least to some people (e.g. the deserving victors of the competitive game).

Tyranny

Capitalism, under its liberal description, is not only the actual master of our collective fate; it *ought* to be this master, extending its power in all directions. "This tendency, this push toward mastery", as Castoriadis remarks, is not "something exclusively specific to Capitalism."[517] Rather, with capitalism, "this push toward mastery is not merely oriented toward 'foreign' conquest but intends just as much and still more the totality of society… education, law, political life, and so on", as emblematically revealed by all the natural and social realities that, whether publicly owned or merely freely available in nature and society, have been turned, partially or *in toto*, into priced commodities to be owned and traded privately for the sake of profit-making (e.g. clean air, entertainment, healthcare).[518]

Pervasive and decisive, the value orientation of capitalism is liberticidal, indeed tyrannical, for it aims at controlling every aspect of human life to increase efficiency of output. Anything that escapes it is a waste, a missed business opportunity, an obstacle to be overcome, if not even a potential threat. Thus, whereas democracy has typically implied pluralism and indeterminacy of ends within a basic constitutional framework, capitalism cannot support them, for there can be only one economic system, driven by the goal of the maximisation of profit. Emblematically, today's chief managers of large business enterprises are said to have a "fiduciary duty" to this end. As McMurtry summarises it, "The market God is, above all, a jealous God. No other economic idea may be put before it."[519]

Divine power is demonstrated most eminently by the sins that God is willing to forgive. According to Max Weber's (1864–1920) famous study *The Protestant Ethics and the Spirit of Capitalism*,[520] it was once typical that the Catholic Church should be prone to punish the heretic, but indulgent to the sinner. The same is true now of the so-called "free market", which accepts corruption (e.g. German enterprises declaring bribes *qua* legitimate expenses deductible for tax purposes) and mendacity (e.g. commonplace untruthfulness of private companies' bookkeeping), as long as they do not disturb profit opportunities, and even praises immoral self-aggrandisement as clever opportunism.

Consistently with its tyrannical tendency, Castoriadis claims that, in its struggle with feudalism, capitalism's "push toward mastery gives itself new means—means of a special character ('rational,' that is to say, 'economic' ones)… [such as]…

- The blossoming of science…
- The birth and the consolidation of the modern State…
- The formation of modern nations."[521] And
- A new mind-set. In the Europe of the industrial revolution, "economic motivation tended to supplant all other motives. The human being became *homo economicus*, that is to say, *homo computans*."[522]

On such a new human being, Edmund Burke, who was not a revolutionary or radical thinker, had already uttered a word of caution to his contemporaries: "Even commerce, and trade, and manufacture, the gods of our economical politicians, are themselves perhaps but creatures; are themselves but effects, which as first causes, we choose to worship… They too may decay with their natural protecting principles."[523] Burke refers here to the venerable cultural, moral and religious traditions inherited from centuries of British history as the "natural protecting principles" of "the gods of our economical politicians" themselves, many of which were not the result of prolonged adaptation to the environmental conditions of the country and successful provision to the ends of the population, but rather of prolonged oppression and exploitation by the British nobility. Still, some of these alleged "gods" were so—most notably the Poor Laws, significantly abolished by the free-market Liberals in 1834—and doing away with them meant throwing away centuries of emancipatory wisdom, not just domination and superstition: "all the decent drapery of life is to be rudely torn off" in lieu of a novel age "of sophisters, economists, and calculators" annihilating "that generous loyalty to rank and sex, that proud submission, that dignified obedience, that subordination of the heart, which kept alive, even in servitude itself, the spirit of an exalted freedom."[524]

It is not relevant here to inquire in the extent to which Burke's depictions of the Middle Ages, its diffuse sense of fealty, and its peaks of civil gentlemanship and religious piety are accurate. Rather, it is interesting to notice how they shed light on the *homo novus* of the early capitalist age, who calculated that it was appropriate to challenge the existing legal and political institutions in the name of democracy (as the Frenchmen dreaded by Burke had done with ample shedding of blood) and, above all, private property. It is only in this perspective, i.e. as an instrumental relationship, that capitalism chose—in addition to science, statehood and nationhood —"the resumption of the ancient movement toward autonomy" i.e. the means of democratic rule.[525] Constrained by the pre-existing feudal institutions, this resumption "manifested at the outset as a protobourgeois movement whose intention was to establish the independence of the commons", becoming later a properly bourgeois movement capable of calling into question the existing political and legal structures of the existing polities and of reshaping them to suit its own ends and purposes.[526]

As a self-aware expression of human creative freedom capable of critical activity, democracy could no longer be appreciated by capitalism once the latter was firmly established. As soon as no alternative economic system is left on the scene, the memory and the possibility of human creative freedom, capable of critical activity concerning economic systems themselves, must be erased, so that "capitalism's domination of the modern era does not appear then as what it is—namely, arbitrary creation of a particular humanity—but as fated phase of all historical movement, at once fated and welcome."[527]

Instrumentality

Like Galileo's new science, the first centralised, bureaucratically cohesive, nationally defined Western State appeared on the scene before any mature bourgeoisie, i.e. around the 17th century (i.e. the so-called "Westphalian" State). These states, run by absolute monarchs and filled with feudal significations and institutions, fought against the protobourgeois democracies of their time and forced them into oligarchic retreat. Yet, the later industrial-financial bourgeoisie of Europe seized hold of these significations and institutions and used them to pursue its own ends. The relationship of capitalism to science, modern statehood and nationhood is, like that to democracy, extrinsic, and specifically instrumental.

The intrinsic character of capitalism is not scientific, State-centred, national, or democratic: it is economic, that is, profit-centred. Were the circumstances to change, the relationship of capitalism with these four instruments could change and, as a matter of historical fact, it has changed. Contemporary capitalism has opposed:

- Unprofitable and dissenting science (e.g. early versions of electric cars, research suggesting the dangerousness of genetically modified organisms, the teaching of humanities inside universities, the science of climate change);
- The modern State (e.g. *via* global free movement of financial capital, subtraction of resources by siphoning revenues to fiscal havens, blackmailing governments by off-sourcing threats)
- Nationhood (e.g. by marketing international standardised dress codes, promotion of English as the world's *lingua franca*, continued pressure for international integration), and
- Democracy (e.g. by enmity to tax-centred egalitarian redistribution of wealth, political lobbying for intervention into countries where socialist governments were democratically elected, superseding popular representation by supranational trade agreements).

Here is the heart of the critique of Castoriadis. Despite all the *a posteriori* claims of inevitability, capitalism and democracy arose together in modern times contingently, and their marriage is far from being a smooth, serene one.

First of all, "the adoption of capitalism does not entail a liberal political regime—as Japan shows us… from 1860 to 1945, or South

Korea after the war."[528] Not only were there democratic experiments prior to capitalism—Castoriadis as a Greek, and myself as a Genoese, are most aware of this fact—but there has been plenty of capitalism without democratic institutions: several Latin American countries and contemporary China can be added to the examples of Japan and South Korea. Capitalism has made use of democracy when and because it was instrumental to the achievement of its goals in certain historical contexts.

Secondly, even in those contexts, as soon as these goals were realised, democracy turned regularly into a secondary matter, if not even a nuisance, an impediment, a menace to further profits. One must simply recall the fierce resistance that liberal states posited against "the resumption of the ancient movement toward autonomy… in the various species of the democratic and workers' movement" in the late 19th century and in the first half of the 20th.[529] In Greece and in Italy, this resistance meant respectively military and fascist dictatorships. Paupers, women, Jews and various other ethnic minorities had to fight long and hard for the recognition of those basic civil and legal rights that the bourgeoisie had extorted from the ruling class of the *ancien régime* one or even two centuries before them. Typically, what all the excluded groups fighting for recognition had in common was not to own significant shares of the available property—the aristocratic anarchist Piotr A. Kropotkin (1842–1921) being then the exception, not the rule. The liberal bourgeoisie even formed alliances with the former aristocratic rulers aimed at preventing further enlargement of the legal-political franchise and the granting of rights at large, especially social, economic and cultural ones.[530]

Thirdly, the result of these prolonged struggles has not been full-fledged democracy; rather, "regimes of liberal oligarchy [i.e.] the compromise our societies have reached between capitalism properly speaking and the emancipatory struggles that have attempted to transform or liberalize capitalism."[531] Such regimes foster democratic autonomy in proportion to its ability to serve capitalism. As Castoriadis writes: "In the effectively actual social-historical reality of contemporary capitalism, these [democratic] liberties function more and more as the mere instrumental complement of the mechanisms that maximize individual 'enjoyments' [*jouissances*]. And these 'enjoyments' are the sole substantive content of the 'individualism' being pounded into our heads these days", i.e. as though the citizen and the consumer were identical notions.[532]

Contingency

Friedrich August Hayek and Ayn Rand, two pivotal figures in promoting the neoliberal paradigm during the 20th century, did have some good reasons to argue that the civil and political freedoms of the liberal tradition were significantly related to the economic freedoms commended by the classical economists. Individual self-affirmation, for example, can express itself through entrepreneurial activity, whilst the interconnected global world of free trade creates opportunities for self-expression previously not available to the individual. Also, successful entrepreneurial activity implies certain forms of freedom, such as: degrees of unhindered intellectual research and circulation of technical or even scientific-technological information; reliable and possibly capillary transportation networks; opportunities for independent judgment and autonomous activity. Moreover, two parallel insights characterise political liberalism and economic capitalism, i.e. that the individual (political as well as economic) may know best what should be done in order to pursue her self-interest; and that a society where successful enterprises flourish is likely to be a prosperous society, analogously to the society allowing its individual members to pursue their life-plans unimpeded.

Even when the value of these reasons is granted, however, there appears to be no essential link yet between democracy and capitalism, including its textbook depiction in neoclassical economics. Consider the unashamed marriage of leading theorists such as Hayek himself, Milton Friedman and James M. Buchanan (1919–2013) with Latin American dictator Augusto Pinochet, under whose tyrannical regime trade unions were made illegal and the universal public provision of social goods such as health and education impossible, no matter how the majority of the Chilean citizens might have wanted to associate with one another and wished to choose freely and democratically. To these thinkers, infringements on private property, free trade and the risk of inflation were more severe and pressing dangers than political persecution, despotic government or even apartheid, in line with Austrian economist Ludwig von Mises' earlier endorsement of European fascism *qua* praiseworthy bulwark against the threat of Soviet socialism: "It cannot be denied that Fascism and similar movements aiming at the establishment of dictatorships are full of the best intentions and that their intervention has, for the moment, saved European civilization. The merit that Fascism has thereby won for itself will live on eternally in history."[533]

Though imperfect and temporary, murderous dictatorships are welcomed by such eminent liberal economists, if property and trade are protected by them. As long as the propertied class retains its wealth and sufficient market opportunity to increase it, the other tenets of the liberal tradition can be toyed with and, at times, neglected altogether. Again and again, in the 19th and 20th century, the scope of democratic self-government was radically limited in the name of so-called "market freedom", and actual persons were jailed, tortured, killed, and even thrown into the ocean.[534] Thus work the "regimes of liberal oligarchy" discussed by Castoriadis.

Autonomy

Political liberalism, though democratic to some relevant extent, is not the only form of democracy possible, nor does it guarantee *a priori* the highest degree imaginable of popular self-determination, which Castoriadis takes as the defining element of democracy. Another way to cast this divergence of value was identified by Immanuel Kant (1724–1804) in his *Groundwork of the Metaphysics of Morals*:

> In the kingdom of ends everything has either a *price* or a *dignity*. What has a price can be replaced by something else

as its *equivalent*; what on the other hand is above all price and therefore admits of no equivalent has a dignity. What is related to general human inclinations and needs has a *market price*; that which, even without presupposing a need, conforms with a certain taste, that is, with a delight in the mere purposeless play of our mental powers, has a *fancy price*; but that which constitutes the condition under which alone something can be an end in itself has not merely a relative worth, that is, a price, but an inner worth, that is, *dignity*.[535]

By valuing human beings merely as means to an end, i.e. the creation of profit, and indeed as commodities for profit (e.g. the concrete reality of markets for non-unionised, defenceless labour), capitalism does not acknowledge the intrinsic worth of the human being, which democracy, for Kant and many other democratic thinkers, aims at enshrining within a just legal framework aimed precisely at securing their freedom, for it is only free men and women that can be said to enjoy full dignity.

Castoriadis shares with Kant and, for that matter, with Marx, the desire to guarantee the conditions allowing all human beings to be valued as ends in themselves and enjoy real opportunities to cultivate their faculties in the non-harmful directions chosen by each freely, i.e. autonomously. Castoriadis' critically qualified acceptance of Marxism and, at the same time, his rejection of Stalinism and Real Socialism, are motivated by the fact that socialist policies, variously interpreted and implemented, can move in the desired direction, but also in the opposite one. Analogously, Castoriadis' critique of capitalism, especially in its contemporary consumerist expression, is born out of the conviction that the tyrannical, constitutive pursuit of profit works against both individual and social autonomy, which ought to be employed in unprofitable ways for the sake of human dignity (e.g. by privileging full employment over efficiency as prime target for the State's economic policy, public green areas to privately-contracted high-density urban development, welfare-enhancing redistributive fiscal policies to socially-polarising fiscal minimalism, non-consumerist enjoyment of leisure time over the purchase of leisure opportunities through priced-goods and services). In experienced reality, whenever private property and profitability are at issue: "capitalism has need not of autonomy but of conformism."[536]

Optimistically, Karl Marx argued that capitalism digs its own grave by producing continuous revolutions that it cannot control. One of these revolutions, the proletarians', is bound to burst capitalism asunder, eventually. Castoriadis agrees with Marx on the self-defying character of capitalism which, historically, did promote democracy itself as "the possibility of and the capacity for calling the established institutions and significations into question", yet opposing it when contradicting the in-built founding principle of the novel economic system, i.e. the pursuit of profit in all spheres of human existence. Democracy, then, could be capitalism's grave-digger, which explains why von Mises or Hayek could tolerate fascism and dictatorship in the face of popular opposition to capitalism. Seen from Castoriadis' angle, democracy is capitalism's short-circuit, not the "two-way street" commended by Bill Clinton. It is a double-edged knife that served capitalism in the past in order to cut its ties with feudal Europe; yet it can be used as well by capitalism's victims to chop the capitalist's newly crowned head.

Whether this regicide will ever happen, however, is nothing fated; it is up to actual human communities:

> For as a productive/economic system, capitalism is not exportable just like that, and the liberal-oligarchic regime, fallaciously called democracy, is not exportable, either. No immanent tendency pushes human societies toward all-out 'rationalization' of production to the detriment of all else, or toward political regimes that accept certain overt forms of intestine conflict while securing certain liberties. Historical creations, these two forms [capitalism and democracy] have nothing fated about them.[537]

On a more specific note, Castoriadis claims that contemporary capitalism is destroying the two anthropological conditions that have made it possible for capitalism to affirm itself in modern times.

On the one hand, the worldwide affirmation of the neoliberal agenda has been weakening trade unions and workers' associations, i.e. the main source of the social and political struggles that have corrected capitalism's self-destructive quest for omnipotence, as exemplified by the ominous post-1929 global crisis, and brought about some mitigating corrective mechanisms (e.g. Keynesian countercyclical State intervention and politically-decided regulation of international currency flows).[538]

On the other hand, the global consumerist society promoted by the same capitalist agenda has been erasing the pre-capitalist "series of anthropological types [capitalism] did not create and could not itself have created: incorruptible judges, honest Weberian-style civil servants, teachers devoted to their vocation, workers with at least a minimum of conscientiousness about their work, and so on."[539] Indeed, with the growth of the virtual economy above and beyond the real economy, it has also been demolishing the one and only true capitalist anthropological type, i.e. "the Schumpeter-style entrepreneur".[540] In lieu of these types, contemporary capitalism has contributed to the generation of the eternal teenager, stupefied by endless adverts and focused only upon the satisfaction of her selfish, shallow impulses; as well as the regeneration of the Weberian ruthless "pirate", whether in the form of financial speculators, self-serving top managers, or business-savvy Sicilian Mafiosi and Colombian drug-lords.[541]

Heteronomy

Not only is the neoliberal coupling of capitalism and democracy not natural; capitalism as such, contrarily to what many neoliberals may say, is not natural either. As Castoriadis observes, "almost the totality of human history has unfolded within regimes where economic 'efficiency,' maximization of the 'product,' and so on were in no way the central bearings for social activities."[542] The liberal and neoliberal alleged anthropological *data* of self-maximisation and non-satiety have very little to do with most recorded human life: "almost always, on a given technological level, social life unfolds with a wholly different set of preoccupations than that of improving the 'productivity' of labor through technical inventions or through rearrangements of work methods and production relations."[543]

Even if there may have been frequently a merchant class, some degree of financial activity, and various forms of private accumulation of wealth, "those sectors of social activity were subordinated to and integrated within others that were considered, each time, to embody the main finalities of human life."[544] Anyone who walks into the Scrovegni Chapel of Padua, gloriously decorated by Giotto (1267–1337), can sense the guilt of wealthy medieval merchants attempting to purify themselves from the sinful filth of money-making, as their economic existence was a fragment of a larger personal and social setting, i.e. their Christian life. Indeed, famous medievalist Jacques Le Goff (1924–2014) argues that the notion of Purgatory developed around the 11th century to serve the needs of a bourgeoning Christian merchant class caught between the pursuit of earthly wealth and the aspiration to a divine Heaven that was forbidden to the rich person by admonition of Jesus Christ himself.[545]

Things are very different today, as the same anthropological *data* seem to depict the motivations and the aspirations of a conspicuous part of the world's population. Rappers walking out of fancy SUVs and pop singers commending money, sometimes above love itself, may well be the popular manifestation of this mind-set. Contemporary female rhythm & blues band *Pussycat Dolls* sing: *"The best things in life are free / But you can keep 'em for the birds and bees / Money / That's what I want..."*; twenty years earlier Madonna had already extolled the virtues of the "material girl" in a song with the same title; one can even step back to Marilyn Monroe's claim that "diamonds are a girl's best friend". Since the inception of post-war consumerist capitalism, there has been no paucity of popular expressions of the anthropological model endorsed by neoliberalism, which Christianity would describe as sinful tokens of avarice or greed.

According to Castoriadis, this popularity constitutes no valid substantiation of the liberal and neoliberal assumption of their naturalness, for "the justification is circular. In the 'wealthy' countries, people 'want' these [consumer] goods because they are raised from their tenderest years to want them (go visit an elementary school today, if you doubt it) and because the regime prevents them, in a thousand and one ways, from wanting anything else."[546] The tyrannical and perplexingly named *"free* market" conditions the subject from the cradle to the grave, as any market expert would state candidly and shamelessly, in order to cause people to mistake artificially-instilled cravings for actual needs.[547]

Praising Italian designer Giorgio Armani (b. 1934), fashion commentator Amy M. Spindler innocently displays how unnatural this process is: "selling fashion means *creating new needs*, and most men do not need another classic jacket. Armani is an expert at creating new needs"[548] After conditioning young minds into premeditate sets of unneeded needs, these people are set 'free' in the happy realm of so-called "consumer sovereignty", where they are trained to measure their worth by what they appear to be able to afford, analogously to the 14th-century parish priest educating the child to be a good Christian, certain that the psychological pressure of her parishioners would then keep her on the straight path for the rest of her life.[549]

John Kenneth Galbraith had already commented on this issue in the 1950s, when the pervasive means of indoctrination manufactured by the medieval Church and later perfected in Benito Mussolini's (1883–1945) Italy and Joseph Stalin's Soviet Union were finding their modern analogue *qua* sophisticated bamboozling by scientifically crafted "advertising" and omni-pervasive media strategies "managing the behaviour of the consumer" in the then-booming consumer societies of Europe and North America.[550] This bamboozling runs deeper than the artificial instillation of desire to conformity/distinction *qua* perceived need, whether for the enjoyment of the purchased good *per se* or of the status that it supposedly guarantees.[551] It is by bamboozlement that the near totality of the system of signs itself is enforced and reinforced, which ascribes utility—absolute as well as marginal—to priced goods and services conferring status to those who own it and making those who do not contemptible or pitiable—what Thorstein Veblen called a person's "pecuniary standard of decency".[552]

As a practicing psychotherapist, Castoriadis was aware of the tremendous amount of pain that this system imposes upon the so-called "losers" in the system, who cannot afford and/or achieve the material symbols of success and/or are pushed to the margins of society because unwilling and/or unable to conform. Mechanisms for social exclusion have always existed, and very painful ones too, but never before the age of television was the propagation of the dominant mind-set so pervasive and uninterrupted.

Whether aware of it or not, whether seeking higher status or simply prevention from suffering public humiliation, the masses—across all classes—still participate today in the growth of a consumer economy no longer able to generate happiness.[553] And in the midst of humiliated lower classes, frustrated middle classes and self-conscious upper classes, these media strategies seem to be at least as powerful as the older tyrants, if not more: "In all [affluent] countries", Castoriadis adds, "they [the consumers] want them [the goods] because, while capitalism did not invent *ab ovo* what is called the demonstration effect, it has raised it to a hitherto unknown degree of power."[554] The reader should ponder seriously on the fact that an average US child is exposed to 40,000 TV commercial a year, not to mention billboards and vicarious advertising.[555] What genuine freedom can the individual enjoy, if she is raised since birth to respond instinctively to deeply conditioned commands?

As Castoriadis observes: "The atomization of individuals is not autonomy. When an individual buys a fridge or a car, he does what forty million other individuals do; there is here neither individuality nor autonomy. This is, as a matter of fact, one of the mystifications of contemporary advertising: 'Personalize yourself, buy Brand X laundry detergent.' And millions of individuals go out and 'personalize' (!) themselves by buying the same detergent."[556]

Concerning the role of television in less affluent countries, Castoriadis remarks: "Televisions, too, rank among these gifts [from

Europe]... allowing... [the] sergeant... [that] seize[s] power and proclaim[s] a socialist people's revolution while massacring a fair proportion of his compatriots... to go about stupefying the population."[557] Although Castoriadis does not assert that "televisual" propaganda annihilates critical thought and free will, he endorses the notion that it does bamboozle its target audience to a noticeable extent.

Concluding Remarks

To Castoriadis' "demonstration effect" due to massive media- and peer-pressured brainwashing, we should also add the active destruction of non-capitalist economies and forms of social life by diverse means, including the threat or the use of military force and large-scale financial usury. For a system so often saluted as the harbinger of liberty, capitalism leaves very little freedom to choose alternative economic orders.

Besides, Castoriadis' awareness of the non-naturalness, anthropic, socio-historical, artificial *ergo* modifiable character of capitalism allows us to connect his work with life-value onto-axiology and shed further light upon the fundamental contradiction between capitalism and freedom. As Castoriadis states: "For the moment, capitalism still manages somehow or other to deliver these [consumer] goods. Here, the discussion can only stop: as long as people want this *pile of junk, which is accumulating in a more and more haphazard way for a growing number of people*, and with which they one day may or may not become saturated, the situation will not change."[558]

This quoted passage, and the remark about the hazardous junk in particular, reveal a fairly simple but most important notion: certain goods are 'bads', in a way that the free market and the *homines oeconomici* do not often, if ever, grasp. The so-called "goods" that they talk about, want, produce, advertise, trade and exchange profitably can be bad for the environment, bad for the many non-human life-forms inhabiting the same environment, bad for people's mental and physical health, bad for people's children and children's children, and bad for their hopes of self-rule and autonomy. Insofar as more and more sales of such bads are still pursued for the sake of profit, the aims of capitalism prove themselves not to correspond to those of biological, spiritual and political life, which, instead, democracy wishes to serve by granting people the ability to shape freely the free society in which to live *qua* free individuals, so as to increase their chances to be content, if not even happy. This is the core of McMurtry's critical analysis of neoliberalism, which I have extensively covered in the previous chapters.

As value theorist and political philosopher Jeff Noonan observes, life-value onto-axiology brings to the fore a long history of actual demands by human societies, whose members have fought for wider access to, and distribution of, means of life, typically controlled by and exploited for the benefit of the ruling oligarchies, including liberal ones.[559] These struggles, which Castoriadis would describe as "emancipatory", have aimed typically at securing that which McMurtry calls "civil commons", i.e. "the organized, unified, and community-funded capacity of universally accessible resources of society to protect and to enable the lives of its members as an end in itself."[560]

Today's environmentalism is another token of precisely such fights. Will it win, though? The answer lies in the sort of rationality that is going to prevail in the public sphere. From an epistemological point of view, the ontological and axiological dimensions of life and life-needs have not been and cannot be computed by the Newtonian-physics-modelled econometrics of either classical or neoclassical market theory, both of which deal with "uniform, invariant sequences" of "externally observable and quantifiable" objects.[561] Life is blinkered out *a priori* by such standard systems of economic calculus, for life does not display the necessary features of the particular objects that can be handled by it, namely inanimate objects following unvarying patterns of behaviour. Indeed, the ontocidal, automatic exclusion of these vital dimensions of reality itself, which are the pre-conditions for the existence of any market economy, explains why many institutions have sometimes proceeded to the creation of alternative econometrics, including McMurtry's WBI.

If, from a logical point of view, the disconnection of the money-capital from the life-capital does not imply necessarily any conflict between them, the same disconnection does not imply mutual flourishing either. And insofar as autonomy—i.e. freedom or democratic means of self-rule—is a means of life, then it does not possess any necessary connection with capitalism. Theoretically, the variable of life is simply alien to money-capital sequences. In practice, the conflict between the two capitals is endemic, to the point that McMurtry speaks of "value wars".

In line with Castoriadis' own assessment, in the last thirty years of worldwide liberalisation and privatisation, money-capital has been taken more and more often as the only structure of understanding directing any allegedly rational and scientific process of policy-making. In other words, neoclassical economics has become much more than a possible interpretation of certain social phenomena: it has become the paradigm of human rationality itself and the basis upon which any form of collective progress can be achieved, including political emancipation.

Nonetheless, as creative social animals capable of autonomy in reason as well as in action, we are not bound to succumb to a myopic, if not mistaken, form of rationality, which can be questioned, revised and, if necessary, rejected, superseded, or supplanted. Not only do Castoriadis and McMurtry share their paramount concern about the fate of the planet's LSS, but also the hope that the severity of the damages suffered by the existing LSS may lead to a significant political response, notwithstanding the incessant corporate media bamboozling that, for example, has made climate-change denial rhetorically acceptable and politically viable in the public sphere, despite its blatant scientific inadequacy.

On this last point, in an interview entitled "The Revolutionary Force of Ecology", Castoriadis praises the growing awareness of "the havoc capitalism ha[s] wreaked upon the environment" and argues that such an awareness has a better chance of bringing down capitalism than "traditional Marxism".[562] Starting from life-grounded concerns, McMurtry's life-value onto-axiology pursues the same aim. Future history, though not one overly remote to us, will tell whether their optimism was misplaced or not.

Chapter 11: The Price of Tranquillity: Cruelty and Death in Adam Smith's Liberalism

Death as the conclusion of a person's earthly life is a barrier that science and technology have not yet succeeded to overcome. Death still ends and defines *ipso facto*, if not *ipso fato*, human existence as nothing else is capable of, whether we realise it or not. In his works, Cornelius Castoriadis often muses upon, and approves of, the ancient Greeks' notion of the human person *qua* sole true *mortal* creature, for she is aware of her own finitude, unlike the immortal gods of high and the doomed but obtuse lowly beasts.[563] Castoriadis even regards the West's abandonment of this ancient and profound sense of mortality as a sign of cultural decadence, which, according to him, has reached its lowest point in the ritual disappearance of death in contemporary market societies. Driven by an exaggerated confidence in techno-science and endless productive capacity—the "pseudorational pseudomastery" of modern capitalism—today's Western societies cultivate the fraudulent myth of eternal youth by means of consumers' *juvénilisation*, while at the same time they hide the inevitable facts of old age and eventual death in the carefully sheltered realms of medical expertise and for-profit funeral services.

On the contrary, Homer, his epic heroes and the tragic poets of classical Athens were willing to face death for what it was, and despised what little immortality there could be in Hades: a dark and hopeless pit, as *per* Achilles' speech in the *Odyssey*. Under this respect, Castoriadis claims as well that a new conception of mortality gained prominence only as of the so-called "golden age" of Athenian philosophy, which marks for him the decline of truly classical Greek culture. *Contra* the traditional brave acceptance of mortality and death, Socrates and his disciples began arguing for the possibility that a privileged part of the human being, the soul, could survive happily after the body's demise.

Partially constructed upon older religious beliefs, this possibility was certainly taken most seriously in the ensuing centuries and a conspicuous number of theologians and philosophers contributed to its further elaboration. Christianity, moreover, made it central to its overall worldview and to its body of doctrine. In the West, it remained mainstream until the 19th century, academia included. Being a faithful 18th-century Scottish Presbyterian throughout his life, to the point of rejecting his beloved mother's attempts at raising him an Episcopalian, Adam Smith was no exception. He was duly aware of this long-lived and sizeable conception within the history of his academic discipline of choice, philosophy. He acknowledges it amply in the erudite account of several ethical schools, both old and new, offered in part VII of his celebrated *Theory of Moral Sentiments*. He acknowledges it as well in his lesser-known accounts of ancient philosophy comprised within the posthumous *Essays on Philosophical Subjects*:[564]

> [T]hough all individuals were... perishable, and constantly decaying, every species was immortal, because the subject matter out of which they were made, and the revolution of the Heavens, the cause of their successive generations, were always the same... indissoluble and immortal, and inseparably united to that sphere which it inhabited.[565]
>
> [...]
>
> Philosophy, which accustoms it to consider the general Essence of things only, and to abstract from all their particular and sensible circumstances, was, upon this account, regarded as the great purifier of the soul. As death separated the soul from the body, and from the bodily senses and passions, it restored it to that intellectual world, from whence it had originally descended, where no sensible Species called off its attention from those general Essences of things. Philosophy, in this life, habituating it to the same considerations, brings it, in some degree, to that state of happiness and perfection, to which death restores the souls of just men in a life to come.[566]

Adam Smith did have something to say about this conception, though indirectly. Neither death nor mortality as such was the sort of topic for which he shows prime concern in his famous lengthy treatises, or in his uneven and unburnt essays (many others, which he did not deem good enough, he destroyed before dying).[567] What interested Smith *in primis* were some pivotal individual and collective dimensions of being that these phenomena affect, e.g. eloquence, imagination, orderly peace, and the good of commercial societies. This is evident already in the quotes above, which suggest the association of "death" and "a life to come" with human "happiness and perfection", both of which, as it is to become clear in what follows, boil down for Smith to *healthy private tranquillity of mind in providentially violent public bodies.*

This chapter maps and outlines in seven thematic sections Smith's disparate thoughts on death and mortality. By so doing, this chapter shows how his understanding of death and mortality can also reveal thorny aspects of his thought that the received views of his liberalism tend to neglect or even forget about, e.g. the therapeutic aim of philosophical and scientific studies, the acceptance of dreadful evil in light of divine providence's greater scheme, and the instrumental worth of living individuals. Because of these thorny aspects, the recurrent and somewhat callous biocidal character of Smith's liberalism is thus further highlighted.

Rhetoric and Aesthetics

A first collective dimension affected by death and mortality is the field of beauty and, as the aesthetics of linguistic communication is concerned, of eloquence, which Smith addresses in his *Lectures on Rhetoric and Belles Lettres*.[568] Classical rhetoric identified three standard contexts for beautiful, eloquent oratory: the lawyer's harangue, the politician's address and the mourner's eulogy, such as Smith's own note "To the Memory of Mr. William Craufurd, Merchant in Glasgow, the Friend of Mr. Hamilton" (an appendix to his 1758 "Dedication to William Hamilton's *Poems on Several Occasions*"). Each of these contexts relates to important aspects of human life, such as justice, happiness and mortality—the last one being the most dramatic of the three. The end of human life, since ancient times, has thus been a fertile ground for orators, poets and writers, historians included, whose stylistic devices Smith analyses and assesses for their inventiveness and effectiveness, in accordance with two of the five canons of classical rhetoric, namely *dispositio* (i.e. structure; lectures 12–30) and *elocutio* (i.e. style; lectures 2–11).

Among Smith's cited sources on death and mortality are renowned English literati such as "Mr. Pope",[569] "Nathaniel Lee"[570] and "Addison".[571] Above all, Smith refers to Latin authors such as "Velleius Paterculus… Florus… Virgil",[572] "Sallust",[573] "Cicero"[574] and, often, "Tacitus".[575] The last one was probably one of Smith's favourite Latin historians, and he is singled out for developing an innovative, psychologically richer style at a time when "[t]he people" of Rome "enjoyed greater internall Tranquillity and Security… Luxury… Refinement of manners… free Liberty of disposing of their wealth", hence being likely to "turn their attention" from issues of personal and public safety "to the motions of the human mind".[576] In the same lecture, Smith observes also the strong effect that focussing upon an individual person's "calamity", her "death" included, can have on the audience or on the readership, whilst focussing upon the calamities and deaths affecting larger multitudes leads to the dissipation of sympathetic identification.[577]

Within the context of rhetoric, Smith wrote as well about Rousseau's 1755 *Discourse upon the Origin and Foundation of the Inequality amongst Mankind*. In a review of his *Discourse*, Smith calls Rousseau a verily "ingenious and eloquent" writer.[578] Smith judges Rousseau's *Discourse* conceptually original, stylistically vibrant and, theoretically, a morally improved version of the doctrine of socially constructive unintended consequences presented by the Dutch philosopher Bernard Mandeville (1670–1733) in his satirical "Fable of the Bees", the "corruption and licentiousness" of which Smith loathed.[579] No deeper philosophical analysis is present, for Smith deems the *Discourse* "a work which consists almost entirely of rhetoric and description", written by "a republican carried a little too far".[580] Still, Smith translates a handful of passages from

Rousseau's text, including a presently relevant one. In it, free and slothful savages are described as preferring "cruel deaths" to civilised life, in which instead the common "citizen… labours on till his death, …even hastens it, in order to put himself in a condition to live, or renounces life to acquire immortality".[581]

As the dramatic character of death can give rise to great eloquence, when the "proper" techniques are employed, so is it capable of producing great "Statuary" under stricter formal conditions of propriety of "imitation", e.g. "the miserable death of Laocoon" and "the dying gladiator" of ancient times.[582] Unlike "Painting", "Statuary… cannot, without degrading itself, stoop to represent any thing that is offensive, or mean, or even indifferent."[583] When proficiently executed, yet, each art, in keeping with its established aesthetic standards, can transform the normally repulsive and terrifying experiences of human frailty and mortality into objects of beauty. As regards drama, it is "death" alone and not even "pain" *per se*, albeit "exquisite", the key-ingredient of "the Greek tragedies" that Smith finds "so agreeable to the imagination", which is a second dimension recurrently associated with mortality in his works.[584]

Imagination and Moral Psychology

The recurrence of this psychological dimension is not at all surprising, given that imagination plays a pivotal role in Smith's *Theory of Moral Sentiments* (TMS). According to the account given in this book, which I can only summarise here, the fundamental ethical power of the human soul consists in imagining how other people might feel when acting ("direct sympathy") or acted upon ("indirect sympathy") and in giving rise within our bosoms to germane feelings in response that may ("concord") or may not ("dissonance") correspond to those people's actual experiences and circumstances. "Pleasure" or, at least, the lessening of "pain" ensue in proportion to the "concord" that is attained. This process is almost instinctive within us and does not require necessarily any articulate thought. To a significant extent, it is part of our make-up *qua* social creatures and, in ordinary life, it just happens.

On top of it, thanks to our imaginative abilities, we are also able to perform a number of additional morally relevant activities, such as to:

- Conceptualise a plethora of morally significant sentiments that are innate to us and that we can yet modify, either by perfecting them or by corrupting them, e.g. *via* exposure to local traditions ("custom") and socially higher-placed role-models ("fashion");
- Acquire morally relevant skills conferring lucid self-reflection ("conscience"), candid self-awareness ("magnanimity"), and sensible self-control ("prudence" and "temperance"), so as to grow in mastery over these sentiments in our minds and hearts ("wisdom" and "virtue");
- Act upon the right sentiments in the right proportion to their cause ("propriety") in habitual ways that we and our fellows deem worthy ("virtues");
- Adapt successfully to an almost infinite number of diverse and complex circumstances ("fortune") that escape any attempt at producing definitive rules for moral living ("casuistry"); and
- Behave in socially accepted ways that inspire positive feelings in our fellows ("approbation"), or fail to do so—either way, God makes sure that the social good follows always and invariably, individual failures notwithstanding ("Providence").

It is then primarily within TMS that Smith gathers many observations or, as he would call them, "illustrations" about death, mortality, and the workings of the imagination thereupon.[585] For example, Smith writes that, thanks to the calming and reflexive aloofness that our imaginative powers allow for, we may accept other people's laughter and frivolity, even if we are in a "grave humour".[586] Similarly, in a more cheerful mood, we can "approve" of the "grief" of a total stranger who "has just received the news of the death of his father", i.e. another and farther removed total stranger.[587] In all such cases, we imagine what those individuals must or should be feeling and discern the correct emotional responses which, in Smith's considered opinion, reflect the character of the viewer rather than that of the viewed person. This is because, according to Smith, we do not actually feel what others feel, but project our feelings onto them as we observe them, based on past experiences, social expectations and cultural norms.

The same intellectual power makes people "voluntarily throw… away life to acquire after death a renown which they could no longer enjoy. Their imagination, in the meantime, anticipated that fame which was in future times to be bestowed upon them".[588] Under more altruistic circumstances, human imagination can lead to self-sacrifice. As Smith writes: a "soldier who throws away his life in order to defend that of his officer" or "exposes his life to acquire some inconsiderable addition to the dominions of his sovereign" instantiates a splendid display of steadfast "military character".[589] The same power of the mind makes the innocent person that is unjustly accused of a hideous crime fear dishonour more than "death" itself.[590] The thought of *post-mortem* humiliation, which she would not truly experience in reality, haunts her intensely nonetheless: imagination does reach deep within the psyche and very far in time, according to Smith. In nearly all cases but rare socio-pathological monstrosities, this imaginative power underpins that universal moral drive, which Smith dubs "sympathy" and claims to be so broad as to extend to the deceased too, for whom we feel genuine "sorrow", even if they cannot feel anything in their state.[591]

Albeit quasi-universal, sympathy is not equally distributed. Firstly, there are more and less capable persons, i.e. wiser and less wise individuals. Differently gifted and/or trained, these are persons who can imagine in better or worse ways what other people may feel. Therefore, they can identify with those people more or less successfully, i.e. they reach more or less effectively an adequately harmonious coincidence of sentiments, and correspondingly result socially proper or improper to a varying degree. Secondly, the closer people are to us, the stronger the drive of sympathy becomes within us. Hence the social phenomenon follows, whereby normally disturbing potent "feelings" that "go beyond the bounds of propriety" can be socially acceptable nonetheless, whenever "pain, sickness, approaching death, poverty, disgrace, etc." afflict "our parents, our children, our brothers and sisters, our intimate friends" rather than a stranger, whom we would normally find unpleasant in her unashamed expression of emotional turbulence.[592] Not to mention one's own misfortunes. Nobody is closer to oneself, according to Smith, than she herself is (or, in keeping with Smith's custom, *him*self): "Every man… is much more deeply interested in whatever immediately concerns himself, than in what concerns any other man: and to hear, perhaps, of the death of another person, with whom we have no particular connexion, will give us less concern, will spoil our stomach, or break our rest much less than a very insignificant disaster which has befallen ourselves."[593]

Smith's acknowledgment of human self-centredness is not reason enough for him to make self-love or selfishness the only motive of human action or the basis of all moral behaviour, *pace* the success enjoyed in the 18th century by the ethical doctrine of "Dr. Mandeville", whom Smith criticises again in part VII of TMS.[594] Quite the opposite, Smith frequently remarks in both public and private writings upon the inherent worth of self-sacrifice and altruism, to the actual point of death. For instance, giving one's own life for King and Empire is a truly honourable way to leave this world: "As your Brother dyed in the service of his country, you have the best and the noblest consolation: That since it has pleased God to deprive you of the satisfaction you might have expected from the continuance of his life, it has at least been so ordered that the manner of his death does you honour."[595]

As mortality is concerned, Smith was fascinated by how many sympathetic responses we seem capable of experiencing and enduring in connection with death, and especially in proportion to the relative personal proximity of the deceased. More broadly, Smith notes also death's intimate relationship with the "heart" of the human being, including "the most violent and convulsive emotions" of which we are capable.[596] For instance, Smith was intrigued by the fact that something positive such as a sudden joy could lead to a person's death. At the same time, on the other end of the sentimental spectrum, recurrent and prolonged "sorrow" and "melancholy" caused by the temporally close deaths of a series of beloved persons could make a person less responsive to yet another normally major cause of "grief".[597] In this depressed state of mind, even a "greater… loss", such as "the death of the last" of that person's "several [dead] children", could be perceived as less traumatic.[598]

Meta-philosophy and Gnoseology

Smith's numerous and insightful "illustrations" constitute a remarkable phenomenology of morality that was not meant to be merely a token of descriptive science. It had a normative, indeed curative purpose too. Like many philosophers before and after him, Smith assigned a therapeutic role to philosophy. Aside from any truth, which might perhaps lie beyond the grasp of our puny minds, Smith did claim that all worthy philosophical endeavours should construct pictures of reality *qua* inherently orderly and broadly beneficial, in order to soothe our worries, offer us a modicum of hope, and grant us an adequate degree of contentment:

> Nature, after the largest experience that common observation can acquire, seems to abound with events which appear solitary and incoherent with all that go before them, which therefore disturb the easy movement of the imagination… Philosophy, by representing the invisible chains which bind together all these disjointed objects, endeavours to introduce order into this chaos of jarring and discordant appearances, to allay this tumult of the imagination, and to restore it, when it surveys the great revolutions of the universe, to that tone of tranquillity and composure, which is both most agreeable in itself, and most suitable to its nature.[599]

Reminiscent of Roman stoicism, Smith's statement suggests that it is not the pursuit of *veritas* that animates chiefly philosophical inquiry, but the pursuit of *tranquillitas*, as exemplified by Seneca's (4 BC–65 AD) *De tranquillitate animi*.[600] The reassuring eventual composition of disparate elements is claimed to be the focus-point of intellectual inquiry, not clutching reality firmly at its joints. Centuries later, the great Hungarian chemist Michael Polanyi will be claiming something analogous, namely that scientific inquiries are sense-making and sense-giving *gestalten* that we decide to believe as true by way of personal acts of intellectual faith in an inherited social practice.[601]

As Smith writes: "the repose and tranquillity of the imagination is the ultimate end of philosophy… [I]t is the end of philosophy, to allay that wonder, which either the unusual or seemingly disjointed appearances of nature excite".[602] Tranquillity was very important in Smith's worldview, and the term itself is recurrent throughout his oeuvre. As Smith affirms in *The Imitative Arts*: "the natural state of the mind" is the one "in which we are neither elated nor dejected, the state of sedateness, tranquility, and composure".[603] That philosophy, whilst studying nature, may aim at leading the mind to its natural state, seems only… natural; and it seems equally natural that Smith, *qua* professed philosopher, should talk frequently of tranquillity.

It should be specified that, for Smith, "philosophy" was not only the sort of intellectual endeavour pursued by the likes of him, Christian Wolff (1679–1754) or Giambattista Vico (1668–1744). It was also the intellectual endeavour which we would call today "science", whether "hard" or "natural". The separation between humanities and sciences, as well as that between *Natur-* and *Geisteswissenschaften*, were not yet an intellectual given: such distinctions, though commonplace today, occurred later. 18th-century thinkers could be vehemently factional and ferociously litigious, but the petty turf wars of modern academia or the urgency of rebranding long-lived arts and humanities into some sort of "human" or "social sciences" were unknown to them. Henceforth, the term "philosophy" extended to the likes of Galileo Galilei (1564–1642), Evangelista Torricelli (1608–1647) and Isaac Newton (1642–1726), consistently with the common English parlance in Smith's day and with Newton's self-understanding as a full-fledged philosopher, and not just a "natural" one.

It is widely known that the title of Newton's ground-breaking masterpiece reads *Philosophiae Naturalis Principia Mathematica*, i.e. mathematical principles of natural *philosophy*. In addition to this branch of philosophy, however, Newton also wrote extensively on theological matters, Church history, Biblical chronology, and he penned an extensive commentary on Saint John's *Apocalypse*. In line with this inclusive and, back then, far-from-uncommon open-ended notion of philosophy, Smith remarks in the concluding paragraph of his *Astronomy*: "the system of Sir Isaac Newton" is one of the many "philosophical systems" developed in human history, i.e. "mere inventions of the imagination" striving "to connect together the otherwise disjointed and discordant phaenomena of nature".[604] Whether these inventions are also true, including Smith's own ones, it is an issue that he settles neither in that book nor elsewhere.

Needless to say, endless scholarship has ensued on this issue, which Smith left unsettled. For example, Smith scholar Andy Denis states:

> The fragment commonly known as Smith's 'History of Astronomy' is more properly called, in full, *The Principles which Lead and Direct Philosophical Enquiries; Illustrated by the History of Astronomy; by the History of the Ancient Physics; and by the History of the Ancient Logics and Metaphysics*. The full title makes clear that Smith's intention is to set out his conception of scientific method. For Smith, in his discussion of successive schools of thought in these *Histories*, the purpose of a system of thought is not to disclose the truth of how the world is, but to soothe the imagination, previously agitated by wonder at the marvels of the world.[605]

As odd as it may sound to contemporary ears, which are accustomed to frequent claims of scientific objectivity and knowledge, Denis argues that Smith understood his own work in this therapeutic light—and exclusively in this light. According to Denis,

Smith's TMS and WN were pursued intentionally as tranquillising synthetic depictions of history. Insofar as they mixed Stoic and Christian conceptual elements to invoke a divine, natural logic to the unfolding of this history, Smith's depictions were, at heart, theodicies. As positively realistic as they might seem to some readers, TMS and WN were written only, in Denis' view, as rhetorically apt treatises for individuals and societies that would benefit from apprehending the universe, and our life in it, not solely as a meaningful totality, but also as a totality that is inherently orderly and advantageous to most.

This is so bold an argument, that alone I single it out from the enormous literature about Smith and submit to the reader, for it is as intriguing as it is controversial and, in my opinion, unanswerable, unless yet undiscovered manuscripts or correspondence should pop up in some library or archive to resolve the matter.

Politics and Equity

The therapeutic composition of discordant elements is certainly palpable in the way in which Smith, like a novel Scottish Pangloss, could accept with composure the apparent injustices of luck, the recurrent confusion of human hearts and minds and, above all, the frequent and widespread violent deaths of vast multitudes throughout human history. These deaths include the gruesome massacres perpetrated by the most ferocious political leaders known to humankind. According to Smith, they all play a positive role in God's hidden yet wise cosmic architecture:

> Fortune has... great influence over the moral sentiments of mankind, and, according as she is either favourable or adverse, can render the same character the object, either of general love and admiration, or of universal hatred and contempt. This great disorder in our moral sentiments is by no means, however, without its utility; and we may on this as well as on many other occasions, admire the wisdom of God even in the weakness and folly of man. Our admiration

of success is founded upon the same principle with our respect for wealth and greatness, and is equally necessary for establishing the distinction of ranks and the order of society. By this admiration of success we are taught to submit more easily to those superiors, whom the course of human affairs may assign to us; to regard with reverence, and sometimes even with a sort of respectful affection, that fortunate violence which we are no longer capable of resisting; not only the violence of such splendid characters as those of a Caesar or an Alexander, but often that of the most brutal and savage barbarians, of an Attila, a Gengis, or a Tamerlane.[606]

In a similar vein, inequalities in social status and income, which in history have led to the deaths of many, both young and old, could also be understood and accepted by Smith with notable poise. He never denies the discomfort and the suffering that they involve, as seen also in the previous chapter: "The order of proprietors may, perhaps, gain more by the prosperity of the society, than that of labourers: but there is no order that suffers so cruelly from its decline".[607] Nor does Smith deny that remedies are conceivable and even sought after, though generally in vain, for the downtrodden are bound to be ignorant, ignored, or manipulated by the very same people that tread upon them as a matter of course, and upon each other as a matter of honour, sport, or advantage:

> But though the interest of the labourer is strictly connected with that of the society, he is incapable either of comprehending that interest, or of understanding its connection with his own. His condition leaves him no time to receive the necessary information, and his education and habits are commonly such as to render him unfit to judge even though he was fully informed. In the publick deliberations, therefore, his voice is little heard and less regarded, except upon some particular occasions, when his clamour is animated, set on, and supported by his

employers, not for his, but their own particular purposes.[608]

Yet, all these sorrowful conditions are themselves but a subtle, unseen and benign state of affairs, whose aim is to secure long-term order, laboriousness and peaceful coexistence within society, no matter what popular "moralists" of all ages may have said against them:

> Moralists... warn us against the fascination of greatness. This fascination, indeed, is so powerful, that the rich and the great are too often preferred to the wise and the virtuous. Nature has wisely judged that the distinction of ranks, the peace and order of society would rest more securely upon the plain and palpable difference of birth and fortune, than upon the invisible and often uncertain difference of wisdom and virtue. The undistinguishing eyes of the great mob of mankind can well enough perceive the former: it is with difficulty that the nice discernment of the wise and the virtuous can sometimes distinguish the latter.[609]
>
> [...]
>
> We favour all their inclinations, and forward all their wishes. What pity, we think, that anything should spoil and corrupt so agreeable a situation! We could even wish them immortal; and it seems hard to us, that death should at last put an end to such perfect enjoyment. It is cruel, we think, in Nature to compel them from their exalted stations to that humble, but hospitable home, which she has provided for all her children. Great King, live for ever!.[610]

Individual lives can and ought to be sacrificed to "the peace and order of society", according to Smith, for "[t]he peace and order of society is of more importance than even the relief of the miserable".[611] Let the unfortunate minorities perish if, by so doing, the majority can prosper. There is such a thing as an expendable human being.

In fact, there are many such human beings. The good, the

happiness and the perfection that matter in the end are those of society at large, not those of each and every individual living in it. Smith was no human rights advocate. He was an advocate for an austere, 18th-century Presbyterian divine providence, which may well decree the instrumental destruction of lives, so that more lives may spring in a more prosperous setting. Wise, decent mortals ought actually to stand ready, like "[g]ood soldiers", to sacrifice their "own private interest" for the sake of others' "public interest" (e.g. "the state or sovereignty"), confiding in God's superior wisdom in all matters:

> No conductor of an army can deserve more unlimited trust, more ardent and zealous affection, than the great Conductor of the universe. In the greatest public as well as private disasters, a wise man ought to consider that he himself, his friends and countrymen, have only been ordered upon the forlorn station of the universe; that had it not been necessary for the good of the whole, they would not have been so ordered; and that it is their duty, not only with humble resignation to submit to this allotment, but to endeavour to embrace it with alacrity and joy. A wise man should surely be capable of doing what a good soldier holds himself at all times in readiness to do. The idea of that divine Being, whose benevolence and wisdom have, from all eternity, contrived and conducted the immense machine of the universe, so as at all times to produce the greatest possible quantity of happiness, is certainly of all the objects of human contemplation by far the most sublime. Every other thought necessarily appears mean in the comparison.[612]

Smith could not only understand and accept coolly the inequalities in social status and income, as well as their attendant lot of suffering and death, in terms of a long-term super-personal peaceful order of society; also, he instructed that they should be suffered gladly, in a more immediate inter-personal display of the sort of virtuous fortitude that Smith exalts throughout TMS. At some point, the wise and virtuous person should come to realise and embrace the truth whereby it is also through small-scale individual misfortunes that significant large-scale happiness can be achieved. Sometimes, they are our own individual misfortunes. Sometimes, they are someone else's.

Under the latter respect, Smith's WN recalls with great equanimity the stern and lethal way in which "the demand for labour", in a well-functioning economy, regulates its demographics and brings about an optimal balance; as the reader has already read in this book, Smith stated that "among the inferior ranks of people… the scantiness of subsistence can set limits to the further multiplication of the human species; and it can do so in no other way than by destroying a great part of the children which their fruitful marriages produce."[613]

Smith acknowledges no alternative for the ignorant and prolific "race of labourers".[614] Their best hopes are neither political action nor forlorn indolence. Instead, their best hopes consist in working hard under the illusion of 'making it to the top' in either an already-developed "European" nation or, better still, in a fast-growing economy like the American one, where wages are bound to improve considerably over time and kick-start a virtuous circularity of increasing demand and supply at all social levels:

> The liberal reward of labour, therefore, as it is the necessary effect, so it is the natural symptom of increasing national wealth. The scanty maintenance of the labouring poor, on the other hand, is the natural symptom that things are at a stand, and their starving condition that they are going fast backwards… The liberal reward of labour, therefore, as it is the effect of increasing wealth, so it is the cause of increasing population. To complain of it is to lament over the necessary effect and cause of the greatest publick prosperity.[615]

In either case, the "race of labourers" are said to be far better off than the great majority of the most powerful "African king[s], the absolute master[s] of the lives and liberties of ten thousand naked savages".[616]

Whether in Europe or in America, the members of the same race are also said to be better off than millions of people living in the stagnating economy of imperial China, where "[a]ny carrion, the carcase of a dead dog or cat… though half putrid and stinking, is as welcome to them as the most wholesome food to the people of other countries" and innumerable "children are every night exposed in the street, or drowned like puppies in the water".[617] Not to mention declining economies like that of "Bengal", where the monopoly enjoyed by the governing British corporation translates into "the labouring poor['s] starving condition".[618] Death, there, is everywhere to be seen.

"Want, famine, and mortality", read in this light, are simply means whereby the overall equilibrium of a prosperous economy is positively secured, either in marginal areas of a happy nation's economic life or upon occasional crises.[619] "Want, famine, and mortality" are worrisome only when a much greater number of people is affected by them, for in that case they signal that the economy is failing. This failure, according to Smith, is due primarily to institutions that have become unhinged from the divinely ordained natural principles of private property and free trade, which secure "happiness and tranquility".[620]

The criticised unhinging comes about because of "[t]he capricious ambition of kings and ministers", or of "the impertinent jealousy of merchants and manufacturers", whose "violence and injustice" and greedy "spirit of monopoly" run "directly opposite" to the "interest… of the great body of the people".[621] For Smith, "the good of the whole", rather than of each individual or select group thereof, constitutes the axiological horizon determining whether a society is happy or not. Not even the preferences of the wealthiest or most powerful élites can contradict this fundamental notion:

> [W]hat improves the circumstances of the greater part can never be regarded as an inconveniency to the whole.

> No society can surely be flourishing and happy, of which the far greater part of the members are poor and miserable. It is but equity, besides, that they who feed, clothe, and lodge the whole body of the people, should have such a share of the produce of their own labour as to be themselves tolerably well fed, clothed, and lodged.[622]

"Equity", i.e. actual fairness or justice whatever the existing laws may be, is mentioned by Smith, but remains secondary (cf. "besides" in the preceding quote) to the vast aggregate happiness ordained by God's wisdom. This hierarchy of value is epitomised by the "unfortunate law of slavery"[623] whose contribution to "the profits" of many "colonies" and of all their direct and indirect beneficiaries in the homelands is what truly counts in the big picture painted by Smith, who muses: "The late resolution of the Quakers in Pennsylvania to set at liberty all their negro slaves, may satisfy us that their number cannot be very great".[624]

Equity is even less relevant *vis-à-vis* the astounding number of persons murdered in the Americas, when not 'merely' enslaved, by European conquerors and colonists. Even these deaths can be understood and accepted dispassionately by Smith. As he writes: "In spite of the cruel destruction of the natives", the lands that they once occupied had been turned into the home of vast herds of "European cattle" and a "more populous" breed of more productive human beings: "we must acknowledge, I apprehend, that the Spanish creoles are in many respects superior to the ancient Indians".[625]

Smith claims as well that foreign "savages and barbarians", who had undergone "a sort of Spartan discipline" throughout their primitive existence, did not suffer too much in being mercilessly exterminated, or at least not as much as a civilised person would suffer.[626] "[H]abituate[d]" as they are "to every sort of distress", the "savages in North America, we are told, assume upon all occasions the greatest indifference" and are capable of "magnanimity and selfcommand… beyond the conception of Europeans", because "[w]hen a savage is made prisoner of war, and receives, as is usual, the sentence of death from his conquerors, he hears it without expressing any emotion, and afterwards submits to the most dreadful torments, without ever bemoaning himself, or discovering any other passion but contempt of his enemies."[627]

Colonialism, despite its lethal brutality on a genocidal scale, could thus be applauded by Smith as a further token of divinely sanctioned "fortunate violence". Like "[t]he heroes of ancient and modern history" or the "wise man" praised by the ancient Stoics, the indigenous persons wiped out by other, European persons can, "upon the approach of death, preserve [their] tranquillity unaltered" and thus deserve "a very high degree of admiration".[628] As Smith repeatedly remarks in his works: "no character is more admired than that of the man who faces death with intrepidity, and maintains his tranquillity and presence of mind amidst the most dreadful dangers".[629] Admirable and admired, these stoical primitives can and may therefore be exterminated, "as is usual", but without the sort of pain that exterminating a civilised nation would involve.

At the same time, "[t]he progress of all the European colonies in wealth, population, and improvement" should be welcomed too, for it "has accordingly been very great."[630] Killing the natives may be "cruel". Yet, in the greater scheme of things, worse would be not "to convert… dead stock into active and productive stock" since, as it is argued throughout WN, it is by establishing private property and making it work *via* free trade that "the good of the whole" is best served.[631]

Eschatology and Eudemonia

Slavery, violent conquest and genocidal exterminations have been common throughout human history. Can we really think that "the great Conductor of the universe" cannot educe "good from ill"?[632] Smith clearly does not think so. Similarly, inequalities in social status and income, and their attendant miseries and deaths, have been the norm in history, not the exception. According to Smith, they are *ipso facto* part and parcel of God's hidden yet wise architecture of the universe:

The rich only select from the heap what is most precious and agreeable. They consume little more than the poor, and in spite of their natural selfishness and rapacity, though they mean only their own conveniency, though the sole end which they propose from the labours of all the thousands whom they employ, be the gratification of their own vain and insatiable desires, they divide with the poor the produce of all their improvements. They are led by an invisible hand to make nearly the same distribution of the necessaries of life, which would have been made, had the earth been divided into equal portions among all its inhabitants, and thus without intending it, without knowing it, advance the interest of the society, and afford means to the multiplication of the species.[633]

As greedy as they can be, the wealthy bring about enough prosperity for the greatest number to participate in and, albeit to conspicuously different degrees, benefit from. Even the wealthy's extravagance trickles down to the destitute and leads to laudable social outcomes. God's providential "invisible hand" ensures it.

There exists veritably a vast and recent scholarly industry that has been attempting to interpret Smith's work as actually devoid of any theological underpinning and make him sound like the sort of 20th- and 21st-century secular liberal, if not even libertarian, economists who worship today his pro-market stances. I believe such attempts to be grossly mistaken from a historical point of view, essentially futile from a logical one, and either intellectually dishonest or naïve. The passages from TMS so far cited in this chapter are already adequate proof of Smith's adherence to commonplace conceptions of much 18th-century Protestant Christianity, especially among educated Scots like himself. More passages that reveal further his adherence follow as well.

Smith was a 'realist', 'right-thinking' man of his time. Unlike 'radical' Rousseau, Smith had no qualms in justifying colonialism, slavery, the poorest workers' death by starvation, and their children's identical doom. Unlike 'radical' Rousseau, Smith had a generally unimaginative notion of future social possibilities (e.g. the abolition of trade barriers within the UK). Today he would be among the pundits who cannot conceive of a world without fossil fuels or of wellbeing without endless economic growth. For Smith, who observed world events from the vantage point of Scotland's central belt, the existing economic system should better be kept as it was, for it was beneficial enough—at least to him and to his peers. Thorstein Veblen's claim that classical economists were primarily the mouthpiece of well-established 18th-century entrepreneurial interests and no visionary prophets of yet-to-come industrialists does plausibly apply to Smith.[634]

Even Smith's celebrated idea of self-interested behaviour leading to general prosperity was in tune with the economic thought of his day, i.e. the doctrine of unintended consequences known today as "the invisible hand", which is a metaphor that Smith uses three times in his entire oeuvre (all of which are cited in this chapter). Apart from being a reiteration of the traditional Christian notion of divine providence and a trope familiar to British educated persons since at least William Shakespeare's (1564–1616) *Macbeth*, its socio-economic characterisation had already been explored by Mandeville, whose "Fable of the Bees" is mentioned repeatedly by Smith in his works, yet in a negative tone. Analogous considerations can be found in Richard Cantillon's (ca.1680–1734) *Essai sur la Nature du Commerce en Général*, which is perhaps largely ignored today, but was very popular in its day and known to Smith and to the British intelligentsia of his time.[635]

As Smith's own notion of the "invisible hand" is concerned, it should be noted that it is fundamentally built upon a tautology: the economic order of private property and free trade commended by him is beneficial because it benefits those who are benefitted from it. In Smith's theodicy, the benefit is universal, insofar as even those who do suffer "most cruelly" from it can enjoy at least the perfect happiness of death's deep "tranquillity" (more on this later), e.g. the countless exterminated natives of the Americas and the millions of Africans enslaved in order to take their place. In later secular versions such as the socio-Darwinist ones (e.g. Herbert Spencer's), however, it is not: losers in the competitive or evolutionary realm of human life are expected to be the case, so that our species may progress further by weeding out the weakest members.

According to Smith, the least fortunate in society ought to be content with their station, for they do not lack that which really matters in life. Once more, God's "invisible hand" takes care of it:

> When Providence divided the earth among a few lordly masters, it neither forgot nor abandoned those who seemed to have been left out in the partition. These last too enjoy their share of all that it produces. In what constitutes the real happiness of human life, they are in no respect inferior to those who would seem so much above them. In ease of body and peace of mind, all the different ranks of life are nearly upon a level, and the beggar, who suns himself by the side of the highway, possesses that security which kings are fighting for.[636]

In Smith's view, the poor and destitute ought not to complain, for God has blessed them too. Accordingly, any rancorous envy directed at those in a better position within society is to be avoided. Take a better look, says Smith, and you will realise that the luxuries of the rich are not much in themselves: "[t]hey keep off the summer shower, not the winter storm, but leave [the rich] always as much, and sometimes more exposed than before, to anxiety, to fear, and to sorrow; to diseases, to danger, and to death."[637] The social standing decreed by divine will can, may and ought to be accepted gladly by each of us, especially if we belong to the lower ranks, for genuine "happiness and tranquility" are close at hand. Rocking the boat only makes things worse for everyone:

> The great source of both the misery and disorders of human life, seems to arise from over-rating the difference between one permanent situation and another. Avarice over-rates the difference between poverty and riches... The person under the influence of [it] is not only miserable in

his actual situation, but is often disposed to disturb the peace of society, in order to arrive at that which he so foolishly admires... In all the most glittering and exalted situation that our idle fancy can hold out to us, the pleasures from which we derive our happiness, are almost the same with those which, in our actual, though humble station, we have at all times at hand, and in our power. Except the frivolous pleasures of vanity and superiority, we may find, in the most humble station, where there is only personal liberty, every other which the most exalted can afford; and the pleasures of vanity and superiority are seldom consistent with perfect tranquillity, the principle and foundation of all real and satisfactory enjoyment.[638]

As to those who find humility an impossible virtue to uphold, they too end up playing a good role in God's wisely designed universe:

> The poor man's son, whom heaven in its anger has visited with ambition... admires the condition of the rich... and, in order to arrive at it, he devotes himself for ever to the pursuit of wealth and greatness... Through the whole of his life he pursues the idea of a certain artificial and elegant repose which he may never arrive at, for which he sacrifices a real tranquillity, that is at all times in his power, and which, if in the extremity of old age he should at last attain to it, he will find to be in no respect preferable to that humble security and contentment which he had abandoned for it... [W]ealth and greatness are mere trinkets of frivolous utility... And it is well that nature imposes upon us in this manner. It is this deception which rouses and keeps in motion the industry of mankind.[639]

Upon reflection, within as wisely organised a universe as the one depicted by Smith, no living man or woman can sensibly express truly justified disappointment.

Whether those brought to a "cruel" death, such as the natives of the Americas discussed by Smith in WN, may have a justified claim to complain, it is not as clear. Steadfastness in the face of death and resilience to physical discomfort may be reasons to admire distant savages and dispatch them with equanimity. It is doubtful that Smith would have been equally cavalier with regard to snuffing persons closer to him that displayed identically virtuous stoicism, such as the poet William Hamilton (1704–1754) or the friend and fellow philosopher David Hume.[640] Still, since they are all dead, perhaps they do not count *vis-à-vis* calculating "the greatest possible quantity of happiness" in societies blessed by "fortunate violence".

Furthermore, as I had anticipated, the dead now enjoy eternal peace, i.e. the highest form of bliss. Far from "the stormy ocean of human life", they have reached the condition that the Stoics described as "the safe and quiet harbour of death".[641] According to Smith, we commonly worry about the dead because we put ourselves into their shoes as though they were still alive, which they are not. Quite the opposite, they have reached a level of tranquillity that no human "calamity" can damage:

> We sympathize even with the dead, and overlooking what is of real importance in their situation, that awful futurity which awaits them, we are chiefly affected by those circumstances which strike our senses, but can have no influence upon their happiness. It is miserable, we think, to be deprived of the light of the sun; to be shut out from life and conversation; to be laid in the cold grave, a prey to corruption and the reptiles of the earth; to be no more thought of in this world, but to be obliterated, in a little time, from the affections, and almost from the memory, of their dearest friends and relations. Surely, we imagine, we can never feel too much for those who have suffered so dreadful a calamity... The happiness of the dead, however, most assuredly, is affected by none of these circumstances; nor is it the thought of these things which can ever disturb the profound security of their repose... It is from this very

illusion of the imagination, that the foresight of our own dissolution is so terrible to us, and that the idea of those circumstances, which undoubtedly can give us no pain when we are dead, makes us miserable while we are alive.[642]

God's benevolence can derive the good from every and any evil, death included. It is impossible to find any aspect of reality, no matter how lethal or unpleasant, that escapes "the Deity" and her "plan of Providence",[643] which "contrived the system of human affections, as well as that of every other part of nature".[644] According to Smith, "every part of nature, when attentively surveyed, equally demonstrates the providential care of its Author, and we may admire the wisdom and goodness of God even in the weakness and folly of man".[645]

Fear of death is itself one such example: "one of the most important principles in human nature, the dread of death, the great poison to the happiness" is equally "the great restraint upon the injustice of mankind, which, while it afflicts and mortifies the individual, guards and protects the society."[646] Analogously, the hope of *post-mortem* immortality demonstrates as well the benign workings of the same "plan of Providence":

> Our happiness in this life is... upon many occasions, dependent on the humble hope and expectation of a life to come: a hope and expectation deeply rooted in human nature; which can alone support its lofty ideas of its own dignity; can alone illumine the dreary prospect of its continually approaching mortality, and maintain its cheerfulness under all the heaviest calamities to which, from the disorders of this life, it may sometimes be exposed.[647]

Imbued with the cosmic optimism that faith in the divine ordering of human affairs can engender, TMS depicts a universe that would be good no matter what sort of human action occurs within it.

Fearing death, seeking it, looking forward to it as a door that will let us enter a blissful new condition: no matter how we respond to our mortality, God's "invisible hand" will turn our choices into something good for society (in his *Astronomy*, Smith calls it "the invisible hand of Jupiter" that the ancient philosophers never "apprehended").[648]

Economics and Justice

Human action extends to the forms of economic organisation that a society develops. In a providentially led universe, there can be no order of property and trade, out of which "the Deity" could not derive eventual human happiness. *Pace* Smith's own defence of private property and free trade in WN, or his followers' vocal advocacy of *laissez faire*, TMS makes it clear that God is both benevolent and omnipotent, to the point of having an all-encompassing providential plan in place, in which any course of human action leads to eventual positive outcomes. While human beings ought to do their part in the universe and try to be decent persons, family members, friends and citizens, God does His own part, which is to secure that good prevails always, no matter the circumstances:

> The administration of the great system of the universe, however, the care of the universal happiness of all rational and sensible beings, is the business of God and not of man. To man is allotted a much humbler department, but one much more suitable to the weakness of his powers, and to the narrowness of his comprehension; the care of his own happiness, of that of his family, his friends, his country.[649]

Consistently with this standard Christian conception, *all* kinds of human actions are covered by "Providence", which extracts *ex malo bonum* under any condition. Smith himself refers to "weakness and folly", as well as to more reasonable behaviours, including some that would clearly interfere with the regularly unequal and often deadly allotment of wealth that we observe in human societies:

> [M]an is by Nature directed to correct, in some measure, that distribution of things which she herself would otherwise have made. The rules which for this purpose she prompts him to follow, are different from those which she herself follows… The rules which she follows are fit for her; those which he follows for him: but both are calculated to promote the same great end, the order of the world, and the perfection and happiness of human nature.[650]

Smith resisted vocally such interferences, possibly out of political partisanship rather than philosophical rigour, religious allegiance and strict logic. According to his own unrestricted application of providential extraction of good from ill, if madmen can produce positive outcomes, why shouldn't too greedy merchants and interfering administrators?

Besides, Smith was not a die-hard libertarian, at least as this term is commonly understood today in Anglophone countries. In WN, for example, Smith speaks favourably of State laws, law enforcement, courts of law, the public regulation of banks and working conditions in order to avoid the mental and physical devastation of the labourers, public education, public armies and navies (as opposed to private mercenaries), large-scale public works that no private person could afford either individually or jointly with others, diplomatic and governing bodies, as well as of progressive taxation of income aimed at providing the financial means to see to all of the above. Combined with Smith's labour theory of value, 19th-century socialists like Karl Marx derived from Smith's writings notions aimed at criticising some of the most life-harming aspects of the Industrial Revolution, which Smith witnessed in its earliest infancy and insightfully assessed in both its potential for increased productivity (i.e. the 'miracles' of the division of labour) and human affliction (i.e. the physical and mental destructiveness of factory life).

Nevertheless, it is absolutely true that Smith's overall picture of a well-functioning economy stipulates that the small boat of the common-good-aimed State ought to sail over a much larger ocean of free, self-interested private initiative. Smith was a liberal, at least as this term is normally understood in European countries. Consistently, God's "invisible hand" is said to be the best means of optimal allocation of resources, not conscious human agency, even if well-meaning and occasionally correct:

> By preferring the support of domestick to that of foreign industry, [every individual] intends only his own security; and by directing that industry in such a manner as its produce may be of the greatest value, he intends only his own gain, and he is in this, as in many other cases, led by an invisible hand to promote an end which was no part of his intention. Nor is it always the worse for society that it was no part of it. By pursuing his own interest he frequently promotes that of the society more effectually than when he really intends to promote it.[651]

As corollaries of this claim, Smith targets a number of historically commonplace interferences, of which he disapproves, since divinely ordained nature can be trusted to see to the overall balance of nations and their economies.[652] The visible and, at times, heavy hand of the State and its bureaucracy is one of these interferences:

> What is the species of domestic industry which his capital can employ, and of which the produce is likely to be of the greatest value, every individual, it is evident, can, in his local situation, judge much better than any statesman or lawgiver can do for him. The statesman, who should attempt to direct private people in what manner they ought to employ their capitals, would not only load himself with a most unnecessary attention, but assume an authority which could safely be trusted, not only to no single person, but to no council or senate whatever, and which would no-where be so dangerous as in the hands of a man who had folly and presumption enough to fancy himself fit to exercise it. To

give the monopoly of the home-market to the produce of domestic industry, in any particular art or manufacture, is in some measure to direct private people in what manner they ought to employ their capitals, and must, in almost all cases, be either a useless or a hurtful regulation.[653]

Revolutions and political upheavals are also condemned, even when philosophical reason may justify politically motivated murders, especially tyrannicide—a tyrant being nothing less than the "one who deprives the people of their liberty, levies armies and taxes, and puts the citizens to death as he pleases".[654] As Smith writes: "That kings are the servants of the people, to be obeyed, resisted, deposed, or punished, as the public conveniency may require, is the doctrine of reason and philosophy; but it is not the doctrine of Nature. Nature would teach us to submit to them for their own sake, to tremble and bow down before their exalted station."[655]

Of all crimes, however, it is theft, which redistributes forcibly the existing wealth, the one that is most vocally rejected. According to Smith, it is even worse "than death" itself:

> The poor man must neither defraud nor steal from the rich, though the acquisition might be much more beneficial to the one than the loss could be hurtful to the other... [for] he renders himself the proper object of the contempt and indignation of mankind; as well as of the punishment which that contempt and indignation must naturally dispose them to inflict, for having thus violated one of those sacred rules, upon the tolerable observation of which depend the whole security and peace of human society. There is no commonly honest man who does not more dread the inward disgrace of such an action, the indelible stain which it would for ever stamp upon his own mind, than the greatest external calamity which, without any fault of his own, could possibly befal him... [theft] is more contrary to nature, than death, than poverty, than pain, than all the misfortunes which can affect him.[656]

Under this perspective, whilst equity is secondary throughout TMS and WN, justice, i.e. fairness according to the existing laws, is not. For Smith, it possesses an important instrumental character associated with the securing of private property, free trade and, *a fortiori,* the generation of social prosperity. As we have already seen in the previous chapter, Smith argues that the original and fundamental function of laws and civil institutions, which have dispensed capital punishments for generations across the world, is precisely to establish and protect private property, especially from the poorer masses that may want it redistributed, either lawfully or unlawfully: "Civil government, so far as it is instituted for the security of property, is in reality instituted for the defence of the rich against the poor, or of those who have some property against those who have none at all."[657]

Jurisprudence and Legal Psychology

Death and mortality come up frequently in Smith's works whenever dealing with the realm of diplomacy and law, e.g. the legal implications resulting from someone's and/or many people's death, such as wills and inheritances,[658] debt settlements,[659] monarchic successions,[660] the care of orphans,[661] the end of marriages (including polygamy)[662] and the commencement of wars.[663]

Another area of legal reality closely associated with death is the penal sphere. For example, Smith cites "[t]he ancient Athenians, who solemnly punished the axe which had accidentally been the cause of the death of a man".[664] Apart from showing a primitive, superstitious outlook, this sort of behaviour reveals as well how deeply shocking the wanton destruction of another person's life can be to the minds and hearts of her peers: "Death is the greatest evil which one man can inflict upon another, and excites the highest degree of resentment in those who are immediately connected with the slain. Murder, therefore, is the most atrocious of all crimes which affect individuals only, in the sight both of mankind, and of the person who has committed it."[665] The mere attempt at taking someone's life can instil so much "terror" that the "resentment of mankind" dictates that the suitable punishment "ought in all countries to be capital".[666]

According to Smith, a violent emotional response to all such severe faults is entirely natural; "the most dreadful crimes" call for "vengeance", which even people "of the most detestable character" may later seek upon themselves in the unlikely hope of atonement.[667] Even when admitting of cases of "furious resentment" whereby an injured party may judge "the death of his enemy… a small compensation for the wrong", Smith shows neither perplexity nor disapproval at the vengeful "pleasure" that people take "to burn or destroy… [a]nimals" or even an inanimate "instrument which had accidentally been the cause of the death of a friend".[668] "The distress" of a "man of humanity" who caused a fatal accident without fault is expected to be deep and intense.[669] Failing to experience such deep and violent emotions in one's heart makes Smith talk of "inhumanity".[670]

Horrible crimes should normally elicit, among the interested persons, adequately strong feelings of vengeance and guilt. Smith writes that "Nature" herself "teaches us to hope" that these horrible deeds, if they are not punished in this life, must certainly meet with their comeuppance in the next.[671] Religions, on their part, reinforce such beliefs, which are conducive to social order, i.e. that recurring long-term, collective axiological horizon that plays a pivotal role in Smith's worldview and allows him to accept in an aloof and generally positive manner even the cruellest deaths:

> Our sense of its ill desert pursues it, if I may say so, even beyond the grave, though the example of its punishment there cannot serve to deter the rest of mankind, who see it not, who know it not, from being guilty of the like practices here. The justice of God, however, we think, still requires, that he should hereafter avenge the injuries of the widow and the fatherless, who are here so often insulted with impunity. In every religion, and in every superstition that the world has ever beheld, accordingly, there has been a Tartarus as well as an Elysium; a place provided for the

punishment of the wicked, as well as one for the reward of the just.⁶⁷²

Much weaker resentment is prompted by actions that we regard as potentially calamitous for society at large and punish accordingly, though this time upon rational bases rather than emotional ones. A calculated extinction of life is not as easily justifiable as an emotionally laden one. For example:

> [W]e both punish and approve of punishment, merely from a view to the general interest of society, which, we imagine, cannot otherwise be secured… A centinel, for example, who falls asleep upon his watch, suffers death by the laws of war, because such carelessness might endanger the whole army. This severity may, upon many occasions, appear necessary, and, for that reason, just and proper. When the preservation of an individual is inconsistent with the safety of a multitude, nothing can be more just than that the many should be preferred to the one. Yet this punishment, how necessary soever, always appears to be excessively severe.⁶⁷³

As to the most severe of legal chastisements, Smith' *Lectures on Jurisprudence* mention frequently capital punishment, which he considered fully justified in civilised nations when dealing with, *inter alia*, murderers and rapists.⁶⁷⁴ On the other hand, he condemns its use in connection with crimes that were minor in either consequence or degree than the "revenge" to be reasonably expected by "an impartial spectator", such as the illegal "exportation of wool" (to which the British population responded by refusing to serve as "jurors" and "informants", hence hindering its concrete application).⁶⁷⁵ The "fellow feeling" of "resentment" or revenge is the psychological and social foundation of criminal law, though it must not be the entirety of the rationale for its institutional practice, which is revenge *cum grano salis*.⁶⁷⁶

Capital punishment is claimed to mirror the stage of civilisation of a nation. Not only is it very common in the early stages of development;[677] also, it reflects the sophistication of the property regime thereby enacted *vis-à-vis* the most valuable assets, *ergo* of the economy itself. For instance, Smith mentions capital punishment for female adultery in ancient Rome[678] and for theft of livestock in pastoral "Tartary" (as opposed to the hunter-gatherer societies of "North America").[679] These economically pivotal assets are usually held by the most powerful members of each society, e.g. the "lands" of feudal lords,[680] the "bill[s] or bond[s]" that are sometimes "forge[d]" by capitally punished criminals in Britain,[681] and the "theft" of large sums of money in England and Scotland.[682]

According to Smith, those who hold the power of life and death over the others can be said to be their rulers in the purest sense possible, whether they are then distinguished from the rest of society because of "aristocraticall" lineage, constitutional distinction or ethnicity.[683] The more absolute is this *potestas vitae necisque*, the starker is the social disparity, e.g. the owner's power to have "a slave… put… to death on the smallest transgression".[684] On this subject, Smith claims also that the exercise of capital punishment by public authorities originated in "the age of shepherds" and that it is necessary in complex economies, insofar as these require public authorities to "preserve the property of the individuals", given that private property, albeit necessary for prosperity, is also the supreme source of embittering inequality and bitter disputes or, in Smith's own words, "the grand fund of all dispute".[685]

Echoing Rousseau, Smith regards deadly violence as occasional and rare in primitive, *de facto* communist societies. On the contrary, as private-property-based civilisation unfolds, "laws and government" become utterly necessary: "[I]ndeed in every case as a combination of the rich to oppress the poor, and preserve to themselves the inequality of the goods which would otherwise be soon destroyed by the attacks of the poor, who if not hindered by the government would soon reduce the others to an equality with themselves by open violence."[686]

The severity of punishments reflects as well the degree of concentration of power in the sovereign's hands, which can be as blood-stained as any private slave-owner's. As Smith observes, in his time and age, only Britain and, even more so, "the republics of Holland and Switzerland" did not punish with death "the author… the writer, printer, or publisher or spreader of… libels and abusive papers",[687] often under the accusation of "treason".[688] Abuses and exaggerated uses of capital punishment are recorded by Smith, including the continuation of punishing as treason, hence even by death, those British subjects that are "so silly as to prefer the Roman Catholick to the Protestant religion."[689] The cruel practices of infanticide under ancient *patria potestas* and modern China are also recorded,[690] as well as the extremely high child mortality among "the meaner and poorer sort" and the slaves, ancient as well as modern, whose life has always been the most expendable.[691]

Concluding Remarks

Death and mortality are everywhere to be found. Not only in Smith's works, but in the very world which these works depict. The commercial society that he praises is, in fact, built upon countless dead bodies of exterminated savages, plus the hard-toiling ones of the labouring masses, whether enslaved or formally free. Nevertheless, this is no reason for despair. There is no doubt, at least to anyone reading TMS in its entirety and with integrity, that Smith presents therein some kind of theodicy, which can make positive sense of all these deaths, even the most callous ones and on the grandest scale imaginable, and of the hard toil endured by the "race of labourers". Whether it is the extermination of the American natives or their replacement by captive slaves, condemned to a life of unfree drudgery, hope is never lost by Smith. Divine providence is at work, whatever ill may seemingly plague humankind on Earth, as Smith's own mentor in moral philosophy, Francis Hutcheson (1694–1746), taught in Glasgow, i.e. one of the main maritime hubs of the growing Atlantic trade in 18th-century Britain.

Whether Smith believed in such a reassuring theodicy, however, it is unclear. According to his own *Astronomy*, philosophy's fundamental aim is to secure as calm an order within each soul as it should be attained within each society. To this end, as Smith argued, natural and moral philosophers produce imaginative (or imaginary?) systems making sense of a reality that is, either *prima facie* or inherently, a bundle of discordant impressions. In this light, TMS and, probably, WN might well tell not what the world is like, perhaps for the simple reason that nobody can do that. Rather, they certainly portray a reassuring orderly picture of the universe. Whether such a picture is or can be true, it is not stated. As Smith observes, each generation of philosophers (*ergo* scientists too) have believed to have reached the "summit of perfection" in the knowledge of the universe.[692] As Smith also acknowledges, different generations have hailed and admired different geniuses and their allegedly definitive accounts. Why should his generation, or ours for that matter, be any closer to the "summit"?

Smith's *Astronomy* leaves the question unanswered. Nor does the question return clearly in any of his other known works. Perhaps that is all that Smith wanted to say on the matter. As to Smith's actual beliefs, therefore, we can only speculate. That the ultimate truths about reality may be unknowable to us was taught by Smith's own Presbyterian creed, which reserved such truths to God's higher intelligence alone. Unknowability of reality was also held by the "sceptical" tenets of successful Scottish Enlightenment thinkers, such as Smith's close friend David Hume.[693] Yet, who would write dense, vast and demanding tomes such as TMS and WN, without believing that he or she could grasp the world for what it is really like? How plausible can it be that Adam Smith was aiming at authoring clever, comprehensive, therapeutic works, the truth of which he would not genuinely warrant himself? We do not possess the answers to these interrogatives, which emerge from a hypothesis that is as intriguing as it is controversial, especially if we consider how many of today's self-declared admirers of Smith often regard a certain streak of economics as the pivotal social science that is capable of grasping reality for what it is and, *a fortiori*, the one that can help us to give shape to a prosperous society.

It can be observed that, possibly because of Smith's attempt at making positive sense of human life at all levels, including the horrifying deaths of millions and our fear of death, TMS and WN have been popular ever since. In particular, since Smith's works regularly justify the wealth of the wealthy and the wealthy's right to defend their wealth against the poor's desire to get part or all of it, both TMS and WN have enjoyed an enduring status *qua* intellectual masterpieces and political Polar Stars among the most powerful sectors of societies in which inequality exists and persists. Ours today is one such society: it is then not overly surprising that Smith is regarded therein as canonical in the disciplines of philosophy, economics and politics.

Whether inherently correct or not, the instrumental appeal of Smith's views to the wealthy and the powerful has occasionally been noted by scholars and, notably, by John Kenneth Galbraith, who was the descendant of Scottish settlers in Canada and, more to the point, tackled in his works the history of economics *qua* sophisticated intellectual apparatus aimed at legitimising the powers that were and that are. It was Galbraith's reasoned belief that most economists, and especially the academically best-entrenched orthodox ones, operated in his day in a way strikingly analogous to Aristotle's, who provided philosophical justifications of slavery in ancient Greece, where slave labour was the rule, and Thomas Aquinas' (1225–1274), who provided theological justifications of private property in the Middle Ages of Western Christendom, when the Church was the single largest landowner in Europe.[694] In particular, in his 1983 book *The Anatomy of Power*, Galbraith addresses the ways in which classical and neoclassical economists assumed the workings of capitalism to be the workings of nature itself.[695]

Thus, David Ricardo is said to have connoted the laws of economics resulting from the study of 18th- and 19th-century British society as essentially consonant with the laws of physics, rather than as the result of local historical arrangements, hence making context-dependant laws, and the contingent economic order they presuppose, seemingly timeless and universal. Reverend Thomas R. Malthus (1766–1834), on his part, blamed the wretched poverty of the working classes of his day on the poor's unrestrained lust and fertility, as though their poverty's aetiology had nothing to do with the economic order of the age. Jeremy Bentham (1748–1832) and the utilitarians equated human happiness with aggregate economic output, thus resisting any social policy that could hinder it. Herbert Spencer and the social Darwinists regarded poverty as the poor's own fault: they were nothing but the weak losers in the competitive game, hence they were being selected out by nature *qua* least fit members of the species; at the same time, their sorry fate was to be accepted as a necessary tool for the species' self-improvement. William S. Jevons, instead, turned hedonistic individualism into a methodological presupposition for the discipline of economics, thus erasing from view *ab ovo* a host of long-lived social and cultural institutions (e.g. the civil commons of 'cleared', clan- and village-based Scottish Highlanders; or the Aristotelian-Thomist concept of the common good *qua* precondition for just economic activity). On top of that, Pareto recorded an unvarying level of inequality throughout human history: hence, according to him, fighting for equality was a futile exercise. Self-professed "progressive" Alfred Marshall, eventually, gave an abstract, logical and compelling mathematical expression to this set of beliefs, the socio-political and ethico-religious roots of which were thus buried behind seemingly neutral and objective symbolic formulae, which are even more commonplace in contemporary economics.

Under this institutionalist, perhaps cynical perspective that Galbraith offers in his works, Adam Smith comes across as a clever and rather prolix hagiographer of the commercial interests that, by the mid-18th century, had already established themselves firmly in Britain as a power to be reckoned with, and the only truly capable of challenging the predominance of the older landed aristocracy that, in association with the Crown, had been the masters of the fate of millions of labouring Britons and colonial subjects. These millions being "they who feed, clothe, and lodge the whole body of the people" even if, as Smith himself acknowledges with his usual composure, they are often denied "such a share of the produce of their own labour as to be themselves tolerably well fed, clothed, and lodged".

Chapter 12: Adam Smith Can Never Be Wrong

The international economic crisis following the 2008 collapse of Lehman Brothers unleashed a flood of *fiat* money by selectively prodigal central banks that have seen fit to keep over-indebted private banks afloat, protect the value of financial assets from inflation, and plunge the world into a prolonged slump.[696] The same crisis also unleashed an outburst of academic literature on the crisis itself, its causes, its effects and its possible solutions. With this literature, a modicum of doubt has re-entered the mainstream of public discourse on topics such as globalisation, capitalism and the free market, to the point that even major national and international newspapers have reported renowned liberals' and conservatives' statements that, until few years ago, would have been associated with leftist 'radicals', right-wing 'nationalists', or 'anachronistic' religious leaders, and generally ignored by mainstream media:

- "The doctrine of the dictatorship of the market is dead" (Nicolas Sarkozy, former President of the French Republic);[697]
- "We need… humaneness… rules… and abandoning the idea of… massive profits" (MIT Nobel-laureate economist Paul A. Samuelson (1915–2009));[698]
- "The dictatorship of the [credit] spread… nullifies… universal suffrage… [because] those who hold economic power… have every decisional power" (former MP and head of Italy's securities and exchange commission [CONSOB] Giuseppe Vegas (b. 1951));[699]
- "There emerge... in civil Europe the first signs of a new type of fascism: financial fascism, white fascism" (Italy's MP and former Finance Minister Giulio Tremonti).[700]

Such statements, though notable, remain uncommon. International economic crises and their dramatic outcomes notwithstanding, certain long-lived, deeply rooted beliefs are truly hard to die. Thus we hear leading politicians and revered economic advisors calling for a return to growth and asserting that structural 'reforms' are imperative, so that market confidence may be re-established and increased competitiveness achieved, without ever pondering upon the fact that these aims are precisely those that guided the global economy before the crisis.[701] Could it ever be that endless growth, market confidence and increased competitiveness are under-defined or even misguided aims for the world's economies (cf. Castoriadis' claim of capitalist "pseudorational pseudomastery")? If even worldwide meltdowns under the technologically most advanced trading conditions and the academically most mature school of orthodox economics cannot undermine the belief in these aims as self-evident and justified, what else can do it?

In this chapter I address one of these resilient beliefs. Specifically, in the traditional philosophical way initiated by Socrates, I assess some conceptual knots arising from a specific hypothesis, that is, the commonplace liberal notion that the so-called "free market" possesses a unique capacity to generate "prosperity". This hypothesis is highly generic, diversely instantiated and potentially vague. In fact, its being highly generic, and *ergo* vague, explains part of the hypothesis' success: since it can apply to many different circumstances, it can be called upon under all or any of them in conveniently tweaked interpretations. Whilst logically perplexing, it can be rhetorically most effective.

Nevertheless, for all its conceptual shiftiness, this hypothesis is worth tackling, for it pervades the whole spectrum of the liberal conceptions of the economy, not only at the level of political rhetoric, but also at the academic level, as exemplified by the microeconomic textbook category of "market imperfections", according to which explaining is needed when the outcomes of market transactions are *not* optimal.[702] Similar considerations apply to macroeconomic stochastic models describing disequilibria as the result of external shocks on an otherwise peaceful ocean of market equilibrium.[703] This hypothesis informs also Adam Smith's canonical "invisible hand", i.e. the doctrine of unintended consequences whereby the individual's pursuit of self-interest results regularly, though not always, in collective wellbeing.

I select here one representative liberal formulation of the hypothesis at issue and deal with those conceptual knots that I deem most evocative. The formulation hereby selected appears in a recent book chapter written by the Swiss liberal thinker Martin Rhonheimer (b. 1950), who claims that the "free market" is "a *necessary* condition" of human prosperity.[704] In his eloquent account of Walter Eucken's (1891–1950) characteristically German ordoliberalism, whereby economic liberalism is twinned with powerful monitoring and corrective public institutions, and the related critique of Anglo-American *laissez-faire* liberalism, Rhonheimer offers in support of his claim one elucidation and one generic token of empirical proof.

The elucidation is that no central planner would be able to coordinate all economic activities as efficiently as the "free market", in which individual agents pursue their own particular self-interest and, by so doing, unintentionally produce prosperity, in accordance with Smith's principle of the "invisible hand".[705] Though not all conditions for prosperity may arise this way, none would arise without it. The "free market" is a necessary condition for prosperity, albeit not a sufficient one, which is instead what more trenchant *laissez-faire* liberals believe. States must also be involved, according to ordoliberalism and few other streaks of liberalism, in order to secure fair market transactions, enforce beneficial rules, correct market distortions, or redress socially and morally harmful market outcomes. Exemplarily, Austrian economist Friedrich A. Hayek himself argued back in 1944 that "there is no doubt that some minimum of food, shelter, and clothing, sufficient to preserve health and the ability to work" should be guaranteed by public institutions, "[n]or is there any reason why the state should not assist the individuals in providing for those common hazards of life against which, because of their uncertainty, few individuals can make adequate provision."[706] However, as Rhonheimer rejoinders, to think that "central planning and state regulation… through several government-run agencies" could ever achieve any prosperity without the "free market" is a foolish notion to be discarded at once.[707]

The generic token of empirical proof is that "history teaches" all this: "a capitalist economy based on a free market, entrepreneurial activity, and free trade without tariff barriers is more realistic and in the long run beneficial for everybody".[708] In this respect, the unrealised failure of Roosevelt's New Deal and a passing reference to the Soviet Union are the two cases of "socialism" that the author utilises to give strength to his point.[709] So obviously flawed and so doomed is the case for socialism that Rhonheimer does not deem it necessary to dwell much on it. Perhaps, it is conventional wisdom, since Rhonheimer writes as though the audience that he addresses with his chapter were most likely to share in the same belief without any hesitation.[710] In this, Rhonheimer follows the tenets of classical rhetoric, which teaches to start from premises that are immediately acceptable to the audience, even if they may not be demonstrated to be true or be simply false.[711]

Indemonstrability

As regards the generic token of empirical proof, the choice of the failed failure of Roosevelt's New Deal strikes as odd, since it is admitted that it was *not* a failure, thanks to the gigantic multiplier effect induced by the war effort of 1939–1945. The choice of the Soviet Union is far more commonplace yet at least as facile, since it ignores the vast literature by Trotskyites and libertarian socialists,[712] as well as by market- and alternative socialists, criticising the URSS' so-called "real socialism" as State capitalism, i.e. a system differing from the Western one in one crucial element alone: State bureaucrats, not shareholders and/or managers, led the wage-labour economy fostering class antagonism.[713]

As regards Rhonheimer's elucidation, though commonly heard, it is not much of an empirical proof. At best, it is an enthymeme, i.e. a rhetorical proof.[714] To make it stick more convincingly, it would require itself many further empirical proofs for adequate scientific substantiation. However, here emerges a severe and frequently unflinchingly by-passed methodological issue. How can anyone prove as binding and comprehensive a thesis as the one presented in

Rhonheimer's essay and, in general, upheld by the liberal community?[715]

The answer is frustratingly simple and scientifically disheartening. The *necessary* character of any economic system cannot be determined in a scientific way, for we have only one planet, one humankind and one very short historical span at our disposal for any empirical verification and/or falsification of the beneficence of the "free market" or, for that matter, of "socialism". For any claim of such a necessary character to be ascertained, we should investigate a set of entirely alternative and separate systems over a certain period of time, probably a very long one, so as to determine that only the ones operating upon the "free market" produce prosperity, at least under certain definitions of it. Unfortunately, to this day, such a test has been impossible to perform.

As the past is concerned, in fact, we know for sure that some civilisations have made it this far. In this connection, we might think of prehistoric, ancient and medieval Earth, let us say before the age of European exploration, as a plausible set of sufficiently separate and alternative economic systems to allows us to conduct a comparative study. Yet, apart from the fact that hardly any of the known ones would count as a free-market or socialist system, we know far too little, if anything, about most of them to make any valid scientific comparison, whatever notion of prosperity we may wish to employ.[716]

If we look at what history has produced until now, we may be in a better position to determine which system has been the most ruthless, hence the one that has imposed itself over the others *via*, say, conquest, extortion, enslavement or mass slaughter. However, that would be a banal and, I suspect, degrading notion of superiority, not to consider the thin or absent link that such a superiority may have to genuine human needs or prosperity. Furthermore, Rhonheimer seems oblivious of the contingent origins and historical development of global market structures themselves, which emerged through a prolonged process involving political, legal, military, monetary and industrial planning by public authorities.[717] Not to mention the socio-cultural and anthropological changes required for actual human beings to think of themselves, and lead their lives as, entrepreneurs, employees, speculators, self-interested individuals, etc. rather than heathen priests, slaves, legionaries, or loyal members of a certain clan or *gens*.[718]

As the present is concerned, there may be alternative but no separate systems, given that even the most isolated indigenous communities in the world are being affected by the environmental changes produced by the advanced economies of the planet.[719] As the future is concerned, unless we deny the ability of humankind to change creatively its collective organisation, which has varied enormously throughout the known history of our species, we cannot even begin to fathom what awaits our descendants: a Star-Trek-like society without money, need and greed; or a Mad-Max-like post-atomic age of competitive barbarism? Yet this is the province of science-fiction, not of science.

Focussing onto the "market" *versus* "socialist" dichotomy is also fundamentally misleading *vis-à-vis* the history of humankind as such, since it shifts the gaze away from what is undeniably necessary for the meaningful survival of our species, i.e. the continued satisfaction of genuine human needs across generational time, as poignantly argued by life-value onto-axiology. That is the prime end, whatever additional feature we may wish to add to the notion of prosperity, such as "freedom" or "political rights": economies are the means to attain *in primis* this prime end.[720]

On this point, the UN's Committee on Economic, Social and Cultural Rights (CESCR) has long espoused an aim-driven approach, rather than a means-driven one. The specific economic system of each member nation is not important, as long as the proper steps are taken and human rights are therefore protected, respected and fulfilled:

> [T]he undertaking "to take steps… by all appropriate means including particularly the adoption of legislative measures" neither requires nor precludes any particular form of government or economic system being used as the

vehicle for the steps in question, provided only that it is democratic and that all human rights are thereby respected. Thus, in terms of political and economic systems, the Covenant [on Economic, Social and Cultural Rights] is neutral and its principles cannot accurately be described as being predicated exclusively upon the need for, or the desirability of a socialist or a capitalist system, or a mixed, centrally planned, or laissez-faire economy, or upon any particular approach.[721]

I deem the CESCR's approach as a paradigm of intellectual openness and life-grounded acumen, especially if we consider how civil commons institutions have been widespread, long before any capitalist, liberal, communist or socialist economic order came into being.

Whose and Which Prosperity?

If we follow Rhonheimer's representative formulation and understand prosperity as "*consumption*, that is, the satisfaction of the needs of *all* the persons living in a determinate territory", we quite simply lack information about most human communities in most parts of the world throughout most of human history.[722] Presently, the past is closed to us; and so is the future, for we cannot predict with exactitude what will happen on our planet tomorrow, not to mention in two years or two centuries. At best, we can infer from the worldwide depletion of natural and social LSS that continuing along the current path of extraction, transformation, marketing, sale, consumption and disposal of commodities does not bode well for future life, which is being destroyed in many ways, including one of the largest mass extinction of animal species known to us.[723]

Also, as the history of today's world is concerned i.e. the so-called "global market", which is usually claimed to be an imperfect instantiation of the "free market" (Rhonheimer himself does so at times), we know for sure the following: it fails to satisfy the *needs* of *all* the persons living on the planet, as the UN's annual statistics on death by malnourishment and starvation regularly report.[724]

While failing these persons' needs, the current imperfect instantiation of the "free market" also caters to artificially instilled *wants* of *some*, including the profitable and profited desires for carcinogenic cigarettes and life-shortening junk food.[725] The global market fails not only to secure planet-wide need-satisfaction, which is what Rhonheimer appears to be taking as "consumption", but also to distinguish between, say, the need for bread of starving paupers and the desire for golden toilets of oil tycoons, so as to prioritise the former above the latter. No distinction between genuine human needs and sheer subjective wants is built firmly within current liberal economics.[726] Quite the opposite, what sets in motion the "free market" in both theory and practice is money-backed demand, i.e. subjective preferences or wants of market agents endowed with pecuniary means, not the vital necessities of humans and societies, not to mention other living beings, whose possession of pecuniary means may be nil.

What is more, many a subjective preference and want are the result of artificial conditioning by the most sophisticated marketing techniques, without which they are unlikely to arise.[727] To top it all, under present conditions, wealth can be accumulated by some to unprecedented heights, while at the same time access to basic sanitation or healthcare is denied to others.[728] Money-backed demand, not need, is what determines consumption in today's world, *pace* Rhonheimer's noteworthy equation.

Revealingly, mainstream economists and, above all, the actual economy of many countries, treat both food and luxury items as priced, marketable goods.[729] No axiological compass is present for basic distinctions between that which is of real value and that which is not, or that which is good and that which is bad. Economic ordinalism may depict a night in which all cows are black, but neither any so-called economic "good", nor all so-called economic "goods", are good. Some are bad. For example, financial speculation over the price of staples such as rice and wheat may be deemed economically rational and itself a form of standard wealth creation, indeed to enormous nominal levels, but it does increase malnutrition and illnesses, which are clear tokens of badness.[730]

Axiologically, the invisible hand seems to possess an invisible brain, which is why ordoliberals *à la* Rhonheimer, unlike libertarians and *laissez-faire* liberals, have long recognised the importance of at least some State intervention. State intervention is *per se* no guarantee of fairness, equality or prosperity, since it may, *inter alia*, favour select clients, bail out private businesses at the expense of the population at large, or lead to disastrous wars. Rather, State intervention flags out the need for guiding, integrating and/or constraining non-economic values and rationalities (e.g. religious, moral, political, aesthetic, biomedical).[731] A visible brain is required for the hand, whether visible or invisible, not to cause harm.

Imperfections

In connection with the importance of State intervention, Rhonheimer himself introduces a number of additional qualifications that cause the "free market" to come across as more inefficient than initially stated. Albeit he claims it to be a necessary one, the "free market" is not a sufficient condition for prosperity or consumption. It is said that it "frequently" leads to prosperity, i.e. not always.[732] It is incapable of providing many "public goods" (i.e. serving as genuine civil commons).[733] It is prone to "failures".[734] If the State does not intervene, it generates inevitably "cartels".[735] Indeed it possesses inherently "a tendency to destroy itself", given also that it causes major social "problems" such as "inequality" i.e. the root-cause of all major political upheavals and violent revolutions.[736]

These qualifications are unlikely to sound surprising to ordoliberals and many liberals, for, in varying degrees, the near-totality of them have long acknowledged that imperfections, even lethal ones, do affect the market system, including Adam Smith, Thorstein Veblen,[737] and Vilfredo Pareto.[738] They sound even less surprising to professed socialists like Albert Einstein and Cornelius Castoriadis, who remarked persistently upon market economies' self-destructive tendencies. These tendencies have ranged from Marx's allegedly inexorable doom by falling rate of profit[739] to the promotion of anthropological traits such as short-term greed and infantile hedonism, which run counter to those personal virtues of "honesty, integrity, responsibility, care for one's work, respect for others" that market economies inherited from previous societies, built themselves upon, and are yet "incapable of reproducing" to a comparable extent.[740]

However, it is perplexing to notice that qualifications of the actual market economies such as the ones listed by Rhonheimer are generally not seen for what they are, i.e. features of the human-made markets, which consist of living individuals engaging in mutual exchanges under certain types of selectively chosen and enforced norms.[741] On the contrary, in a strange twist of logic, they are seen as exceptions to the implicit rule, which assumes markets to be perfect, even if they are not perfect and have proven repeatedly not to be so in many and sometimes most dramatic ways.

Indeed, few years before his death, John Kenneth Galbraith argued the very talk of "free market" or "market system" to be nothing but a "fraud" (in the title of his last book) aimed at hiding the historical fact of "capitalism", that is to say, a much more fitting descriptor of real market economies, in which there have always been:[742]

- At least one powerful group of players planning the economy to suit their own advantage (e.g. merchants, industrialists, absentee owners, corporate managers, financial managers); as well as
- Conspicuous market manipulation (including creating demand by operant conditioning techniques); and
- Conditions of monopoly and oligopoly covering key-areas of the economic arena (e.g. credit), if not most of it.

After about fifty years of activity as one of the world's best-known economists, Galbraith reached a conclusion that, until now, has been thoroughly ignored by most of his colleagues, for accepting it to any significant extent would demand a Copernican revolution within his discipline. According to him, contemporary economics and business studies teach a number of fraudulent notions that make economists popular among the rich and powerful, and are so commonly repeated and commended that most economists accept them uncritically, thus making these lies "innocent" (again, in the very title of the book). The lies are that:

- There exists a market system, rather than capitalism (the just-seen "renaming");[743]
- Consumers are the price-determining sovereign, rather than corporate pawns being moulded through and through by the most sophisticated marketing techniques;[744]
- Annual GDP marks progress, despite past greatness in poorer societies and present environmental devastation in richer ones;[745]
- "Work" applies equally to the poor, for whom unemployment means destitution and blame, and the rich, for whom it means leisure and distinction;[746]
- States alone have self-serving bureaucracies, not private corporations;[747]
- Individual entrepreneurs are the standard economic agent, rather than large corporate entities, and that the two are equivalent anyway;[748]
- Shareholders have decisional power, rather than the managerial class;[749]
- The public sector is separate from, and interferes with, the private one, whilst corporate interests have hijacked public bodies at all levels (e.g. the military-industrial complex in the US);[750]
- Business-friendly deregulation is good for growth, rather than the root of larcenous private abuse over the public at large;[751]
- Finance experts monitor and forecast likely economic trends, which are unknown and unknowable by definition;[752]
- Market discipline is the rule, whilst those who bear the brunt of economic failures are innocent employees and their families, not the wealthier actual decision-makers;[753]

- Monetary policy matters, whilst central banks are largely ceremonial, for businesses start borrowing again, and banks lending, when profits are foreseen, irrespective of central banks' decisions.[754]

Textbooks often refer to methodological convenience when explaining why economists assume abstract, unreal, perfect market conditions.[755] Though understandable, such a prioritisation of methodological convenience over empirical evidence is a grave departure from standard scientific methodology, as Veblen had already acknowledged one century ago.[756] Galileo may have invited the scientific inquirer to reason *ex hypothesi*, but he never maintained that contrary evidence should be systematically side-stepped in order not to change the starting hypothesis.[757] In the natural sciences, hypotheses are meant to be tested and revised in light of empirical evidence, as done, for example, by system theorists Vitali, Glattfeder and Battiston with regard to "the network of global corporate control" that characterises today's world economy.[758] Facts, as unpleasant as they may be, should be the backbone of scientific inquiry. Only the formal sciences, i.e. logic and mathematics, content themselves with coherent theoretical constructs.[759]

Referents?

The absence of exact instantiations of the growingly unempirical "free market" is only the beginning. If we allow for some State intervention, as Rhonheimer does, what should count then as truly "free market" and "socialist" economies? Where should we draw the line of demarcation?

These two terms are almost omnipresent in both recent political history and scholarship, yet their actual separation is far from obvious. Indeed, from a conservative perspective, liberals and socialists can be hardly distinguishable from each other, as the political critiques by Pope Pius X (1835–1914) and Friedrich Nietzsche exemplify.[760] Furthermore, before the 20th century, most societies in human history had not been market societies. They may have contained some markets, such as slave trade in the ancient Mediterranean, but most of their members did not participate in them.[761] As far as we can ascertain, subsistence, redistribution and reciprocity were their main features.[762] These features were reflected also in these societies' cultures, which kept the analogues of today's economic rationality as secondary instruments to other primary social goals, such as community status, personal honour, or the salvation of the believer's immortal soul.[763]

It should be observed that great achievements were possible in these older societies, whether in the fine arts, philosophy, mathematics, architecture, poetry, drama, law or religious life. Such human accomplishments seem to have little to do with "free markets" or the size of a country's GDP, and perhaps may be unrelated to whatever broad prosperity the liberal hypothesis at issue implies. Still, it is not aimless to ponder upon the fact that even the great scientific discoveries that led to the technologies whereby 20th-century human populations boomed worldwide, in both self-proclaimed "capitalist" and "socialist" economies, were made in countries with smaller GDPs than today and, often, limited or quasi-absent market systems.[764]

Moreover, modern societies, in which commercial and financial markets have become much more extensive and influential, have often retained—sometimes up to the present day—significant elements of subsistence, redistribution and reciprocity (e.g. small-scale farms in Scotland, Poland and India; national and international poverty alleviation programmes; 'old pals" networks and 'revolving doors' inside corporate bureaucracies),[765] as well as many development-spurring elements of public ownership and planning, such as: independent Venice's pioneering, publicly owned merchant and military fleets; George C. Marshall's (1880–1959) post-WWII European Recovery Program; or Germany's, Brazil's, North Dakota's and communist China's public banks.[766] Rhonheimer himself claims that genuine free markets existed worldwide only for a brief period of time, i.e. "between 1850 and 1870", and that the self-proclaimed "free market" post-WWII US have resembled post-WWI Germany in maintaining the State-centred structures inherited from their war economies, which still allow the State, for one, to bail out bankrupt private firms.[767]

Given Rhonheimer's own standards, the issue of identifying genuinely "free market" and "socialist" economies is not an easy one by any stretch of imagination. Not even the post-war US may count as a decent token of the former type of economy, at least according to Rhonheimer, who compares them to the historical champion of cartel-friendly organised capitalism, i.e. Wilhelmine Germany.[768] Any firm, trenchant scientific evaluation of the historical experience of concrete societies seems therefore less and less likely, at least if we take Rhonheimer's considerations seriously, since we lack clear referents for the key-terms of "market" and "socialist" economies.[769]

Non-existence

The distance from concrete societies increases further whenever it is asserted, as Rhonheimer does, that the "free market" is an ideal, i.e. something that does not truly exist in reality (I do not dwell on the contradiction entailed by his claim about free markets having existed worldwide only for a brief period of time in the 19th century).[770] In other words, it is a purely theoretical construct, an empirical impossibility: the human being is actually incapable of operating according to it. Perfect markets, in whatever Hyperuranion they may be located, are therefore not to be blamed for crises, unemployment or any other misfortune that may befall upon us. People are. The former are not around. The latter are.

Rhonheimer seems not to notice the troublesome implications of such an approach, for not only does it mean that there is no clear empirical evidence that free markets are the one, necessary way to prosperity, but also that there cannot be any, for they have never been truly present, since they are not suited to "the human condition", as he writes.[771] Moreover, he does not seem to notice that his approach is analogous to that of many 20th-century Marxist zealots who, when confronted with the failures of Eastern Europe's "real socialism", argued that their theory was correct, since its practice alone had failed, given various and varying human flaws. In this manner, no amount of contrary empirical evidence could disprove their theoretical stance.

Unfalsifiability

The Marxist zealots' case leads us to the most fundamental and most intractable conceptual knot of the liberal position with regard to the markets' unique ability to generate prosperity. This knot can be summarised as follows:

- If the genuine "free market" cannot be established, for it is a theoretical construct inconsistent with "the human condition", and
- If the actual historical experience of what is commonly referred to as the "free market", i.e. the history of mostly Western developed countries over the past three centuries, is one of considerably imperfect applications involving significant elements of State intervention (e.g. post-bellic Germany and US),
- Then, why is the market system *necessarily* responsible for wealth and, to some extent, wellbeing (i.e. prosperity), whereas, say, significant State intervention and public ownership of strategic resources are not? Why not the two of them together, on a par?[772] Or why not either of them, or other factors (e.g. literacy, patriotism, military strength, science-technology), depending on the specific circumstances of each particular case, duly investigated by means of close historical, economic, legal, medical, sociological, anthropological, environmental and axiological analyses? Principled comparisons are possible, but they must rest on solid empirical ground. Reality may well be messy, diverse and complex. Why should there be one necessary source of prosperity for all cases?[773]

By his own account and qualifications, Rhonheimer has no

answer to offer to these questions. Quite simply, he states his thesis and uses it to read history in order to be allowed to state it. In other words, Rhonheimer is assuming *a priori* that the "free market" produces necessarily wealth and, at least to some extent, wellbeing. By means of that assumption he then reads human history as its verification—State-led development, recurrent crises, vast environmental degradation and social tragedies notwithstanding. No proof of whether or which causes of wealth and wellbeing is sought, for history cannot be interpreted in any other manner *ab initio*.

This is not just a case of rash oversimplification, which it certainly is too, such that it would be necessary to pause and specify which forms of market transactions are beneficial in which ways to which groups of people under which circumstances. It is also a profound methodological flaw. It does not apply solely to Rhonheimer's essay, but also to political liberalism and mainstream economic thinking in general—and that is why it is being discussed in this chapter. In effect, it does begin with Adam Smith's WN and reaches its highest peak in *laissez-faire* economics, which argues that the "free market" is the necessary *and* sufficient condition for human prosperity. In all of its forms, it is an example of scientific unfalsifiability, or pseudo-science, for such an assumption, whereby "free markets" are bound to generate prosperity, admits of *no* counterevidence whatsoever. Specifically, the structure of the underlying paralogism is as follows:[774]

(a) First of all, insofar as it is assumed that unhindered markets bring about prosperity, if we do not have prosperity now, then we must simply wait and abstain from causing undue hindrance. As Christians and Marxists have long known, eschatology calls for patience; hence the recurrent future-driven phrases commonly attached to so-called "market reforms", which are assumed to be proven and justified by benefits that do not yet exist and might never exist: "transition", "in the long run", "long-term benefits", "children and grandchildren", etc.[775]

(b) Secondly, if waiting is not a practicable option, then someone else but the market can always be blamed, such as the government (e.g. recurrent accusatory phrases involving public authorities' "corruption", "red tape", "interference", "distortion"), the trade unions (*qua* common and often sole textbook example of "rent-seeking special interest group") or some dishonest private actors (e.g. "crony capitalism", "State capture by private interests", "bad apples"), for being unfaithful to the spirit of "free markets" and causing hindrance. Markets fail not; people do—although one can legitimately wonder what markets may be if not people transacting with one another within a certain normative setting.[776]

(c) Thirdly, insofar as Smith's followers and ordoliberals *à la* Rhonheimer argue as well for the desirability of at least some State intervention (e.g. Smith's progressive taxation, Presbyterian-style education of the youth, public regulation of banks and mentally destructive working conditions; Eucken's redressing of socially detrimental market outcomes), they corner public authorities in a hopeless argumentative position. Given the starting point, growth and prosperity can always be seen as the result of the markets' enduring degree of freedom rather than the State's intervention, while crisis and misery can always be blamed onto the State, i.e. not onto the markets being actually unable to generate growth or genuine prosperity. Even the recent financial collapse of 2007–2008 has been blamed on insufficient State regulation and supervision, despite deregulation and freedom from State interference being precisely the policies that self-proclaimed free-market advocates had been promoting, successfully, for decades.[777]

(d) Operating under such an assumption, markets can never be wrong, whatever major environmental or social ills may have arisen, and eliminate *a priori* the need for serious empirical investigation. If things go well, it is because markets have been allowed to work out their so-called "magic" (hence self-maximising rational agents are said to have responded to incentives, entrepreneurship and innovation to have been rewarded, etc.): a textbook case. If things do not go well, then the guilty party is always someone or something else, including protectionism,[778] unpredictable "financial tsunamis"[779] and excessive cocaine intake.[780] Mainstream economics proceeds as though market agents become immediately something else as soon as their behaviour is not conducive to the expected results. Yet those agents, amongst whom there may certainly be cocaine-addicted bankers and brokers, are actually the market actors whose behaviour the empirical scientist should observe, describe and predict, probabilistically or in even weaker ways, but always *a posteriori*. On the contrary, by operating as an *a priori* science, the unintended consequences detected by orthodox economics are such that, if they are positive, their intended premise is the free market; if negative, instead, it is invariably something else.

(e) *A fortiori*, if the markets do not deliver the promised bounty, it is because there have not been enough, or they have not been "free" enough; hence the cure can only be more of the same.[781] Unsurprisingly, this is exactly what happens in Rhonheimer's 2012 essay: "markets", he says, are *"normally* and *as a matter of principle* the solution".[782] Similarly, leading statesmen, politicians and economic advisors seek more of the same, even after promoting market-oriented policies for decades (e.g. the EU's competition policies).[783] If these policies have not been glaringly successful—they cannot but conclude, given the starting assumption—it is because there is still too limited a market system in place (e.g. former EU competition commissioner Mario Monti).[784]

John Quiggin (b. 1956) dubs "zombie" those economic beliefs that, despite contrary evidence, creep back relentlessly.[785] The unfalsifiability of the liberal hypothesis discussed in the present text explains why this 'non-death' occurs, such that even after the recent disastrous deregulation experiment in the financial sector, or the older catastrophes of 1914 and 1929, free-market adherents may still believe that "the more… interfering with the market system, the greater the insecurity".[786]

Spill-overs

Rhonheimer's essay is fallacious because of the self-contradictory morass resulting from (i) insisting upon the markets' necessary beneficence, whilst also (ii) piling up observations and qualifications that point precisely to the opposite conclusion and (iii) to the empirical non-testability of (i). Representative of analogous liberal assessments, his essay is built upon an unfalsifiable hypothesis that has made him—and many liberals—unable to:

(a) Read historical experience in ways that might (a1) acknowledge a much higher level of complexity (e.g. the role of trade unions' demands in forcing capitalism to become civilised and allowing for a higher share of the existing wealth to reach the population at large and improve overall living conditions;[787] the analogous role of socialist, religious and/or conservative agendas in civilising capitalism;[788] the prevailing mixed[789] as well as oligo- and monopolistic character of modern capitalism[790]), or (a2) contradict the original assumption (e.g. ecological collapse[791] and waste accumulation;[792] recurrent economic crises;[793] enduring unemployment;[794] the failure of most businesses and products launched every year;[795] successful national development and/or post-war reconstruction by public planning of industrial production or strategic subsidies[796]);

(b) Avoid engaging in pseudo-scientific (b1) *ad hoc* explanations (e.g. the State's pro-market legislation, deregulation, liberalisation and privatisation are to blame, for they were erroneous, corrupt or insufficient; State institutions are to blame for financial crashes, because of some minor change in the laws that unleashed an otherwise impossible flood of private greed; Mexican, Korean, Russian, Icelandic... *X* culture is not ready or adequate for a well-functioning "free market" economy),[797] or (b2) sweeping *de facto* exculpations, so as not to perform serious empirical studies and possibly revise the original assumption (e.g. people fail markets, not *vice versa*; capitalists fail, not capitalism; human nature itself is not suited to the actual application of the "free market" and therefore leads to its historical failure);[798]

(c) Envision different, hybrid, pragmatic, contingent or case-specific solutions to socio-economic problems (e.g. context-based mixed economies; voluntary communes, cooperatives and social enterprises; State ownership of strategic assets *qua* cost-abating additional factor of production; Georgist taxation of economic rent from natural resources; socially constructive cooperation with oligopolies; ritual debt cancellation; sustainable retreat by carbon rationing; market socialism) that are typically pushed forth by other actors (e.g. trade unions, religious groups, philanthropists, green parties) for reasons that have little or nothing to do with so-called "free markets" (e.g. better salaries, social cohesion, national prestige, fear of revolt, humaneness, conservationism);[799]

(d) Conceive of alternative systems, whether based on past experiences or untested and novel ones—freedom entailing creativity and change that cannot be predicted in advance. Despite its recurrent talk of "liberty" and "freedom", and its systemic avoidance of insufferable facts notwithstanding, the liberal mind-set castrates imagination *ab initio* by assuming the received conditions to be somehow rational and only limitedly perfectible, but not something that could or should be overcome altogether.[800] Under this respect, Adam Smith's WN prefigures and exemplifies the unimaginative character of liberal 'realism' by dismissing 'utopian' ideas such as the worldwide abolition of slavery, universal literacy, democratic constitutions, the UK-wide abolition of commercial barriers, the humane treatment of primitive colonial subjects, or preventing poor workers and their families from being wiped out by famines and disease in times of crisis.

Concluding Remarks

If my argument is sound, then contemporary politics, influential policies and entire academic programmes are built upon an unscientific assumption. I do not object to having unscientific assumptions. Indeed, some of the most important dimensions of human existence are built upon unscientific assumptions, such as intimate love and religious life. I do object to doing so, though, and not admitting it.

Were liberals, and mainstream economists in particular, to state that, given some partially successful partial instantiations of the market system, they *hope* or have *faith* that the markets, left largely unhindered, may provide us (or some of us) with future prosperity, then they would be intellectually honest. They could follow in the steps of Richard Rorty (1931–2007), who advocates political liberalism *qua* hopeful civil religion of democracy.[801] They would be consistent with Friedrich A. Hayek's characterisation of the market order as "transcendent" and comparable to the religious one in assuming that its own unfathomable will, "not mine" i.e. humankind's, "be done".[802] They would bear witness to Keynes' claim that non-rational passions determine market trends and his warning that his own future-driven theory might be merely "a visionary hope".[803] They would be reminiscent of the Providential character of Adam Smith's "invisible hand".[804] But how many liberals and mainstream economists could even barely commence to fathom doing anything like it?

By pursuing mathematics-like *a priori* deductive science and mixing it with enough conveniently selected data, mainstream economists claim to have reached the peak of reliability and 'hardness' in the social sciences, which they are likely to criticise for being far too often far too 'soft', i.e. vaguer and far less predictive than physics and chemistry. If there is any totem that they bow to most frequently, that is a somewhat mythical notion of science, not plain old-fashioned religion. Though a strong quasi-religious element is present in their discipline since at least Adam Smith's day, as this has been identified by the likes of Galbraith,[805] Hobsbawm,[806] McMurtry[807] and Robert H. Nelson (b. 1944),[808] its adherents have no knowledge or awareness of it. Standard textbooks in economics say nothing about it. On the contrary, they:

- Assume the free markets' existence, which is itself empirically doubtful and at best historically limited, as *per* Rhonheimer's own statements;
- Assume away any shortcoming by presupposing methodologically the free markets' perfection; and
- Ascribe to the free markets the necessary generation of prosperity, whatever contrary evidence there has been in human experience, such as: State-led development (e.g. communist China); prosperous cartel-intensive economies (e.g. Bismarck's Germany); the collapse of the first age of market globalisation and the ensuing Great War and Great Depression; the growing populations and living standards of 20th-century constitutionally "socialist" nations (e.g. Viet Nam); or the worldwide depletion of natural and human LSS upon which "the life and health of the billions [are] supported".[809]

Such a reticence about economic reality and the unfalsifiable assumption at issue are not only unscientific; they are also unprofessional. In truth, they are tantamount to a lie. And lying is, under normal circumstances, unethical. I doubt that there is any vulgarly hypocritical self-serving intention to lie or avoid the truth systematically in the writings and statements of committed free-market liberals and mainstream economists, as some unorthodox economists have sometimes argued.[810] Too many and too frequent are the public utterances about the free market's unique ability to generate prosperity. Mendaciousness, double standards and Jesuitical hypocrisy on such a scale would require an incredible amount of inter-subjective coordination and group discipline. Albeit logically possible, it seems practically improbable.

The uncritical acceptance of the hypothesis at issue is much more similar to an embedded structure of superstition, or an internalised religious dogma, rooted deeply in the consciousness of the adherents to liberalism, to the point of becoming a Burkean "prejudice" (i.e. habitual belief without reflexive judgment), a tacit criterion for professional selection and self-censorship or, to use Veblen's famous phrase, a "trained incapacity" to think outside the box inside which they have caged their own minds.[811] It is analogous to the largely unquestioned and openly unquestionable belief in God's existence to be found in Europe's medieval mind-set, amongst both simple laymen and sophisticated scholars. Under this respect, contemporary economics is strikingly analogous to medieval scholastic theology: in its institutional success; in its display of technical skill; in its appeal to young keen minds; in its discussion of unreal perfect abstractions that justify *de iure* and do not challenge *de facto* the *status quo* and those who benefit most from it; in its scornful neglect of uninfluential heretics and in its virulent attacks against the influential ones. Then, the very suggestion that free markets may not be a necessary source of prosperity must sound preposterous, if not ungodly, to their ears: a prank at best; a blasphemy at worst. God only knows whether a reformation of their ways, such as the one invoked long ago by Thorstein Veblen, will ever succeed among them.[812]

Chapter 13: Five Books of Economic History

I. *Francesco Boldizzoni,* The Poverty of Clio: Resurrecting Economic History, *2011*
II. *Stephen J. Collier,* Post-Soviet Social: Neoliberalism, Social Modernity, Biopolitics, *2011*
III. *Andreas Kruck,* Private Ratings, Public Regulations: Credit Rating Agencies and Global Financial Governance, *2011*
IV. *William N. Goetzmann,* Money Changes Everything: How Finance Made Civilization Possible, *2016*
V. *Volker R. Berghahn*, American Big Business in Britain and Germany: A Comparative History of Two "Special Relationships" in the 20th Century, *2016*

If it were possible to crystallise into a sentence the principal thesis of Francesco Boldizzoni's (b. 1979) slender yet comprehensive assessment of the current state of health of economic history, then it would be the following statement: "One cannot write economic history that is not at the same time social and cultural history".[813]

According to Boldizzoni, economic history in Europe is not only surviving, and even flourishing occasionally, but it is also facing the growing threat of professional marginalisation, due to the seemingly unstoppable popularity of Anglophone cliometrics. Boldizzoni claims that the increasing number of PhD graduates from US universities who establish themselves in European academic institutions and research centres, the enduring social prestige enjoyed by mainstream economists amongst and above their colleagues in different academic disciplines, and the same economists' intentional colonisation of study areas that belonged traditionally to the humanities and other social sciences (e.g., family, religion, education), have all been promoting the affirmation of this US-born school of thought far beyond its genuine scientific merit.

From the 1950s onwards, cliometrics has based itself on the theoretical presuppositions (e.g., market-based price formation, self-maximising rationality) and analytical tools (e.g., regression analysis, deductive mathematical models) of contemporary economics in the investigation of past civilisations and past societies. By doing so, cliometricians have pampered their own convictions that these theoretical presuppositions capture the deepest and unvarying propensities of human nature across space and time, and therefore that the economist's standard conceptual-methodological toolkit is what one needs in order to grasp the truth about our ancestors, their ways of life and, above all, their economies.

As a consequence of their approach, cliometricians have been dismissive of traditional methodologies in economic history. Competence in ancient or foreign languages, archaeology, familiarity with anthropology and sociology, as well as careful and extensive archival and textual research are deemed secondary, if not irrelevant. After all, by assuming *a priori* given traits of human behaviour and by building upon them formally consistent models, one can offer a self-reinforcing picture of past events that is strikingly similar to our contemporary view of things, as though past peoples and past economies were very much like us and ours, irrespective of whether they were actually so or not.

The issue is not a new one. Adam Smith himself derived his conception of a well-functioning commercial society on the assumption of a fundamental human propensity to truck, barter and exchange, which he considered so typical of our anthropology as to speak of "bargaining savages", in spite of older statements to the contrary (e.g., Tacitus on the Fennians).[814] Over the centuries, ethnographers and anthropologists such as Franz Boas (1858–1942), Bronislaw Malinowski (1884–1942), Ruth Benedict (1887–1948) and Marshall Sahlins (b. 1930) have brought forth copious and conspicuous evidence contradicting this univocal picture, but mainstream economists seem quite simply to have paid no notice whatsoever. Indeed, they seem to have ignored, side-lined or forgotten those very economists who rejected the anachronistic and clearly anti-historical approach of much of their discipline. Among the latter Boldizzoni cites Georg F. List (1789–1846), Richard Jones (1790–1855), Gustav von Schmoller (1838–1917), William

Cunningham (1849–1919), Arnold Toynbee (1852–1883), John Maynard Keynes, Karl Polanyi, Gunnar Myrdal and Carlo Cipolla, to whom we could add Veblen and the two Galbraiths. It was the likes of David Ricardo, Carl Menger (1840–1921), Alfred Marshall, Léon Walras (1834–1910), and Vilfredo Pareto who defined what is "classic" (and "neoclassic") in their discipline.

As to Boldizzoni's assessment of today's cliometricians, they are said to have invested their inventiveness and somewhat comical abnegation into reconstructing past events and past economies as though they were anticipating 20th-century US economic mentalities and institutions. Yet would that show that those events and economies were truly like the latter? Empirical research alone can answer this question, but that is something that cliometricians do not seem to appreciate or understand in its full ramifications. Who needs the historian's cautious and sensitive interpretations of long-lost worlds and archaic world-views, developed through time-consuming, taxing and complex investigations of remote and often fragmentary sources in dead languages and dusty artefacts? Perhaps one needs only a few of these historians, conveniently cherry-picked from the secondary literature, whom cliometricians so often discredit as antiquarian, pedantic, and unable to grasp basic economic laws. Formal adherence to self-contained models concocted by up-to-date economists can do the rest.

Many perplexing, sometimes involuntarily facetious, results of the ahistorical, or even plainly anti-historical cliometric approach are presented and criticised with great care and intellectual verve by Boldizzoni (see in particular chapter 3, "The Fanciful World of Clio", and chapters 4–5, "The World We Have Lost: Microeconomic History" and "Macroeconomic Perspectives"), whose line of argument is double-pronged. On the one hand, his book contains several critical considerations that apply to standard economics in general, not just to cliometrics, such as:

- The self-enclosed non-falsifiability of formal economic models for which all sorts of *ad hoc* adjustments have been devised (e.g., "implicit markets", "invisible transactions",

- "shadow costs");[815]
- The excessive abstractedness of the economist's categories of thought from socio-cultural determinants of human action;
- The dogmatic and rather crude philosophical anthropology underpinning their depiction of the human being (cf. chapter 2, "Economics with a Human Face?").

On the other hand, chapters 4 and 5 strike a powerful blow to the notion that today's market societies, their economic structures, forms of agency, and material and immaterial institutions may serve as a credible template to describe the primitive and ancient world, the feudal world, most of modern Europe, and even much of 20th-century Eastern Europe, Asia, Oceania and Africa. Reciprocity, redistribution, central planning, autarkic self-reliance, slavery, serfdom, irrelevance of the profit motive, socially determined price formation and many other non-market-based features of those economies have been demonstrated incessantly by actual empirical research, to which Boldizzoni refers across disciplinary and linguistic domains.

Boldizzoni's book reminds us and, above all, the cliometricians themselves, that by enthusiastically serving self-assertive mainstream economics and by abandoning history's adherence to empirical research and context-specific interpretation, Robert Solow's (b. 1924) worst fear *vis-à-vis* his own discipline has materialised: "we are at the point where economics has nothing to learn from economic history but the bad habits it has taught to economic history".[816]

From this dire perspective, it is refreshing to come across an acute, complex account of post-communist urban economy in Russia. Stephen Collier's book, also published by Princeton University Press, is the result of much fieldwork in provincial Russia and first-person poring over original Soviet and Russian documents. What emerges is an account of the noticeably partial transition of former Soviet economies, especially at the local and regional level, to Western-style liberal principles and markets (e.g., heating services).[817] Its being only a partial transition is explained by a variety of factors, which reveal both the resilience of Soviet material (e.g., the actual pipes) and immaterial institutions (e.g., the conception of all individuals as citizens with the same basic needs to be met rather than preference-ranking incentive-responsive market agents), as well as the diversity and context-specific adaptability of officially liberal agendas implemented over the 1990s and 2000s (e.g., the World Bank's limited implementation of infrastructure 'reforms').

In contrast to Collier's study, Andreas Kruck's account of the powerful affirmation of private rating agencies over the past decades falls short of providing a convincing study of this phenomenon. The book is laudably informed and informative (especially chapter 2), for it contains vast and valuable data on how public regulators incorporate private rating agencies into their governance functions and how these functions have been formalised both at State- and international levels (e.g., BIS, OECD, APEC). Thus, Kruck's account is commendable for outlining the legal and institutional frameworks through which "credit rating agencies have been empowered and granted political authority by regulators".[818] However, his study falls into the pit of needless abstraction, using chapters 3–5, out of a total of 6 chapters, to attempt to generate and validate a theoretical model of the private-public governance system of financial markets, created over the past few decades by certain governments and government officials, who allowed the financial sector to become its own regulator and its main, if not sole, supervisor.

It is unquestionably true that, until the publication of Kruck's *Private Ratings*, no "thorough theory-based explanation of the use of credit ratings by public regulatory bodies" was available.[819] Still, it is not difficult to see why. What use is theory if one does not tackle the far more empirical and perhaps unsavourily grittier issues of revolving doors, lack of transparency, oligopolistic syndicate, fraudulent and predatory practices, insider trading, lobbying, political corruption, and ideological myopia underpinning the legal and institutional frameworks listed in the second chapter of the book?

These issues are mentioned frequently yet episodically, especially in connection with the recent collapse of international finance, but the theoretical model that dominates the volume bears little direct hermeneutical and explanatory power on these matters. Indeed, even the recurring references to the post-2008 global economic crisis seem to be somewhat unrelated, as though they were added after the development of the model itself (the author states that when he "started to work on this book, the US mortgage crisis was just beginning").[820] Such shortcomings notwithstanding, Kruck's work is a welcome contribution to a much-needed debate on the role played by private businesses in general, not just credit agencies, in replacing the State in many of its traditional operations—that is, the "transformations of the state"—the subject addressed by this book and the series to which it belongs.[821]

The title of Goetzmann's book states: "Money changes everything".[822] This much rings true; and it probably is. Goetzmann's volume offers compelling evidence in support of the thesis stated in the title from a variety of interesting, informative and illustrative cases in world history. In four clearly written parts of uneven length, we read about, *inter alia*: lending and accounting in ancient Mesopotamia (part I); minting and litigating in classical Greece (part I); incorporating and tax-farming in late-republican and imperial Rome (part I); governmental steering of the money supply and issuing of paper money in ancient and medieval China (part II); experimenting with public and private finance in medieval and early-modern Europe (notably Genoa, Venice, Holland, France and the UK; part III); participating in the first age of financial globalisation in late-19th- and early-20th-century China, Russia and US (part IV).

Berghahn's book supplies additional evidence in support of the same thesis. This time, however, this comes with exclusive regard to the financial and industrial triangle comprising the US, the UK and the various political manifestations of capitalist Germany between the late 19th century and 1957. This is the year marking the diplomatic conclusion of the Suez Crisis, hence the internationally tangible termination of "the age of European colonialism and of Empire", and the financial as well as military institution of *"Pax*

Americana" over much of the world.[823] Given all this evidence, it becomes clear and uncontroversial to argue that, once the genie of money (i.e. credit, bookkeeping, banking and attendant financial techniques) is left out of the bottle—a metaphor that Goetzmann employs repeatedly in his book—, the history of human societies is no longer the same; and this is so to a significant extent. John Kenneth Galbraith and Stephen A. Zarlenga (1941–2017), namely two scholars who attempted in the past analogous sweeping accounts of world finance, could not agree more.[824]

Although Goetzmann's book is far from being a slender one, the subject matter is considerably bigger. Consequently, Goetzmann can only offer several historical vignettes, some of which are more detailed than others. These vignettes are peppered with Goetzmann's personal recollections *qua* financial historian and archaeologist, iconic references to artistic sources, and a number of noble opinions from minor as well as major commentators. The pleasure of investigation and the thrill of discovery are communicated vividly to the reader, *pace* the well-established academic convention requiring the living author to feign non-existence. Stylistically, the choice pays off. Whilst *prima facie* the book's sheer size and subject matter may be intimidating, its actual content is anything but stuffy, dense or turgid. Quite the opposite, its light prose, beautiful illustrations and first-person tone mean that the book can serve as an entertaining read for the non-specialist.

Much more unlikely to appeal to non-specialists is Berghahn's book. His shorter volume is judiciously researched and thoroughly referenced. It is patiently articulated over six time-periods and as many chapters (late 1800s–1901 in chapter 1, 1902–1914 in chapter 2, 1914–1922 in chapter 3, 1923–1933 in chapter 4, 1933–1941 in chapter 5, 1941–1957 in chapter 6). It is intelligently built upon pre-existing quantitative sources and, above all, it presents originally vetted qualitative sources, which grant the book a "bottom up" character that is normally associated with minority studies rather than business history.[825] As such, it can explain why and under which socio-political circumstances did the business relations between the US, the UK and Germany unfold, and not just that they did so and to what measurable extent. Its detached, academic tone and the broad spectrum of views and voices combined within it make Berghahn's book an interesting read to the academically initiated. Readers unfamiliar with 20th-century European and US history, though, may find it difficult to navigate the book's rich and thoughtfully constructed polyphony.

Specialists, on their part, will find Goetzmann's tome self-admittedly too cavalier towards too great a number of issues. The book's author spends few lines, if any, dealing with themes that he himself introduces as relevant. These include, for instance: the empirically informed subtleties of "Scholastic philosophy" about "usury" and "just compensation for risk";[826] the possible relevance of papal proclamations for medieval "maritime trade";[827] the thorny and sometimes violent civic struggles over direct and indirect forms of taxation (e.g. the Republic of Genoa's "salt tax");[828] and "Marx and a century of Marxist scholarship" plus the diverse economic experiments of allegedly Marxist countries.[829]

Still, a vast canvas as the one chosen by Goetzmann can only be painted by means of very broad strokes. One book, however long, is all that he has got, and he does succeed in making it an amusing one, notwithstanding the perplexingly nonchalant treatment of the French and, above all, Italian languages. Berghahn, on his part, deals with a more narrowly defined time and place in world history, pays painstaking attention to giving enough room to all the significant issues that he mentions, justifies patiently the absence of coverage of some others, and makes it certain that the spelling of non-English terms, especially German ones, is accurate.

Goetzmann's book states in its subtitle: "How finance made civilization possible". This much rings true too; but that is all. If anything, Berghahn's book makes the reader pause and ponder more than once, for it is, perhaps unintentionally, a meticulous study of how large and influential sectors of world finance, commerce and industry promoted and/or profited from ruthless colonial rule, total warfare and even Adolf Hitler's (1889–1945) murderous dictatorship (cf. in particular chapter 5, sections 10, 11 and 13).

In contrast, Goetzmann's large volume offers primarily evidence in support of his latter thesis. The book's author is so candidly partial to it, that he frequently dismisses with a sleight of hand many critiques of finance *qua*: deeply rooted conservative drives aimed at preserving "the status quo" at all costs;[830] fallacious "ad hominem attacks" rather than reasoned arguments;[831] sexist defences of a "male-dominated realm" from "female investors";[832] "populist rhetoric" instead of plausible or sensible policy;[833] obtuse "religious backlash" rather than identification of moral failure;[834] the "jealous" expression of "a long grudge against the rational mind" held by a more primitive "part of the brain";[835] the nostrum of "human nature", an all-purpose rhetorical topic, for "stand[ing] in the way of rational choice";[836] and political resentment at the success of daring "modernizers" that public authorities could not control.[837] Among the many men and the very few women cited in the book, including merciless tyrants and scheming crooks, the only person whom Goetzmann says openly that he cannot fully "forgive" is Karl Marx.[838] Astonishingly for Goetzmann, the author of *Das Kapital* was willing to do away with modern "bankocracy" (Marx's cited derogatory term for London-based international finance), even if it meant Marx's own pecuniary loss as a petty 19th-century shareholder.[839]

Despite Goetzmann's likely familiarity with the *Annales* school's historians (cf. "Jacques Le Goff" and "long durée"), Goetzmann is at a loss when confronted with *mentalities*—another key-concept of theirs—that stray too far away from textbook economic rationality.[840] Goetzmann does not deny the existence of: sovereigns forgiving their subjects' debts on political grounds (e.g. ancient Mesopotamia); bureaucrats imbued with a deep sense of duty and integrity (e.g. Confucian mandarins and Christian Templars); jurists arguing in favour of rational regulations based upon "natural law" (*ergo* a different "human nature" and "rationality" than those endorsed by Goetzmann);[841] socialists aspiring to an alternative economic order (e.g. Russian Bolsheviks); and prosperous peoples applying their community-focussed "traditional values" to natural resources from which higher private profits could be extracted (e.g. "Norwegian society").[842] Nevertheless, even if it means suggesting duplicity, stupidity or hypocrisy, Goetzmann can never take these human beings seriously on their own terms. He must explain them in other terms, which are closer to standard textbook economic rationality (e.g. self-promotion with the uncouth masses, fear of punishment, protection of the selfishly advantageous "social order"), or as emotionally compromised if not altogether irrational behaviour (the religious mind-set seems especially foreign to Goetzmann, despite its preponderance throughout human history).[843]

Emblematically, Goetzmann expresses utmost surprise at the fact that "Harry Markowitz did not copyright or patent his [investment portfolio] optimizer" and "gave it away to the world as an appendix to his book."[844] Selflessness, whether motivated by humanitarian altruism, religious piety, moral duty or intellectual loftiness, is seemingly inconceivable in Goetzmann's worldview or, at least, it goes unmentioned. In contrast, Berghahn tries to give each and every voice that he encounters a charitable interpretation, which presupposes a modicum of rationality and a degree of justifiability even *vis-à-vis* the least popular stances presented in his book. Thus, the reader finds a succinct, clear and aloof account of "Hitler's ideology of conquest and ultimate war aims", its roots in "Social Darwinism", and the historical circumstances of its mass appeal.[845]

Ideological and motivational partiality aside, as a serious historian of finance and business life, Goetzmann cannot simply deny the numerous and blatant material proofs of finance's hand in unmaking civilisations or, at least, in making civilised life a miserable one for very many people. On three occasions, he is adamant and detailed about it. They are:

(1) The booming slave trade of the "Projecting Age", which Goetzmann dubs "one of the most egregious, systematic sins of humanity";[846]

(2) The militarily enforced "opium trade" between British India and China in the 19th century, i.e. "one of the most shameful episodes in the history of finance";[847] and

(3) The "economic collapse" in the US after "the wreckage of 1929", which "alerted Americans to the uncertainty of financial

markets".[848]

On other occasions, the uncivil face of finance must be detected behind the lines, either timidly hinted at or briefly mentioned as a hermeneutical option among others, and frequently drowned amid profusions of rhetorical questions and possible rejoinders diminishing its plausibility. In this verbose and oblique manner, Goetzmann acknowledges finance's role in: forcing "[d]ebtors… to sell themselves into slavery" *via* usurious loans throughout ancient societies;[849] spurring or at least facilitating the Western conquest and exploitation, if not outright extermination, of "native tribes" all over the planet during the Renaissance and in modern times;[850] and the repetition of "the same story of debt and servitude played out since ancient time" in modern time's North-South sovereign credit relations.[851]

Trusting in finance's creative energy, Goetzmann salutes most positively many a "New Era" and innovation prompted by its heralds.[852] He shows genuine enthusiasm about the "exciting… fireworks" of financial markets that get "speculative juices flowing" in ebullient times of experimentation.[853] He even combines, controversially, the growth of Greek finance with the rise of Athenian "democracy", not elitist oligarchy, and in spite of his own references to "Solon's proclamation that Athenians could not contract on their personal freedom", i.e. an early case of "equity aversion and regulatory restraints".[854] Furthermore, Goetzmann regularly highlights the responsibility of politicians and "lawmakers" *vis-à-vis* financial crises, instead of targeting the recklessness and greed of financial agents *in primis*.[855] Somehow, he cannot get around the notion that the politicians' unwillingness or inability to prevent financial enthusiasm, and their desire to profit from it in licit and sometimes illicit ways, stems precisely from the kind of individualistic and self-maximising rationality that he commends, whereas sensible regulation requires a forward-looking gallant integrity belonging to other rationalities (e.g. the one explored by the natural law tradition of the Middle Ages, which he dismisses as religious twaddle).

Nonetheless, compelled by historical fact and intellectual rigour, Goetzmann is not blindly unaware of the ambiguous character displayed by finance in concrete world societies. Insights from critical works by John A. Hobson (1858–1940), Vladimir I. Lenin (1870–1924) and Thomas Piketty (b. 1971), for example, are cited. In the concluding pages of his work, Goetzmann even states that, when "fac[ing] trade-offs between profit maximization and national interest, it is only right that [States] serve their citizens first", inasmuch as States "have a fiduciary duty to their citizens", even though it may be difficult to understand how the individuals operating within State institutions should be guided by such a selfless and incorruptible sense of duty, which differs and diverges from the atomistic economic rationality that Goetzmann recognises elsewhere as the only one that he can make sense of.[856]

What Goetzmann's account lacks, in essence, is a clearer axiological compass. Such a compass would allow Goetzmann to explain when and why finance can be welcomed as a means of progress, which he claims finance to have been often and overall, or resisted as a means of life-depletion. In his own impersonal manner, Berghahn's scholarly neutral and multi-faceted account cannot help the reader in this quest either. No clear axiological compass is present therein. To retrieve this type of insight, which the topics discussed in both books at issue urgently call for, one must refer to a different breed of thinkers, such as Arthur F. Utz (1908–2001) and John McMurtry, or the above-mentioned Galbraith and Zarlenga.

Chapter 14: A History of Economics

The ongoing global economic crisis kick-started by Lehman Brothers' collapse in 2008 has led to a modicum of soul-searching amongst a few economists—e.g. Ha-Joon Chang's *23 Things Economists Don't Tell You About Capitalism*—and of increased visibility for prescient non-economists—e.g. the second edition of John McMurtry's *Cancer Stage of Capitalism*. Much of this soul-searching would not be necessary, had most economists' purview, as well as economics and business degree lines at large, included *de rigueur* a conspicuous amount of economic history and the works of non-orthodox masters such as Thorstein Veblen, Joan Robinson, Cornelius Castoriadis and John Kenneth Galbraith (I do not use 'unorthodox' or 'heterodox' for both sound somewhat belittling or, as Jeremy Bentham would have written, dyslogistic).

Yet, that has not been the case. Economic history has been left primarily to historians or reduced to theory-driven cliometrics, as Francesco Boldizzoni explains in his book, *The Poverty of Clio*. Not even the well-tested wisdom of John Maynard Keynes is being restored to its primacy in a time of crisis that is strikingly akin to the 1930s.[857] Häring's and Douglas' book is therefore yet another attempt to breach through the wall of economic orthodoxy, the resilience of which before repeated large-scale meltdowns is either the result of the unfalsifiable assumption of the unfettered markets' inherent ability to bring about prosperity (cf. chapter 12) or, as Häring and Douglas less kindly suggest, of the self-serving character of much modern economics *qua* rent-seeking profession.

Given the prolonged ridiculing and side-lining of alternative views since Veblen's days, I suspect that their clear and well-argued book is going to remain as marginal as, say, Galbraith's pre-crisis *Economics of Innocent Fraud* or Jonathan Schlefer's post-crisis *The Assumptions Economists Make*. After all, albeit unintentionally, their volume is in essence a much-needed contemporary token of economic institutionalism *à la* Veblen, whom mainstream economists have long condemned to the status of embalmed "lone wolf", in line with their professional training's unwritten aim of keeping reality at a safe distance.[858]

The first chapter of the book explains how this peculiar disciplinary feature has arisen, given that it traces the history of "modern mainstream economics" as a doctrine that, since embracing free-trade advocacy in the 18th century, has been gradually either abstracting or assuming itself away from socio-political reality and empirical data that might contradict the most cherished beliefs of the dominant business élites, not to mention challenge their interests.[859] To begin with, free-trade champions Davis Hume and Adam Smith conveniently ignored how mercantilism had contributed decisively to making Britain the "industrial world leader".[860] Their point is reminiscent of Veblen's claim that 18th-century liberals were the legitimising mouthpiece of a newly established dominant economic force, not visionaries who bravely defied the enduring feudal powers of the age.[861] Then, in the late 19th-century, Jevons, Marshall, Menger, Clark (1847–1938) and Walras spearheaded mathematical marginalism "against Marxist assaults and socialist tendencies" and proclaimed an allegedly "'scientific' and value-free" understanding of economic life that "de-emphasized the production side" and "eliminated the element of social interaction" within fictional models of "equilibrium" that were worthy of "Robinson Crusoe".[862] By so doing, they reduced "individuals" into "the 'atoms' of society" in which "workers would receive the fair value of what they produced", as though political power, social prestige or inherited privilege did not exist or matter in the sphere of economic agency.[863]

At the same time, the authors note that the alternative school of institutionalism—which did take power, prestige and privilege very seriously—started being pushed into insignificance through peer pressure, academic blacklisting and direct "political inquisition", which continued well into the 20th century under "McCarthyism" and created a professional body of economists devoted to staunch self-censorship and prone to leaving "heresy" to "lesser journals".[864] The additional acquisition of ordinalist concepts elaborated by Italy's Pareto, Britain's Robbins (1898–1984), and Austria's Menger and von Mises further contributed to drawing economists into formally manageable grand schemes and yet away from concrete reality, including vital "need" or "the fairness or wisdom or sanity of general patterns of allocation in society", since it became a standard assumption within the discipline "that no one can reliably compare *individual* differences of preferences. Instead [economics] now focuses all resources upon maximizing the efficiency of the economic machine, on the basis that a rising tide lifts all boats".[865] By this ordinalist move, economists "depersonalized economics… making the wellbeing of the economic machine the priority above all else, including long-term sustainability or the human beings inside the machine."[866] Later in the century, "Nobel Memorial Prize winners Kenneth Arrow and Gerard Debreu" brought this approach to its utmost level of mathematical skill and empirical irrelevance, given that the so-called "'SMD conditions" upon which their theorem is based "are extremely demanding and hardly ever fulfilled in reality".[867]

Funded by business groups and/or anti-socialist Cold-War governments, 20th-century mainstream economists embraced also Tullock's (1922–2014) and Buchanan's atomistic and anomic anthropological model called "rational choice" theory, which has led at least two generations of "economists… economics and business students… [and] policymakers" to adopt and internalise "different values than people on average" and become far more selfish and less prone to cooperation and altruism than most other human beings.[868] This model was exported, like many other things American, in those parts of "Europe and Asia" that came under the US sphere of influence after the two World Wars.[869]

Amongst the items of disciplinary export was also "GDP as *the* measure of economic success of a nation", so as "to eliminate distributional issues from the core of the economic discipline" and despite the GDP's blatant blindness to factors that are important for human life and *a fortiori* for economic activity, such as "institutional childcare… chronic illnesses… child wellbeing".[870] This choice of criteria made the US economy look like the paradigm of virtue to be emulated by all others, even if GDP measurements continue to be marred by their inherent arbitrariness, as with the cases of the "quadratic weighting" and "hedonic method" discussed by the authors.[871]

Such problematic issues notwithstanding, and in spite of repeated crises on a massive scale, "the mixture of dogma and self-censorship" of mainstream modern economics sails on unaffected, probably because "[t]he status quo is highly favourable to mainstream economists", who enjoy better "influence", "funding", "employment" rates and "average pay" than all other social scientists, thanks to their "[b]eing able to give… answers that do not offend the people holding the purse strings".[872]

As a sort of Zen slap to the reader and, in particular, to mainstream economists, who still largely evade genuine confrontation with reality in lieu of abstract models based upon unlikely presuppositions, the whole second chapter is devoted to the exemplification of how "Money is Power" to determine events in one's own as well as in others' life, irrespective of mainstream economics' notions of perfect competition, fair distribution, clearing markets, perfect information, consumer sovereignty, market prices, rational expectations, market discipline, etc.[873] Empirically and relentlessly, money is used precisely to prevent genuine market conditions from appearing, as long recognised and discussed at length by economic institutionalism.[874] As a regular denial of market principles, dominant financial conglomerates have been regularly:

- Enjoying "short side power on the credit market";[875]
- "Control[ing] vast sums of other people's money";[876]
- Circulating "insider information" in abundance despite legal prohibition;[877]
- Erecting "barriers to entry" in existing markets so as to establish oligopolies and "the power to determine prices";[878]
- Extracting "profits from trading against naïve investors";[879]
- Exerting "collusion between asset management firms and companies" to have "stock price pumped up by increasing demand";[880]
- Pushing "bankers on the boards of non-financial companies [to] take advantage of their board seats by extracting information", "manipulate investor demand", "bribe[-]

managers", and generally "break the fiduciary trust of their customers";[881]
- Establishing "hedge funds" that are "almost completely opaque about what they do" and make vast amounts of money in fees despite their limited actual profitability;[882]
- Securing the assistance of "the regulators" in "fend[ing] off any impediment to their dangerous business practices";[883]
- Paying for "the blessing of the rating agencies" upon their "junk assets".[884]

"Financial institutions" have a long history of keeping "regulators and lawmakers" from "stepping in".[885] Whether by selective use of contributions to parties and politicians (e.g. Barack Obama (B. 1961)), outright bribes or indirect ones through the revolving doors system (e.g. Hank Paulson (b. 1946), Nicholas Brady (b. 1930) and Robert Rubin (b. 1938)), direct involvement in politics (e.g. Robert Morris (1734–1806), Alexander Hamilton (1757–1804), Andrew Mellon (1855–1937)), or ties of friendship or blood relations with political leaders (e.g. the House of Medici and the Rothschilds), the power of money has been exercised throughout the history of both feudal and so-called "free-market" ages, so as to secure "five hundred years of bankers' rule".[886]

The deep roots of the bankers' rule lie in their ability to "issue money and to determine the value of currency… either in cooperation with the government or with the tacit and later explicit permission of the government".[887] Under this respect, Häring and Douglas recount the history of private and central banking in Western countries, its role in generating money and, with it, diverse forms of profitability, some of which fostering production and consumption, others fostering instead speculation and related boom-bust cycles.[888] *En passant*, they slap once more today's mainstream economists: "the privilege of private banks to create money is no longer seriously debated. The degree of avoidance of the subject smacks of a taboo."[889] Veblen's great spiritual heir John Kenneth Galbraith may have written a famous history of money and maverick intellectual Stephen Zarlenga may have continued his effort in our time, but mainstream "[e]conomists and participants in discussions of economic policies take this [present] state of affairs as a given. Yet a look at the early monetary histories of China and of the US clearly shows that the system has never been without alternative."[890]

In the third chapter, the authors delve deeper into the real world of economic affairs and the issues of power, prestige and privilege characterising it. This time, however, their focus is upon the modern corporation, not just the financial sector, which certainly dominates today's economies. In particular, their keen lens of analysis is cast upon the licit and illicit self-serving practices of the managerial class, whose "old boys' networks" allow its affiliates to receive huge salaries and bonuses independently of performance and of shareholders' contrary opinion.[891] References to several representative episodes and extensive empirical studies make their case compelling and convincing. In the process, many assumptions of mainstream modern economists are exploded from within:

- "[M]arkets" as "the best judges of performance";[892]
- "[M]onetary incentives" as conducive to performance;[893]
- "'[P]erformance-related' pay packages" as fair and proportionate;[894]
- "[R]isk taking" and managerial ability as rewarded or punished by "market forces";[895]
- Owners as able to "supervise managers";[896]
- Accountability to "regulators" or "the board";[897]
- The "outraged" public acting as an actual constraint on managers' behaviour;[898]
- "[I]llegal activity" being exceptional rather than normal;[899]
- "[O]ptimal contracting" conditions;[900]
- "[S]hareholder value" as a reliable criterion for corporate performance and governance;[901]
- "[F]inancial institutions and their analysts" as reliable and objective;[902]
- And corporate "accounting" as reliable and objective.[903]

Even the unorthodox ordoliberal and Thomist notion of "worker representatives" on corporate boards serving as a check on managerial malpractice is abated.[904] None of the claims above stands the test of reality.

The fourth chapter appeals once more to economic reality, yet to disprove this time the "simple version of neoclassical textbook economics" that so many "accept as the essence of economic reason"—especially politicians and policy advisors with basic training in economics or business studies.[905] These are the makers of the rules of the economic game in the real world, not high-level economists, many of whom should have acquired the knowledge needed to move past the "textbook-presented caricature that most students of economics, and even more of those who take only the basic economic courses" are taught instead.[906] For one, "profit", which "competition between companies" should drive "down to zero" is seen as enduring in the real world and, indeed, as the main open aim of economic life in the near-totality of current economic systems.[907] "Rising marginal costs" are shown to be the norm only in "nonmechanized labor-intensive industries such as subsistence farming", as Piero Sraffa (1898–1983) had already discussed in the 1920s, but they are still assumed in neoclassical textbooks rather than facing "the problems that make real-life competition work less than perfectly".[908] Striking instances of such regularly eschewed or underplayed problems are:

- The omnipresent location-based monopolies and price-determining oligopolies of corporate economies;
- The careful management of craftily manufactured consumer preferences;
- The resilience of long-lived inefficient producers endowed with conspicuous market power;
- The regular monopsony enjoyed by most employers over the labour market; and
- The endless barriers to the entry and survival of new competitors in existing markets.[909]

The authors challenge further commonplace textbook notions by discussing how well-tested historical experiences have demonstrated that monopolies can be good at times, including public ones, since they offer as valid services or goods and at better prices than firms operating under a regime of private competition (e.g. fire insurances, water supply and sewerage services).[910]

The authors' attack on mainstream textbook economics does not end here, though, for they address as well the way in which neoclassical economics, starting with John Bates Clark, has avoided the problem of determining "how much each worker in a team contributes to revenue" by "defining it away" through the concept of "labor unit".[911] The authors argue that this avoidance has been due quite simply to the fact that neoclassical economics has no way whatsoever to resolve it, as Vilfredo Pareto had "already pointed out" to some extent and the "famous Big Mac index" poignantly reveals.[912] As ordinary fast food is concerned, in fact, neoclassical economics does not possess the conceptual tools to explain successfully why "entry-level workers at McDonalds in underdeveloped countries have to work up twelve times as long to buy one of the Big Macs they produce than workers in some industrialized countries… even though they do the exact same job with virtually the same equipment".[913] Moreover, the notion of "capital", upon which mainstream textbook economics functions, is "ill-defined and usage of more capital is consistent with either a higher or a lower remuneration of capital", meaning that the actual distribution of income cannot be explained in its peculiar technical terms, since textbook economics does not explore as obvious and crucial a factor as "the negotiating power of the various social classes", which is instead what "first year classes in practical business skills" teach their students.[914]

The fifth chapter takes the next step in this line of analysis and enters the territory of industrial relations, with its plethora of strikes, lockdowns, diverse strategies for effective staff management, selfless and risky worker solidarity, complex processes for reputation-building, frequent calls for social responsibility, sticky issues of social cohesion, repeated forms of exploitation and discrimination, and inevitable matters of sheer luck *vis-à-vis* success in business, such as "being at the right place at the right time".[915] Several historical examples and empirical studies are discussed in order to attack this time the naïve and mistaken philosophical anthropology presupposed by textbook economics, which relies upon the notion of the self-maximising individual, or *homo economicus*, that is contradicted by "hundreds of thousands of years" of social "norms and preferences that… enable us to live together in prosperous societies" and that "encourage us to put aside narrow self-interest, to act pro-socially and to punish those who don't."[916]

Once again, the book's authors come across as reminiscent of Veblen's extensive incursions into the remotest past of our species, when the fundamental habits and dispositions of the human being were forged.[917] The aim of the authors is not antiquarian, though. Rather, they provide a complex characterisation of human nature and motivation, in order to argue that, if we want to make sense of employer-employee relations in the real world, power structures as well as moral and socio-political considerations must be reintroduced in the economic picture. This much-needed integration is precisely what mainstream economists have carefully avoided for decades by relying upon "the self-interest-centred theory" of human nature and by assuming in "textbook economics" that:

> [L]abor markets function no differently than the market for potatoes. The employer and the worker trade units of labor at a price that is determined by the law of demand and supply. A unit of labor of a given quantity is well defined, according to this view, just like a potato of given size and quality is well defined. Also the standard requirements for perfect competition need to hold: there can be no transaction costs, information must be complete and contracts can be perfectly enforced without cost.[918]

Yet, "this is not the norm".[919] Indeed, the relevance of a more articulate and candid approach to economic reality becomes crucial when "policies and institutions" are being "revisited" and the role of "rules" and "unions" is being assessed.[920] A more open-minded and informed approach can limit the harms of top-down theory-driven dogmatism, e.g. the 1994 OECD vocal call for union-dismantling "structural reforms" that was notably downgraded in the 2004 and 2007 OECD job studies, given the mounting counterevidence on income distribution and economic performance.[921] As the "six decades" necessary for "economists to switch sides" on the issue of minimum wage signal as well, reality may not be kept at a safe distance forever, but it can certainly be so kept for a long time.[922] Meanwhile, lives are impoverished or even lost.

The sixth and concluding chapter addresses the political level as such, thus achieving the climax of the ideal itinerary of the whole book, which comprises three essential steps:

(A) It starts with the critique of overly abstract and largely unempirical mainstream economics;
(B) It continues with the presentation of conspicuous power structures within the actual economies of the world that contradict both the assumptions and the conclusions of mainstream economists; and
(C) It argues that we cannot make sense of how economies operate unless we take these structures into proper account.

The authors do not aim at the abandonment of economics. They are not echoing Pareto's disillusionment with economics' predictive abilities and eventual move into sociology. Rather, they attempt at bringing the discipline back to its origins, whether as *fin-de-siècle* institutionalism or even older political economy. Significantly, the chapter opens with an account of why it is reasonable for people to participate in the democratic process, which "rational choice-inspired economics has struggled and largely failed to explain".[923] To do so, the authors present the gradual rediscovery of long-forbidden, if not altogether forgotten, individual preferences in "probabilistic voting theory".[924] Then, the authors address the issues of revolving doors, "conflict of interest", and "lobbying and contributions" in order to show that, even if economists may not like government 'interference', business people love it, as long as it is in their favour.[925]

Once again, this is *nihil novum sub sole*, since Adam Smith had already denounced it; but the authors proceed to make suggestions to strengthen and protect political systems—the authors focus on the US one—*via* "'cobweb cleaning' committee[s]", "working toward a transparent and accountable political system and an independent media", and "the automatic publication of everything that happens to a policymaker".[926] Minimising governments is not advocated, for the known result is to make them even weaker *qua* countervailing power and therefore more likely of capture or substitution by the largest private interest groups. Once again, the authors believe this not to be 'sheer' political science or something else than economics. If the wisdom of the book's final chapter had to be crystallised into one sentence, then it would be the following: how, by whom, and which rules of the economic game are written, it is an issue that no serious economist should avoid tackling.

Epilogue: Good and Bad Capitalism

The world has been facing a major economic crisis. There is no doubt about it. Mainstream media sources talk openly about it. The IMF, which had been promoting worldwide financial deregulation for the past thirty years, now reckons that an astounding loss of wealth occurred as a result of the 2008 collapse and that future generations are to be affected by the losses in employment, living standards, wellbeing, security and opportunity arisen from it: "The world economy is entering a major downturn in the biggest financial crisis since the 1930s, said the International Monetary Fund".[927] Revealingly, in the wake of the global crisis unleashed by deregulated capital trade, the IMF started suggesting policies that it had opposed for thirty years, such as increasing public spending and the number of civil servants.[928] Similarly, in an interview with Maurizio Molinari, Nobel-prize winner Robert Solow invited the newly-elect American President Barack Obama to increase public expenditures to restart and sustain growth.[929] Given the abrupt change of views amongst mainstream institutions and economists, Serge Halimi (b. 1955) remarks: "So, everything was possible after all. Governments could take radical action in the financial sector. The constraints of the European stability pact could be forgotten. Central banks could kowtow to governments and stimulate the economy. Tax havens could be blacklisted. Everything was possible because the banks had to be rescued."[930]

The implications of the unfolding crisis have been as grim as they were obvious. Much was going to be lost in terms of livelihoods, living standards, life savings, and access to vital goods and services. Significantly, during the eventful month of October 2008, comparisons with the depression of the 1930s became commonplace amongst journalists, researchers and politicians. The "economic abyss" that swallowed our grandparents and caused the "fall of liberalism" was reappearing under our feet, this time disclosing the flaws of neoliberalism.[931] Conservative politicians, heads of State and economists started uttering phrases that until September 2008 were heard solely from socialists, the latest three popes of the Catholic Church, and few marginalised proponents of alternative forms of globalisation. Faced by the mounting economic crisis, the British government decided to increase taxation on the income of highest-earning Britons for the first time in thirty years, acting upon well-tested Keynesian wisdom, but violating one of the dogmas of neoliberal economic policy.[932]

At the same time, another major crisis has been set firmly on the world's political agenda for at least fifteen years: "Human activities inflict harsh and often irreversible damage on the environment and on critical resources. If not checked, many of our current practices put at serious risk the future that we wish for human society and the plant and animal kingdoms".[933] As repeatedly denounced by the international scientific community at its highest and most representative levels, human civilisation has become for the first time in its history a threat to the planetary environment that allows for humanity's own existence. There is no aspect of the Earth's environment that has not been depleted in the three centuries that have seen the affirmation of capitalism, both private- and State-led, worldwide: the biosphere-protecting ozone-layer, breathable-air producing and reproducing pluvial forests and oceanic life-systems, self-regenerating water aquifers, nourishing-food-producing arable spaces, and natural-equilibrium-maintaining and science- and technology-inspiring biodiversity. Denials of this dramatic situation, albeit somewhat popular and sometimes politically convenient, smack of intellectual dishonesty. As a matter of fact, the causal link between the pursuit of profit and environmental degradation becomes visible every time environmental regulation is resisted as "too costly", by-passed by illicit behaviour, or avoided by outsourcing productive activities to countries that have actually little such regulation or none at all. In its willingness to cause illness and death, the self-maximising ethos preached and practiced by orthodox economists, and taken by them as the only essential psychological given within their simplistic philosophical anthropology, resembles eerily the ethos of gangsters, usurers, drug dealers and pimps, whose enterprises are typically modelled along the lines of for-profit business.[934] This resemblance is revealed further by the recurrent examples of illicit behaviour occurring daily in the business world, even amidst 'respected' and well-established enterprises, e.g. German giant Siemens' prolonged policy of bribing governments worldwide, for which the company accepted in December 2008 to pay an 800,000,000 USD fine to the Department of Justice of the United States of America.[935]

Life-value Onto-axiology

What can philosophy do in a time of crisis? Typically, philosophy would provide consolation to the individuals affected by the crisis. Alternatively, philosophy would attempt to sketch a comprehensive picture of phenomena that are likely to be perceived as separate issues and treated as such by non-philosophers. In this book, the reader has encountered a contemporary token of the latter type of philosophical endeavour, namely life-value onto-axiology. The reason for this choice should have become evident by now, as the reader considers that, as McMurtry states in *The Cancer Stage of Capitalism*: "[F]inancial crises always follow from money-value delinked from real value, which has many names but no understanding of the principle at its deepest levels."[936]

When dealing with financial matters, crises included, we are likely to think of value in terms of money. The value of an item is the price that it can get on the market. After all, that is exactly what is exemplified by the British Broadcasting Corporation's article serving as incipit for this epilogue, filled as it is with references to "global economic growth", "surging oil and food prices" and "rates of inflation". Is this a correct interpretation of "value", though?

First of all, McMurtry's statement about financial crises reminds us of the rather obvious but often neglected fact that there may be values that are not expressed in terms of money, such as ethical, aesthetic, epistemic, religious, existential, etc. In point of fact, money-value may even be glaringly absent, intentionally underplayed, side-lined, or actively resisted so as to express another value. For instance: a man jumps into a river to save another's life without considering whether he is self-maximising in the short-, medium- or long term; fragile natural wonders are protected by tradition and by law from mass tourism and unruly development; potentially contaminated food is recalled and destroyed to avoid harming the public; holy sacraments and rites are freely offered to the believer.

Secondly, McMurtry's statement hints at the possibility of determining a deeper and truer form of value. Such a more profound understanding of value has been grasped partially in many instances of human culture. For example, confronted with the tragedies of another victim of financial wizardry, i.e. post-1929 American society, Franklin Delano Roosevelt (1882–1945) affirmed: "The measure of the restoration lies in the extent to which we apply social values more noble than mere monetary profit".[937] F.D. Roosevelt's successor Henry S. Truman (1884–1972) echoed his message in the electoral campaign of 1948: "You remember the big boom and the great crash of 1929… the Democratic party puts human rights and human welfare first… these Republican gluttons of privilege are cold men. They are cunning men… They want a return of the Wall Street economic dictatorship."[938] Further examples of the same awareness are not too difficult to concoct, such as the conventional distinctions between: so-called "virtual" and "real" economies (i.e. gambling money for short-term gain should be less important than the stability of long-term sources of mass employment); wealth and wellbeing (i.e. being rich does not guarantee happiness in life, which one supposedly achieves by other means); negative and positive freedoms (i.e. the citizen's formal rights are meaningless without the satisfaction of certain material conditions that make them actually enjoyable). Not to mention the limits adopted by religious or legal traditions to the pursuit and accumulation of wealth, from the sin of simony in the Christian world to the nations' diverse and diversely enforced restrictions on, say, the trade of toxic and addictive substances, armaments and firearms, endangered animal species, archaeological specimens, etc.

There are things in our life to which we commonly refer as "priceless" and to which we ascribe the utmost value; things such as health, the air we breathe, free time, the beauty of a sunset, the sight of our children playing at kindergarten, a quiet old age, the depths of learning, the meaningfulness of a job that we have chosen as a life-mission. In truth, when any of these items is turned into a priced good or, as often said, "commodified", some may even experience a sense of uneasiness, as though something improper or even sacrilegious had occurred. Whether this subjective reaction takes place or not, the "commodification" of any valuable reality previously unpriced implies two major problems, of which we may be also more or less aware subjectively.

First of all, these items, when priced, are no longer available to as many people as before, but only to those who can afford to pay for them. Secondly, these items, when priced, can easily push life goods out of the market to sell more at less money-cost, as with worse-quality food catered in schools as cost-saving hence profit-making stratagem for the service suppliers. Money-value can trump life-value at every turn. Thus, a child can buy junk food at the expense of his health; a childish adult can buy a noisy snow-bike at the expense of the experience of a glacier's majestic silence; a gang of profit-seeking firms can buy a nation's natural resources and savings at the expense of a whole society's enduring wellbeing. Certainly, the commodification of diverse entities is not a trait unique to modern neoliberal capitalism, nor are hoarding and plundering, but they become most forceful within it, for neoliberalism assumes that the social optimum can only be attained by letting profit-driven markets rule over as many areas of human life as possible, rather than a select set thereof. Classical liberal economists, for example, would have never recommended the privatisation of either domestic or foreign security provision, which has increasingly become a feature of late-modern capitalism.[939]

Differing, deeper and truer forms of value can be disclosed fully and most explicitly. Life-value onto-axiology can tell us how to distinguish good from bad, or at least where to look when we try to distinguish between them. This theory of value, by revealing the deeper and truer form of value from which all others spring, would then show us, or at least steer us *vis-à-vis*, whether and when anything is either good or bad: eating, making money, losing money, inflation, equality, left- and right-wing policies, sex, 'Schumpeter-esque' creative destruction, etc. Undoubtedly, in making such a claim, McMurtry has taken an exceptionally bold step. If one considers the dominant trends within Anglophone value theory of the second half of the 20th century, which have largely eschewed any commitment to substantial notions of value, then life-value onto-axiology does appear unorthodox and daring—and, for this very reason, extremely interesting. Normally, Anglophone theorists of value of the second half of the 20th century, possibly terrified by the consequences of Stalinist and fascist uncompromising statements of value, regularly preferred much looser interpretations of value. In Germany, according to Michel Foucault (1926–1984), the prolonged experience of top-down determination of social values by the State, from "Bismarck's state socialism" to "National Socialism", was a crucial factor in the development of German neoliberalism, most notably Hayek's work, which is famous for its emphasis upon individual independence in value options by way of the principle of free choice in the free market.[940]

Whether Anglophone, German or else, contemporary axiologists have regularly understood value as being ultimately subjective (i.e. different individuals have different values), atomistic (i.e. societies' values are aggregates of individuals' values) and human (i.e. human beings ascribe value to non-human beings, which would otherwise possess none). Harvard professor Ralph Barton Perry (1876–1957) argues: "a thing—anything—has value or is valuable in the original and generic sense, when it is the object of interest—any interest."[941] Nicholas Rescher (b. 1928), the German-American champion of the Anglophone analytic tradition, rarefies further the notion of value and reduces it to the status of linguistic rationalisation of individual yens: "A value represents a slogan capable of providing for the rationalization of action by encapsulating a positive attitude toward a purportedly beneficial state of affairs."[942] Even more abstract and uncommitted is Zdzislaw Najder's (b. 1930) option, according to which: "M is an axiological value if and only if M is a judgement, ascribing the quality of valuableness to objects, properties or states of affairs, and constituting within the given value-system a final justification of other judgements of the system."[943]

In doing so, all these axiologists mirror the dominant liberal conception of economic value of their age, whereby the individual's preference satisfaction determines value by exercise of seemingly universal and neutral money-demand in the free market. Yet, within any capitalist economy, this allegedly universal and neutral unit of value-measurement comes with thick strings attached. Specifically, economic activity aims at maximising whichever starting capital there may be, and not just at expressing it in monetary terms. As Adam Smith had already assumed in the 18th century, such an aim is what a rational human being strives for by nature.

McMurtry is aware of his own academic exceptionality and does not deny the dangers that are regularly associated with any objective determination of value: "As the recent history of philosophy discloses, the multiplying particular bearings of language games, specific practices, incommensurable epistemic perspectives, anti-foundationalist conversations and poststructural principles of difference have overwhelmed the very idea of a unifying value ground as in principle wrong, and oppressive in consequence."[944] However, after pondering upon the recurrent economic crises of the post-Bretton-Woods age and upon the immense ecological losses accompanying them, he claims as well: "What is required is a life-grounded value foundation beneath our constructed divisions, a value ground that values our means of life and living fully above all else."[945] Since the formal and relativist options debated in mainstream axiology have proven tragically useless *vis-à-vis* both economic and ecological crises, McMurtry endeavours to provide a substantial and objective alternative, which pivots around the key-notions discussed in the first section of the present volume: the life-ground (i.e. what is required for us to take the next breath), life needs (as distinguished from preferences or wants), civil commons (i.e. all those social constructs allowing universal access to life good whereby to satisfy one's life needs), and the wellbeing index (i.e. the life-goods required to meet genuine life needs).

Liberal Echoes

Each and every key-notion of life-value onto-axiology is original in its wording and ability to join together dots that one normally finds disconnectedly disseminated all over the philosophical and scientific literature. At the same time, however, these key-notions capture fundamental truths about human life that reverberate in a countless number of sources, both old and new; sometimes in unexpected liberal ones too, i.e. sources emphasising individual liberty, free choice and even money-value well above life-value.

As the notion of life need is concerned, it is fascinating to recall liberal icon Isaiah Berlin, who remarks in his most famous work: "It is true that to offer political rights, or safeguards against intervention by the state, to men who are half-naked, illiterate, underfed, and diseased is to mock their condition… What is freedom to those who cannot make use of it? Without adequate conditions for the use of freedom, what is the value of freedom?".[946] Recalling an unspecified "nineteenth-century Russian radical writer", Berlin adds: "First things come first: there are situations… in which boots are superior to the works of Shakespeare; individual freedom is not everyone's primary need."[947]

Additionally, Berlin is fully aware of the material deprivations that a liberal economic system generates: "[T]he minority who possess it [liberty] have gained it by exploiting, or, at least, averting their gaze from, the vast majority who do not."[948] From this awareness, he derives a moral obligation to intervene, even at the cost of the much-cherished individual freedom: "If my brothers are to remain in poverty, squalor, and chains—then I do not want it [liberty] for myself… To avoid glaring inequality or widespread misery I am ready to sacrifice some, or all, of my freedom… I should be guilt-stricken, and rightly so, if I were not."[949]

As common for political liberals, Berlin restates in all of his most important essays the noble truth according to which my freedom ends where your nose begins. Yet, at the same time, he reminds us of the fact that for that noble truth to apply, all noses must be put first on a par. As long as the noses are not on a par, for the bodies that they stand attached to are not equally nourished and cared for, then one must think of why it is so and what can be done to redress the situation. Somebody's freedom can become a dis-value, if it implies another's misery, wretchedness and oppression, as with the financial speculator's freedom to gamble with the stability of a nation's economy providing adequate livelihood to millions that have never dreamt of engaging in any such gambling. In this, Berlin is reminiscent in turn of John Stuart Mill, the male champion of women's rights in the 19th-century UK, a staunch proponent of individual freedom *versus* State oppression, and the liberal master who considered private property itself a mere human arrangement aimed at securing people's wellbeing: "Private property, as an institution… owe its origin… to repress violence and terminate quarrels."[950] As a consequence, private property ought to be as likely to undergo modification and limitation as any other human arrangement—for the superior sake of people's freedom and wellbeing. For instance, "besides property in the produce of labour, and property in land, there are other things which are or have been subjects of property, in which no proprietary rights ought to exist at all… At the head of them, is propriety in human beings… Properties in public trusts… In a right of taxing the public… [In t]he brevet or privilege."[951]

Mystical Echoes

Such liberal echoes do suggest that life-value onto-axiology may actually touch upon something truly basic and fundamental, i.e. logically sound, empirically cogent and cross-cultural. In quasi-Kantian terms, life-value onto-axiology sets in place the conditions for the possibility of value itself, henceforth that which is valuable beyond comparison. After all, to deny the life-ground's import is a token of utter hypocrisy. Whoever wished to deny or suspend the judgment about the pivotal importance of meeting the prerequisites for prolonged survival and adequate individual and social existence, would be able to do so only by having benefited from meeting such prerequisites for a considerable length of time. This being the time necessary for her to become: a linguistically competent individual; trained in the complex social techniques of public debate; and sufficiently free from the worry of having to meet those prerequisites so as to participate in a public debate on the life-ground.

A person willing to deplete her health and eventually die in order to express her denial or her scepticism would carry the only credible denial or sceptical stance. It is doubtful that there may be many candidates for this role, though. In the sceptical tradition, the only philosopher ever to endanger his own life because of claims of ignorance was its mythical founder Pyrrho (ca.360–ca.270 BC), whom friends prevented from falling off cliffs and into wells or walking under galloping horses. Not even mystical and religious traditions, which emphasise spiritual and otherworldly values above material and this-worldly values, deny the importance of preserving bodies and minds alive and well, or at least well enough as necessary to be able to grasp the spiritual values that these traditions promote. Significantly, the communal sharing of means of life, whether unleavened bread, rice, beverages or children's education, is present in many religious rituals and symbolic formulations, Eastern as well as Western. Metaphors of life-giving, feeding, thirst-quenching, open and luminous space, rest, peace of mind, vital wisdom and communal existence colour Christianity as well as Andean polytheism, Buddhism as well as Greek Gnosticism. Even death, ultimate sacrifices and pessimistic life-escapes are repeatedly justified by referring to another, fuller life that possesses utmost value.[952]

National Echoes

Three countries are mentioned often in McMurtry's books.

(1) Norway is praised for funding its social programmes by publicly owned oil-based revenues, whilst oil consumption itself is being phased out progressively at the same time. The Norwegian case highlights how strategic assets may and probably should be controlled by the State rather than by private companies in order to maximise the likelihood that they may benefit as large a share of

society's members as possible and operate consistently along environmentally sound goals.

(2) Malaysia is recalled as a rare token of re-regulation of the financial sector before the current crisis exploded. It is well-known to experts in the financial sector that, in the mid-1990s, Malaysia was the only south-east-Asian country to set strict standards on foreign investments, openly against the advice of the World Bank and of the IMF. In this manner, Malaysia was the least affected and the promptest to recover from the meltdowns that brought down the so-called "tiger" economies of the region in those year, which experienced, among other things, a disastrous increase in deforestation and loss of biodiversity for the sake of short-term money-valued recovery. Alone, and with the growing giants of so-called "Chindia" on the background, Malaysia denounced the senselessness of deregulated international financial trade, which invades countries, produces speculative bubbles, causes them to burst, brings whole societies onto their knees, indebts them further, and colonises them to the benefit of foreign bankers and corporate shareholders.

(3) Finally, the small nation of Cuba is singled out for being able to maintain a high-level social infrastructure despite prolonged isolation by US-mandated economic blockade, thus showing how public services do not require alleged free trade, or indeed any private system of ownership and profit to exist, and unmasking also the empty rhetoric that claims universal education and public healthcare to be "unaffordable" and "too costly" in countries that are much more prosperous than Cuba.[953]

These three nations, as strikingly different as they are, exemplify nonetheless how, from a life-grounded perspective, an economically successful country is one that can boast high-quality education and healthcare provision, long life-expectancy rates, humane working hours and conditions, free or affordable recreational opportunities, environmentally sound industrial and urban development, steadfast job security, widespread opportunities for meaningful employment, and widespread high levels of perceived happiness.

Concluding Remarks

Vital needs do not solely set the bottom line under which an individual or a social arrangement should never go. Also, these needs indicate the parameters for the sort of growth that ought to be pursued. A good economic system must secure first of all the long-term provision of vital goods for as many citizens as possible. Secondly, it must generate the conditions for a fuller enjoyment of life, which is not confined to the sole sphere of biological movement. The life-ground sets the criteria to assess the performance of the economy. As for today's dominant model, the life-ground reminds us that good capitalism serves life; bad capitalism does not. Adherents to life-value onto-axiology, and John McMurtry's in particular, are therefore rich in advice concerning how to make sure that capitalism be good. Among them are:

- Truly and thoroughly applying environmental, health and safety regulations;
- Introducing a Tobin tax to protect countries from currency speculation and create a fund to help them when devastated by it;
- Applying fiscal measures capable of redistributing wealth across the impoverished sectors of society;
- Facilitating access and payback of credit for small- and medium-size, real-economy, employment-creating, environmentally sound enterprises;
- "Green taxes" i.e. taxing goods and services in proportion to environmental criteria;
- Prohibiting the production and/or trade of most obvious life-destructive commodities, including speculative financial products and (ab)use of currency;
- Introducing a 100% reserve requirement for credit-issuing banks and strict State regulation of banking and financial activities;
- Scheduling re-payment of foreign debt in ways consistent with the healthy and sustainable growth of the debtor;

- Re-scheduling re-payment of foreign debt and linking it to growing employment and preservation of the existing public sector;
- Suspending re-payment of foreign debt as a case of national emergency;
- Refusing further re-payment of foreign debt as a case of odious debt;
- Issuing altogether new notes constitutionally recognised as legal tender for job-creating, environmentally sound enterprises, along the line of the US Colonial Script and Abraham Lincoln's (1809–1865) greenbacks;
- Securing public sector initiatives to protect and enable the lives of citizens as rent for the money circulating in each country;
- Allowing for international lending of money between States at extremely low rates of interest and for the sake of true, healthy economic development.

Some of these measures are not unheard of. Indeed, some recall regulatory frameworks instituted in many countries after the collapse of Wall Street in 1929 and the subsequent prolonged economic crisis. Similarly, some echo further measures introduced to allow for the economic recovery of war-savaged countries in the golden years of Keynesianism. A few resemble policies implemented with considerable life-enablement in Brazil during the 2000s. Two characteristic features colour all of these proposed solutions.

First of all, they are aimed at guaranteeing existing environmental, health, safety and welfare protections or at improving them. In this direction, the prolonged diverting of public money towards private, for-profit entities is to be reverted. Without such a shift, achieving the peaceful and ecologically sustainable form of development aimed-for by leading international institutions is likely to result impossible.

Secondly, all these proposals display a clear anti-speculation aim, i.e. they target the virtual economy as the leading area of contemporary capitalist activity *qua* leading source of life-destructive praxes. The urgency of generating short-term capital gains for investors, i.e. the management's only and paramount fiduciary duty, is what causes cost-cutting measures even in productive and competitive sectors of the real economy and forces governments to cut public spending in order to guarantee returns for the private sector as tax rebates, FDI-attractive measures, research and development grants, and further *ad hoc* giveaways to for-profit enterprises, national and foreign, which are far from being institutionally committed to the wellbeing of the Earth's ecosystems or populations.

The same urgency is causally related to the astounding ordinariness of dubious and fraudulent practices, whether in the very common forms of sham bookkeeping or massive tax avoidance and evasion.[954] Currency speculation, which threatened in the early 1990s countries as wealthy as Italy and the UK, is capable of devastating societies in very short spans of time. As a matter of fact, the 1990s saw the birth of a new term aimed at describing a new phenomenon, namely the sudden collapse of an entire society because of massive speculative waves: "meltdown". The list of countries affected by this new form of Biblical flood is long and, of late, it comprises developed countries too. The liquid capital accumulated since the 1970s and freely, swiftly transferable by computer is the genie that has escaped from the neoliberal lamp, bringing havoc wherever it goes, and showing no desire to be bottled back into the lamp. Fleeting and destructive, this genie is capable of condemning entire sectors of a nation's population to misery and insecurity, and of compelling them to plunge their seas, forests, rivers and natural beauties for the sake of economic recovery and survival (e.g. over-fished Atlantic waters and disappearing Indonesian pluvial forests). The insatiable thirst for profit of the virtual economy does not affect the real economy alone, but also the LSS upon which the latter stands. In this manner too, the virtual economy can hasten the collapse of the world's environment.[955]

The reasons for the strong anti-speculation tone of such corrective policies are not based solely and strictly upon environmental concerns. Political concerns are also paramount. None less than the (in)famous speculator George Soros (b. 1930) believes that democracy is at stake, whenever huge flows of liquid capital can flood, or vanish abruptly from, a sovereign nation.[956] Such huge flows are a threat to the ability of democratically elected governments to respond to their electors, rather than to bankers, foreign creditors and impersonal, globetrotting markets which seek only profit opportunities.

On this point, Thorstein Veblen had already observed how "ownership… rests not on a natural right of workmanship but on the ancient feudalistic ground of privilege and prescriptive tenure, vested interest, which runs back to the right of seizure by force and collusion… [and it] confers a legal right to sabotage".[957] Those who own privately considerable amounts of wealth can wrest away the power of elected governments by denying support to productive enterprises, causing mass unemployment, and/or speculating against a nation's currency and public assets. Thus, they can even force a government to bail out their own poorly run enterprises with taxpayers' money, lest more enterprises be left to crash. The undemocratic power of a "moneyed aristocracy" had already been identified by US President Thomas Jefferson (1743–1826),[958] who claimed private "banking institutions" to be "more dangerous to our liberties than standing armies".[959] Analogous considerations were made by William Lyon MacKenzie King (1874–1950), former Prime Minister of Canada, who affirmed: "Until control of the issue of currency and credit is restored to government and recognised as its most conspicuous and sacred responsibility, all talk of the sovereignty of Parliament and of democracy is idle and futile... Once a nation parts with control of its credit, it matters not who makes the nation's laws... Usury once in control will wreck any nation."[960]

Anyone interested in the fate of democratic institutions should ponder upon the words of the longest-serving Prime Minister of a country of the British Commonwealth. These institutions, under the label of "just form of life", are themselves part of McMurtry's Well-Being Index, i.e. the complete and universal set of needs that all humans require to be met in order to flourish.

Endnotes

[1] Cf. John McMurtry, *The Structure of Marx's World-View*, Princeton: Princeton University Press, 1978.

[2] To exemplify the relevance of non-academic media exposure, the interviews with McMurtry contained in Peter Joseph's 2011 film have been aired frequently on *La Cosa Web TV*, i.e. the web channel associated with Beppe Grillo's (b. 1948) *Movimento 5 Stelle*, i.e. Italy's second largest party since 2013. Though no direct causation can be established, it is remarkable that many policy proposals of this party are blatantly reminiscent of McMurtry's own philosophy and policy proposals for financial reform.

[3] John Maynard Keynes, *The General Theory of Employment, Interest and Money*, 1936, chapter 12, § 5, <https://www.marxists.org/reference/subject/economics/keynes/general-theory/>.

[4] Alan D. Morrison and William J. Wilhelm, Jr., *Investment Banking. Institutions, Law and Politics*, Oxford: Oxford University Press, 2007, 187 & 225.

[5] Self-declared free-market advocate Alan Greenspan brushes away crashes like the latest one and that of 1929 as "notably rare exceptions" ("U.S. Debt and the Greece Analogy", *Wall Street Journal*, 18th June 2010,<http://online.wsj.com/article/SB10001424052748704198004575310962247772540.html>).

[6] Cambridge: Cambridge University Press, 2013.

[7] I contacted both authors, who, in a further proof of academia's astounding ability for self-seclusion, confirmed that they were unaware of McMurtry's twenty-year-older term and concept.

[8] Regarding the endnotes, I made use of the Chicago Style Citation standard, i.e. the most common among Anglophone academic philosophers, though purged of some of its more quixotic aspects.

[9] John McMurtry, *The Cancer Stage of Capitalism*, London: Pluto Press, 1999, 17 (notes carrying no subtitle refer to the 1999 first edition of the book, not the 2013 second edition).

[10] Cf. ibid., xi–xii.

[11] Toronto: Garamond Press, 1998, 325–30; cf. *The Cancer Stage of Capitalism*, 151–79, for a slightly revised version.

[12] Before publishing *The Cancer Stage of Capitalism*, John McMurtry had devoted a book, entitled *Understanding War* (Toronto: Science for Peace & Samuel Stevens, 1989), to the axiological study of this specific type of life-destructive for-profit business.

[13] This distinction between types of money sequence can only be made from the standpoint of life-value, a standpoint not available to the Marxist framework of analysis, which posits production forces as such as nominally determining, and repels throughout this normative ground that McMurtry's analysis works from.

[14] On this point, Luciano Gallino (cf. *Finanzcapitalismo*, Milan: Einaudi, 2011) speaks aptly of corporations such as FIAT and General Motors as "banks that make cars".

[15] John McMurtry, *The Cancer Stage of Capitalism*, viii.

[16] Ibid., 45.

[17] Ibid., 50.
[18] Ibid., 114.
[19] Ibid., 151.
[20] Ibid., 153.
[21] Cf. ibid., 164–71 & 178–9.
[22] Ibid., x.
[23] Ibid., 214.
[24] Ibid., 204.
[25] Ibid.
[26] Cf. ibid., 204–14.
[27] Ibid., 209.
[28] Ibid., 218.
[29] Ibid., 231.
[30] Ibid., 202.
[31] Cf. ibid., 238–54.
[32] Cf. ibid., viii–xiv.
[33] Cf. ibid., 45.
[34] Cf. ibid., 206–7.
[35] John McMurtry, *Value Wars: The Global Market Versus the Life Economy*, London: Pluto Press, 2002, 5.
[36] Ibid., 98.
[37] Ibid., 126.
[38] Ibid., 129.
[39] Ibid., 151.
[40] Ibid., 166.
[41] Ibid.
[42] Ibid.
[43] Ibid.
[44] Ibid.
[45] Ibid., 167.
[46] Ibid., 223 n13.
[47] Ibid.
[48] Ibid., 243 n49.
[49] Ibid., 111–7.
[50] Ibid., 155–7.
[51] Ibid., 101 & 104–5.
[52] Cf. ibid., 100–9.
[53] Cf. ibid., 133–4.
[54] Cf. ibid., 46–8.
[55] Ibid., 54.
[56] Ibid., 48–55.
[57] Cf. ibid., 98, 135 & 151.
[58] Cf. ibid., 261 n72.
[59] Cf. ibid., 96.
[60] Cf. ibid., 245 n60 & 162–4.
[61] Cf. ibid., 172–7.
[62] Cf. ibid., 193–8.
[63] Cf. ibid., 113.
[64] Cf. ibid., 245 n60.

[65] Cf. ibid., 165–9, 202–5, 214–5, 227 n38 & 259–60 n66.
[66] Cf. ibid., 181–6 & 214–5.
[67] Ibid., 204.
[68] Cf. Ibid., 165–7, 172–7 & 214–9.
[69] Ibid., 186–8.
[70] Ibid., 150–4.
[71] Ibid., 161–77.
[72] Cf. ibid., 150–4.
[73] Cf. ibid., 190–8.
[74] Cf. ibid., 198–202.
[75] Cf. ibid., 219–20.
[76] Ibid., 214–5.
[77] Cf. ibid., 259–60 n66.
[78] Princeton: Princeton University Press, 2007.
[79] Cf. Karl Popper, *Cattiva maestra televisione*, edited and translated by Giancarlo Bosetti, Venice: Marsilio, 2002.
[80] John McMurtry, *The Cancer Stage of Capitalism: From Crisis to Cure*, London: Pluto Press, 2013, 12.
[81] Ibid., 11.
[82] Ibid., 51.
[83] As cited in ibid., 226.
[84] Ibid., 4.
[85] Ibid., 237–42.
[86] Ibid.
[87] Ibid., 144–6.
[88] Ibid., 256–7.
[89] Ibid., 338 n115.
[90] John McMurtry, "Glossary", in *Philosophy and World Problems*, part of UNESCO, *Encyclopedia of Life Support Systems*, Paris & Oxford: Eolss, 2009–2010, <www.eolss.net>.
[91] John McMurtry, *The Cancer Stage of Capitalism: From Crisis to Cure*, 42.
[92] Ibid., 255–6.
[93] Ibid., 19.
[94] Ibid., 202–3.
[95] Ibid., 179.
[96] As cited in ibid., 115.
[97] Ibid., 99.
[98] Ibid., 169
[99] Ibid., 3–4 & 14.
[100] Ibid., 6.
[101] Ibid., 147–9.
[102] Ibid., 237–42.
[103] Ibid.
[104] Ibid., 6.
[105] Ibid., 10.
[106] Ibid., 16 & 118–24.
[107] Ibid., 42.
[108] Ibid., 313ff.
[109] Ibid., 296.

[110] Ibid., 262–5.
[111] Ibid., 268–72.
[112] Ibid., 286–94.
[113] Ibid., 295–9.
[114] Ibid., 20.
[115] Ibid., 162–3.
[116] Ibid., 288.
[117] Cf. Ibid., 320–1.
[118] Ibid., 30.
[119] Ibid., 28.
[120] Ibid., 28 & 218–9.
[121] Ibid., 295.
[122] Ibid., 15 & 107.
[123] Cf. ibid., 229–30.
[124] Chaïm Perelman and Lucie Olbrechts-Tyteca, *The New Rhetoric: A Treatise on Argumentation*, translated by John Wilkinson and Purcell Weaver, Notre Dame: Notre Dame University Press, 1969, 93.
[125] Ibid., 86–109.
[126] Albert O. Hirschman, *The Rhetoric of Reaction: Futility Perversity, Jeopardy*, Cambridge, MA: Belknap Press, 1991.
[127] Cf. Slavoj Žižek, *First as Tragedy, Then as Farce*, London: Verso, 2009.
[128] Donald Gibson, *Environmentalism: Ideology and Power*, Huntington: Nova Science, 2002.
[129] Hans Jonas, "Sul razzismo", *Il concetto di Dio dopo Auscwitz. Una voce ebraica*, translated by Carlo Angelino, Genoa: Il melangolo, 1993, 48.
[130] Hans Jonas, *The Imperative of Responsibility. In Search of an Ethics for the Technological Age*, Chicago: The University of Chicago Press, 1984, 168.
[131] Ibid., 31.
[132] Ibid., 140.
[133] Hans Jonas, "Philosophical Reflections on Experimenting with Human Subjects", *Daedalus*, 98(2), 1969, 243.
[134] Ibid., 224.
[135] Ibid.
[136] Hans Jonas, *Philosophical Essays: From Ancient Creed to Technological Man*, Chicago: The University of Chicago Press, 1974.
[137] Hans Jonas, "Philosophical Reflections on Experimenting with Human Subjects", 243.
[138] Ibid.
[139] Ibid.
[140] Ibid., 230.
[141] Hans Jonas, *The Imperative of Responsibility*, 122.
[142] Jonas' own work was not secular, but informed by religious belief, such as the "reverence of creation" and "cosmic piety" discussed in D. Levy, *Hans Jonas: The Integrity of Thinking* (Columbia & London: University of Missouri Press, 2002) and the Biblical wisdom cited by Jonas and discussed in E. Cohen, "Conservative Bioethics and the Search for Wisdom" (*The Hastings Center Report*, 36(1), 2006, 44–56).
[143] Hans Jonas, *The Imperative of Responsibility*, 22.
[144] Ibid., 32.

¹⁴⁵ Hans Jonas, "Philosophical Reflections on Experimenting with Human Subjects", 230.
¹⁴⁶ Hans Jonas, *The Imperative of Responsibility,* 36 & 204 (emphasis added).
¹⁴⁷ Hans Jonas, *Dio è un matematico? Sul senso del metabolismo*, translated by Carlo Angelino, Genova: Il melangolo, 1995, 60–2.
¹⁴⁸ Ibid., 41.
¹⁴⁹ Ibid., 61.
¹⁵⁰ Jonas' conservatism was not dogmatic, as discussed in L. Vogel, "Natural law Judaism? The Genesis of Bioethics in Hans Jonas, Leo Strauss, and Leon Kass" (*The Hastings Center Report*, 36(3), 2006, 32–44).
¹⁵¹ Jonas valued human freedom, the biological preconditions of which he recognised and cherished, as discussed in E. Mendieta, "Communicative Freedom and Genetic Engineering" (*Logos*, 2(1), 2003, 124–40).
¹⁵² Hans Jonas, *The Imperative of Responsibility*, 145.
¹⁵³ Ibid.
¹⁵⁴ Ibid., 185.
¹⁵⁵ Soviet environmental history is rife with dramatic events, as discussed in in M. Deutsch, M. Feschbach and A. Friendly Jr., *Ecocide in the USSR: The Looming Disaster in Soviet Health and Environment* (New York: Basic Books, 1968). It is true that Chapter 2, Article 18 of the 1977 constitution of Soviet Union did contain clear references to "future generations" and the sound conservation of natural resources and pristine environments, but often they were disregarded, as discussed in C.E. Ziegler, *Environmental Policy in the USSR* (Amherst: University of Massachusetts Press, 1990).
¹⁵⁶ Hans Jonas, "Sul razzismo", 46.
¹⁵⁷ Ibid., 47.
¹⁵⁸ Ibid.
¹⁵⁹ Ibid., 47–8.
¹⁶⁰ Ibid., 48.
¹⁶¹ Ibid.
¹⁶² Ibid., 48–9.
¹⁶³ Hans Jonas paid no heed to the deniers of climate change. In this book, I follow his lead.
¹⁶⁴ Ki-moon Ban, *UN Secretary-General Ban Ki-moon's message for the World Environment Day*, 2009, SG/SM/12265ENV/DEV/1055 OBV/788.
¹⁶⁵ Hans Jonas, *The Imperative of Responsibility*, 145.
¹⁶⁶ Andrew Jacobs, "In China, Pollution Worsens Despite New Efforts", *The New York Times,* 28th July 2010, <http://www.nytimes.com/2010/07/29/world/asia/29china.html>.
¹⁶⁷ This phenomenon has come to be known under the simple term "austerity".
¹⁶⁸ Lawrence H. Summers, "The Memo" [internal memorandum circulated on 12th December 1991], <http://www.whirledbank.org/ourwords/summers.html>; cf. also Kevin Smith, "'Obscenity' of Carbon Trading", *BBC News*, 4th April 2007, <http://news.bbc.co.uk/2/hi/science/nature/6132826.stm>.
¹⁶⁹ Fyodor M. Dostoyevsky, *Note invernali su impressioni estive*, translated by Serena Prina, Milan: Feltrinelli, 1993, 49.

[170] The inherently homicidal character of liberalism has deep historical roots. Consider, for example, the classical liberal Drummond professor of political economy William Nassau Senior (1790–1864) who, when told that a million Irishmen had already died in the potato famine (1845–1849), famously replied: "It is not enough!"—the iron law of supply and demand had not yet run its full course (cf. US economist Michael Hudson, "Breakup of the euro?" (26th May 2011), <http://michael-hudson.com/2011/05/eu-politics-financialized-economies-privatized/>).

[171] Herbert Spencer, *The Man* versus *the State*, Caldwell: The Caxton Press, 1960, 162 (published originally in 1884).

[172] Lawrence H. Summers, "The Memo".

[173] Ibid.

[174] Cf. Arthur Fridolin Utz, *Wirtschaftsethik* (Bonn: Scientia Humana Institut, 1994) for a concise and precise articulation of the Aristotelian-Thomist notion of justice (i.e. particular—distributive and commutative—and general or social) and its application to modern economic orders.

[175] Lawrence H. Summers, "The Memo".

[176] Ibid.

[177] Ibid.

[178] Cf. "Harvard Students Rip New President Lawrence Summers on Toxic Waste Memo", *Boston Globe*, 13 March 2001.

[179] Cf. "Toxic Memo", *Harvard Magazine*, 5 January 2001.

[180] Cf. Jay Johnson, Gary Pecquet and Leon Taylor, "Potential Gains from Trade in Dirty Industries: Revisiting Lawrence Summers' Memo", *Cato Journal*, 27, 3 (2007): 397–410.

[181] UNESCO, *Encyclopedia of Life Support Systems*, "Definitions", 2002, § 2.

[182] John McMurtry, "What is Good? What is Bad? The Value of All Values across Time, Place and Theories", *Encyclopedia of Life Support Systems*, 2009–2010, § 5.34.10.

[183] John McMurtry, *The Cancer Stage of Capitalism*, 206–7.

[184] John McMurtry, "What is Good? What is Bad?", Glossary.

[185] Ibid., § 6.2.1 (emphasis in the original).

[186] Ibid., Glossary.

[187] Ibid., § 6.3 (emphasis in the original).

[188] John McMurtry, *Unequal Freedoms*, 164.

[189] Human needs balance mutually, as argued in Noonan' book entitled *Democratic Society and Human Needs* (Montreal & Kingston: McGill's-Queen's University Press, 2006). For example, the need for water is balanced out by the need to urinate; whilst the need to be educated can only turn into pathological solipsism if it is not balanced out by the needs to rest and socialise.

[190] John McMurtry, *Value Wars*, 156.

[191] Cf. Martha Nussbaum, "Nature, Functioning and Capability: Aristotle on Political Distribution", *Oxford Studies in Ancient Philosophy*, 6, suppl., 1988, 145–84 and Amartya Sen, *Commodities and Capabilities*, Amsterdam: North-Holland, 1985.

[192] John McMurtry, "Principles of the Good Life: The Primary Theorems of Economic Reason", 2005 [Unpublished manuscript circulated amongst EOLSS contributors].

[193] John McMurtry, *The Cancer Stage of Capitalism*, 242.

[194] Edmund Burke, *Reflections on the Revolution in France*, 1791, § 134, <http://bartelby.org/24/3/>.
[195] José C. Escudero, "What is Said, What is Silenced, What is Obscured: The Report of the Commission on the Social Determinants of Health", *Social Medicine*, 4(3), 2009, 183.
[196] John McMurtry, "Principles of the Good Life".
[197] In the 1970s, UK's trade unionists coined the acronym "TINA" to ridicule PM Margaret Thatcher's (1925–2013) catchphrase "There Is No Alternative", *pace* her frequent references to "liberty" and "freedom".
[198] Cf. Jeff Noonan, *Democratic Society and Human Needs*: the history of democracy is a history of rising civil commons.
[199] It should be noted that property rights extend to social institutions such as non-living for-profit legal persons, i.e. the modern corporation, to which belongs the lion's share of contemporary world trade.
[200] Robert Nozick, *Anarchy, State, and Utopia*, New York: Basic Books, 1974, 179.
[201] Cf. Arthur Fridolin Utz, *Wirtschaftsethik*.
[202] Hans Jonas, *The Imperative of Responsibility*, 130.
[203] Ibid., 100–1 (emphasis added).
[204] Ibid., 130.
[205] Ibid., 131.
[206] Ibid.
[207] Ibid., 11.
[208] Cf. Paul G. Kuntz, "Augustine: From *Homo Erro* to *Homo Viator*", *Augustinian Studies*, 11, 1980, 79–89.
[209] Cf. Gabriel Marcel, *Homo Viator* (translated by E. Craufurd, New York: Harper Torchbooks, 1962) and *The Philosophy of Existentialism* (translated by Manya Harari, New York: The Citadel, 1967).
[210] Gabriel Marcel, *The Philosophy of Existentialism*, 28.
[211] Ibid.
[212] Gabriel Marcel, *Homo Viator*, 43 (emphasis added).
[213] Ibid. (emphasis added).
[214] Ibid., 38–9.
[215] Ibid., 36.
[216] Cf. Jill G. Hernandez, *Gabriel Marcel's Ethics of Hope: Evil, God and Virtue* (London: Continuum, 2011) and Brendan Sweetman, *The Vision of Gabriel Marcel. Epistemology, Human Person, the Transcendent* (Amsterdam: Rodopi, 2008).
[217] UNWTO, *Global Code of Ethics for Tourism*, 1999, 1, A/RES/406(XIII) & A/RES/56/212, <http://www.unwto.org/ethics/full_text/en/pdf/Codigo_Etico_Ing.pdf>.
[218] John McMurtry, "What is Good? What is Bad?", § 1.16 (emphasis added).
[219] Ibid., § 6.2.1.
[220] Cf. James E. Lovelock, "Gaia as Seen through the Atmosphere", *Atmospheric Environment*, 6(8), 1972, 579–80.
[221] Cf. Giorgio Baruchello, "Western Philosophy and the Life-ground", *Encyclopedia of Life Support Systems*, Paris & Oxford: Eolss, 2007, <http://www.eolss.net>.
[222] John McMurtry, "What is Good? What is Bad?", § 6.1.4.

[223] Ibid., § 6.1.
[224] Ibid., § 6.3 (emphasis removed).
[225] Ibid., § 6.1 (emphasis removed).
[226] John McMurtry, *The Cancer Stage of Capitalism: From Crisis to Cure*, 42.
[227] John McMurtry, *Unequal Freedoms*, 164.
[228] John McMurtry, *The Cancer Stage of Capitalism: From Crisis to Cure*, 19.
[229] Ibid., 1.
[230] Jeff Noonan, *Democratic Society and Human Needs*, xiv.
[231] Ibid.
[232] Ibid., 57.
[233] John McMurtry, *Value Wars*, 156 (emphasis removed).
[234] John McMurtry, "What is Good? What is Bad?", § 10.10.4.
[235] John McMurtry, *Value Wars*, 156.
[236] John McMurtry, "Glossary".
[237] John McMurtry, *The Cancer Stage of Capitalism: From Crisis to Cure*, 240.
[238] Ibid., 199 (emphasis removed).
[239] Ibid., 239; cf. Garrett Hardin, "The Tragedy of the Commons", *Science*, 162, 1968, 1243–8.
[240] Warren Buffett, "Berkshire Hathaway Inc. 2002 Annual Report", 2003, 15, <http://www.berkshirehathaway.com/2002ar/2002ar.pdf>.
[241] Cf. Elizabeth Johnson and Harlan Morehouse, "After the Anthropocene: Politics and Geographic Inquiry for a New Epoch", *Progress in Human Geography*, 38(3), 2014, 439–56.
[242] UNWTO, *Global Code of Ethics for Tourism*, title page.
[243] Ibid., 5 (emphasis added).
[244] John McMurtry, *The Cancer Stage of Capitalism: From Crisis to Cure*, 170.
[245] UNWTO, *Global Code of Ethics for Tourism*, 2.
[246] Ibid.
[247] Ibid. (emphasis added).
[248] Ibid.
[249] John McMurtry, *The Cancer Stage of Capitalism: From Crisis to Cure*, 256–7.
[250] Cf. Intergovernmental Panel on Climate Change (IPCC) *Managing the Risks of Extreme Events and Disasters to Advance Climate Change Adaptation*, 2012, <http://www.ipcc-wg2.gov/SREX/>.
[251] John McMurtry, *The Cancer Stage of Capitalism: From Crisis to Cure*, 9 & 179 (emphasis removed).
[252] As cited in ibid., 115 (emphasis removed).
[253] UNWTO, *Global Code of Ethics for Tourism*, 3, art. 3(1) (emphasis added).
[254] John McMurtry, *The Cancer Stage of Capitalism: From Crisis to Cure*, 11 (emphasis removed).
[255] Ibid., 188 (emphasis removed).
[256] Ibid., 169.
[257] Ibid., 3–4 & 14 (emphasis in the original).

[258] The literature substantiating this conclusion is massive. Cf., *inter alia*, Stephen G. Cecchetti, Madhusudan S. Mohanty and Fabrizio Zampolli, "The Real Effects of Debt" (Bank of International Settlements' (BIS) Working Papers, 352, 2011, <http://www.bis.org/publ/work352.htm>); The Center for Human Rights in Practice, *Reports on the Impact of Public Spending Cuts on Different Disadvantaged Groups within the UK* (2013, <http://www2.warwick.ac.uk/fac/soc/law/chrp/projects/spendingcuts/resources/database/reportsgroups/>); The European Commission, *EUROPA – Food Safety – Chemical Safety of Food – Food Contaminants* (2013, <http://ec.europa.eu/food/food/chemicalsafety/contaminants/index_en.htm>); IPCC, *Managing the Risks of Extreme Events and Disasters to Advance Climate Change Adaptation* (2012, <http://www.ipcc-wg2.gov/SREX/>); The House of Commons' Environment, Food and Rural Affairs Committee (HC 141), "Food Contamination, Vol. 1" (London: The Stationery Office, 2013 [fifth report of session 2013–4, incorporating HC 1035-i-ii, session 2012–3]); The House of Lords' Select Committee on Economic Affairs (HL 48), "Tackling Corporate Tax Avoidance in a Global Economy: Is a New Approach Needed?" (London: The Stationery Office, 2013 [first report of session 2013–4]); Institute for Fiscal Studies (IFS), "Food Expenditure and Nutritional Quality over the Great Recession" (IFS Briefing Note BN143, 2013, <www.ifs.org.uk/bns/bn143.pdf>); International Labour Organization (ILO), *Public Sector Shock: The Impact of Policy Retrenchment in Europe* (Geneva: ILO, 2013); Organisation for Economic Cooperation and Development (OECD), *Divided We Stand: Why Inequality Keeps Rising* (2011, <DOI:10.1787/9789264119536-en>), *Addressing Base Erosion and Profit Shifting* (2013, <DOI:10.1787/9789264192744-en>) & "Crisis Squeezes Income and Puts Pressure on Inequality and Poverty" (2013, <http://www.oecd.org/els/soc/OECD2013-Inequality-and-Poverty-8p.pdf>); Trust for America's Health, *F as in Fat. How Obesity Threatens America's Future* (2011, <http://healthyamericans.org/reports/obesity2011/Obesity2011Report.pdf>); UN, "Political Declaration of the High-level Meeting of the General Assembly on the Prevention and Control of Non-communicable Diseases" (adopted 24th January 2012, G.A. Res. 66/2, UN GAOR, 66th Sess., Agenda item 117, UN Doc. A/RES/66/2); World Health Organization (WHO), *Noncommunicable Diseases. Country Profiles 2011* (2011, <www.who.int/nmh/publications/ncd_profiles_report.pdf>).

[259] John McMurtry, *The Cancer Stage of Capitalism: From Crisis to Cure*, 288.
[260] Ibid., 20ff.
[261] Ibid., 62–3.
[262] Ibid., 262–5.
[263] Ibid., 268–72.
[264] Ibid., 286–94.
[265] Ibid., 295–9.
[266] Ibid., 258–60 & 300.
[267] UNWTO, *Global Code of Ethics for Tourism*, 2.
[268] Pope Francis, EVANGELII GAUDIUM [apostolic exhortation given at Saint Peter's in Rome on 24th November 2013], § 56, <http://w2.vatican.va/content/francesco/en/apost_exhortations/documents/papa-francesco_esortazione-ap_20131124_evangelii-gaudium.html>.
[269] UNWTO, *Global Code of Ethics for Tourism*, 2 & 5, art. 7(2).
[270] Ibid., 6, arts 8(4), 9(1) & 10(2).
[271] Ibid., 3, art. 3(2) & 4, art. 4(2).

²⁷² John McMurtry, *The Cancer Stage of Capitalism: From Crisis to Cure*, 310 (emphasis removed).
²⁷³ The poignant term "toxic asset" was coined by Angelo Mozilo, founder of Countrywide Financial (cf. Tom Petruno, "Mozilo knew hazardous waste when he saw it", *Los Angeles Times*, 4ᵗʰ June 2009, <http://latimesblogs.latimes.com/money_co/2009/06/the-use-of-toxic-to-describe-high-risk-mortgages-has-been-de-rigueur-for-the-last-two-years-now-it-looks-like-countrywide.html>). I was not able to determine the paternity of "banking cancer" and "financial metastasis".
²⁷⁴ Eric J. Hobsbawm, "Il marxismo e il movimento operaio: il secolo lungo", *Come cambiare il mondo: Perchè riscoprire l'eredità del marxismo*, Milan: BUR, 2011, 413–6 (translation mine; the English translation was necessary because about two-thirds of the material contained in the 2011 BUR book have never been published in Hobsbawm's native tongue, including the essay cited here).
²⁷⁵ Martha Nussbaum, *Not for Profit: Why Democracy Needs the Humanities*, Princeton: Princeton University Press, 2.
²⁷⁶ Paul Krugman, "Blooey", *The Conscience of a Liberal*, blog entry, 19ᵗʰ November 2011, 8:39am (emphasis added) and "The Яussians Are Coming! The Яussians Are Coming!" [sic], *The Conscience of a Liberal*, blog entry, 18ᵗʰ March 2013, 11:35am (emphasis added).
²⁷⁷ Cf. Robert E. Tucker, "Figure, Ground and Presence: A Phenomenology of Meaning in Rhetoric", *Quarterly Journal of Speech*, 87(4), 2001, 396–414.
²⁷⁸ Cf. Friedrich Nietzsche, "Lecture Notes on Rhetoric", *Philosophy and Rhetoric*, 16, 1983, 94–129 (lectures prepared originally in the 1860s).
²⁷⁹ Cf. Andrew Ortony, *Metaphor and Thought*, Cambridge: Cambridge University Press, 1993.
²⁸⁰ Cf. Bernard Mandeville, *The Fable of the Bees or Private Vices, Publick Benefits*, 1732, vol. 1, <http://oll.libertyfund.org/index.php?option=com_staticxt&staticfile=show.php&title=846&search=%22body+politick%22&layout=html#a_1631121>.
²⁸¹ Cf. Nils Bohr, "On the Constitution of Atoms and Molecules, Part II: Systems Containing Only a Single Nucleus", *Philosophical Magazine*, 26(153), 1913, 476–502.
²⁸² Cf. Aesop, "The Belly and the Members", *Aesop's Fables*, #130, 33, <http://history-world.org/Aesops_Fables_NT.pdf>. Axel Honneth's recent attempt at revamping socialism makes use of this image and envisions a "society of the future" operating like "an organic whole of independent yet purposefully cooperating functions in which the members act for each other in social freedom." (*The Idea of Socialism*, translated by Joseph Ganahal, Cambridge: Polity Press, 2017, 93).
²⁸³ Cf. Alan G. Gross, *The Rhetoric of Science*, Cambridge, Mass.: Harvard University Press, 1990.
²⁸⁴ Cf. Deirdre McCloskey, *The Rhetoric of Economics* (Madison: University of Wisconsin Press, 1985) and Albert O. Hirschman, *The Rhetoric of Reaction*.
²⁸⁵ E.g. David Humphreys, "Life Protective or Carcinogenic Challenge? Global Forests Governance under Advanced Capitalism", *Global Environmental Politics*, 3(2), 2003, 40–55.
²⁸⁶ Cf. Stefania Vitali, James B. Glattfelder and Stefano Battiston, "The Network of Global Corporate Control", *PLoS*, 6(10), 2011, <http://www.plosone.org/article/info%3Adoi%2F10.1371%2Fjournal.pone.0025995>.

[287] Cf. Andrew Glyn, *Capitalism Unleashed: Globalization, Finance and Welfare*, Oxford: Oxford University Press, 2006.
[288] E.g. Sampat Mukherjee, *Modern Economic Theory*, New Dehli: New Age International, 2002, 11–2.
[289] Cf. ibid and Norbert Häring and Njall Douglas, *Economists and the Powerful. Convenient Theories, Distorted Facts, Ample Rewards* (London: Anthem Press, 2012).
[290] Cf. Kenyon R. Stebbins, "Garbage Imperialism: Health Implications of Dumping Hazardous Wastes into Third World Countries", *Medical Anthropology*, 15(1), 1992, 81–102.
[291] Cf. Greg Palast, Maggie O'Kane and Chavala Madlena, "Vulture Funds Await Jersey Decision on Poor Countries' Debts", *The Guardian*, 15th November 2011, <http://www.guardian.co.uk/global-development/2011/nov/15/vulture-funds-jersey-decision>.
[292] Cf. Nicholas Shaxton, *Treasure Islands*, London: Bodley Head, 2011.
[293] Cf. Cornelius Castoriadis, "The Dilapidation of the West", *The Rising Tide of Insignificancy*, 2003, 73–108, <http://www.notbored.org/RTI.html> (the English translations of Castoriadis' works available on this website are anonymous and provided as a public service. Their quality and, above all, their accessibility, are higher than the alternatives available; hence my choice of them).
[294] Cf. John Kenneth Galbraith, *The Economics of Innocent Fraud: Truth for Our Time*, Boston: Allen Lane, 2004.
[295] Cf. Cornelius Castoriadis, "Imaginary and Imagination at the Crossroads", *Figures of the Thinkable*, 123–52, <http://www.notbored.org/FTPK.pdf>.
[296] Revealingly, few years after the publication of *The Cancer Stage of Capitalism*, McMurtry was invited by UNESCO to serve as Honorary Theme Editor for EOLSS.
[297] Cf. Thomas I. Palley, "America's Exhausted Paradigm: Macroeconomic Causes of the Financial Crisis and Great Recession" (*The New American Contract*, June 2009, <http://www.newamerica.net/files/Thomas_Palley_America's_Exhausted_Paradigm.pdf>) and Luciano Gallino, *Finanzcapitalismo*.
[298] Cf. Michael Hudson, *The Bubble and Beyond*, Dresden: Islet, 2012.
[299] Aulis Aarnio, "Statutory Interpretation in Finland", in *Interpreting Statutes. A Comparative Study*, edited by D. N. MacCormick and R. S. Summers, Aldershot: Dartmouth, 1991, 123.
[300] Cf. Cornelius Castoriadis, "The 'Rationality' of Capitalism", *Figures of the Thinkable*, 81–122.
[301] Cf. Judith M. Dean, Mary E. Lovely and Hua Wang, "Are Foreign Investors Attracted to Weak Environmental Regulations? Evaluating the Evidence from China", The World Bank Working Papers and Research Publications, 2005 (ref. 3505).
[302] Donella H. Meadows, Dennis L. Meadows, Jorgen Randers and William W. Behrens III, *The Limits to Growth*, Milan: Universe, 1972.
[303] E.g. Tim Jackson, *Prosperity Without Growth. Economics for a Finite Planet* (London: Earthscan, 2009) and Rob Dietz, Dan O'Neill and Herman Daily, *Enough is Enough. Building a Sustainable Economy in a World of Finite Resources* (London: Routledge, 2012).

[304] Cf. James Crotty, "Structural Contradictions of the Global Neoliberal Regime" [paper presented at the meetings of the Union for Radical Political Economics at the Allied Social Sciences Association in Boston, 7th–9th January 2000], <http://people.umass.edu/crotty/assa-final-jan00.pdf>.
[305] Cornelius Castoriadis, "Imaginary and Imagination at the Crossroads", 129.
[306] John McMurtry, "The Social Immune System and the Cancer Stage of Capitalism", *Social Justice*, Special issue: Public Health in the 1990s, 22(4), 1995, 1–25.
[307] John McMurtry, *The Cancer Stage of Capitalism: From Crisis to Cure*, 22.
[308] E.g. Wolfgang Streeck, "Four Books on Capitalism", *Socio-Economic Review*, 7(4), 2009, 741–54.
[309] John McMurtry, *The Cancer Stage of Capitalism: From Crisis to Cure*, 22–4 (emphasis added).
[310] Ibid., 22–5.
[311] Ibid., 30–40 & 167–78 (emphasis removed).
[312] E.g. ibid., 46–63 on Chile, the US, Iraq, Canada and Japan; 138–40 on Canada; 141 on New Zealand; 156–8 on former Yugoslavia, sub-Saharan Africa and Guatemala; 163–4 & 223 on Mexico; 26–8, 190–1, 226–7, 251–2 & 278–86 on the EU; 193–5 on post-communist countries; 224 on Peru; 224–6 on Rwanda; 274–7 on Japan; 286–7 on Libya.
[313] Cf. Ibid., 76–7 & 152–3.
[314] E.g. ibid., 226 (Giulio Tremonti), 229–30 (Nicolas Sarkozy), 234 (Pat Buchanan and Bob Dole), 234–5 (Robert Reich), 236 (George Soros), 247 (Bill Clinton), 250 (Aung San Suu Kyi) & 308 ("Lula" da Silva).
[315] Ibid., 212–6.
[316] Ibid., 202–3.
[317] As cited in ibid., 17.
[318] Ibid., 128; cf. also 247.
[319] Ibid., 245.
[320] Ibid., 169.
[321] Ibid., 99.
[322] Ibid., 170.
[323] Ibid., 78.
[324] Ibid., 19.
[325] As cited in ibid., 170.
[326] Ibid. (emphasis removed).
[327] Ibid. (emphasis removed).
[328] Ibid., 17 (emphasis removed).
[329] Ibid., 51 (emphasis removed).
[330] Ibid., 106 (emphasis in the original).
[331] Ibid., 3.
[332] Ibid., 180 (emphasis in the original).
[333] Ibid., 123 (emphasis removed).
[334] E.g. O. Ferrell, M. Hartline, G. Lucas and D. Luck, *Marketing Strategy*, Orlando: Dryden, 1998.
[335] Citibank Chief Economist Willem Buiter as cited in John McMurtry, *The Cancer Stage of Capitalism: From Crisis to Cure*, 12 (emphasis removed).
[336] Ibid., 6 (emphasis in the original).
[337] Ibid., 232–4.

338 Ibid., 156.
339 Economist Peter Drucker as cited in ibid., 127.
340 Ibid., 189 (emphasis removed).
341 Ibid., 6; cf. also 269.
342 Ibid., 109.
343 Ibid., 128–30.
344 Ibid., 90.
345 Ibid., 6.
346 Ibid., 8.
347 Ibid., 10.
348 Ibid., 28–9.
349 Ibid., 45 (emphasis removed).
350 Ibid., 188.
351 Ibid., 5.
352 Ibid., 15.
353 Ibid., 20.
354 Ibid., 41.
355 Ibid., 133 & 246.
356 Ibid., 189.
357 Ibid., 201–2.
358 Ibid., 224–6.
359 Ibid., 8.
360 Ibid., 16.
361 Ibid., 102.
362 Ibid., 118–24.
363 Ibid., 35, 183 & 202–3.
364 Ibid., 19.
365 Ibid., 21.
366 Ibid., 42.
367 Ibid., 102.
368 Ibid., 3 & 124–5.
369 Ibid., 190.
370 Ibid., 208–10.
371 Ibid., 218.
372 Ibid., 15 (emphasis added).
373 Ibid., 20.
374 Ibid., 162–3.
375 Ibid., 19.
376 Ibid., 182–3 (emphasis removed).
377 Cf. S.R. Lakhani, S.A. Dilly and C.J. Finlayson, *Basic Pathology, an Introduction to the Mechanisms of Disease* (4th ed.), London: Hodder Arnold, 2009.
378 Cf. L.B. Peppas and J.O. Blanchette, "Nanoparticle and Targeted Systems for Cancer Therapy", *Advanced Drug Delivery Reviews*, 56, 2004, 1649–59.
379 Cf. V. Pinsolle, A. Ravaud and J. Baudet, "Does Surgery Promote the Development of Metastasis in Melanoma?", *Annales de Chirurgie Plastique Esthétique*, 45(4), 2000, 485–93.

[380] Cf. Elísabet Hjörleifsdóttir *et al.*, "Living with Cancer and Perception of Care: Icelandic Oncology Outpatients, a Qualitative Study", *Support Care Cancer*, 16, 2008, 515–24.

[381] John Maynard Keynes, *The General Theory of Employment, Interest and Money*, chapter 24, § 2.

[382] Cf. Harold J. Berman, *Law and Revolution: The Formation of the Western Legal Tradition*, Cambridge, Mass: Harvard University Press, 1983.

[383] Cf. Páll Skúlason, *A Critique of Universities*, Reykjavík: Háskólaútgafan, 2015.

[384] New York: Harper and Row, 1969, 264–9 (Drucker himself was drawing inspiration from Fritz Machlup's 1962 book *Production and Distribution of Knowledge in the United States*, Princeton: Princeton University Press).

[385] Ibid., 271–7.

[386] Ibid., 277–8.

[387] I refer in this chapter to *An Inquiry into the Nature and Causes of the Wealth of Nations* (WN) by book, chapter and paragraph numbers; and specifically to the 1904 Cannan edition of Smith's work, published by Methuen in London and available online on the *Library of Economics and Liberty*.

[388] Alan Greenspan, "Remarks by Chairman Alan Greenspan. Economic Flexibility", *The Federal Reserve Board* [speech given before the National Italian American Foundation in Washington D.C. on the 12th October 2005], <http://www.federalreserve.gov/boarddocs/speeches/2005/20051012/default.htm>. Cf. also Alan Greenspan's 2007, hence pre-crisis, book *The Age of Turbulence: Adventures in a New World* (Penguin, New York) for further instantiations of the same points (15, 89, photographic insert 1 page 5, 276, 325, 488, 502, and especially 260–6 & 367–70).

[389] In this chapter, I interpret Smith's favoured economic system to be an ideal rather than a historical given, for he claims it in WN to be an expression of actual human nature, but also one that other expressions of human nature oppose relentlessly and repeatedly, thus making it "an Oceana or Utopia" to ever unfold *in toto*, even in his native land (IV.ii.43).

[390] Alan Greenspan, "Remarks by Chairman Alan Greenspan. Economic Flexibility".

[391] Wall Street top financiers are known as "masters of the universe" because of a popular 1987 novel by Tom Wolfe, *The Bonfire of Vanities* (New York: Bantam).

[392] Exemplarily, influential businessmen such as Goldman Sachs chairman Lloyd Blankfein (b. 1954) and Barclays CEO Bob Diamond (b. 1951), who had embodied the competitive ethos of unmitigated self-aggrandisement as a supreme aim, started issuing public apologies and calls for ethical behaviour (cf. Christine Harper and Matt Townsend, "Blankfein Apologizes for Goldman Sachs Role in Crisis", *Bloomberg*, 17th November 2009, <http://www.bloomberg.com/apps/news?pid= newsarchive&sid=aeV9jwqKKrEw>).

[393] As cited in Andrew Clark and Jill Treanor, "Greenspan — I Was Wrong About the Economy. Sort of", *The Guardian*, 24th October 2008, <http://www.guardian.co.uk/business/2008/oct/24/economics-creditcrunch-federal-reserve-greenspan>.

[394] Cf. Charles Bean, "The Great Moderation, the Great Panic, and the Great Contraction", *The Bank of England* [speech given at the Annual Congress of the European Economic Association, Barcelona, 25th August 2009], <http://www.bankofengland.co.uk/publications/Documents/speeches/2009/speech399.pdf>.

[395] In private e-mail exchanges with Dr. Maria Pia Paganelli, she describes and criticises the present chapter as "Marxist", but accepts as correct the use that has been made of her work. I thank her hereby for her help.

[396] Cf. also David Harvey, *A Brief History of Neoliberalism*, Oxford: Oxford University Press, 2005.

[397] Adam Smith, WN, IV.vii.129.

[398] Maria Pia Paganelli, "Is a Beautiful System Dying? A Possible Smithian Take on the Financial Crisis", *Adam Smith Review*, 6, 2011, 269.

[399] Cf. Alan Greenspan, *The Age of Turbulence*, 40–1, 51–3 & 134.

[400] Cf. Adam Smith, *The Theory of Moral Sentiments*. London: Millar, 1790.

[401] Cf. Maria Pia Paganelli, "*In Medio Stat Virtus*: An Alternative View of Usury in Adam Smith's Thinking", *History of Political Economy*, 35(1), 2003, 21–48.

[402] Cf. Maria Pia Paganelli, "Approbation and the Desire to Better One's Condition in Adam Smith", *Journal of the History of Economic Thought*, 31(1), 2009, 79–92.

[403] Maria Pia Paganelli, "Is a Beautiful System Dying?", 271.

[404] Cf. also John Kenneth Galbraith, *The Age of Uncertainty*, London: BBC, 1977, 279, in which corporate apparatchiks are described as seeking "constructive cooperation between government and industry" i.e. "socialism for the rich".

[405] As far as bullying is concerned, WHO Director-General Margret Chan (b. 1947) has recently denounced how "high-profile commercial and investment arbitrations targeting Uruguay and Australia are deliberately designed to instill fear in other countries wishing to introduce similarly tough tobacco control measures. Numerous other countries are being subjected to the same kind of aggressive scare tactics. It is hard for any country to bear the financial burden of this kind of litigation, but most especially so for small countries." ("Maintaining Momentum in an Era of Austerity" [speech delivered on 10th October 2011], <http://www.who.int/dg/speeches/2011/wpro_10_10/en/>).

[406] Cf. Maria Pia Paganelli and Andrew Farrant, "Are Two Knaves Better Than One? Every Man a Knave: Hume, Buchanan, and Musgrave's Views on Economics and Government", *History of Political Economy*, 37, Supplement 1, 2005, 71–90.

[407] Maria Pia Paganelli, "Is a Beautiful System Dying?", 274.

[408] E.g. Adam Smith, WN, V.i.107.

[409] Cf. also Sankar Muthu, "Adam Smith's Critique of International Trading Companies. Theorizing 'Globalization' in the Age of Enlightenment", *Political Theory*, 36, 2008, 185–212.

[410] E.g. Maria Pia Paganelli, "David Hume on Monetary Policy: A Retrospective Approach", *Journal of Scottish Philosophy*, 7(1), 2009, 65–85.

[411] Cf. Adolf Berle and Gardiner Means, *The Modern Corporation and Private Property* (Piscataway: Transaction, 1932) and Michael Jensen and William Meckling, "Theory of the Firm: Managerial Behavior, Agency Costs and Ownership Structure" (*Journal of Financial Economics* 3(4), 1976, 305–60).

⁴¹² Cf. Alfred Chandler, *Scale and Scope. The Dynamics of Industrial Capitalism* (Cambridge, MA: Belknap, 1994) and James Hawley and Andrew Williams, *The Rise of Fiduciary Capitalism. How Institutional Investors Can Make Corporate America More Democratic* (Philadelphia: University of Pennsylvania Press, 2000).
⁴¹³ Cf. John Kenneth Galbraith, *The Age of Uncertainty* and Patrick K. O'Brien and Armand Clesse (eds.), *Two Hegemonies: Britain 1846–1914 and The United States 1941–2001* (Aldershot: Ashgate, 2002).
⁴¹⁴ Cf. Luciano Gallino *Finanzcapitalismo*, 55ff, which sheds light upon the last descriptor, offering data on the stark predominance of finance in world trade: the approximate 2007 ratio of internationally recorded on-balance financial assets over world GDP was 4.4, whilst the likely ratio of off-balance financial assets (mostly derivatives) over world GDP was 12.6. Besides, the near-totality of these assets was designed, traded and/or owned by a handful of financial holdings, which also controlled significant stakes in non-financial corporations as direct or indirect shareholders (e.g. through investment funds) or as sources of credit and insurance. On top of this, they often operated *via* opaque ownership structures making use of foreign tax havens.
⁴¹⁵ Cf. John Crowley, *The Privileges of Independence. Neomercantilism and the American Revolution* (Baltimore: The Johns Hopkins University Press, 1993), Joseph Stancliffe Davis, *Essays in the Earlier History of American Corporations* (Clark: The Lawbook Exchange, 2006; originally published in 1917), Jeffry Frieden, *Global Capitalism. Its Fall and Rise in the Twentieth Century* (London: Norton, 2006) and Michael Hudson, *America's Protectionist Take-Off 1815–1914. The Neglected American School of Political Economy* (Hobart: Islet, 2010; 2ⁿᵈ ed.).
⁴¹⁶ E.g. Henry George, *Progress and Poverty* (London: Penguin, 2000; originally published in 1879), Thorstein Veblen, *Ownership and Business Enterprise in Recent Times. The Case of America* (New York: Kelley, 1964; originally published in 1923), John Kenneth Galbraith, *The New Industrial State* (Princeton: Princeton University Press, 2007; originally published in 1967) and Michael Hudson, *Super Imperialism, The Economic Strategy of American Empire* (London: Pluto Press, 2003; 2ⁿᵈ ed.).
⁴¹⁷ Smith as cited in Chomsky as cited in Milan Rai, "Market Values and Libertarian Socialist Values", in *The Cambridge Companion to Chomsky* (edited by James McGilvray, Cambridge: Cambridge University Press, 2005, 225–39), 228–9 & 231. Chomsky's quote from Smith's WN reads "need to truck and barter", but Smith (WN, I.ii.1, 4 & 5) actually wrote of a "propensity", "disposition" and "power" to "truck, barter and exchange", namely a token of rhetorical *interpretatio*, hence the amended quote in the text. Cf. also Noam Chomsky, *Understanding Power. The Indispensable Chomsky* (edited by Peter Mitchell and John Schoeffel, London: Vintage, 2002), 221.
⁴¹⁸ Maria Pia Paganelli, "Is a Beautiful System Dying?", 269.
⁴¹⁹ Cf. Noam Chomsky, *Understanding Power*, 346–48.
⁴²⁰ Cf. ibid., 390–95.
⁴²¹ Cf. ibid., 222; cf. also Andrew Terjesen, "Adam Smith Cared, So Why Can't Modern Economics?" (in *Applying Care Ethics to Business*, edited by Maurice Hamington and Maureen Sander-Staudt, Dordrecht: Springer, 2011, 55–72, 2011).
⁴²² Cf. Adam Smith, WN, IV.vii.29 & V.i.39.
⁴²³ Ibid., I.xi.263.

[424] Cf. ibid., I.i.11.
[425] Ibid., III.i.1.
[426] Ibid., V.i.178.
[427] Cf. John Kenneth Galbraith, *Tout savoir — ou presque — sur l'economie* (Paris: Editions du Seuil, 1978), who doubted whether market competition *à la* Smith could be the case in a modern economy, where gargantuan corporations lead the game. He observed that competition, albeit much praised, is regularly eschewed: (a) by shareholders and owners, who lobby governments on national as well as international levels to be secured revenue or establish oligopolies and *de facto* cartels; (b) by top managers, who pay themselves stellar salaries settling them for life after a short spell at a company; and (c) workers, who seek favourable contracts *via* trade unions' bargaining—all three groups seeking advantages irrespective of performance.
[428] Cf. Noam Chomsky, *Understanding Power*, 42–3.
[429] Cf. ibid., 140–3 & 203–4.
[430] Contemporary countries whose markets were forcibly opened to corporatisation recall lethally poor resource-rich Bengal in Smith's WN, i.e. the chief example of a declining economy by way of a joint-stock company's mismanagement and overexploitation (I.viii.26).
[431] Cf. Noam Chomsky, *Understanding Power*, 255–8.
[432] Cf. ibid., 191–2, 280–4 & 344–6; cf. also Milan Rai, "Market Values and Libertarian Socialist Values", 230–1.
[433] Cf. Noam Chomsky, *Understanding Power*, 251–5.
[434] As cited in Milan Rai, "Market Values and Libertarian Socialist Values", 229–30. Austere, Austrian free-market advocates of the Ludwig von Mises Institute were aware of the "confusing... rhetoric" of Ronald Reagan, whom Sheldon Richman defines as "the most protectionist president since Herbert Hoover" ("Ronald Reagan: Protectionist", *The Free Market*, 6(5), 1988, <http://mises.org/freemarket_detail.aspx?control=489>).
[435] Cf. Noam Chomsky, *Understanding Power*, 251–5.
[436] McMurtry's main source on the existence of global oligopolies is uncontroversial: *The Economist*.
[437] McMurtry remarks that the "average life" of today's commodities is 42 days and "most investment is in financial vehicles with no labour input and no production of material commodity at all" (*The Cancer Stage of Capitalism*, 44). What is more, these financial vehicles change hands every 20–22 seconds (cf. Michael Hudson, "Higher taxes on top 1% equals higher productivity" [interview with *The Real News*, 1st January 2011], <http://therealnews.com/t2/index.php?option=com_content&task=view&id=31&Itemid=74&jumival=6000.2011>).
[438] As Adam Smith commends in WN "the wealth of nations as consisting, not in the unconsumable riches of money, but in the consumable goods annually reproduced by the labour of the society." (IV.ix.38).
[439] McMurtry cites "downsizing, job-shedding, sector dismantling", the financialisation of enterprises and the vagaries of speculative capital trade as crucial causes of a long trail of unemployed, underemployed and low-paid labour (*The Cancer Stage of Capitalism*, 44), whose increasing annual revenues were for Adam Smith a key-indicator of a nation's growing wealth (cf. WN, IV.iii.32).

[440] McMurtry observes how many of today's "business-friendly" governments have promoted "flat taxation, taxation of the majority ... serving ... transnational investors and corporations, competitive lowering of corporate taxation ... tax-havens for the rich ... reduction of income taxes on the wealthy"; in brief, they have reduced progressive taxation in lieu of regressive taxation (e.g. US payroll taxes, value-added and sales taxes), shifting its burden off rent-seeking incumbents (e.g. landowners, large recipients of capital gains) and onto productive structures, while at the same time providing devoted infrastructure and services, subsidies, special credit lines and bail-out money to corporations that have been contributing less and less tax money to the public purse (e.g. 1980s US bank bailouts; *The Cancer Stage of Capitalism*, 44ff).

[441] Adam Smith, WN, V.ii.8.

[442] Cf. ibid., IV.ii.6.

[443] Ibid., II.iii.2.

[444] Cf. Vincent W. Bladen, "Adam Smith on Productive and Unproductive Labour. A Theory of Full Development", *Canadian Journal of Economics and Political Science*, 26(4), 1960, 625–30.

[445] Cf. Milan Rai, "Market Values and Libertarian Socialist Values", 227–8.

[446] Cf. Noam Chomsky, *Understanding Power*, 216–7.

[447] Cf. ibid.

[448] Ibid., 261.

[449] Ibid. 355–62.

[450] Cf. José Atilano Pena López and José Manuel Sánchez Santos, "El problema de Smith y la relación entre moral y economía", *Isegoría. Revista de Filosofía Moral y Política*, 36, 2007, 81–103.

[451] Cf. Noam Chomsky, *Understanding Power*, 72–3 & 240–2.

[452] Cf. ibid., 61–4, 85–7, 96–101, 106, 111–5, 183–4 & 203–11.

[453] Cf. ibid., 195–9 & 222; cf. also Milan Rai, "Market Values and Libertarian Socialist Values", 234–5.

[454] I mention here examples of historical changes that Smith did not deem possible or likely to occur.

[455] Cf. Noam Chomsky, *Understanding Power*, 177–80 & 186–7.

[456] Albert Einstein, "Why Socialism?", *Monthly Review*, May 1949, <https://monthlyreview.org/2009/05/01/why-socialism/>. An analogous form of socialism can be retrieved today in the work of Frankfurt School's third-generation champion, Axel Honneth, who claims "unused potentials for social renewal" to be best unleashed "through a process of communication which is as unrestricted as possible", as also notably argued, in his view, by John Dewey (1859–1952), Emile Durkheim (1858–1917) and Jürgen Habermas (*The Idea of Socialism*, 96).

[457] John McMurtry, *Value Wars*, 49.

[458] Ibid., 87.

[459] Ibid., 50.

[460] Cf. ibid., 54.

[461] Cf. ibid., 50.

[462] Ibid., 48.

[463] Cf. John McMurtry, *The Cancer Stage of Capitalism*, 39.

[464] John McMurtry, "Understanding Market Theology", in *The Invisible Hand and the Common Good*, edited by Bernard Hodgson, Dordrecht: Springer, 2004, 151–82. Chapter 11 of the present book contains ample textual evidence of how Smith's "invisible hand" should be understood as a deistic conception of benevolent providence, as also argued by Paul Oslington in *Adam Smith as Theologian* (London: Routledge, 2011).

[465] The unfalsifiability of the invisible-hand hypothesis is articulated in chapter 12 of this book.

[466] Cf. also Karl Polanyi, *The Great Transformation: The Political and Economic Origins of Our Time* (Boston: Beacon Press, 2002, 2nd ed.; originally published in 1944) and John Quiggin, "Common Property Rights in the Economics of the Environment" (*Journal of Economic Issues*, 22(4), 2002, 1071–87).

[467] Adam Smith, WN, IV.vii.59.

[468] Ibid., IV.i.33 & I.viii.37–8.

[469] Noam Chomsky, *Understanding Power*, 58.

[470] Ibid.

[471] Ibid.

[472] Ibid., II.ii.94.

[473] As shown in chapter 11 of the present book, Adam Smith's attribution of value to human life was more often instrumental than intrinsic.

[474] Chicago: University of Chicago Press.

[475] Adam Smith had already used the term "free trade" to describe what we have come to know as "capitalism", which is a term born in the 19th century. The latest edition of the *Oxford English Dictionary* locates its first usage in English in 1854 by William Makepeace Thackeray (1811–1863) in his novel, *The Newcomes*. In French, however, the term had already been in use for a longer time. The 1992 edition *Dictionnaire historique de la langue française*, edited by Alain Rey and published in Paris by Le Robert, records its first usage in 1753. In German, as perhaps to be expected, Karl Marx makes use of the term *Kapitalismus* in the first volume of *Das Kapital* (1867), though, perhaps unexpectedly to the readers, only twice. It is only with the historian Werner Sombart (1863–1941) and his 1902 work *Der modern Kapitalismus* that the word becomes mainstream.

[476] Bill Clinton, *Between Hope and History*, New York: Random House, 1996, 36. I chose a quote by a political world leader from the left, for neoliberal policies are commonly associated with right-wing parties and politicians, notably Margaret Thatcher and Ronald Reagan, but in effect became much more widespread in the 1990s across the whole political spectrum, becoming eventually the conventional wisdom of most 21st-century decision-makers and world leaders, particularly in Europe and North America.

[477] Cf. Pia Guldager Bilde and Vladimir F. Stolba (eds.), *Surveying the Greek Chora. The Black Sea Region in a Comparative Perspective*, Aarhus: Aarhus University Press, Black Sea Studies 4, 2006.

[478] Cornelius Castoriadis, "First Institution of Society and Second-Order Institutions", in *Figures of the Thinkable*, 162. Historical research suggests that risk-averse family farmers were behind democratic and republican regimes in ancient Greece and Italy, rather than protobourgeois merchants, as in Medieval Europe (cf. A. W. Griswold, *Farming and Democracy* (New Haven: Yale University Press, 1948) and V. D. Hanson, *The Other Greeks: The Family Farm and the Agrarian Roots of Western Civilization* (New York: The Free Press, 1995)).
[479] Cornelius Castoriadis, "Imaginary and Imagination at the Crossroads", 129.
[480] Ibid.
[481] Cf. William N. Goetzmann, *Money Changes Everything: How Finance Made Civilization Possible*, Princeton: Princeton University Press, 2016.
[482] E.g. Giuseppe Gallo, *La Repubblica di Genova tra nobili e popolari*, Genoa: De Ferrari, 1997.
[483] Cornelius Castoriadis, "The 'Rationality' of Capitalism", 87 (emphasis mine).
[484] Cornelius Castoriadis, "Third World, Third Worldism, Democracy", *The Rising Tide of Insignificancy*, 53.
[485] The hypothetical *datum* at issue is very hypothetical and historically most dubious (see following note), yet it has become part of the public mind-set, analogously to the way in which the saintliness of the first Christian Emperor Constantine was a widespread yet utterly false belief upheld by Christians until the 18th century.
[486] The commonplace rhetorical twinning of capitalism and democracy blossomed in the 1990s, in spite of capitalist economies having prospered under fascist and military dictatorships, e.g. Mussolini's Italy, Hitler's Germany, Pinochet's Chile (cf. Eric Hobsbawm, *Age of Extremes: The Short Twentieth Century: 1914–1991*, London: Michael Joseph, 1994/Abacus, 1995).
[487] Cornelius Castoriadis, "Democracy as Procedure, Democracy as Regime", *The Rising Tide of Insignificancy*, 350.
[488] Cornelius Castoriadis, "The Dilapidation of the West", 88.
[489] Cf. Cornelius Castoriadis, "The 'Rationality' of Capitalism".
[490] Adam Smith, WN, I.xi.163–4.
[491] A commendable exception to this oblivion is Jeff Noonan's *Democratic Society and Human Needs*, where the differences and the conflicts between the liberal and the republican movements in the late 18th century and throughout the 19th century are outlined most clearly and analysed as orbiting around a struggle between the centrality of property rights *versus* life needs.
[492] Camillo Cavour, book review of *History of Piedmont: Carlo Alberto's Kingdom* by Angelo Brofferio, *Il Risorgimento*, III, 797, 27th July 1850, 3–4.
[493] Adam Smith, WN, I.xi.261–3.
[494] Ibid.
[495] Ibid., I.viii.38.
[496] Ibid., I.xi.263.
[497] Ibid.
[498] Ibid., V.i.55.
[499] Cf. Leonard Trelawny Hobhouse, *Liberalism*, London: Williams & Northgate, 1911, <http://socserv2.socsci.mcmaster.ca/econ/ugcm/3ll3/hobhouse/liberalism.pdf>.
[500] Cornelius Castoriadis, "The 'Rationality' of Capitalism", 88.

[501] Ibid., 87–8. An interesting exception to this trend was constituted by Vilfredo Pareto, who was not only a staunch liberal, but also one of the decisive figures in the history of economics *vis-à-vis* the formalisation and mathematical symbolisation of this discipline. Although he never abandoned the idea that mathematical economics could give us some rough yet useful general picture of economic life, he did realise in his maturity that the tools of economics, even when cast in as "scientific" terms as possible, fell short of comprehending and explaining human behaviour, both individual and collective (cf. Joseph Femia, *Pareto and Political Theory*, London: Routledge, 2006). Too complex, unpredictable and irrational, human behaviour needed additional and alternative means of comprehension and explanation, which Pareto endeavoured to provide in his monumental 1916 *Trattato di sociologia generale* (translated in 1935 into English by Andrew Bongiorno, Arthur Livingstone and James Harvey Rogers as *The Mind and Society*, London: Jonathan Cape). Belated and yet little aware of the intrinsic limitations of neoclassical economics comes the late-20th-century study of so-called "market irrationality", which sneeringly assumes that human beings who do not operate according to the principles posited by classical and neoclassical economists are not rational.
[502] Cornelius Castoriadis, "The 'Rationality' of Capitalism, 91.
[503] Cf. Oscar Wilde, "The Soul of Man under Socialism", 1891, <https://www.marxists.org/reference/archive/wilde-oscar/soul-man/>.
[504] Karl Marx and Friedrich Engels, *The Communist Manifesto*, translated by A.J.P. Taylor, London: Penguin Classics, 1998, 97.
[505] Cornelius Castoriadis, "The 'Rationality' of Capitalism", 89.
[506] Ibid., 91.
[507] Ibid., 89.
[508] Ibid., 89–90.
[509] Ibid., 91.
[510] Ibid., 92.
[511] Ibid.
[512] Cornelius Castoriadis, "Unending Interrogation", *The Rising Tide of Insignificancy*, 274.
[513] Cornelius Castoriadis, "The 'Rationality' of Capitalism", 93.
[514] Cornelius Castoriadis, "The Rising Tide of Insignificancy", 135.
[515] Similar points about the birth and development of religion were made later by Friedrich Nietzsche (1844–1900) and Sigmund Freud (1856–1939).
[516] John McMurtry, "Understanding Market Theology", 157.
[517] Cornelius Castoriadis, "The 'Rationality' of Capitalism", 93.
[518] Ibid.
[519] John McMurtry, "Understanding Market Theology", 174.
[520] London: Routledge, 2001.
[521] Cornelius Castoriadis, "The 'Rationality' of Capitalism", 93–5.
[522] Ibid., 96.
[523] Edmund Burke, *Reflections on the Revolution in France,* § 134.
[524] Ibid., §§ 128 & 126.
[525] Cornelius Castoriadis, "The 'Rationality' of Capitalism", 96.
[526] Ibid.
[527] Cornelius Castoriadis, "Third World, Third Worldism, Democracy", 48.
[528] Ibid., 52.

[529] Cornelius Castoriadis, "The 'Rationality' of Capitalism", 96.
[530] Cf. J.A. Mayer, *The Persistence of the Old Regime*, New York: Pantheon Books, 1981.
[531] Cornelius Castoriadis, "Anthropology, Philosophy, Politics", *The Rising Tide of Insignificancy*, 205.
[532] Cornelius Castoriadis, "The Dilapidation of the West", 79.
[533] Ludwig von Mises, *Liberalism*, 1927, chapter 1, § 10, <https://mises.org/library/liberalism-classical-tradition/html>.
[534] Cf. Renée Sallas, "Leader and Master of Liberalism" (*El Mercuro*, 12th April 1981, D8–9) and Greg Grandin, *The Last Colonial Massacre: Latin America in the Cold War* (Chicago: University of Chicago Press, 2011).
[535] Immanuel Kant, *Groundwork of the Metaphysics of Morals*, translated and edited by Mary Gregor, New York: Cambridge University Press, 1998, 42–3 (emphases in the original).
[536] Cornelius Castoriadis, "The Rising Tide of Insignificancy", 149.
[537] Cornelius Castoriadis, "Third World, Third Worldism, Democracy", 51–2.
[538] Cf. Cornelius Castoriadis, "The 'Rationality' of Capitalism".
[539] Cornelius Castoriadis, "The Dilapidation of the West", 87–8.
[540] Ibid.
[541] Cf. Antonio Nicaso and Lee Lamothe, *Global Mafia: The New World Order of Organized Crime* (Toronto: Macmillan, 1995) and John Dickie, Cosa Nostra: *A History of the Sicilian Mafia* (London: Hodder & Stoughton, 2004). Indeed, the contemporary Mafioso, who bullies others into submission, smashes competitors and destroys lives for the sake of personal aggrandisement—hence the chilling phrase "it is nothing personal, it is just business"—whilst diversifying her portfolio with a keen eye for the most profitable investments, exemplifies unnoticed the successful anthropological type that neoliberalism implies.
[542] Cornelius Castoriadis, "The 'Rationality' of Capitalism", 90.
[543] Ibid.
[544] Ibid.
[545] Cf. Jacques LeGoff, *La bourse et la vie*, Paris: Hachette, 1986.
[546] Cornelius Castoriadis, "The 'Rationality' of Capitalism", 115.
[547] Cf. Jeremy Rifkin, *The Age of Access: the New Culture of Hypercapitalism Where All of Life Is a Paid-for Experience*, New York: Tarcher/putnam, 2000.
[548] Amy M. Spindler, "Review/Fashion; In Milan, Bold Visions And a Softer Silhouette", 1st July 1993, <www.nytimes.com>, (emphasis mine).
[549] Cf. Benjamin Barber, *Consumed: How Markets Corrupt Children, Infantilize Adults, and Swallow Citizens Whole*, New York: Norton, 2007.
[550] John K. Galbraith, *The New Industrial State*, 144.
[551] Cf. Jean Baudrillard, *La Société de consummation*, Paris: Éditions Denoël, 1970.
[552] Thorstein Veblen, *Theory of the Leisure Class: An Economic Study in the Evolution of Institutions*, London: Penguin, 1994 (originally published in 1899).
[553] Cf. Bruno Frey and Alois Stutzer, *Happiness and Economics* (Princeton: Princeton University Press, 2002) and Joseph Heath and Andrew Potter, *The Rebel Sell. How the Counterculture Became Consumer Culture* (Chichester: Capstone, 2005).
[554] Cornelius Castoriadis, "The 'Rationality' of Capitalism", 115.

555 Cf. Eric Clark, *The Real Toy Story: Inside the Ruthless Battle for America's Youngest Consumers*, New York: Free Press, 2007.
556 Cornelius Castoriadis, "The Rising Tide of Insignificancy", 148–9.
557 Cornelius Castoriadis, "Third World, Third Worldism, Democracy", 51.
558 Cornelius Castoriadis, "The 'Rationality' of Capitalism", 115 (emphasis mine).
559 Cf. Jeff Noonan, *Democratic Society and Human Needs.*
560 John McMurtry, *Unequal Freedoms*, 376.
561 John McMurtry, *Value Wars,* 101 & 104–5.
562 Cornelius Castoriadis, "The Revolutionary Force of Ecology", *The Rising Tide of Insignificancy*, 115.
563 Cf. especially Cornelius Castoriadis, *Figures of the Thinkable.*
564 For all the works by Smith cited in this chapter, cf. the definitive 1981–7 Glasgow edition of his works and correspondence, i.e. Adam Smith, *The Glasgow Edition of the Works and Correspondence of Adam Smith*, Indianapolis: Liberty Fund, 1982, <http://oll.libertyfund.org/title/197>, which comprises: *The Theory of Moral Sentiments*, edited by D.D. Raphael and A.L. Macfie (vol. I), <http://oll.libertyfund.org/title/192>; *An Inquiry Into the Nature and Causes of the Wealth of Nations*, 2 Vols., edited by R. H. Campbell and A. S. Skinner (vol. II), <http://oll.libertyfund.org/title/220>; *Essays on Philosophical Subjects*, edited by W. P. D. Wightman and J. C. Bryce (vol. III), <http://oll.libertyfund.org/title/201>; *Lectures On Rhetoric and Belles Lettres*, edited by J. C. Bryce (vol. IV), <http://oll.libertyfund.org/title/202>; *Lectures On Jurisprudence*, edited by R.. L. Meek, D. D. Raphael and P. G. Stein (vol. V), <http://oll.libertyfund.org/title/196>; *Correspondence of Adam Smith*, ed. E. C. Mossner and I. S. Ross (vol. VI), <http://oll.libertyfund.org/title/203>.
565 Adam Smith, "The Principles Which Lead and Direct Philosophical Enquiries; Illustrated by the History of the Ancient Physics" (commonly abbreviated as *Ancient Physics*), §§ 8–9.
566 Adam Smith, "The Principles Which Lead and Direct Philosophical Enquiries; Illustrated by the History of the Ancient Logics and Metaphysics" (commonly abbreviated as *Ancient Logics*), § 4.
567 Smith's *Inquiry into the Nature and Causes of the Wealth of Nations* (1776, Cannan ed.) has already been abbreviated as WN. Since from this chapter onwards I am going to cite as frequently also his *Theory of Moral Sentiments* (1759; 6th ed., 1790), then I abbreviate it as TMS. TMS being more quixotic than WN in its internal subdivisions into parts, sections and chapters, I specify further in this chapter all such subdivisions for both books. Thus the reader should find it easier to retrieve the original sources, which are cited here.
568 The full title reads also: "delivered in the University of Glasgow and reported by a student, 1762–3".
569 Ibid., lecture 2, 19th November 1762, §§ 7–8 & n4.
570 Ibid., lecture 6, 29th November 1762, n11.
571 Ibid., lecture 8, December 1762, n14.
572 Ibid., lecture 7, 1st December 1762, § 83; and lecture 13, 20th December 1762, §§ 174–5 & n14.
573 Ibid., lecture 17, 5th January 1763, § 20.
574 Ibid., lecture 26, 31st January 1763, § 171 & n8.
575 E.g. ibid., lecture 7, 1st December 1762, § 83.
576 Ibid., lecture 20, 12th January 1763, §§ 63–4, 66 & 68.

577 Ibid., §§ 66–7.
578 Adam Smith, *Considerations Concerning the First Formation of Languages*, 1761, § 2.
579 Adam Smith, "A Letter to the Authors of the *Edinburgh Review*", 1755, § 11. Unlike Mandeville, Smith believed enlightened, moral self-interest to bring about prosperity, rather than outright selfishness and even knavery. Furthermore, Mandeville thought public authorities able to steer such selfishness and knavery towards the common good, while Smith was far more sceptical about public interferences in private affairs.
580 Ibid., § 12.
581 Ibid., § 15.
582 Adam Smith, "Of the Nature of that Imitation Which Takes Place in What Are Called the Imitative Arts" (commonly abbreviated as *The Imitative Arts*), part I, § 7.
583 Ibid.
584 Adam Smith, TMS, part II, section ii, chapter 1, § 11.
585 Ibid., "Advertisement", § 1.
586 Ibid., part I, section i, chapter 3, § 3.
587 Ibid., part I, section i, chapter 3, § 4.
588 Ibid., part III, chapter 2, § 5.
589 Ibid., part IV, chapter 2, §§ 10–1 & part V, chapter 2, § 6; cf. also part VI, section iii, § 7.
590 Ibid., part III, chapter 2, §§ 11–2.
591 Ibid., part I, section iii, chapter 2, § 1.
592 Ibid., part III, chapter 3, § 12.
593 Ibid., part II, section ii, chapter 2, § 1.
594 Cf. ibid., part II, section ii, chapter 4, § 6.
595 Adam Smith, "Letter to Charles Townshend", 17th September 1759.
596 Adam Smith, "The Principles Which Lead and Direct Philosophical Enquiries; Illustrated by the History of Astronomy" (commonly abbreviated as *Astronomy*), section I, "Of the Effect of Unexpectedness, or of Surprise", §§ 2 & 6.
597 Ibid., §§ 6 & 9.
598 Ibid.
599 Adam Smith, *Astronomy*, section II, "Of Wonder, or of the Effects of Novelty", § 11.
600 Cf. <http://www.thelatinlibrary.com/sen/sen.tranq.shtml>.
601 Cf. Michael Polanyi, *Personal Knowledge. Towards a Post-critical Philosophy*, London: Routledge & Keagan Paul, 1958.
602 Adam Smith, *Astronomy*, section IV, "The History of Astronomy", §§ 13 & 33.
603 Adam Smith, *The Imitative Arts*, part II, § 20.
604 Adam Smith, *Astronomy*, section IV, § 76.
605 Andy Denis, "The Invisible Hand of God in Adam Smith", *Research in the History of Economic Thought and Methodology*, 23, 2005, § 3.
606 Adam Smith, TMS, part VI, section iii, § 30. As commonplace in the 18th century, Smith called "savages" the hunter-gatherers, "barbarians" the pastoral nomads, "civilised" those peoples capable of farming, "polished" the trading ones such as the Dutch and the British.
607 Adam Smith, WN, book I, chapter xi, conclusion, § 9.
608 Ibid.

[609] Adam Smith, TMS, part VI, section ii, chapter 1, § 20.
[610] Ibid., part I, section iii, chapter 2, § 2.
[611] Ibid.
[612] Ibid., part VI, section ii, chapter 3, §§ 3–5.
[613] Adam Smith, WN, book I, chapter viii, §§ 38–9.
[614] Ibid., book I, chapter xi, conclusion, § 8.
[615] Ibid., book I, chapter viii, §§ 26 & 41.
[616] Ibid., book I, chapter i, § 11.
[617] Ibid., book I, chapter viii, § 24.
[618] Ibid., book I, chapter viii, § 26.
[619] Ibid.
[620] Ibid., book V, chapter iii, § 90.
[621] Ibid., book IV, chapter iii, part 2, §§ 9–10.
[622] Ibid., book I, chapter i, § 35.
[623] Ibid., book IV, chapter vii, part 2, § 54.
[624] Ibid., book III, chapter ii, § 10.
[625] Ibid., book IV, chapter vii, part 2, § 7.
[626] Adam Smith, TMS, part V, chapter 2, § 9.
[627] Ibid.
[628] Ibid., part VI, section iii, § 5 & part VII, section ii, chapter 1, § 20.
[629] Ibid., part VI, section iii, § 17.
[630] Adam Smith, WN, book IV, chapter vii, part 2, § 6.
[631] Ibid., book II, chapter ii, § 86.
[632] Adam Smith, TMS, part I, section ii, chapter 3, § 4.
[633] Ibid., part IV, chapter 1, § 10.
[634] Cf. Thorstein Veblen, *The Instinct of Workmanship and the State of Industrial Arts*, New Brunswick: Transaction, 1990 (originally published in 1914).
[635] Cf. Richard Cantillon, *Essai sur la Nature du Commerce en Général*, 1755, <http://www.institutcoppet.org/wp-content/uploads/2011/12/Essai-sur-la-nature-du-commerce-en-gener-Richard-Cantillon.pdf>
[636] Adam Smith, TMS, part IV, chapter 1, § 10.
[637] Ibid., part IV, chapter 1, § 8.
[638] Ibid., part III, chapter 3, § 31.
[639] Ibid., part IV, chapter 1, §§ 8–10.
[640] Adam Smith, "Dedication to William Hamilton's *Poems on Several Occasions*", § 1, & "Letter to David Hume", 22nd August 1776.
[641] Adam Smith, TMS, part VII, section ii, chapter 1, § 25.
[642] Ibid., part I, section i, chapter 1, § 13.
[643] Ibid., part III, chapter 5, § 7.
[644] Ibid., part VI, section ii, chapter 2, § 4.
[645] Ibid., part II, section iii, chapter 3, § 2.
[646] Ibid., part I, section i, chapter 1, § 13; oddly enough, Smith acknowledges elsewhere the existence of people "who had been created without the natural fear of death" (ibid., part III, chapter 3, § 44).
[647] Ibid., part III, chapter 2, § 33.
[648] Adam Smith, *Astronomy*, section III, "Of the Origin of Philosophy", § 2.
[649] Adam Smith, TMS, part VI, section ii, chapter 3, § 6.
[650] Ibid., part III, chapter 5, § 9.
[651] Adam Smith, WN, book IV, chapter ii, § 9.

[652] Cf. Adam Smith, *Lectures on Jurisprudence*, 30th March 1763.
[653] Adam Smith, WN, book IV, chapter ii, §§ 10–1.
[654] Adam Smith, *Notes from the Lectures on Justice, Police, Revenue, and Arms delivered in the University of Glasgow*, henceforth abbreviated as *Lectures on Justice*, "Of public jurisprudence", 1766, § 66.
[655] Adam Smith, TMS, part I, section iii, chapter 2, § 3; cf. also *Lectures on Jurisprudence*, 14th March 1763.
[656] Adam Smith, TMS, part III, chapter 3, § 6.
[657] Adam Smith, WN, book V, chapter i, part 2, § 11.
[658] Cf. Adam Smith, *Lectures on Jurisprudence*, 6th, 10th & 17th January 1763 & 11th February 1763; cf. also "Private law".
[659] Cf. ibid., 17th January 1763, "Pledges", "Domestic law" & "Private law".
[660] Cf. ibid., 10th January 1763, 8th February 1763, 8th & 17th March 1763; cf. also "Of public jurisprudence".
[661] Cf. ibid., 10th & 11th February 1763.
[662] Cf. ibid., 8th & 10th February 1763, 10th March 1763.
[663] Cf. ibid., "Of the laws of nations".
[664] Adam Smith, *Astronomy*, section III, § 2.
[665] Adam Smith, TMS, part II, section ii, § 2.
[666] Ibid., part II, section iii, chapter 2, § 4; cf. also *Lectures on Jurisprudence*, 10th March 1763.
[667] Adam Smith, TMS, part III, chapter 2, § 9.
[668] Ibid., part III, chapter 4, § 12, & part II, section iii, chapter 1, §§ 1 & 3.
[669] Ibid., part II, section iii, chapter 3, §§ 4–5.
[670] Ibid., § 1; cf. also *Lectures of Jurisprudence*, 21st February 1762.
[671] Adam Smith, TMS, part II, section ii, chapter 3, § 12.
[672] Ibid.
[673] Ibid., part II, section ii, chapter 3, § 11.
[674] E.g. 21st January 1763, "Delinquency", especially §§ 2, 5–10, 13, 15, 18 & 21.
[675] Ibid., § 2; cf. also, "Of contract".
[676] Ibid., 10th March 1763, § 2.
[677] Cf. ibid., 3rd February 1763.
[678] Cf. ibid., 8th February 1763; cf. also "Domestic law".
[679] Ibid., 24th December 1762, "Of Occupation", § 7; cf. also 23rd February 1763.
[680] Ibid., 4th March 1763, §§ 1–2.
[681] Ibid., 21st January 1763, "Delinquency", § 6.
[682] Ibid., 3rd February 1763, §§ 4–5; cf. also "Of contract".
[683] Ibid., § 13.
[684] Ibid., 15th February 1763, § 4; cf. also 16th February 1763.
[685] Ibid., 22nd February 1763, § 4.
[686] Ibid., § 5.
[687] Ibid., 21st January 1763, "Delinquency", § 21.
[688] Ibid., 15th March 1763, § 4.
[689] Ibid., 16th March 1763, § 1; cf. also 15th March 1763.
[690] Ibid., 14th February 1763.
[691] Ibid., 16th February 1763, § 6; cf. also "Domestic law".
[692] Adam Smith, *Astronomy*, section II, § 11.
[693] Ibid., section IV, § 76.

[694] Cf. John Kenneth Galbraith, *A History of Economics: The Past as the Present*, London: Penguin, 1991.
[695] Boston: Houghton Mifflin.
[696] Cf. Michael Hudson, *The Bubble and Beyond*.
[697] Nikolas Sarkozy, "Morta ideologia della dittatura dei mercati", *La Repubblica*, 23rd October 2008.
[698] Paul Samuelson, "È' l'ultimo regalo dell'era Bush", *La Repubblica*, 2008, <http://rassegna.governo.it/testo.asp?d=33912628>; all translations from Italian into English are mine.
[699] Giuseppe Vegas, "Vegas: 'C'e' il rischio dittatura dello spread'", *Il Sole 24 Ore*, 14th May 2012, <http://www.ilsole24ore.com/art/finanza-e-mercati/2012-05-14/relazione-consob-vegas-lancia-110722.shtml?uuid=AbXHvNcF>.
[700] Giulio Tremonti, *Uscita di sicurezza*, Milan: Rizzoli, 2012, 14.
[701] E.g. Mario Monti, "Lo spot elettorale di Mario Monti", *Post*, 6th February 2013, <http://www.ilpost.it/2013/02/06/video-elettorale-monti-scelta-civica/>. I write "reforms" between single brackets because the institutional and historical meaning of, say, privatised pension schemes, flexible labour contracts and outsourced provision of formerly public services is typically a return to 19th-century or even earlier arrangements. "Counter-reforms" would be a more exact term, though rhetorically less appealing.
[702] E.g. John Sloman, *Economics*, Upper Saddle River: Prentice Hall, 2006 (6th ed.).
[703] Cf. Jonathan Schlefer, *The Assumptions Economists Make*, Cambridge, Mass.: Belknap, 2012.
[704] Martin Rhonheimer, "Capitalism, Free Market Economy, and the Common Good: The Role of State Authorities in the Economic Sector", in *Free Markets and the Culture of Common Good*, edited by M. Schlag & J.A. Mercado, Dordrecht: Springer, 2012, 9 (emphasis in the original). Rhonheimer's chapter has the merit of condensing into one text a great variety of claims about the capitalist economic order that liberals have made in support and in praise of it.
[705] Ibid., 9–10.
[706] Friedrich A. Hayek, *The Road to Serfdom*, London: Routledge, 2001, 124–5.
[707] Martin Rhonheimer, "Capitalism, Free Market Economy, and the Common Good", 5.
[708] Ibid., 24.
[709] Ibid., 4–7.
[710] The volume *Free Markets and the Culture of Common Good* comprises contributions from several participants in a conference of the same title and include, *inter alia*, a former minister of a right-wing government of the Italian republic, a former director of the IMF, and one of Europe's wealthiest bankers.
[711] Cf. Chaïm Perelman and Lucie Olbrechts-Tyteca, *The New Rhetoric*.
[712] E.g. Cornelius Castoriadis, *La societé bureaucratique: Ecrits politiques, 1945–1997*, Paris: Christian Bourgois, 2000.
[713] E.g. the chapters by Lawler, Ollman, Ticktin and Schweickart in *Market Socialism. The Debate among Socialists*, edited by B. Ollman, London: Routledge, 1997.
[714] Cf. Jennifer Richards, *Rhetoric. The New Critical Idiom*, London: Routledge, 2008.

[715] It is not necessary to address here the evidence running contrary to his claim, e.g. the demographic decline of free-market post-communist Russia under Boris Yeltsin and its partial recovery *via* a far less liberal economic system under Vladimir Putin (b. 1952; cf. M. Todorova and Z. Gille (eds.), *Post-Communist Nostalgia*, New York: Berghahn, 2010).

[716] Cf. Francesco Boldizzoni, *The Poverty of Clio: Resurrecting Economic History*, Princeton: Princeton University Press, 2011.

[717] Cf. Karl Polanyi, *The Great Transformation*.

[718] Cf. Mark S. Weiner, *The Rule of the Clan*, New York: Farrar, Straus & Giroux, 2013.

[719] E.g. Itkadmin, *Inuit Recommend Changes to Canadian Environmental Protection Act*, Inuit Nunangat: Inuit Tapiriit Kanatami, 2007.

[720] Isaiah Berlin, *Four Essays on Liberty*, Oxford: Oxford University Press, 1969, 124.

[721] CESCR, General Comment No. 3, "The nature of states parties' obligations", 1990, § 8, <http://daccess-dds-ny.un.org/doc/UNDOC/GEN/G08/422/35/PDF/G0842235.pdf?OpenElement>.

[722] Martin Rhonheimer, "Capitalism, Free Market Economy, and the Common Good", 19 (emphasis in the original).

[723] Cf. UNESCO, *Encyclopedia of Life Support Systems*.

[724] Cf. FAO, *FAO Hunger Portal*, 2013, <http://www.fao.org/hunger/en/>.

[725] E.g. Martin O'Flaherty *et al.*, "Potential Cardiovascular Mortality Reductions with Stricter Food Policies in the United Kingdom of Great Britain and Northern Ireland", *Bulletin of the World Health Organization*, 90, 2012, 522–31.

[726] Cf. John Quiggin, "Existence Value and Benefit-Cost Analysis: A Third View", *Journal of Policy Analysis and Management*, 12(1), 1993, 195–9.

[727] Cf. John Kenneth Galbraith, *The Economics of Innocent Fraud*.

[728] Cf. OECD, "Income Inequality and Growth: The Role of Taxes and Transfers", *OECD Economics Department Policy Notes*, No. 9, 2012, <http://www.oecd.org/eco/public-finance/49417295.pdf>.

[729] E.g. M. Parkin, M. Powell, and K. Matthews, *Economics*, Harlow: Pearson, 2008 (7th ed.). Nonetheless, it must be acknowledged that there exist countries that publicly provide or subsidise vital staples and services outside market transactions, hence *ipso facto* following a civil-commons logic and countering "privatisations" and "market liberalisations" that, by definition, indicate the deprivation of some individuals (i.e. what is private is not public) and the axiological homogenisation of such staples and services (i.e. they turn into priced market items, exactly like non-vital luxury and carcinogenic 'goods').

[730] 19th-century social Darwinists, sadists and Pyrrhonian sceptics may not agree on malnourishment and illness being clearly bad, though I know of no member of these groups who has sought either for herself.

[731] Cf. John Kenneth Galbraith, *The New Industrial State*.

[732] Martin Rhonheimer, "Capitalism, Free Market Economy, and the Common Good", 10.

[733] Ibid., 14.

[734] Ibid., 13.

[735] Ibid., 15.

[736] Ibid, 15 & 25. States can increase inequality by means of fiscal and monetary policy, financial (de)regulation and *ad hoc* legal norms favouring the wealthy over the poor (cf. OECD, "Income Inequality and Growth").

[737] E.g. Thorstein Veblen, *Absentee Ownership and Business Enterprise in Recent Times: The Case of America*, London: George Allen & Unwin, 1924.

[738] E.g. Vilfredo Pareto, *The Mind and Society*.

[739] Cf. Karl Marx, *Da Kapital*, vol. III, 1894, <http://www.marxists.org/archive/marx/works/1894-c3/>.

[740] Cornelius Castoriadis, ""What Democracy?", *Figures of the Thinkable*, 242. In a recent essay of hers ("Commercial Relations: From Adam Smith to Field Experiments", in *The Oxford Handbook of Adam Smith*, edited by C.J. Berry, M.P. Paganelli and C. Smith, Oxford: Oxford University Press, 2013, 333–51), Maria Pia Paganelli discusses field experiments showing how the interpersonal commercial activities can foster morality, but fails to notice how far predominant impersonal consumer and corporate activities do exactly the opposite, thereby destroying moral propensities cultivated in prior stages of civilisation (cf. Andrew Terjesen, "Adam Smith Cared, So Why Can't Modern Economics?").

[741] Cf. Garrett Barden and Tim Murphy, *Law and Justice in Community*, Oxford: Oxford University Press, 2010.

[742] John Kenneth Galbraith, *The Economics of Innocent Fraud* (especially chapters 2 & 3).

[743] Ibid., chapter 2.

[744] Cf. ibid., chapters 3 & 6.

[745] Cf. ibid., chapters 9 & 10.

[746] Cf. ibid., chapter 4.

[747] Cf. ibid., chapters 5 & 7.

[748] Cf. ibid., chapters 2 & 9.

[749] Cf. ibid., chapters 5, 6 & 10.

[750] Cf. ibid., chapters 7 & 11.

[751] Cf. ibid., chapters 7, 8 & 10.

[752] Cf. ibid., chapter 8.

[753] Cf. ibid., chapter 4.

[754] Cf. ibid., chapter 8.

[755] Cf. Norbert Häring and Njall Douglas, *Economists and the Powerful*.

[756] Cf. E.S. Reinert and F.L. Viano (eds.), *Thorstein Veblen. Economics for an Age of Crises* (London: Anthem, 2012) and David Reisman, *The Social Economics of Thorstein Veblen* (Cheltenham: Edward Elgar, 2012). Cf. also the extensive work of self-appointed liberal champion Deirdre McCloskey (e.g. *The Secret Sins of Economics*, Cambridge: Prickly Paradigm Press. 2002), who nonetheless criticises orthodox economists' existence theorems for assuming the unproven and therefore avoiding *ab initio* socio-historical reality and its murky complexities.

[757] Cf. Jonathan Schlefer, *The Assumptions Economists Make*. On the liberal economic scene, the so-called Cambridge school of economics did nothing of the sort, but it was marginalised by the neoliberal school, especially in America, to the point of producing what Paul Krugman calls the "Dark Ages" of his discipline ("The Dark Ages, Returned In Full", blog entry, 17th November 2010, 8:56am, *The Conscience of a Liberal*, <http://krugman.blogs.nytimes.com/2010/11/17/the-dark-ages-returned-in-full/?_r=0>), i.e. ignorance of economic history and major alternative or older doctrines (cf. also Cornelius Castoriadis, "The 'Rationality' of Capitalism").

[758] Stefania Vitali, James B. Glattfelder and Stefano Battiston, "The Network of Global Corporate Control".

[759] Cf. Jaakko Hintikka *et al.* (eds.), *Theory Change, Ancient Axiomatics, and Galileo's Methodology*, vol. I, Leiden: Springer, 1981.

[760] Cf. Pious X, *Pascendi dominici gregis* (encyclical letter, 1907, <http://www.vatican.va/holy_father/pius_x/encyclicals/documents/hf_p-x_enc_19070908_pascendi-dominici-gregis_en.html>) and Friedrich Nietzsche, "The Greek State", *On The Genealogy of Morality*, Cambridge: Cambridge University Press, 2006, 164–73 (originally published in 1872).

[761] Cf. Francesco Boldizzoni, *The Poverty of Clio*.

[762] Cf. Karl Polanyi, *The Great Transformation*.

[763] Cf. Gilbert K. Chesterton, "Reflections on a Rotten Apple", *In Defense of Sanity*, 1935, San Francisco: Ignatius, 260–9 (originally published in 1935).

[764] Cf. John Kenneth Galbraith, *The Economics of Innocent Fraud*.

[765] Cf. John Quiggin, "Common Property Rights in the Economics of the Environment" (*Journal of Economic Issues* 22(4), 1988, 1071–87) and Mark S. Weiner, *The Rule of the Clan*.

[766] My choice of examples signals how reciprocity, redistribution and market exchange can be good as well as bad. No fixed axiological standard is inherent to each or any of them; rather, it is imposed onto them from the outside (e.g. by legislation, politics, religion, moral education).

[767] Martin Rhonheimer, "Capitalism, Free Market Economy, and the Common Good", 21.

[768] Cf. Thorstein Veblen, *Imperial Germany and The Industrial Revolution* (Kitchener: Batoche, 2003; originally published in 1915) and Lee McGowan, *The Antitrust Revolution in Europe: Exploring the European Commission's Cartel Policy* (Cheltenham: Edward Elgar, 2010).

[769] Many different, hybrid forms of economic organisation developed in the long life of the former communist block itself (cf. Michail S. Gorbachev, *Memoirs*, London: Doubleday, 1995; and G. Ofer, "Soviet Economic Growth: 1928-1985", *Journal of Economic Literature*, 25(4), 1987, 1767–833).

[770] Martin Rhonheimer, "Capitalism, Free Market Economy, and the Common Good", 15.

[771] Ibid.

[772] This point is characteristic of the ordoliberal tradition, which finds a contemporary non-German expression in Raghuram Rajan and Luigi Zingales, *Saving Capitalism from the Capitalists: Unleashing the Power of Financial Markets to Create Wealth and Spread Opportunity* (New York: Random House, 2003), in which it is argued that a duly steered international financial market could be the engine of international wellbeing.

[773] The peculiarity of different types of successful economic development shows in studies such as F. Hodne's researches on Norway (*An Economic History of Norway, 1815–1970*, Trondheim: Tapir, 1975; and *The Norwegian Economy, 1920–1980*, London: Croom Helm & St. Martin's, 1983) and V. Lintner's and S. Mazey's on post-WWII Europe (*The European Community: Economic and Political Aspects*, New York: McGraw-Hill, 1991).

[774] The principle of falsification has been crucial in the history of science since at least the 17th century and was famously crystallised in the philosophy of science of Karl Popper (*Conjectures and Refutations*, London: Routledge & Keagan Paul, 1963).

[775] E.g. Mario Monti, "Italy to return to growth in 2013", *Reuters*, 10 September 2012, <http://www.reuters.com/article/2012/09/10/italy-gdp-idUSL1E8KAH6720120910>.

[776] Cf. Garrett Barden and Tim Murphy, *Law and Justice in Community*.

[777] Cf. Michael Hudson, *The Bubble and Beyond*.

[778] Paralogisms engender paralogisms. Mistaking effects for causes, Friedrich A. Hayek blames the mass unemployment of the 1930s on "the striving for security" by "restrictionism", i.e. the protectionist worldwide response to the Great Depression, as though no import whatsoever should be ascribed to the first Golden Age of free capital trade unleashed by European imperialism and the gold standard (1860s–1914), its deflationary effects and eventual crash, its novel crash at the end of the Roaring Twenties because of its reintroduction, and the ensuing mass liquidations recommended by liberals like himself (*The Road to Serfdom*, 132–3; cf. Karl Polanyi, *The Great Transformation*).

[779] Yet Marxism teaches since the 19th century that capitalism leads inevitably to crises, as also argued by the French regulation school (cf. Michel Aglietta, *A Theory of Capitalist Regulation: The US Experience*, London: Verso, 1976; and Michel Aglietta and Antoine Rébérioux, *Dérives du capitalisme financier*, Paris: Albin Michel, 2004). Crashes and meltdowns are to be expected, and are expected and even predicted by some students of economics, but their orthodox colleagues dissent. Hence, even if proved right by the collapse of 2008, unorthodox Marxists, post-Keynesians and institutionalists remain mere "unpersons" to the eyes of standard professors (James K. Galbraith, "Who Are These Economists, Anyway?", *Thought and Action*, Fall 2009, 85).

[780] As peculiar as it may sound, British neuropsychopharmacologist David Nutt claimed widespread cocaine consumption by bankers to be the cause of the 2008 financial crisis, for it led to excessive risk-taking (cf. R. Williams, "Financial meltdown was caused by too many bankers taking cocaine, says former drugs tsar Prof David Nutt", *The Independent*, 15th April 2013, <http://www.independent.co.uk/news/uk/home-news/financial-meltdown-was-caused-by-too-many-bankers-taking-cocaine-says-former-government-drugs-tsar-prof-david-nutt-8572948.html>).

[781] An unassailable comprehensive rational explanation allowing for no serious doubt and no possible change of conduct is a standard token of lunacy, according to G.K. Chesterton (cf. *Orthodoxy*, New York: Dodd, Mead & Co, 1908, 10ff).

[782] Martin Rhonheimer, "Capitalism, Free Market Economy, and the Common Good", 12 (emphasis in the original). A corollary of the unfalsifiable hypothesis at issue is the notion of self-correcting markets.

[783] Cf. Lee McGowan, *The Antitrust Revolution in Europe*.

[784] Mario Monti, "Italy to return to growth in 2013".
[785] John Quiggin, *Zombie Economics: How Dead Ideas Still Walk Among Us*, Princeton: Princeton University Press, 2010.
[786] Friedrich A. Hayek, *The Road to Serfdom*, 134.
[787] In his *General Theory of Employment, Interest and Money*, Keynes claims workers' demands for better salaries to spur economic activity. If correct, so-called "labour reforms" causing the precarisation and pauperisation of large sways of workers since the 1970s would then harm actual economic growth, as argued for instance by British historian Eric Hobsbawm in his book *Come cambiare il mondo*.
[788] E.g. Gibson's *Environmentalism: Ideology and Power* on the conservative roots of environmentalism.
[789] Hayek is paradigmatic in his anti-historical claim that planning and free market systems are "irreconciliable", as well as in assuming the actual existence of such ideal types (*The Road to Serfdom*, 130).
[790] Krugman, Obstfeld and Melitz photograph candidly this given, which Veblen and Robinson had already observed and discussed extensively in their lifetime (cf. *International Economics: Theory & Policy*, Upper Saddle River: Prentice Hall, 2011, 9th ed.).
[791] Awareness of looming environmental disaster is as old as the Club of Rome's denunciation of the *Limits to Growth*. Considerable progress has been achieved in "green" economics by the likes of Jackson (*Prosperity Without Growth*) Dietz, O'Neill and Daily (*Enough is Enough*), or Weston & Bollier (*Green Governance*). However, all this intellectual production has not dented neoclassical orthodoxy and, above all, standard textbooks, upon which is formed the knowledge of economics of most businesspeople, politicians, as well as economic and political advisors, i.e. crucial decision-makers, who still claim "growth" to be the supreme end.
[792] Already denounced by Veblen and Gailbraith, the vastly wasteful character of today's market economies is addressed by T. Stuart in his 2009 book *Waste: Uncovering the Global Food Scandal* (London: Norton).
[793] Supra, n5.
[794] Eric Hobsbawm notes in *Come cambiare il mondo* how mainstream economics has abandoned the Keynesian principle of full employment for the Friedmanite 'natural' rate of unemployment, which inspires policies that allow for unemployment in order to avoid higher inflation. Prices are kept low by keeping people out of jobs.
[795] National statistics bureaux register the failure and voluntary closure of most businesses launched annually after only few years of activity, e.g. the US Census Bureau (*Business Dynamics Statistics*, <http://www.census.gov/ces/dataproducts/bds/data_firm.html>).
[796] Massimo Florio offers an extensive account of State-led reconstruction in post-war Britain and an extensive welfare comparison with the economic and social outcomes of Thatcherite privatisations in his book *The Great Divestiture. Evaluating the Welfare Impact of the British Privatizations 1979–1997*, Cambridge, Mass.: MIT Press, 2004.

[797] Business and financial presses print these explanations and exculpations most commonly, but they are not absent from academic discourse either, e.g. S. Linz's 2000 working paper for the William Davidson Institute entitled "Are Russians Really Ready for Capitalism?" (<http://wdi.umich.edu/files/publications/workingpapers/wp268.pdf>). Many years before him, Ludwig von Mises had already explained the success of communist revolution in Russia by claiming that it could only happen among "the barbarian peoples on both sides of the Urals, whose relationship to civilization has never been any other than that of marauding denizens of forest and desert accustomed to engage, from time to time, in predatory raids on civilized lands in the hunt for booty" (*Liberalism*, chapter 10, § 1).

[798] The notion of a well-functioning free market abstracted from actual market agents is captured in the title of the 2003 book by Rajan and Zingales, *Saving Capitalism from the Capitalists*.

[799] Cf. Cornelius Castoriadis, "The 'Rationality' of Capitalism". In the 20th and 21st century, liberal economists sponsoring a more hybrid and contingency-based conception of economic activity have often been derided as "socialists" and other disqualifying predicates aimed at preventing wide social acceptance and true intellectual exchange (e.g. D. Luskin, "Paul Krugman: The Prophet of Socialism (The Nobel Laureate Who Has Been Consistently Wrong)", *National Review*, 6th December 2011, <http://www.freerepublic.com/focus/f-news/2733894/posts>).

[800] Cf. Cornelius Castoriadis, "The 'Rationality' of Capitalism".

[801] Cf. Jason Boffetti, "How Richard Rorty Found Religion", *First Things*, May 2004, <https://www.firstthings.com/article/2004/05/how-richard-rorty-found-religion>.

[802] Friedrich A. Hayek, *Collected Works*, vol. I, London: Routledge, 1992, 72.

[803] John Maynard Keynes, *The General Theory of Employment, Interest and Money*, chapter 24, § 5.

[804] Cf. Paul Oslington, *Adam Smith as Theologian*.

[805] Cf. John Kenneth Galbraith, *The Age of Uncertainty*, 272 for an iconic juxtaposition of education in dogmatics: Harvard MBA graduates and Spanish Catholic seminarists (copyright of the BBC):

[806] Cf. Eric Hobsbawm in his introduction to *Come cambiare il mondo*.
[807] Cf. John McMurtry, "Understanding Market Theology".
[808] Cf. Robert H. Nelson. *Economics as Religion: From Samuelson to Chicago and Beyond*, University Park: Penn State University Press, 2001.

[809] Friedrich A. Hayek, *Collected Works*, vol. I, 75.
[810] Cf. John Kenneth Galbraith, *The Economics of Innocent Fraud*; Norbert Häring and Njall Douglas, *Economists and the Powerful*; and Chang Ha-Joon, *23 Things Economists Don't Tell You About Capitalism* (London: Bloomsbury Press, 2012).
[811] Thorstein Veblen, *The Instinct for Workmanship and the State of the Industrial Arts*, 347.
[812] Cf. Thorstein Veblen, "Why Is Economics Not an Evolutionary Science?", *The Quarterly Journal of Economics*, 12, 1898, 373–97.
[813] Francesco Boldizzoni, *The Poverty of Clio,* 136.
[814] Ibid., 106–7.
[815] Ibid., 50.
[816] Ibid., 139.
[817] Stephen J. Collier, *Post-Soviet Social: Neoliberalism, Social Modernity, Biopolitics*. Princeton: Princeton University Press, 2011, 234ff.
[818] Andreas Kruck, *Private Ratings, Public Regulations: Credit Rating Agencies and Global Financial Governance*, Hampshire, UK: Palgrave Macmillan, 2011, 71.
[819] Ibid., 12.
[820] Ibid., xv.
[821] Ibid., iii.
[822] William N. Goetzmann, *Money Changes Everything*.
[823] Volker R. Berghahn, *American Big Business in Britain and Germany: A Comparative History of Two "Special Relationships" in the 20th Century*, Princeton: Princeton University Press, 2016, 341 & 7.
[824] Cf. John Kenneth Galbraith, *Money: Whence It Came, Where It Went* (Princeton: Princeton University Press, 2017; originally published in 1975) and Stephen Zarlenga, *The Lost Science of Money* (Valatie: American Monetary Institute, 2002).
[825] Volker R. Berghahn, *American Big Business in Britain and Germany*, 10.
[826] William N. Goetzmann, *Money Changes Everything*, 235.
[827] Ibid.
[828] Ibid., 291.
[829] Ibid., 408.
[830] Ibid., 8.
[831] Ibid.
[832] Ibid.
[833] Ibid., 191.
[834] Ibid., 233.
[835] Ibid., 379.
[836] Ibid., 514.
[837] Ibid., 439.
[838] Ibid., 411.
[839] Ibid., 408.
[840] Ibid., 233 & 520.
[841] Ibid., 233.
[842] Ibid., 512.
[843] Ibid., 233.
[844] Ibid., 507.
[845] Volker R. Berghahn, *American Big Business in Britain and Germany*, 229.

846 William N. Goetzmann, *Money Changes Everything*, 335.
847 Ibid., 423.
848 Ibid., 481–93.
849 Ibid., 52.
850 Ibid., 389.
851 Ibid., 421.
852 Ibid., 331.
853 Ibid., 324–32.
854 Ibid., 17, 460 & 380.
855 Ibid., 342.
856 Ibid., 516.
857 Cf. Paul Krugman, "Still Say's Law After All These Years", *The Conscience of a Liberal*, blog entry, 10th February 2013, 2.53pm.
858 David Reisman, *The Social Economics of Thorstein Veblen*, 311.
859 Norbert Häring and Njall Douglas, *Economists and the Powerful,* 1.
860 Ibid., 3.
861 Cf. Thorstein Veblen, *The Instinct of Workmanship and the State of the Industrial Arts*, 292.
862 Norbert Häring and Njall Douglas, *Economists and the Powerful,* 5.
863 Ibid., 6.
864 Ibid., 9, 21 & 26.
865 Ibid., 13–4 (emphasis in the original).
866 Ibid., 13.
867 Ibid., 7.
868 Ibid., 21 & 37–8.
869 Ibid., 27.
870 Ibid., 28–9 (emphasis in the original).
871 Ibid., 33.
872 Ibid., 42.
873 Ibid., 47.
874 E.g. Thorstein Veblen, *Absentee Ownership and Business Enterprise in Recent Times*.
875 Norbert Häring and Njall Douglas, *Economists and the Powerful*, 49.
876 Ibid., 50.
877 Ibid., 53.
878 Ibid., 54.
879 Ibid., 55.
880 Ibid., 57.
881 Ibid., 59–63.
882 Ibid., 64–5 & 68.
883 Ibid., 95.
884 Ibid., 97.
885 Ibid., 69.
886 Ibid., 69–72.
887 Ibid., 74.
888 Cf. ibid., 72–96.
889 Ibid., 76.
890 Ibid.
891 Ibid., 116.

[892] Ibid., 108.
[893] Ibid., 109.
[894] Ibid., 111.
[895] Ibid., 116 & 126.
[896] Ibid., 114.
[897] Ibid., 115 & 118.
[898] Ibid., 121.
[899] Ibid., 123.
[900] Ibid., 124.
[901] Ibid., 128.
[902] Ibid., 130.
[903] Ibid., 131.
[904] Ibid., 137.
[905] Ibid., 141.
[906] Ibid.
[907] Ibid., 142.
[908] Ibid., 142–4.
[909] Cf. ibid., 144–54.
[910] Cf. ibid., 151–3.
[911] Ibid., 155.
[912] Ibid., 157–8.
[913] Ibid.
[914] Ibid., 160.
[915] Ibid., 171.
[916] Ibid., 167.
[917] E.g. Thorstein Veblen, *Theory of the Leisure Class*.
[918] Norbert Häring and Njall Douglas, *Economists and the Powerful*, 168 & 173.
[919] Ibid., 167.
[920] Ibid., 188 & 190–1.
[921] Ibid., 189; cf. also 203–4.
[922] Ibid., 193.
[923] Ibid., 211.
[924] Ibid., 213.
[925] Ibid., 215–7.
[926] Ibid., 219.
[927] "'Major Global Downturn' says IMF", *BBC News*, 8th October 2008, <http://news.bbc.co.uk/1/hi/business/7659086.stm>.
[928] Cf. L. Iezzi, "'Più spese e niente tagli alle tasse' ecco la ricetta anti-crisi dell'Fmi", *La Repubblica*. 30th December 2008, <http://www.repubblica.it/2008/12/sezioni/economia/crisi-8/ricetta-fmi/ricetta-fmi.html>.
[929] Cf. Maurizio Molinari and Robert Solow, "Barack non tema il deficit", *La Stampa*, 2008, <http://www.lastampa.it/_web/cmstp/tmplRubriche/giornalisti/grubrica.asp?ID_blog=43&ID_articolo=1067&ID_sezione=58&sezione=>.
[930] Serge Halimi, "Thinking the Unthinkable", *Le Monde Diplomatique*, November 2008, 1A & 5A.
[931] Eric Hobsbawm, *The Age of Extremes,* 89 & 105.
[932] Cf. "Londra, manovra di sostegno. Taglio Iva e più tasse ai ricchi", *La Repubblica*, 25th November 2008, <http://www.repubblica.it/2008/11/sezioni/economia/crisi-mutui-14/piano-gb/piano-gb.html>.

[933] Union of Concerned Scientists, "World Scientists' Call for Action", 1997, § 3, <https://www.eolss.net/worldscientist.aspx>.
[934] Cf. Antonio D'Argenio, "L'Europa invasa dalla cocaina", *La Repubblica*, 5th November 2008, <http://www.repubblica.it/2008/11/sezioni/cronaca/ue-cocaina/ue-cocaina/ue-cocaina.html>.
[935] Cf. "Usa, multa record alla Siemens", *La Repubblica*, 15th December 2008, <http://www.repubblica.it/2008/12/sezioni/economia/siemens-multa/siemens-multa/siemens-multa.html>.
[936] John McMurtry, *The Cancer Stage of Capitalism*, 243.
[937] Frank D. Roosevelt, "The only thing we have to fear is fear itself" [first inaugural address as President of the USA], 1933, § 6, <http://historymatters.gmu.edu/d/5057/>.
[938] As cited in D. McCullogh, *Truman*, New York: Simon & Schuster, 1992, 658–9.
[939] Cf. J.W.E. Sheptycki, *In Search of Transnational Policing* (Aldershot: Ashgate, 2002), D.D. Avant, *The Market for Force: The consequences of privatizing security* (Cambridge: Cambridge University Press, 2005), and *The Changing Face of European Conscription*, edited by P. Joenniemi (Aldershot: Ashgate, 2006).
[940] Michel Foucault, *The Birth of Biopolitics. Lectures at the College of France 1978–79*. New York: Palgrave MacMillan, 101.
[941] Ralph B. Perry. *Realms of Value*, Cambridge: Harvard University Press, 2–3.
[942] Nicholas Rescher, *Introduction to Value Theory*, Englewood Cliffs: Prentice-Hall, 1969, 9.
[943] Zdzisław Najder, *Values and Evaluations*. Oxford: Clarendon Press, 1975, 63–4.
[944] John McMurtry, "What is Good? What is Bad?", § 1.5.3. Even social scientists such as Doyal and Gough, who investigate extensively needs in actual human societies, avoid committing themselves to more than whatever values may be conventionally agreed upon (cf. their 1991 book, *A Theory of Human Need*, London: MacMillan).
[945] Ibid., § 1.9.2.
[946] Isaiah Berlin, *Four Essays on Liberty*, 124.
[947] Ibid.
[948] Ibid., 125.
[949] Ibid.
[950] John Stuart Mill, *Principles of Political Economy with some of their Applications to Social Philosophy*, 1909 (7th ed.; originally published in 1848), § II.I.2, <http://www.econlib.org/library/Mill/mlP.html>.
[951] Ibid., § II.II.7.

⁹⁵² As concerns needs, most university-educated philosophers and social scientists in the Western countries are familiar with the theory of need developed by US psychologist Abraham H. Maslow (1908–1970) after World War Two. His "pyramid" of human needs is reported on standard textbooks of psychology, sociology and economics, and so too is his belief that: "The integrated wholeness of the organism must be one of the foundation stones of motivation theory" ("A Theory of Human Motivation", *Psychological Review*, 50, 1943, 370). However, Maslow's pioneering work is regarded today as self-contained, insufficiently backed by scientific evidence, and treated as a museum piece. The very notion of human need is hardly discussed and articulated in recent literature, to the point of being undistinguishable from the cognate notions of want, preference and desire, i.e. the cornerstones of standard economic psychology. For instance, one of Italy's most used reference websites for students in economics and other social sciences recites: "Needs are a feeling of dissatisfaction due to the want of something. Human needs are unlimited, subjective, resurgent and variable" ("I bisogni", 2007, <http://doc.studenti.it/riassunto/diritto/bisogni-loro-classificazione.html>). Back in the 1960s US, only Rollo May (1909–1994) was alone in challenging subjectivist ophelimity and value-neutral ordinalism by suggesting that value is what satisfies a need, rather than a preference (cf. his 1969 book, *Value Theory and the Behavioural Sciences*, Springfield: Charles C. Thomas).

⁹⁵³ According to the World Wildlife Fund's *The Living Planet Report* 2006, Cuba was in 2003 the only country whose ecological footprint and HDI were consistent with the UN's standards for sustainable development.

⁹⁵⁴ It is a little-known but highly symbolic fact that David and Frederick Barclays (b. 1934), amongst the wealthiest bankers in the world, still hold their legal residence on the small island of Sark, one of the last tracks of thoroughly feudal and tax-free land belonging to Queen Elisabeth II (b. 1926). The only inhabitant of that island paying taxes to the Queen is its lord, Michael Beaumont (1927–2016) at the time of writing, who corresponds to Her Majesty 1.79 GBP a year.

⁹⁵⁵ Revealing of the degree of planetary exhaustion is the recent proposal by Maldivan President Mohamed Nashed (b. 1967) to create a fund whereby to purchase a new homeland for his nation's inhabitants, as their archipelago is foreseen to disappear under water in the near future.

⁹⁵⁶ Cf. George Soros, *The Crisis of Global Capitalism: Open Society Endangered*. Jackson: Public Affairs, 1998.

⁹⁵⁷ Thorstein Veblen, *Absentee Ownership and Business Enterprise in Recent Times,* 51 & 66.

⁹⁵⁸ Thomas Jefferson, Letter to Josephus B. Stuart, ME 15:112, <http://etext.virginia.edu/jefferson/quotations/jeff1325.htm>.

⁹⁵⁹ Thomas Jefferson, Letter to John Taylor, ME 15:23, <http://etext.virginia.edu/jefferson/quotations/jeff1325.htm>.

⁹⁶⁰ As cited in *Monetary Reform*, Summer 1996, 16.

www.ingramcontent.com/pod-product-compliance
Lightning Source LLC
Chambersburg PA
CBHW052050230426
43671CB00011B/1858